Religious Movements in South Asia 600–1800

Oxford in India Readings

DEBATES IN INDIAN HISTORY AND SOCIETY

Series Editors: Sabyasachi Bhattacharya, B.D. Chattopadhyaya, Richard M. Eaton

RAZIUDDIN AQUIL (EDITOR)	*Sufism and Society in Medieval India*
FINBARR BARRY FLOOD (EDITOR)	*Piety and Politics in the Early Indian Mosque*
BISWAMOY PATI (EDITOR)	*The 1857 Rebellion* (OIP)
SCOTT C. LEVI (EDITOR)	*India and Central Asia* Commerce and Culture, 1500–1800
BHAIRABI PRASAD SAHU (EDITOR)	*Iron and Social Change in Early India*
SEEMA ALAVI (EDITOR)	*The Eighteenth Century in India* (OIP)
THOMAS R. TRAUTMANN (EDITOR)	*The Aryan Debate* (OIP)
AMIYA P. SEN (EDITOR)	*Social and Religious Reform* The Hindus of British India (OIP)
G. BALACHANDRAN (EDITOR)	*India and the World Economy 1850–1950* (OIP)
BIDYUT CHAKRABARTY (EDITOR)	*Communal Identity in India* Its Construction and Articulation in the Twentieth Century (OIP)

Religious Movements in South Asia 600–1800

edited by
David N. Lorenzen

OXFORD
UNIVERSITY PRESS

OXFORD
UNIVERSITY PRESS

Oxford University Press is a department of the University of Oxford.
It furthers the University's objective of excellence in research, scholarship, and education by publishing worldwide. Oxford is a registered trademark of Oxford University Press in the UK and in certain other countries

Published in India by
Oxford University Press
22 Workspace, 2nd Floor, 1/22 Asaf Ali Road, New Delhi 110002, India

First Edition published in 2004
Oxford India Paperbacks 2005
20th impression 2023

ISBN-13: 978-0-19-567876-5
ISBN-10: 0-19-567876-1

Typeset in Lalit (Palatino) 10/12.7
by Excellent Laser Typesetters, Pitampura, Delhi 110 034
Printed in India by Replika Press Pvt. Ltd.

Contents

Series Editors' Note

The Debates in Indian History and Society series focuses on the diversity of interpretations in historical discourse. The series address widely debated issues in South Asian history (including contemporary history) through edited volumes centring around sharply-focused themes or seminal writings which have generated arguments and counter-arguments resulting in worthwhile debates. In this context, the debated represent not simply differences in opinions but also offer important interpretative frameworks, which result in them acquiring a certain historiographic status. The approach encourages the interrogation of history, as distinct from representing history as a collection of 'given' facts. The aim to bring to reader significant writings, interpretations, and sources and to open to the students bridge-heads into research.

In this volume, the fourth in the series, a historian of religion addresses a range of debates on religious movements in the medieval and early modern periods and presents the views of several scholars on each debate. The following issues are considered:

What factors led to the inclusion or exclusion of non-Brahmins, even Shudras, in bhakti movements in early and medieval Tamilnad?

What role, if any, was played by Sufis in the conversion of non-Muslims to Islam in medieval India?

Why did Rama cults emerge when and where they did in India's premodern history?

How did essentialized understandings of Islam and Hinduism, which were so characteristic of the late colonial period, serve to explain the rise of nirguna bhakti movements such as those of Kabir, Dadu, and Nanak?

Finally, two contemporary historians offer overviews to our understandings of the bhakti movements and to the conceptual construction of Hinduism itself.

SABYASACHI BHATTACHARYA
B. D. CHATTOPADHYAYA
RICHARD M. EATON

Introduction

David N. Lorenzen

The historical study of religious movements that flourished in South Asia before the year 1800 has not yet received the attention it deserves. Scholars working on South Asian history have mostly concentrated their research on economic and political history or on the study of social movements of a more secular character. These historians have, for instance, written a great deal about the character of ancient South Asian feudalism, including the role of temples as large landholders, but not very much about the ideological aims and social functions of these temples. Particularly in American and European universities, South Asian religion is most often studied not by historians but by scholars associated with religion and language departments. They have generally preferred to work on the religious ideas and literature of the leading figures of religious movements, on mythology and metaphysics, and on the iconography of the gods. They have produced excellent studies of the metaphysics of Sankaracarya, the poetry of Sur Das, and the art and mythology of Krishna, but much less on the organizational structure and social and political concerns of the movements associated with such metaphysicians, poets, and gods.

This is not, of course, the whole story. Good studies of pre-modern religious movements do exist. The shortage is relative, not absolute. The purpose of this volume is to bring together important essays that debate how the religious and worldly aims of different movements are linked and how their ideologies, social bases, and organizational structures have both continued and changed over the course of time. The collection is divided into five parts: Alvars and Nayanars, conversion to Islam, Rama and the Muslims, Kabir and the Sants, and historical overviews. Each part includes two or three essays which present opposing views of important issues, either in the form of direct polemical debate or of significant differences of emphasis.

The aim of the collection is to focus on these issues rather than offer a complete survey of major religious movements in South Asia before 1800. Nonetheless, I should at least mention some of the important movements that are not adequately represented here. In south India, these include the movements of the Tamil Siddhas, the Saiva Siddhantins, and the Virasaivas. With regard to Maharashtra, the Varkari, Mahanubhava, and Ramdasi sectarian movements are mentioned only in passing. Tyagaraja of Andhra is not mentioned, nor are the Prananathis of Gujarat and Madhya Pradesh. In northern South Asia, the most obvious omissions are the movements of the Sikhs, the Vallabhas, the Naths, the Rajasthani followers of Dadu Dayal and Mirabai, and the Bengali followers of Chaitanya. Also omitted are discussions of many Jain, Buddhist, Christian, Dashnami, Tantrik, Muslim, Parsi, and Adivasi movements that were founded in many parts of South Asia between AD 600 and 1800.

Religious Movements

Given the variety of movements discussed in the essays of this volume, it is obvious that the term 'religious movement' is being used here in a rather general way to cover a wide range of religious groups and organizations, some quite tightly organized with a well-defined membership and some much more loosely defined currents or tendencies with a mostly informal and floating membership. Nonetheless, some general limits of this range of groups should be indicated.

To define a movement as 'religious' does not require that we define exactly what we mean by 'religious'. Religion is notoriously difficult to define with any precision, but most readers will, I think, accept that the movements discussed here are primarily religious in character. Nonetheless, whatever the strictly spiritual message of any given religious movement, it is also true that every such movement embodies at least some social, economic, and political attitudes, norms, and goals. Every religious movement is, to some degree, a socio-religious movement. In some movements, the social, economic, and political components may be quite prominent and even dominant. This is true today, for instance, in the cases of the Ravidasi movement and the Vishva Hindu Parishad, however different their social aims may be. It can even be argued that these two are social movements in a religious garb. In other movements, such worldly aims may be less evident, but they are never totally absent. Groups such as the Varkaris in Maharashtra and the Chaitanya movement in Bengal are good examples of groups in which mundane concerns are less prominent.

It is much more difficult, especially in a South Asian context, to specify what we mean by a 'movement', since the degree and style of organization of popular religious groups varies enormously. Some are so loosely structured that they are perhaps better described as religious currents rather than movements. Their followers are difficult to identify and have no formal ties to other members of the group or to its leaders. Other groups have more defined and limited memberships. The followers are often tied to the leaders by religious initiation and to each other by specific codes of religious belief and practice.

In essays and books written in English or European languages, the movements discussed in the essays of the present collection are often called 'sects' or 'sectarian movements'. Scholars have sometimes questioned the appropriateness and accuracy of these terms. The English word 'sect' and its European language equivalents have become associated with a fairly specific set of characteristics. The classic attempt to define and analyse the meaning of 'sect' in a mostly Euro-American and Christian context is that of Ernst Troeltsch (1931), who developed a conceptual contrast between 'sect' and 'church'. Roughly speaking, sects are viewed as small, enthusiastic, and voluntary organizations that impose a great deal of doctrinal and behavioural conformity on their members. Churches, on the other hand, are viewed as large organizations that demand less conformity from their members who usually belong to the church because their parents and grandparents did. Successful sects tend to gradually become churches, a process called 'the transition from sect to church'. Even in a Euro-American and Christian context, these contrasting ideal types do not always fit the empirical characteristics of actual historical sects and churches. To make matters more confusing, scholars have introduced further conceptual categories such as 'denominations', 'cults', 'new religious movements', and various different types of sects in an effort to create more precise typologies (Wilson 1970, Yinger 1970, Hill 1973).

Many of the religious movements discussed in this collection can be described as 'popular' movements. By this I simply mean that most of their followers (though not necessarily their leaders) come from middle- and lower-class groups and not from elite sections of the population. Among Hindus and Sikhs, as well as most South Asian Muslims, caste is in most contexts a more useful measure of social status than economic class, although caste and class boundaries do of course roughly coincide. In a South Asian context, then, a 'popular' religious movement is one whose followers mostly come from middle and low castes. The leaders of the movements, on the other hand, may come from either lower or higher castes. The religious movements in which the leaders come from non-Brahmin castes tend to embody social ideologies opposed to the religious and worldly dominance of upper castes, while movements with leaders from Brahmin castes tend to accept or reinforce such dominance.

The set of terms used in the languages of South Asia to describe religious movements does not correspond closely to these English terms or their European language equivalents. In Hindi, the South Asian language with which I am most familiar, common terms used for religious movements often called 'sects' in English language books and articles are *panth, sampraday, qaum,* and *parampara*. The most common word for a social 'movement,' usually secular, is *andolan*. Wider religious formations corresponding to a 'religion' such as Christianity, Buddhism, or Islam are in Hindi generally called *dharma,* though sometimes the terms *mazahab* and *iman* are used. Sikhs prefer to call their religion 'the' *panth*. A literal but rather neologistic equivalent to the English term 'popular religious movement' is *lok-pracalit dharmik andolan*.

All these Hindi terms have primary or etymological senses that differ considerably from those of English language terms such as 'sect', 'church', 'cult', and 'denomination'. *Panth* is derived from a word meaning 'way' or 'path'. The primary meaning of *sampraday* is close to 'tradition', while that of *qaum* is 'nation' or 'community'. *Parampara* is equivalent to both 'tradition' and 'genealogy'. The term *dharma* is often closely equivalent to 'religion' but also means 'law', 'moral order,' and 'duty.' *Mazahab* is also roughly equivalent to 'religion' but it has an Arabic etymology and a Muslim association whereas *dharma* has a Sanskrit etymology and a Hindu and Buddhist association. *Iman* is another word with an Arabic etymology, and its primary sense is 'belief' or 'creed'.

The differences between religious movements in South Asian and European or American countries are not simply conceptual or semantic, there are also quite real differences in the characters of such movements and the ways in which they have arisen, flourished, and declined. The majority of such movements in South Asia have been Hindu or Muslim rather than Christian (though Christian, Sikh, Jain, Buddhist, and other movements are of course also present), and they have developed in a society whose basic structure and ideology are organized around the caste system. In other words, the religious and social contexts as well as the individual histories of movements in South Asia have differed markedly from the movements in Europe that have provided the raw material for much scholarly theorizing about the nature of popular religious movements and how they develop and function. These contextual differences do not mean that theories about sects and churches in Europe and America are completely inapplicable to South Asian contexts. There do exist significant parallels between religious movements in South Asia and Europe or America. Nonetheless the academic theories about religious movements developed on the basis of the mostly Christian sects of Europe and America need to be rethought in the context of religious movements in South Asia.

Louis Dumont and World Renunciation

Among the few explicitly theoretical studies of Hindu religious movements, Louis Dumont's 1959 article entitled 'World Renunciation in Indian Religions' (1980: 267–86) has had a powerful impact. The influence that it has wielded is a tribute to the subtlety of Dumont's arguments, his rhetorical skill, and the wide acceptance that his Levi-Straussian structuralist approach received in the 1960s and 1970s.

Dumont starts from two basic contrasts: one contrast between Brahmanic Orthodoxy and popular Hindu religion, generally manifested in the form of Hindu sects, and a second contrast between the Brahmin priest and/or the ordinary householder from any caste, on the one hand, and the ascetic renouncer on the other. Dumont then develops these two contrasts—with the help of *varnasrama-dharma*, the traditional theory of the four aims of life (*i.e. kama, artha, dharma*, and *moksa*), and Levi-Straussian structuralism—into a 'unitary definition of Hinduism and even of Buddhist and Jain religions' (1980: 269).

It is evident from Dumont's description of the contrast between Brahmanic orthodoxy and popular Hindu religion that he is implicitly adapting Troeltsch's contrast between Church and sect to Hinduism. Non-sectarian Brahmanism takes the role of 'church,' while more sectarian groups such as *panths, sampradayas*, and *paramparas* take the role of 'sect' (1980: 268–9).

Dumont posits the existence of a set of three 'complementarities' that are present in popular Hinduism but largely absent in Brahmanic orthodoxy. These include, first, 'the complementarity of the pure and the impure, of the superior and the inferior' derived from the caste system and present, in popular Hinduism, even among the gods; second, the direct role of the man who serves as an oracle possessed by a god as an intermediary who informs and directs other men; and, third, 'the complementarity of function between a god and a goddess' commonly present in village cults (1980: 270). According to Dumont: 'Generally speaking, we can say that the complementarities of common religious practice become blurred and indistinct when we move to the level of Brahmanic practice...[while] in Brahmanic theory they tend to disappear altogether' (1980: 271).

Up to this point, Dumont has done little more than reintroduce a traditional and largely unexceptionable distinction between popular Hinduism and Brahmanic orthodoxy using a somewhat different vocabulary. It is when he attempts to integrate the world view and institution of the renouncer as the unique key to understanding the character both of Brahmanic orthodoxy and popular religion that the discussion becomes more problematic and also more interesting. He claims that 'the secret of Hinduism may be found in the dialogue between the renouncer and the man-in-the-world' and sums up his argument with the statement that 'Hinduism, the religion of caste and of renunciation, has developed by integrating—in Brahmanism—and by tolerating—in the sects—the products of the renouncer's thoughts and mysticism' (1980: 270, 285–6).

For Dumont, the contrast between the ascetic renouncer and the householder or Brahman reveals a deeper opposition between an 'individual-outside-the-world' and a caste-bound 'man-in-the-world, who is not an individual' (1980: 275). Dumont argues that 'to say the world of caste is a world of relations is to say that the particular caste and the particular man have no substance: they exist empirically, but they have no reality in thought, no Being' (1980: 272). In Dumont's view, the ascetic renouncer is, on the other hand, an independent individual who has both substance and Being: 'the renouncer leaves the world behind in order to devote himself to his own liberation. He submits himself to his chosen master, or he may even enter a monastic community, but essentially he depends upon no one but himself, he is alone' (1980: 274).

As Dumont's theory partly suggests, empirical investigations by many scholars (e.g. Thapar 1978; van der Veer 1989) have found that one primary motivation of ascetic renunciation is often a rejection of, and escape from, the responsibilities and cares of married life and children, rather than simply a search for spiritual liberation. On the other hand, membership in a monastic community is not an incidental and occasional detail of the renouncer's existence, as Dumont suggests, but rather the basic source of his material security and emotional well-being. Even during their periodic wanderings far from their monasteries, ascetic renouncers most often travel in pairs or small groups as anyone who has traveled on South Asian trains and roads can attest.

In some respects we can even stand Dumont on his head and argue that it is the householder who is the individual, however hemmed in he may be by social and economic responsibilities to his family and caste, while it is the renouncer who loses his individuality when he joins a collective monastic brotherhood and puts on its uniform insignia and dress. Dumont would probably reply that this confuses the merely empirical householder and the merely empirical ascetic with the more essential normative concept or ideal category of each. However, Dumont himself often assumes a more or less close fit between empirical realities and ideal concepts. It is only when empirical reality sharply differs from the ideal concept that he insists he is discussing concepts rather than empirical matters. But when the concepts of non-individual householder and individual religious renouncer are systematically contradicted by the behavior of actual flesh-and-blood householders and ascetics, the claim that the ideal concepts are primary and the empirical realities of secondary importance begins to look quite peculiar.

There are also serious problems with Dumont's analysis even at the level of the ideal normative concepts themselves. As Dumont at one point admits, and then largely discounts, the normative ideal of the renouncer clearly includes the idea that he should dedicate himself to the task of systematically annihilating his ego and his egoism. But what kind of an individual is someone who erases his own ego? Likewise, the normative ideal of the householder includes the idea that once the male householder arrives at the position of the head of his extended family, he becomes responsible to no one and has virtually complete freedom to make decisions about his own life and the lives of his family members. What kind of a non-individual is such an autocratic patriarch?

Dumont's most serious misunderstandings concern the role of bhakti and sects in Hindu religion. Bhakti is, in his opinion, 'a sanyasic development, an invention of the renouncer'. This is because 'this religion of love supposes two perfectly individualized terms; in order to conceive of a personal Lord there must also be a believer who sees himself as an individual' (1980: 282). As we have noted, Dumont believes, wrongly in my opinion, that only the renouncer is able to think of himself as, and hence be, an individual.

Dumont notes that historically 'practically all the sects have been founded by sanyasis and the greater part include, apart from worldly adherents, a sanyasi order constituting the nucleus of the sect.' This is largely correct but there do exist important exceptions. Dumont does not offer any convincing explanation for the logic behind this empirical observation that sects have been founded by renouncers, but instead merely argues that the great influence of the renouncer-gurus of the sects over their lay disciples enables the religion and thought of the renouncers to 'penetrate to the great mass of men-of-the-world' (1980: 284).

In Dumont's theoretical model, Hindu sects become mere instruments for the spreading of the renouncer's world view, but we have no explanation of why lay men-and-women-in-the-world, who generally constitute the bulk of the followers of any given sect, are drawn to these sects, nor what contributions lay thought has made to them. In addition, the model does not explain why several important sects were in fact founded by married men who did not renounce their wives after becoming full-time religious leaders. Among the most obvious is the case of the ten Sikh Gurus; others such as Vallabhacharya and his successors among the Vallabhas, Ghazidas and his successors among the Chhattisgarh Satnamis, and the principal acaryas of the Damakheda branch of the Kabir Panth can also be mentioned.

Two other ways in which sects can be contrasted with orthodox Brahmanism, according to Dumont, are, first, the fact that the sect, unlike Brahmanism, 'is not essentially syncretic but holds to one doctrine, the principle of its unity,' and is in fact often 'monotheist in the true sense,' and second, the fact that 'the sect, whatever its dominant inspiration, transcends caste and, at least in principle, is open to all, as is appropriate in a creation of the renouncer' (1980: 284). Here, once again, Dumont's theory clashes with empirical observations. The distribution of syncretism and monotheism in orthodox Brahmanism and in Hindu sects is, for instance, complex and inconsistent. It is true that most sects focus on worship of a single god or avatar, but the existence, and the lesser but real power, of other gods is not usually denied. Likewise, if we include classical systems of Brahmanic metaphysics such as Vedanta and Samkhya as manifestations of orthodox Brahmanism, we find in them a frequent tendency toward a systematic monotheism. The fact that many bhakti-oriented sects evolved their own schools of Vedanta—complete with Sanskrit commentaries on the Upanishads, *Vedanta-sutras* and *Bhagavad-gita* understandable only to a small elite of high-caste renouncers—only complicates the situation further.

Most curious, is Dumont's assertion that the Hindu sect 'transcends caste and, at least in principle, is open to all.' This fits together nicely with his claim that the renouncer, who is the soul of the sect, should be regarded as an 'individual-outside-the-world,' in other words, outside the caste-system. If the renouncer himself transcends caste then it is only logical that the institutional embodiment of the renouncer's thought, the sect, should transcend caste as well. Unfortunately for this theory, the majority of Hindu sects stoutly defend the caste system including both its ideology, *varnasrama-dharma,* and its institutional practices. The only significant rejection of caste among Hindu sects is found in Virasaivism, in *nirguni* sects such as the Kabir and Ravidas Panths, and to a lesser extent in the Arya Samaj. Even in these cases, the opposition is limited mainly to the realm of ideology rather than practice. Furthermore, Dumont's claim that the sect is, 'at least in principle,' open to all ignores the fact that most sects draw their followers from a quite specific set and range of castes. Several sects, such as the Satnamis of Chhattisgarh and the Ravidasis of Uttar Pradesh draw the vast majority of their followers from a single caste. A principle—like Dumont's claim that sects are open to all—that is systematically violated in practice is hardly worth the name. The relation between the caste membership of different sects and their respective interpretations of *varnasrama-dharma* is a complex topic that is discussed in more detail below.

Sect and Caste

Another influential idea associated with several sociologists and anthropologists including Dumont is the claim that sects in South Asia have historically tended, almost inevitably, to evolve or degenerate into castes. This theory is not found in Dumont's renunciation article, first published in 1959, but it is present in his famous 1966 book, *Homo Hierarchicus* (pp. 184–91). Dumont's collaborator, David Pocock, discusses this issue in some detail in his 1973 book, *Mind, Body and Wealth: A Study of Belief and Practice in an Indian Village,* where he calls it a 'commonplace of Indian history' (p. 151). Another significant discussion is found in David Mandelbaum's *Society in India* (1972: 523–44). Mandelbaum cites several earlier scholars who accept the idea of the inevitable transition from sect to caste, at least in part, including M. N. Srinivas, I. Karve, Jawaharlal Nehru, and Max Weber. In fact, Weber is evidently the original author of the theory, although he is not cited as such by either Dumont or Pocock. Weber's discussion is found in his *Hinduismus und Buddhismus,* a part of his great *Gesammelte Aufsätze zur Religionssoziologie*. This essay on Hinduism and Buddhism, originally published in 1920, was translated into English, and even then not adequately, only in 1958.

What makes this idea of the transition from sect to caste curious is the fact that it bears almost no relation to the empirical evidence of South Asian history. It provides us with an ironic example of the truth, and the falsity, of Derrida's slogan: 'There is nothing outside the text' (*il n'y pas de hors-texte*). Evidently what has happened is that Weber's original idea was picked up and transmitted from scholar to scholar without anyone having submitted it to a critical evaluation against the historical evidence available.

Weber, like many other sociologists and anthropologists, starts his analysis of Hindu religious movements with the reasonable assumption that caste has been the single most dominant institution of Hindu society since at least the middle of the first millenium BCE, and must, therefore, affect the way religious movements arise, develop and, sooner or later, decline. According to Weber and his successors, if we accept the pervasiveness of caste, it is logical to assume that sects have tended to evolve into castes in the same way that other institutions such as tribes, clans, and guilds have done.

Weber presents his theory of the transition from sect to caste as a partial response to the question of why there is little evidence in South Asia of rebellions by lower castes against the Hindu caste order. Hinduism, he says, quickly established its dominance over 'salvation religions' like Buddhism and Jainism because of 'the fact that Hinduism could provide an incomparable religious support for the legitimization interest of the ruling strata'. He continues (1968: 18–19):

> Once established, the assimilative power of Hinduism is so great that it tends even to integrate social forms considered beyond its religious borders. Thus religious movements of expressly anti-Brahmanical and anti-caste character, that is, contrary to one of the fundamentals of Hinduism, have been in all essentials returned to [the] caste order.
>
> The process is not hard to explain. When a principled anti-caste sect recruits former members of various Hindu castes and tears them from the context of their former ritualistic duties, the caste responds by excommunicating all the sect's proselytes.... If the sect permitted a way of life Hinduism considers ritually defiling (beef consumption), the Hindus treat it as a pariah people, and if this condition continues long enough, as an impure caste.... If ritualistic defilement is not indicated, in time (particularly if the activities of the sect members are of a ritualistic nature—and such is usually the case), the sect may take its place among the surrounding castes as one with special ritualistic duties....
>
> In the course of time the sect can be recognized either as a single caste (sect-caste) or as a caste with subcastes of different social rank. This last occurs when the sect members are socially quite heterogeneous.

The only actual historical example Weber gives for this process is the sect of the Lingayats who, he claims, illustrate the gradual development from a socially heterogeneous sect to a 'caste with subcastes' so that now the sect 'demands the registration of its members according to the four classical Hindu castes' (1968: 20). In order to support their later versions of this same basic transition from sect to caste, Dumont and Pocock both give the same Lingayats as their principal example while Mandelbaum discusses the Jains, Lingayats, and Sikhs in the same context. None of them presents a clear example of a single sect gradually developing into a single caste, although the logic of the argument indicates that this should be the simplest and most frequent case. Dumont does allude in passing, however, to the Gosains and Sadhs of Uttar Pradesh as cases in which a sect originally constituted exclusively by male renouncers 'degenerates into a caste' when the renouncers form conjugal unions and sire children. This process is rather different from that envisioned by Weber, who did not consider the possibility of exclusively renouncer sects. In at least the case of the Gosains (or at least those better known as Jogis), however, Dumont's example is plausible. Unfortunately, any reconstruction of the early history of the Sadhs and Gosains can only be based on scholarly speculations since almost no historical evidence exists.[1]

If we look at the relation between Hindu castes and Hindu sects from a more empirical and historical point of view, we find a situation quite different from that proposed by the historical sociologist Weber and by anthropologists such as Dumont and Pocock. For a start, most major Hindu sects—whether Vaishnava, Saiva, or Sakta—have followers who come from a wide range of castes. The vast majority of such sects have shown no significant tendency to evolve into either endogamous castes or self-contained groups of castes. Examples include the Srivaishnavas in the south, the Caitanyas in Bengal, the Vallabhas in western India, the Varakaris in Maharashtra, the Ramanandis in the north, and the Prananathis in central and west India. Most of these religious movements have been founded and led by Brahmin renouncers, but their lay followers have always come from a wide range of castes from Brahmins to middle castes and even, in some cases, to dalits.

The *nirguni* sects of northern South Asia provide examples of several more varied and complex relations between caste and sect. The principal *nirguni* sects are those of the Kabir Panthis, the Ravidasis, the Dadu Panthis, and the Sikhs. All these sects have been founded and led by non-Brahmins. In the case of the Kabir Panthis and Dadu Panthis, the leadership has generally been in the hands of non-Brahmin renouncers. In the case of the Sikhs, the leadership has mostly consisted of learned professionals who are allowed to marry. The leadership of the Ravidasis is harder to define and includes both renouncers and married lay persons. In the cases of the Kabir Panthis, the Dadu Panthis, and the Sikhs, the lay followers have come from a wide range of castes, but have mostly excluded Brahmin castes. Among the Sikhs, however, the Jat caste cluster represents about half the membership. In the case of the Ravidasis, both the leaders and the followers have always come almost exclusively from the traditionally untouchable Chamar caste cluster.

Almost all the larger Hindu sects, whether led by Brahmins or members of other castes, permit marriages between their lay followers and persons who do not belong to the sect, provided that both persons belong to the same caste. Persons belonging to the same sect may be preferred, but the choice of other caste members still remains open. Unlike caste membership ascribed by birth, sect membership is generally determined by individual choice or family tradition and is not always formalized by a ritual initiation. In these circumstances, it is not always clear who is a member of a given sect and who is not.

Among the Lingayats, the Sikhs, and the Jains, however, the choice of marriage partners outside the sect is, for the most part, no longer accepted. In these movements, Weber's sect to caste model does have some applicability. Whether these movements can be classed as fully Hindu, however, is doubtful. Each of them has established a self-identity to some degree independent of Hinduism—less independent in the case of the Lingayats and more independent in the cases of the Jains and Sikhs—and each has also created a sort of independent system of castes existing within the movement. Each has established its own marriage and other life-cycle rituals administered by its own ritual specialists. Nonetheless, in at least the cases of the Jains and the Sikhs, traditional ties to historically related castes outside the religious movements have been partly maintained and interfaith marriages within these castes are sometimes accepted.

Another example of a movement in which caste and sect are closely intertwined is that of the Satnamis of Chhattisgarh, examined in detail in a recent historical and anthropological study by Saurabh Dube (1998). The Satnami sect or Panth was founded among the Chamars of the region early in the nineteenth century. Its doctrines and ritual practices are clearly related to those of the Kabir Panth and *nirguni* tradition. From the moment of its inception, the Satnami movement drew a large majority of its followers from Chamar castes although a minority of members of other low castes also joined. From virtually the beginning, the Satnamis organized themselves as an endogamous caste separate from the Chamars. As Dube indicates (1998: 63), to join the Satnam Panth 'signaled both ... the initiation into a sect and the incorporation into a caste'. Although most Satnamis are now born into the Panth rather than being converts from outside, the rules for the induction of new members into this sect-caste are still unchanged. There has not been any gradual transition from sect to caste such as that the Weber model posits.

The historical evidence about the early stages of popular religious movements founded before 1800 is generally much less precise or reliable than that available for the Satnamis. Nonetheless, the evidence that does exist suggests that in virtually all cases there has been little or no significant change in the nature of the relations between sect and caste over the years. In addition, these relations do not form any consistent pattern. Each case is largely unique. The most that we can say is that in most cases each popular religious movement seems to draw a large majority of its followers from a specific range of castes found in one or two specific cultural and linguistic regions. This range of castes may be wide, as in the case of the Ramanandi movement, or more narrow as in the case of the Kabir Panth. In the case of the Raidasis, most followers come from a single caste cluster. All three movements are relatively widespread, but do draw most of their members from regions where people speak Hindi dialects. For example, most Kabir Panthis come from the Bhojpuri and Chhattisgarhi regions, though some also belong to western UP, Rajasthan, and even Gujarat and eastern Maharashtra. On the other hand, the Sikhs draw most of their support from Punjab, the Dadu Panthis from Rajasthan, the Caitanyas from Bengal, and the Srivaishnavas from Tamil Nadu and each movement is associated with the respective languages of these regions. Internal and external migrations such as the Sikh diaspora have complicated this situation, but the applicability of the general rule is clear enough.

Social Ideologies

Every popular religious movement—whether it is organized as a compact sect or as a more loosely defined religious current—fosters and inculcates a fairly specific social ideology, that is, a normative set of beliefs and attitudes about how the social system should be structured. In a South Asian context, this above all implies interpretations and judgements about the dominant social ideology of *varnasrama-dharma,* the rules and norms of the caste system, and about the proper relations between men and women. Some movements have strongly supported *varnasrama-dharma* and others have strongly opposed it. Virtually all movements have supported a patriarchal model of the relations between men and women, but differences can also be found about such questions as whether or not women are directly eligible for salvation or must be first reborn as men.

Since about the beginning of the Common Era, Hinduism has been dominated by religious devotion or *bhakti* to the various forms and avatars of the gods Vishnu and Siva and their divine wives, consorts, and associates. By about 600, a corpus of roughly standardized myths about these gods and goddesses, codified in the *Mahabharata* and *Ramayana* epics and in the early Puranas, was largely complete. Virtually all the Hindu movements formed after this date have been based on bhakti and have been led, in at least their initial stages, by poet-saints who sang songs and told stories about these same gods. Furthermore, almost all sects and movements inspired by bhakti have fostered interpretations of *varnasrama-dharma* that are, to varying degrees, more egalitarian than the strict hierarchical norms of traditional Brahmanic interpretations of the system as embodied in law books and digests and in customary practices.

In the sects and the looser movements associated with bhakti, social ideologies are transmitted by several means. The most obvious embodiments of ideological messages are the songs, verses, and stories that constitute the literature approved and taught within each movement. Whether these texts have been written down or not, their principal mode of transmission has usually been oral. If we take the Kabir Panth as an example, we find ideas about social norms being transmitted through the vernacular songs (*pad*s and *bhajan*s) and verses (*doha*s or *sakhi*s) attributed to Kabir, in hagiographic stories about Kabir (*katha*s or *caritra*s), and in miscellaneous texts such as religious dialogues (*gosthi*s), commentaries on Kabir's own works (*'ika*s), rulebooks about proper behaviour for lay followers or sadhus (*paddhati*s), public sermons (*pravacan*s), and more private religious conversations (*sat-sang*). Among more mainstream groups such as the Srivaishnavas and Ramanandis, analogous vernacular texts are supplemented by more traditional Sanskrit texts such as the *Bhagavad-gita* and the *Bhagavata-purana*.

The ideological messages of all these sorts of texts can often be quite direct. Many of Kabir's songs, for instance, embody explicit attacks against the discriminatory practices associated with the caste system. Most stories about Kabir contain obvious morals that undermine key values of this system. Ramanandi and Srivaishnava texts, on the other hand, frequently offer defences of the caste system, albeit with liberalized bhakti interpretations. The same is true of more generic bhakti texts, most notably the key texts of the *Bhagavad-gita* and *Bhagavata-purana*. Even more rarified philosophical and theological discussions about such topics as the creation of the universe, the nature and importance of God's grace, and the differences between *nirgun* and *sagun* concepts of God, can have significant social implications (Lorenzen 1987).

In any society, dominant social norms are transmitted as much or more by everyday social practices than by verbal texts whether oral or written. In the context of South Asia and the hierarchical ideology of *varnasrama-dharma,* the transmission is effected by practical rules about who can take water from whom, who can take what sort of food from whom, who can have sex with whom, who can marry whom, who can or cannot wear symbolic items such as the sacred thread, who can perform what ritual functions, and how one person should address and behave towards another. The social ideology of any given religious movement is judged in part by the extent to which its members are encouraged to support, accept, ignore, surreptitiously subvert, or openly reject such everyday social practices.

If a popular religious movement does not accept the dominant ideology embodied in these everyday practices, its possibilities for openly rejecting them are generally limited. This is particularly true of movements whose membership is drawn principally from low-caste and poor people. As Susana Devalle (1985) and James Scott (1990) have indicated, poor and dominated persons often resist the imposition of hierarchical social norms through behaviour such as passive resistance and dissembling that contains 'hidden transcripts' of their rejection of these norms. Another way to subvert these norms, however, is to abandon or reject them in the context of social interactions *within* the membership of a given religious group and in the religious rituals of the group. On the occasion of religious feasts, for instance, all members of a given sect, regardless of caste, are often expected to eat together seated in a single line (*pangat*).

Even in cases where a popular Hindu movement generally accepts the hierarchical norms of *varnasrama-dharma,* the movement may also function as a means of fostering economic and social co-operation among persons of different classes or castes. An employer, for instance, may prefer to hire members of the same sect and then treat or pay them better in exchange for their greater loyalty. Likewise a banker might be more willing to loan money at a better rate of interest to a fellow member of his sect. The role of Hindu sects in fostering these sorts of cross-caste economic and social ties has still not been adequately studied, but one example is found in David Pocock's description of such relations among the followers of a sect of Swami Narayan in Gujarat (1973: 145–57).

Engels and Weber

The theoretical orientations of most modern historical studies of popular religious movements can be traced, directly or indirectly, to one of two sources: the work of Friedrich Engels (1820–95), Karl Marx's long-time collaborator, and that of Max Weber (1864–1920). Particularly relevant to the present discussion are Engels' study of the sixteenth-century Anabaptist leader Thomas Müntzer and his followers in the essay 'The Peasant War in Germany', first published in 1850 (Marx and Engels 1964: 97–118), and Weber's long essay on 'The Sociology of Religion', first published in 1922 (Weber 1963). Although the texts of Engels and Weber were written long ago and have been much criticized since, they continue to have an important influence on contemporary historians who study religious movements (for example, Cohn 1970: 251; Trevor-Roper 1967).

Both Engels and Weber attempted to explain the rise and fall of religious movements through considerations of the social, economic, and political factors that influenced them, and both pay particular attention to the importance of the social bases of the movements. Related more to Engels' approach are studies that aim to place each specific movement in its historical time and place and emphasize the political and material aspects of its historical development. More closely allied to Weber are studies that attempt to place each movement within a larger typology of such movements and emphasize the meanings of the beliefs and practices of religious movements in relation to the social relations that operate in the society as a whole. Engels argued that class struggle usually stood behind ideologies and political conflicts and claimed that 'even the so-called religious wars of the sixteenth century involved primarily positive material class interests...' (Marx and Engels 1964: 98). Weber was more concerned with the affinities of different social classes with different sorts of religious movements and discusses religious wars mostly in the context of struggles between nations and civilizations rather than between different social classes (Weber 1963: 85–9).

Although both Engels and Weber share an interest in the class bases of religious movements, there are two basic points on which they differ. These can be summarized in the contrasts between the concepts of material determination and class affinity, on the one hand, and between class struggle and legitimate domination on the other. Let us take the second contrast first since it is the more obvious one. That Marx and Engels saw class struggle as the motor engine of history is well known. One of their principal aims was to identify the major moments of social crisis when economic, social, and political contradictions lead to major transitions in the social order. Engels' study of the peasant wars in Germany tries to show how the class interests of Thomas Müntzer's followers played a role in the defeat of absolutism and of the remains of the feudal system in sixteenth-century Germany. Weber was more interested in developing a typology of different sorts of legitimate, or legitimized, political and social domination that permitted the political and social system to survive. Since this typology is of limited relevance to Weber's analysis of the class affinities of religious groups, we need not discuss it further here.

The contrast between the concepts of material determination and class affinity in Engels and Weber goes more to the heart of their respective attitudes towards the relation between social groups and classes and popular religion. In his famous preface to his *A Contribution to the Critique of Political Economy* of 1859, Marx argues that in periods of social revolution, the 'material transformation of the economic conditions of production' in some sense directly determines 'the legal, political, religious, aesthetic or philosophic...forms in which men become conscious of this conflict and fight it out' (Marx and Engels 1959: 44). Engels' interpretation of the Anabaptist role in the Peasant War in Germany is clearly based on this idea, although the precise sense in which the infrastructure *determines* the superstructure is not spelled out here or elsewhere by either Engels or Marx.

Weber prefers to argue for an *affinity* between economic

class and religion that essentially avoids the question of determination or priority of one over the other. Weber's famous long essay, 'The Protestant Ethic and the Spirit of Capitalism', argues that modern capitalism is associated particularly with Calvinist Protestants because there was a positive interaction between the worldly asceticism fostered by Calvinism and the need for capital accumulation in the capitalist economic system. Each influences the other, but neither has any necessary priority (Weber 1958). In his essay 'The Sociology of Religion', Weber asserts that the relationships between the urban middle classes and congregational religion 'were not determined exclusively by the distinctive economic patterns of urban life. On the contrary, the causation might go the other way, as is readily apparent.' For the most part, however, in this essay Weber tends to pay more attention to the role of socio-economic class in determining the typical type of popular religious movement than in the influence that the religious movement has on the class behaviour of its adherents, in other words his position is in fact not so far from Engels' as at first it might seem (Lorenzen 1995a: 22–8).

Alvars and Nayanars

Two of the earliest well-documented regional popular religious movements in South Asia are those of the Vaishnava Alvars and the Saivite Nayanars of Tamil Nadu. The founding poet-saints of these movements lived in this region between about the seventh and tenth centuries, but important texts related to their movements continued to be written long afterwards. The principal documentary evidence we have about them and the movements they led are the collections of religious songs they composed, the somewhat later hagiographies about them written by their followers, and the numerous inscriptions found in or near the principal temples associated with the movements. There also exists a somewhat later set of theological texts and commentaries that attempt to give each of the movements a more systematic and scholarly pedigree. Most important in this regard are the works of the Srivaishnava theologians Yamunacarya and Ramanuja.

Two essays on these movements have been included here: 'From Devotion and Dissent to Dominance: The Bhakti of the Tamil Alvars and Nayanars' by R. Champakalakshmi (1996) and 'Social Mobility and Medieval South Indian Hindu Sects' by Burton Stein (1966). Champakalakshmi's essay is the most comprehensive and builds on the earlier work by Stein and others. Nonetheless there are significant differences in the arguments of each essay.

Both essays describe and offer explanations for the rise of the bhakti movements of the Alvars and Nayanars and give particular emphasis to what the authors see as a gradual process of decline in the social and religious dissent evident in the movements. Champakalakshmi emphasizes the importance of royal patronage of the temples associated with the bhakti movement for the extension of agricultural settlements into the hinterland. She links the egalitarian aspects of this bhakti movement more to its rivalry with Jainism and Buddhism than to its connections with kings and Brahmins. She argues that although the poetry of the Alvars and Nayanars does contain 'an element of protest or dissent', nonetheless their movement 'does not reflect a popular character or a broad social base till at least the twelfth century AD' (1996: 143). She notes that there are 'three major themes' in the bhakti hymns: first 'the idea of devotion to a personal god, i.e. *bhakti*', second 'a protest against orthodox Vedic Brahmanism and the exclusiveness of the *brahmana*s in their access to divine grace and salvation,' and, third, 'a vehement denunciation of the Jains and Buddhists as non-believers, heretics, and hence as "heterodox"'. She suggests that the second theme, the opposition to Vedic Brahmins, reflects a conflict between these Brahmins and priests at 'local cult shrines' who were eventually integrated into another 'priestly group called Siva-*brahmanas*' (p. 145).

More important, Champakalakshmi claims, was the conflict of the bhakti movements with the Jains and Buddhists. This conflict was not simply ideological but also involved competition for royal patronage and donations of agricultural land (pp. 157–8):

The hymnists were propagating *bhakti* in a situation of conflict and rivalry with non-orthodox sects like the Jains and Buddhists whose influence

> and dominance in royal and urban centres had been established in the pre-seventh-century period.... *Bhakti* would, therefore, seem to have emanated and spread in a context of rivalry for social dominance and royal patronage as seen in Kancipuram and Madurai, which were the centres of such conflict and change. Presumably, *bhakti*, by throwing open the path of salvation to all, irrespective of caste and social hierarchy, imbibed the ideals of the non-orthodox creeds, namely birth and caste as no obstacles to salvation, and thereby succeeded in rooting out 'heretical' sects.

Finally Champakalakshmi argues that a similar sort of rivalry between the followers of the Vaishnava and Saiva wings of the bhakti movement in Tamil Nadu led to further competition for both royal patronage and popular support in which the Cola kings, in particular, tended to side with the Saivas, possibly because the Saivas had proved more adept at integrating local Tamil deities such as Murukan (Skanda) and Korravai (Durga) into their own fold and because of the Saivas' close alliance with the powerful Velala caste. By the twelfth century this Vaishnava–Saiva rivalry had almost completely supplanted the earlier rivalries of *bhakti* with Vedic Brahmanism, Jainism, and Buddhism. All these rivalries fostered the evolution of a social ideology that favoured the aspirations of lower-caste groups, but Champakalakshmi concludes that the promises of equality were largely unfulfilled: '*Bhakti* ideology... induced messianic expectations among the lower orders of *varna*-based society, presumably by providing a delusion of equality among the low castes, which in reality remained beyond their access...' (p. 158).

Burton Stein's essay has a more limited focus, but continues the story of the south Indian bhakti movement up to the fifteenth century. Stein discusses the incorporation of Sudra functionaries into the important Srivaishnava temples of Srirangam in Tamil Nadu and Tirupati in Andhra Pradesh, beginning with the reforms introduced by Ramanuja (b. AD 1017), and the subsequent exclusion of these same functionaries from these temples at a later period. Although Stein does not attempt to explain why the Sudras were initially incorporated into temple worship, he does discuss the role played by these Sudra functionaries in the context of the rivalry between the two main branches of the

Srivaishnava movement: the Northern School (*Vadagalai*) of Vedanta Desika (b. AD 1269) and the Southern School (*Temgalai*) of Pillai Lokacarya (b. AD 1264) and a parallel rivalry between the *Vaikhanasa* and *Pamcaratra* schools of ritual procedures. On the whole the Northern and Vaikhanasa schools were much more socially conservative and opposed the incorporation of Sudras as important participants in the temple rituals while the Southern and Pamcaratra schools took a much more liberal position on the same issues. According to Stein (1966: 87):

The important ritual roles of Sudras at Srirangam were maintained according to the code of Ramanuja until the Temple was desecrated by Muslims in AD 1323, when the major image was hidden an all services ceased. Ritual at the temple was restored when it was rescued from Muslim control in the 1370s by the expanding power of Vijayanagar.... Under officials appointed by the Vijayanagar rulers, the code of Ramanuja was abandoned...and this undermined the rights and privileges of Sudra functionaries.

In the case of the Tirupati temple, the important role of Sudra functionaries was fostered by the Telugu warrior, Saluva Narasimha, through the leadership of his agent in the administration of the temple, a disciple of the Southern School teacher Manavala. Nonetheless, Stein argues that 'in the course of the sixteenth century, following the death of Saluva Narasimha and his agent at Tirupati, the rank and privileges of Sudras [in the temple] declined' (p. 89). Stein finds that it is difficult to identify the reasons for 'the failure of the Sudra Srivaishnavas to maintain their improved ritual position at either Srirangam or Tirupati', but concludes that this may reflect an effort by the opposing schools to seek an 'internal adjustment necessary for consolidation' (pp. 92–3):

The elimination of significant Sudra influence at Srirangam and Tirupati may therefore be understood as an internal sect adjustment which reduced the tension between Northern and Southern School followers and between the proponents of *Pamcaratra* and *Vaikhanasa*, through consensus on the continued significance of Sanskrit learning and the dominance of properly prepared Brahmans in sect leadership and control.

Conversion to Islam

The issue of proselytism and conversion from one religion to another has provoked a great deal of political debate in recent years. Most complaints have come from spokesmen for Hindu communalist organizations such as the Vishva Hindu Parishad which have accused Christian and Muslim missionaries of 'stealing' Hindus, particularly poor Hindus from the Scheduled Castes and Scheduled Tribes, by means of economic inducements. Very little analysis is needed to see that these complaints are hypocritical and politically motivated efforts to attack and denigrate the Muslim and Christian communities. To mention simply the most obvious fact, Christian missionaries in South Asia mostly gave up efforts at active conversion early in the twentieth century and decided instead to concentrate on public service in education and healthcare. Active Muslim proselytism was abandoned even earlier. It should also be noted that the principal population that is supposedly being stolen, the tribal and dalit groups of marginal rural zones, cannot be called clearly Hindu in the first place unless Hindu means anyone in South Asia who does not belong to another major religion. This recent conversion debate cannot, by any stretch of the imagination, be called academic and will not be considered here.

Nonetheless, the issue of proselytism and conversion before 1800 has spawned serious academic debate. All religions and religious movements have to begin somewhere sometime. In the case of South Asia we can date the start of most religions and religious movements with a fair amount of precision, both those originating in the subcontinent and those originating elsewhere. The one important exception is the religion of the *Rg-veda* and its gradual evolution into Pauranic Hinduism in the early centuries of the Common Era. The origins of Vedic religion are mostly beyond the reach of historical research, and the transition to Hinduism was too gradual and complex to be defined with any precision.

More significant for the proselytism and conversion debate is the fact that most major religions and religious movements, including Vedic religion and Hinduism, have had periods of significant growth by the acquisition of new followers. Wherever the Vedic Aryans came from, early Vedic texts make it clear that they represented only part of the population of the subcontinent. Somehow, either by active proselytizing or gradual acculturation, most of the rest of the population was absorbed into Vedic and Hindu religion. For many centuries in the ancient period, Buddhism, an actively proselytizing religion, competed successfully with Vedic and Hindu religion, only to gradually decline after about 500 or 600 CE. On a smaller scale, the same can be said of Jainism. Sikhism, which began in the early years of the sixteenth century, also grew by active proselytism, but it only gradually established itself as a religion wholly independent of Hinduism.

Islam and Christianity have gained followers in South Asia by a combination of active proselytizing, immigration, and the intermarriage of Muslims and Christians with Hindus and others. The result is that over 30 per cent of the combined populations of India, Pakistan, and Bangladesh are now Muslims and about two per cent Christians. The growth of Islam has provoked academic discussion about how and why Islam had more success in some regions, most notably Pakistan and Bangladesh, than in others, and who, if anyone, were the principal agents of Islamization. These questions are discussed in the essays by Richard M. Eaton and Mohammad Ishaq Khan included in this volume.

Eaton begins his essay with a review of three different theories about how and why many South Asians converted to Islam. One is the 'religion of the sword' theory that claims that many or most South Asians were forced to become Muslims by the threat of force. As Eaton and others have indicated, the evidence for this theory is weak, and it seems 'to have confused conversion to Islam with the extension of Turko-Iranian rule in North India between 1200 and 1765' (p. 106 below; see also Rizvi 1981 and Levtzion 1979). A second, somewhat similar, theory is the 'political patronage' theory. Here the basic idea is that individuals and groups converted to Islam to better their political and economic situation under Muslim rulers and zamindars. As Eaton allows, this theory may help explain some conversions, particularly in urban centres such as Delhi, Agra, and Lucknow, but it fails to account for the much greater concentration of Muslim converts in marginal areas like western Punjab (Pakistan) and eastern Bengal (Bangladesh). A third theory is the 'religion of social liberation', which Eaton says claims 'that the Hindu caste system is a rigidly discriminatory form of social organization and that the lowest and most degraded castes, recognizing in Islam an ideology of social equality, converted to it en masse in order to escape Brahmanical oppression' (p. 109 below). Against this theory, Eaton argues that Indian untouchables did not have any notion of innate human equality and could not actually better their social position by conversions to Islam in any case.

Eaton then proposes his own theory that stresses the fact that the populations of both the Punjab and East Bengal were, at the time of their adoption of Islam, much less Hinduized than the populations of the central Ganges plains and the Deccan. In both regions, the 'preliterate', basically non-Hindu population—one whose economic livelihood was initially more associated with pastoralism and mixed agriculture than with sedentary cultivation—adopted the Islam of their rulers and associated migrants through a gradual process of acculturation (what Eaton calls 'accretion') followed, much later, by a stage of 'reform' leading to full Islamization. In East Bengal, Eaton's primary interest, the opening up of new lands for rice cultivation as a result of the eastern shift of the exit channels of the Ganges led to migration of Muslim peasants to the area and the assimilation of the indigenous population of former pastoralists, forest people, and fishermen to Islam. Eaton has further discussed this process in other publications (1993, 2000).

Eaton next turns to a discussion of the identity of the principal agents who supervised or fostered the two-step conversion of the non-Muslim population to Islam. He notes that previous scholars have tended to emphasize the roles played by three different agents: Muslim merchants, the village Qadi or judge, and the Sufi. Eaton accepts that all three contributed to the process of Islamization, but he gives greatest weight to the Qadis and to the cults dedicated to the tombs of dead Sufis. On the other hand, he minimizes the role of living Sufis, arguing that (p. 117 below), 'in their own writings and in the contemporary biographical accounts of them, [living] Sufis do not appear to have been concerned with conversion'.

Mohammad Ishaq Khan discusses the process of premodern Islamization in the geocultural context of Kashmir, another region far from the main political centres of Turko-Iranian rule. Like Eaton, Khan accepts that full Islamization was a gradual process, but he disagrees with Eaton, sharply and explicitly, about the role of Islam's egalitarian ideology in fostering conversion, and also about the role of living Sufi preachers as the principal agents of proselytizing. Khan's specific focus (p. 128 below) is on the role of 'the founding of an indigenous mystic order, the *Silsilah-i Rishiyyan*, by Shaikh Nuruddin Rishi (AD 1379–1442)' and also on the interesting personal association of Nuruddin with the popular Shaivite woman poet-saint Lal Ded (fourteenth century).

According to Khan (p. 134 below), Nuruddin Rishi, inspired in part by Lal Ded, 'trenchantly espoused' nothing less than 'the idea of the dignity and fundamental equality of man' and it was, at least in part, this social message that helped him to win popular support and to foster conversion to Islam by low-caste people. Khan also emphasizes the importance of the Hindu–Muslim synthesis found in the preaching and practices of Nuruddin, but Khan (p. 131 below) refuses to see this synthesis as either an example of syncretism or as a manifestation of a 'polarity between the so-called Great Tradition of the '*Ulama* and the Little Tradition of "Indian Islam"', a polarity he claims to find implicit in Eaton's account. Instead Khan argues (p. 136) that 'what is unique about the social role of Nuruddin...is his intuitive ability to make profuse and profound use of idiom and vocabulary not only from the Qur'an, but more significantly from traditional Hindu sources, the Vedas, and Upanishads. However, he contrived their use in such a way as to recast their thought content and make them carriers of Islamic values and contents.' For a fuller discussion, one can consult Khan's recent book on Kashmir's transition to Islam (1997).

The disagreements between Eaton and Khan suggest several further questions. Although Eaton has dealt primarily with

Bengal and Khan exclusively with Kashmir, it seems inherently unlikely, though perhaps possible, that the processes of conversion would have been so different in the two regions. Has Eaton somewhat exaggerated the extent to which in Bengal conversion to Islam was the result of a mostly impersonal process of acculturation or has Khan somewhat exaggerated the proselytizing role of living Sufis in Kashmir? To what extent were low caste and dalit persons able to propound, or at least to accept, an egalitarian social ideology? What possible relation existed between the iconoclastic social and religious ideas of Lal Ded and Shaikh Nuruddin Rishi and those of later nirguni poet saints, particularly Kabir (c. 1440–1518)? To what extent were Muslim Sufis able to use Hindu texts and ideas for their own purposes?

The Avatar Rama and the Ramanandis

The question of the relation between the rise in the popularity of the avatar Rama after about CE 1200 and the greater presence of Islam in South Asia after the same date is, to say the least, highly controversial. This is particularly true after the December 1992 destruction of the Babri Masjid in Ayodhya. Apart from its potential to raise religious passions, however, this topic also faces the formidable problem that most evidence for a relation between the rise of Rama and the presence of Islam is enciphered in a mythological code. If one wishes to claim that there is indeed a relation between Rama and Islam after CE 1200, one cannot simply point to the rise in the number of Rama temples and to the increasing popularity of vernacular *Ramayanas*, most notably Tulsi Das' *Ram-carit-manas*, nor can one simply point to the obvious relation between devotion to Rama and anti-Muslim feeling in the statements of present-day Hindu communalists. One has to provide convincing evidence that the medieval Hindus who sponsored and supported the Rama temples and who wrote and read the vernacular *Ramayanas* were consciously comparing and coding Rama's battles against barbarians (*mlecchas*) and demons (*asuras* and *daityas*) with political and social conflicts between the Hindu and Muslim communities.

This is what Sheldon Pollock attempts to do in his essay 'Ramayana and Political Imagination in India'.

Pollock has recourse to three different sorts of evidence to argue his case: archaeological remains of Rama temples and cultic sites, inscriptions that compare or identify ruling kings with Rama, and Sanskrit texts that do the same. With regard to the archaeological evidence, Pollock first stresses the fact that there was an almost complete absence of temples dedicated primarily to Rama before the twelfth century (an absence already noted in 1913 by R. G. Bhandarkar, as Pollock acknowledges). Then Pollock turns to a discussion of 'several major cultic centres devoted to Rama [that] are created or reinvigorated' sometime around CE 1300. His main examples are 'the Rama complex at Ramtek...and the Ramacandra shrine at Vijayanagar' (Pollock 1993: 266). When he turns to inscriptions, Pollock notes a similar absence of references to Rama as an object of religious devotion in inscriptions written before the twelfth century and then cites passages from the Dabhoi inscription of CE 1253 and the Hansi inscription of CE 1168 that compare (in the first case, and then only indirectly) or identify (in the second case) the ruling king with Rama. Both inscriptions refer to these ruling kings' defeat of Turkic (*turuska*) opponents but do not explicitly compare these Turks to Rama's demon enemies. Pollock's textual evidence is likewise drawn primarily from two sources, both written in Sanskrit: Merutunga's *Prabandhacintamani* of CE 1304 and Jayanáka's *Prthvirajavijaya,* written between CE 1178 and 1193. In these texts king Jayasimha Siddharaja of Gujarat (CE 1094–1143) and king Prthviraja Cauhan of Ajmer (d. CE 1193) are both clearly identified with Rama, and their Turkic opponents with Rama's demon opponents (indirectly in the case of Merutunga and more directly in the case of Jayanaka).

After reviewing the history of the spread of Turkic dynasties across northern South Asia in the period from about CE 1000 to 1350, Pollock discusses the affinity of the story of Rama with these political events in terms of two 'special imaginative "resources"' of the story: 'divinization and demonization'. According to Pollock, Valmiki's story (p. 183 below):

offers for the first time a special assessment, or resolution, of the paradox that the political comprises in premodern India. It does this by way of what I think is a new mediation of the religious, that is, the divine or numinous, and the political, by which I mean the nature of life in the human polity. The second heading, the demonization of the Other—a shopworn yet still indispensable phrase—relates to those who stand outside this theologically sanctioned polity. Not only are these two thematics the defining thematics of Valmiki's epic, they are two of the most powerful conceptions of the social-political imagination. The first proclaims that the order of everyday human life is regulated by the active, immanent presence of the divine; the second, that those who would disturb or destroy that order must be enemies of God and not really human.

Given these two special imaginative resources of Rama's story, it is, in Pollock's opinion, only natural that the story became a primary vehicle for conceptualizing the unique challenge to Hindu culture represented by Islamic culture. South Asia hitherto had been able to assimilate the cultures of earlier warrior groups that invaded from the north-west with comparatively little effort. This was not possible in the case of the Islamicized invaders of the eleventh and twelfth centuries. The ensuing crisis occasioned attempts to strengthen and codify 'the Hindu way of life' in *dharmanibandha* texts such as the *Krtyakalpataru* of Laksmidhara (*ca.* CE 1130) and retellings of Rama's story in vernacular texts such as Tulsi Das's *Ramacaritamanasa* (*ca.* CE 1580) (*ibid.*, pp. 286–7). This, in Pollock's view, is the main rationale for the rise of the Rama cult in this period, and evidently also for the adoption of Rama as the tutelary deity of modern Hindu communalism as well.

Brajadulal Chattopadhyaya's extended critique of Pollock's article takes issue with several specific problems with his historical evidence and methodology. Many of Chattopadhyaya's objections are clearly valid, but whether they are sufficient to completely overturn Pollock's main argument—namely that there is an important relation between the story and cult of Rama and the presence of the Muslims in India after AD 1200—is less clear. At least in part, Chattopadhyaya's strong reaction against Pollock's article may stem less from specific problems of evidence and methodology and more from a general reluctance of many historians strongly opposed to communalism such as Chattopadhyaya to accept that the roots of communalism may extend back beyond the colonial period, in other words that communalism may have a sort of pre- or proto-history.

Here anti-communalist historians are undoubtedly reacting, and with reason, against historians with Hindu communalist sympathies who claim, directly or indirectly, that Aurangzeb and age-old Muslim fanaticism are the root causes of the present communalist mess. Pollock, however, is himself strongly opposed to Hindu communalism and clearly would reject any simplistic anti-Aurangzeb style argument. He would also, I think, agree that communalism in South Asia is a basically modern political phenomenon, one that can be traced back directly to the British divide-and-rule tactics such as the first partition of Bengal in 1905 and, less directly but more consequentially, to the introduction of electoral (and hence majority versus minority) politics beginning with the Government of India Act of 1909. One cannot, however, simply assert that everything starts with the British. Clearly communalism built upon and exacerbated an already existing cultural fault line. The importance historians chose to give or not give to this cultural fault line is in fact a quite legitimate question for debate, and it is here that the disagreements between Pollock and Chattopadhyaya become more significant.

One of Chattopadhyaya's more significant criticisms is that Pollock tends to overlook the fact that the rise to prominence, large size, and numerical abundance of Hindu temples largely takes place after CE 500 or even 700, that is, well after the so-called imperial Guptas. To argue, as Pollock does, that sculptural and epigraphic evidence for the Rama cult before these dates is sparse, therefore, is not to say very much. The archaeological evidence for temples after CE 700 but before 1100, the approximate date when Pollock claims that Rama first becomes an important object of cultic devotion, on the other hand, is quite abundant and Pollock clearly is justified in pointing out the lack of Rama temples in this period. Another important point that Chattopadhyaya makes is that Pollock's evidence for the importance of the Rama cult *after* CE 1100 is also weak. As has been indicated above, the key exhibits that Pollock presents in defence of his arguments are in fact remarkably few. Maybe, and here the jury is still out, the Rama cult was not particularly important even well *after* the Turkic conquests.

Chattopadhyaya's most telling criticism is that Pollock ignores the abundance of comparisons of medieval Hindu kings with divine figures (gods, avatars, and sages) other than Rama. Chattopadhyaya cites a number of sources in which Rama is either ignored or included as simply one among many such figures with whom the ruling kings are compared. According to Chattopadhyaya (1998: 110): 'The use of the legendary figure of Rama and the reference to his ideal rule are a part of a complex of motifs, and there is never any suggestion in the records themselves that a particular motif gains precedence over others in a specific context'. In the cases of both Pollock and Chattopadhyaya, however, the evidence of *vernacular* texts relevant to the role of Rama after about CE 1200 is not adequately explored, and many of the arguments that they raise could be pursued further in this light.

This is, in part, what Richard Burghart does in his essay on 'The Founding of the Ramanandi Sect'. Whereas Pollock attempts to describe the rise of a politically-oriented, but vaguely defined, cult dedicated to the avatar Rama starting from about the twelfth century using the evidence of temples and Sanskrit texts, Burghart describes the rise of a specific religious sect called the Ramanandis dedicated to the same avatar starting from about the late fifteenth or early sixteenth century using evidence drawn from both Sanskrit and vernacular texts. Through an ingenious close reading of a set of several different spiritual genealogies of the sect, Burghart attempts to reconstruct several stages in the sect's historical development. One of his principal aims is to argue, against sectarian tradition, that it is unlikely that the fifteenth-century ascetic named Ramanand was actually the founder of the Ramanandi sect. Other scholars have expressed doubts about the need for such radical historical scepticism about the early sectarian traditions relating to Ramanand and his disciples (Caracchi 1999: 23–78; Lorenzen 1991: 3–22, 1999). In the context of the claims of Pollock about counter-Muslim aspects of the rise of a movement of devotion to Rama, however, Burghart's comments provide an interesting contrast.

Burghart argues that the Ramanandis had to compete with a number of other sects in north India for three sources of income and support, all of which were in limited supply (Burghart 1978: 126):

> In order to maintain themselves over time, the ascetics of the various Hindu sects acquired access to three important resources: devotees and disciples, pilgrimage routes and pilgrimage centres, and political patronage. The availability of these resources was limited. Although some ascetic sects were founded in the outerlying regions of the subcontinent, nearly all of them, like the Ramanandi sect, eventually spread to the Ganges basin where, given the number of sects operating on that territory, the competition for these three limited resources was very intense.

In this view, the Ramanandi sect does not arise as a movement of reaction against Islamization, as Pollock's model suggests; rather it becomes simply one of several sects, both Hindu and Muslim, that were in competition for these three scarce resources. Burghart further argues, moreover, that the success of the Ramanandi sect over its rivals is likely due to the fact that it extended its recruitment pool of both devotees and possible ascetics to include persons from low castes, women, and even untouchables and Muslim converts (*ibid.*):

> In the competition for devotees and disciples Ramanand and/or his followers gained a significant advantage over their rival sects. The servant castes, untouchables, women, and former Hindus who had converted by choice or by threat of force to Islam comprised more than three-fourths of the population of the Ganges basin and constituted an immense hitherto unexploited source of devotees and disciples for an ascetic sect.

Kabir and the Sants

According to tradition, Ramananda's direct disciples included several men born into non-Brahmin castes. Most important among them was a low-caste Muslim weaver from Banaras named Kabir. In collaboration with his fellow disciples, especially the untouchable leather-worker named Raidas, Kabir launched a movement of devotion not to Rama, the avatar and king of Ayodhya, but to an impersonal or *nirgun* Ram, a Supreme God who was beyond any anthropomorphic (or theriomorphic) representation. This movement became known as that of the Sants or Nirguni Bhakti.

It quickly spread to other parts of northern South Asia, especially Rajasthan, where the followers of a cotton-carder named Dadu formed the Dadu Panth, and to the Punjab, where Guru Nanak initiated his Sikh Panth.

Much of our knowledge of Kabir and the Sant or Nirguni movement stems from the work of three great mid-twentieth-century scholars: Pitambardatta Barthwal, Parasuram Caturvedi, and Hajariprasad Dvivedi. Selections from Barthwal's 1936 book, *The Nirguna School of Hindi Poetry* (1978) and Dvivedi's famous 1942 study entitled *Kabir* (1971) are included here. Although these texts may now appear dated in some respects, the issues they raise, particularly with regard to the relation of the Sant movement to both Islam and the South Asian caste system, are still being debated. Nowadays this debate generally embodies more cautious and balanced views of both Islam and the caste system, but these earlier texts include a sharper focus on the radical social and political dimensions of the Sant movement and on its break with more traditional *saguni* bhakti.

Barthwal claims that the Sant movement arose among the lower castes of Hindu society mostly as a result of their being caught between a rock and a hard place: oppression by their new rulers bearing a harsh Islamic religion and by high-caste Hindus who imposed caste-based economic and social inequalities. Caught in this difficult situation, Kabir and his followers devised a religious message and practice that attempted to free them from both sorts of oppression. Dvivedi's view is in some respects similar, but he sees the main challenge of Islam and caste Hinduism not so much in terms of their mutual capacity for oppression, to which he also refers, but rather in terms of a set of sharp contrasts between the world-views and styles of life characteristic of each. Juxtaposing Persian-based and Sanskrit-based key terms used in descriptions of Islam and Hinduism, Dvivedi sets out his appreciation of the essential differences in the two religions (1971: 180–1):

Muslim religion [*dharma*] is a 'religion' [*mazahab*]. Its organization was completely contrary to Indian social organization. Indian society kept a caste-associated character and fostered an individualized religious practice. Islam omitted this caste-associated character and fostered a collectivized religious practice. The central point of one was conduct [*caritrya*], that of the other was religious doctrine [*dharma-mat*]. In Indian society it was an accepted fact that whatever one's beliefs might be, if one's conduct was pure, then that individual was worthy, whatever caste he might belong to.... The new [Muslim] religious doctrine that was shaking up the Indian people and society gave no importance at all to conduct. Its organization was completely the opposite.... Although [Muslim] society was exclusionist in religious form, it was inclusionist in social form, while Hindu society was inclusionist in religious form and exclusionist in social form.

Dvivedi, then, sees the problem not so much in terms of economic and social oppression of the common people by Muslim and Hindu elites who use the negative aspects of their respective religions for this purpose, but rather in terms of a radical disjuncture between the basic socio-religious world-views of Islam and Hinduism. This difference between Dvivedi's appreciation of Islam and Hinduism and that of Barthwal also leads to an interesting difference in their respective appreciation of the nature of Sant religion, especially that of Kabir himself. In Barthwal's view, Kabir and the Sants were rebelling against specific oppressive features of Islam and Hinduism and seeking a religion that could combine the positive features of both. Barthwal does not attempt to disguise Kabir's dissatisfaction with Islam and Hinduism as *actually* practised, but he does claim that Kabir was seeking a synthesis of an *ideally* conceptualized model of the two religions. Dvivedi on the other hand, since he postulates such a radical difference between Islam and Hinduism, is virtually obliged to also regard Kabir as having espoused a radical break with both religions. In the case of such radical opposites, no syncretic synthesis was logically possible. In more recent scholarship, a somewhat similar debate has offered differing evaluations of the continuities and discontinuities between the *nirguni* bhakti of the Sants and the *saguni* bhakti of figures like Sur Das and Tulsi (Hawley 1987, 1995; Lorenzen 1995a).

Historical Overviews

Krishna Sharma's essay, 'Towards a New Perspective,' a chapter of her 1987 book *Bhakti and the Bhakti Movement*, and Romila

Thapar's 1989 essay, 'Imagined Religious Communities? Ancient History and the Modern Search for a Hindu Identity,' both present general theoretical arguments about the nature of the bhakti 'movement', of Hindu sects, and the of the construction of Hinduism as a religious concept.

In her essay Krishna Sharma makes three broad claims. The first is that 'what is summed up under the general designation, Bhakti movement, was really an amalgam of a number of devotional movements. A monolithic view of these movements can be taken only if their common denomination, bhakti, is understood in its generic sense' (1987: 7). Specifically, she argues that there exist two distinct schools within this 'generic' bhakti movement: that of the Nirguna devotees (*bhaktas*) and that of the Saguna devotees. The character and conceptual structure of these two movements were, in Sharma's view, quite separate. Her second claim is that scholars have wrongly defined bhakti 'as a monotheism based on devotion to a personal God, and as the opposite pole of the monistic stream of Hindu religious tradition which advocates belief in an impersonal God' (*ibid.*, p. 4). This view, she argues, ignores almost completely the bhakti of the Nirguna devotees. Sharma's third claim is that 'the modern academic definition of bhatkti *sic* was, in fact, formulated in the nineteenth century by some Western scholars regardless of the indigenous understanding of it' (*ibid.*, p. 7).

Regarding these three claims, few would dispute the first. The idea that the Nirguna and Saguna schools or currents of bhakti are distinct clearly exists in the minds of early Nirguna poets such as Kabir, Nanak, Rajjab, and others (Lorenzen 1996: 1–12, 257–61). In a modern academic context, the differences of the Nirguna and Saguna devotees were early recognized by scholars such as J. N. Farquhar (1920), J. Estlin Carpenter (1921), and Kshitimohan Sen (1929). The conceptual divide was then given a more formal conceptualization by two Hindi scholars–Pitambardatta Barthwal and Parasuram Caturvedi (see above). On the other hand, many accounts of Hindu religion aimed at a popular audience, and also some academic studies, still treat all bhakti movements as members of one big family, whatever its internal divisions. Others have argued that the social differences between the followers of popular Nirguna and Saguna movements are more basic to understanding how and why the movements differ than are their merely theological differences (Lorenzen 1995a).

Sharma's second claim is that 'in all academic works... bhakti is defined as a monotheism based on devotion to a personal God' in opposition to a more 'monistic stream of Hindu religious tradition' based on worship of an impersonal God. This claim seems to be true primarily for some scholarly works written before about 1920 or for works written later as text books or for a wide popular audience. Since Farquhar, and certainly since Barthwal, however, most scholars have been well aware of the existence of basic differences between Nirguna and Saguna bhakti, even those who insist that both belong to one big bhakti family.

Sharma's third claim is that the identification of all bhakti with Saguna monotheism is exclusively the work of foreign scholars. This claim is much more controversial. As has just been noted, differences between Ṇirguna Bhakti and Ṣaguna bhakti were noted and discussed by modern scholars of both British and South Asian origin at least as far back as 1920. Sharma is correct that there was a pronounced tendency of Christian writers to conceptualize bhakti in terms of monotheistic devotion to an anthropomorphic God, but this tendency is most evident in books written for a popular audience, not scholarly monographs. Most importantly, the tendency to promote Saguna worship of Vishnu as 'official' Hinduism was also a key project of many nineteenth century Hindu intellectuals such as Harishcandra, as Vasudha Dalmia's excellent recent study makes clear (1999). In her study Dalmia specifically criticizes Sharma on just this point. Hindu intellectuals such as Harishchandra were undoubtedly responding to critiques of Hinduism by Christian writers, but they were also pursuing their own independent agendas. One should also note that even early Christian writers constructed their own interpretations of Hinduism with the help of native intellectuals who had their own ideas about the nature of Hinduism and their own social and religious agendas.

Romila Thapar's essay questioning the concept of imagined religious communities is principally an argument against the projection of communal religious ideologies into the past. Her widely ranging discussion includes such topics as the notion of an Aryan race, Asoka's distinction between Brahmanism and Sramanism, the rise of 'a variety of devotional cults' sometime shortly after CE 1000, royal patronage of these cults and their return role in the legitimization of political authority, the loose and late development of the concepts of Hinduism and Hindu identity, the early history of religious conflicts between Saivism and the Sramanic sects of Jainism and Buddhism, the history of the varied meanings of the word 'Hindu,' and the construction of a modern but suspect concept of Hinduism by western Orientalists and Hindu nationalists. She grants that the fifteenth century vernacular corpus of texts by Kabir 'refers to Hindus and counterposes Hindus and Turuskas in a religious sense' (1989: 224), but she also insists that 'the perception which groups subscribing to Hindu and Islamic symbols had of each other was not in terms of a monolithic religion, but more in terms of distinct and disparate castes and sects along a social continuum. Even the recognition of a religious identity does not automatically establish a religious community' (*ibid.*, p. 225).

Two aspects of Thapar's argument are quite controversial. First is her view of the role of the encounter with Islam in establishing a Hindu identity. Second is her interpretation of the relation between religion and social ideology. The former issue is, as has been noted, discussed in detail in several of the essays included in this collection, particularly those of Barthwal, Dvivedi, Chattopadhyaya and Pollock. Barthwal, Dvivedi and Pollock clearly give greater weight to the role of Islam as Hinduism's significant Other in the creation of a sense of Hindu identity. In comparison, Chattopadhyaya and Thapar attribute less importance to the role of Islam. Thapar instead claims that the 'clashes which on the face of it would now be interpreted as between Hindus and Muslims, would require a deeper investigation to ascertain how far they were clashes between specific castes and sects ...'How compatible this view is with the evidence for conflictive Hindu and Muslim identities found in such texts as the sixteenth century songs and verses of Kabir and Vidyapati's early fifteenth century *Kirtilata* perhaps needs further consideration (Lorenzen 1999).

Thapar's argument that 'the recognition of a religious identity does not automatically establish a religious community' is evidently based on the view that religion is a phenomenon that can be separated, at least in theory, from political and social concerns. Other scholars have argued that religious ideologies are themselves a special category of social ideologies and that religious ideologies necessarily imply distinct membership boundaries, even if these boundaries are no more clearly defined than the difference between 'them' and 'us'. Are religious ideologies mainly concerned with the relation between man and God or are they mainly concerned with the establishment of boundaries and rules of human communities? Although both metaphysical beliefs and community norms are obviously essential to any religion, it does make a big difference which aspect we regard as more important.

Summary

As a general category, then, popular religious movements can be defined as groups of ordinary persons who share a set of religious beliefs and practices and a related set of social, moral, and political norms and goals. Most studies of such movements in South Asia before 1800 have been written from a historical perspective. This tends to limit the range of generalizations found in them, but it also means that the best discussions are sharply focused and empirically well grounded. In this book, I have attempted to collect a representative sample of some of the best of these studies relating to a variety of religious movements from both the south and the north existing in the period from about AD 600 to 1800. Most of the movements are Hindu, but Muslim movements are also represented. Studies of movements before AD 600—whether Brahmanic, Buddhist, or Jain—are best left to a separate volume.

Inevitably, popular religious movements come in many different shapes and sizes. Some have large memberships and are geographically widespread. Others are small and local. Some are highly structured and clearly define who belongs to them and who does not. Others are loosely structured and have no clearly defined membership. Some are led by full-time religious specialists, others are not. Some have a clearly defined social ideology and social base and others do not. Some have quite specific political or economic goals and some have quite imprecise or even surreptitious social and political aims. Some have developed a sophisticated and complex metaphysics, others rely exclusively on simple devotion. Some are otherworldly in orientation, others are thisworldly. Some insist on a strict code of ethics or ascetic restraints and others have a relatively lax or hedonistic attitude to life. Some are long-lived, some are ephemeral. Most movements are associated with one or other major religious tradition—whether Hindu, Muslim, Christian, or Buddhist—but some adhere strictly to their chosen tradition, while others combine elements from two or more different traditions.

What this set of essays shows is that popular religious movements have played key roles in South Asian history from at least Gupta times. Although pre-Gupta movements are less well documented and not discussed here, we do know, for instance, that at least the Buddhist and Jain religions split up quite early into a large number of competing movements or 'sects'. Pre-Gupta Hindu movements were usually organized around either specific philosophical or theological doctrines or around the worship of specific deities. It is difficult, however, to conclude much about their class bases, social ideologies, and specific styles of organization and ritual practices since the evidence is so incomplete. Already in Gupta times, however, we begin to find clearer evidence about the existence of popular Hindu movements such as the Pasupatas and Bhagavatas. Beginning with the Alvars and Nayanars in southern India from about the seventh century, there appears a great profusion of popular religious movements based on devotion to universal deities (even in cases where these deities have more specific local manifestations). These movements have clear spiritual and moral messages but they have also been, and in many cases continue to be, key players in the political and social life of the subcontinent.

Note

1. For an attempt to reconstruct the history of the Sadhs, see Allison 1935. For the Gosains/Jogis, see Vaudeville 1974: 81–9.

References

Allison, W. L. 1935. *The Sadhs*. Calcutta.

Barthwal, P. D. 1978. *Traditions of Indian Mysticism based upon Nirguna School of Hindi Poetry*. New Delhi. First published in 1936 as *The Nirguna School of Hindi Poetry*.

Burghart, Richard. 1978. 'The Founding of the Ramanandi Sect,' *Ethnohistory* 25, 2: 121–39.

———. 1983. 'Renunciation in the Religious Traditions of South Asia,' *Man* (N.S.) 18: 633–53.

Caracchi, Pinuccia. 1999. *Ramananda e lo yoga dei sant*. Alessandria, Italy.

Carpenter, J. Estlin. 1977. *Theism in Medieval India*. New Delhi. First published in 1921.

Champakalakshmi, R. 1996. 'From Devotion and Dissent to Dominance: The Bhakti of the Tamil Alvars and Nayanars', in R. Champakalakshmi and S. Gopal (eds), *Tradition, Dissent, and Ideology: Essays in Honour of Romila Thapar*, pp. 135–63. Delhi.

Chattopadhyaya, Brajadulal. 1998. *Representing the Other? Sanskrit Sources and the Muslims*. New Delhi.

Cohn, Norman. 1970. *The Pursuit of the Millennium: Revolutionary Millenarians and Mystical Anarchists of the Middle Ages*. Rev. ed.; New York. First edition published in 1957.

Dalmia, Vasudha. 1999. *The Nationalization of Hindi Traditions: Bharatendu Harischandra and Nineteenth-Century Banaras*. Delhi. First published in 1997.

Devalle, Susana. 1985. 'Clandestine Culture of Protest in Colonial Situations', *Canberra Anthropology* 8, 1–2: 32–57.

Dube, Saurabh. 1998. *Untouchable Pasts: Religion, Identity, and Power among a Central Indian Community, 1780–1950*. Albany.

Dumont, Louis. 1980. 'World Renunciation in Indian Religions', in his *Homo Hierarchicus: The Caste System and Its Implications*, pp. 267–86 (Appendix B). Translated from French. Chicago. The original French version of the essay was published in 1959. The English version was first published in 1960. The original French edition of the book (without this essay) was published in 1966.

———. 1986. *Essays on Individualism: Modern Ideology in Anthropological Perspective*. Chicago.

Dvivedi, Hajariprasad. 1971. *Kabir*. Delhi. Originally published in 1942.

Eaton, Richard. 1985. 'Approaches to the Study of Conversion to Islam in India', in Richard C. Martin (ed.), *Approaches to Islam in Religious Studies*, pp. 106–23. Tucson.

———. 1993. *The Rise of Islam and the Bengal Frontier, 1204–1760*. Berkeley. Paperback edition 1996.

Eaton, Richard. 2000. 'Who are the Bengal Muslims? Conversion and Islamization in Bengal', in his *Essays on Islam and Indian History*, pp. 249–75. New Delhi.

Farquhar, J. N. 1967. *An Outline of the Religious Literature of India*. Delhi. First published in 1920.

Hawley, John Stratton. 1987. 'The Sant in Sur Das', in K. Schomer and W. H. McLeod (eds), *The Sants: Studies in a Devotional Tradition of India*, pp. 191–211. Delhi.

———. 1995. 'The *Nirgun/Sagun* Distinction in Early Manuscript Anthologies of Hindu Devotion', in David N. Lorenzen (ed.), *Bhakti Religion in North India*, pp. 160–80. Albany/Delhi.

Hill, Michael. 1973. *A Sociology of Religion*. London.

Khan, Mohammad Ishaq. 1997. *Kashmir's Transition to Islam: The Role of Muslim Rishis (Fifteenth to Eighteenth Centuries)*. New Delhi.

———. 2000. 'The Rishi Movement as a Social Force in Medieval Kashmir', in Muzaffar Alam *et al.* (eds), *The Making of Indo-Persian Culture: Indian and French Studies*, pp. 129–47. New Delhi.

Lorenzen, David N. 1987. 'Traditions of Non-Caste Hinduism: The Kabir Panth', *Contributions to Indian Sociology* 21: 264–83.

———. 1991. *Kabir Legends and Ananta-das's Kabir Parachai*. Albany. Also published in Delhi, in 1992.

———. 1995a. 'The Historical Vicissitudes of Bhakti Religion', in David N. Lorenzen (ed.), *Bhakti Religion in North India*, pp. 1–32. Albany/Delhi.

———. 1995b. 'Lives of Nirguni Saints', in David N. Lorenzen (ed.), *Bhakti Religion in North India*, pp. 181–211. Albany/Delhi.

———. 1999. 'The Life of Kabir in Legend', in Alan Entwistle and Carol Solomon (eds), *Studies in Early Modern Indo-Aryan Languages, Literature, and Culture*, pp. 209–26. New Delhi.

———. 1999. 'Who Invented Hinduism?', *Comparative Studies in Society and History* 42: 630–59.

Levtzion, Nehemiah. 1979. *Conversion to Islam*. New York.

Mandelbaum, David G. 1972. *Change and Continuity*, vol. 2 of his *Society in India*. Berkeley, 1972. First published in 1970.

Marx, Karl and Friedrich Engels. 1959. *Basic Writings on Politics and Philosophy*. Ed. Lewis S. Feuer. Garden City.

———. 1964. *On Religion*. Introduction by Reinhold Niebuhr. New York. Engel's 'Peasant War' essay is only partly excerpted here but the book contains a good general selection of writings on religion by both Marx and Engels.

Narayanan, M. G. S. and Veluthat Kesavan. 1987. 'Bhakti Movement in South India', in D. N. Jha (ed.), *Feudal Social Formation in Early India*, pp. 347–75. This essay was earlier published in S. C. Malik (ed.), *Indian Movements: Some Aspects of Dissent, Protest, and Reform*. Simla, 1978.

Pocock, David. 1973. *Mind, Body and Wealth: A Study of Belief and Practice in an Indian Village*.

Pollock, Sheldon. 1993. 'Ramayana and the Political Imagination in India', *Journal of Asian Studies* 52, 2: 261–97.

Rizvi, S. A. A. 1981. 'Islamization in the Indian Subcontinent' in David N. Lorenzen (ed.), *Religious Change and Cultural Domination*. Mexico, pp. 39–60.

Scott, James C. 1990. *Domination and the Arts of Resistance: Hidden Transcripts*. New Haven.

Sen, Kshitimohan. 1974. *Medieval Mysticism of India*. Translated from Bengali. New Delhi. First published in 1929.

Sharma, Krishna. 1987. *Bhakti and Bhakti Movement: A New Perspective*. New Delhi.

Stein, Burton. 1968. 'Social Mobility and Medieval South Indian Hindu Sects', in James Silverberg (ed.), *Social Mobility and the Caste System in India: An Interdisciplinary Symposium*, pp. 78–94. The Hague.

Thapar, Romila. 1978. 'Renunciation: The Making of a Counter-Culture?', in Romila Thapar, *Ancient Indian Social History: Some Interpretations*, pp. 63–104. New Delhi.

———. 1989. 'Imagined Religious Communities? Ancient History and the Modern Search for a Hindu Identity', *Modern Asian Studies* 23: 209–31.

Trevor-Roper, H. R. 1956. *The European Witch-Craze of the Sixteenth and Seventeenth Centuries and Other Essays*. New York.

Troeltsch, Ernst. 1931. *The Social Teaching of the Christian Churches*. 2 vols. Translated from German. New York.

van der Veer, Peter. 1989. *Gods on Earth: The Management of Religious Experience and Identity in a North Indian Pilgrimage Centre*. Delhi.

Vaudeville, Charlotte. 1974. *Kabir*. Oxford.

Weber, Max. 1958. *The Protestant Ethic and the Spirit of Capitalism*. Translated from German. New York.

———. 1958. *The Religion of India: The Sociology of Hinduism and Buddhism*. Translated from German. New York. First published in German in 1920.

———. 1963. *The Sociology of Religion*. Translated from German with an introduction by Talcott Parsons. Boston. First published in German in 1922.

Wilson, Bryan. 1970. *Religious Sects: A Sociological Study*. New York.

Yinger, J. Milton. 1970. *The Scientific Study of Religion*. London.

I

Alvars and Nayanars

1

From Devotion and Dissent to Dominance

The Bhakti of the Tamil Āḷvārs and Nāyanārs*

R. Champakalakshmi

The *bhakti* of the Tamil Āḷvārs and Nāyanārs has been the theme of many scholarly works studying the concept and its impact from various standpoints, namely *bhakti* as a cult under the broad rubric of the development of religion in South India, or as an important element in the sectarian Purāṇic religions, or as the focus of a debate on the nature of bhakti as a protest/dissent against caste hierarchy, status, and privileges. Recent studies

* From R. Champakalakshmi and S. Gopal (eds), *Tradition, Dissent, and Ideology: Essays in Honour of Romila Thapar*, Delhi, 1996, pp. 135–63.

This essay is a revised version of one of the two lectures delivered at various Indian universities under the UGC National Lectures Scheme in 1979 and a paper presented at the 31st International Congress of Human Sciences in Asia and North Africa, Tokyo, 1983. See Proceedings of this Congress published in 1984 (Tokyo), vol. II, ed. Yammo Tatsuro.

have examined the concept, its origins, varied contexts as well as its content, both metaphysical and emotional. Works that dwell upon the rich poetic and aesthetic appeal of *bhakti* literature are also known. Despite the availability of an impressive volume of published literature on the subject, fresh insights may still be gained from a study of the *bhakti* hymns, the nature of the concept and its social impact, its ideological significance, and institutional developments in early medieval Tamiḻakam.

This essay is an attempt to study *bhakti* as a concept evolving first in the hymns of the Vaiṣṇava Āḻvārs, subsequently in those of the Śaiva Nāyanārs, growing into an instrument of protest or dissent against *brāhmaṇa* orthodoxy, existing social norms and inequalities, developing into an ethical/moral principle capable of evolving new value systems, and thus providing the basis for the emergence of a dominant ideology[1] that was to ultimately become the ruling ideology at the hands of powerful dynasts and elite groups, with immense capacities to sustain and revitalize itself during situations of crises.

I

You people
who have gone there to worship,
the name Irunkuṉṟam
has spread far and wide
on this great bustling earth
it boasts fame in ages past
for it is the home of the dear lord
who eradicates delusions
for people who fill their eyes
with his image

[*Paripāṭal*, 15, trans. Norman Cutler, 1993.][2]

Addressing mortals on the earth the poet of this verse from the *Paripāṭal*, a Cankam classic, praises Mālirunkuṉṟam (Tirumāliruñcōlai or Aḻakarmalai near Maturai) as the best of all earth's mountains as it is the god's abode on earth. The *Paripāṭal* introduces us to a new era in Tamil culture, a new milieu to Tamil religion and worship, namely the temple, which was to become one of the major symbols of South Indian tradition. *Bhakti* or devotion appears here for the first time as the central concept, which was to be later developed more fully by the Āḻvārs (and Nāyanārs), and elaborated in the exegesis of the Vaiṣṇava and Śaiva canonical texts of medieval times. The work also brings into Tamil religion the idea of an absolute or universal godhead Māl/Māyōn/Viṣṇu and Murukan—and his abode, the temple, which was to become the most innovative focus of Tamil life and culture.

The *Paripāṭal* is classified as one of the eight Cankam anthologies (*eṭṭuttokai*), but stands apart from the others on account of its religious content and character, somewhat alien to the anthologies. Dated by all serious students of Cankam literature somewhere between the period of the anthologies and the *bhakti* or hymnal literature, that is, in about the fifth to sixth centuries AD,[3] it has more in common with the late Cankam collection, *Kalittokai*, and the epic *Cilappatikāram*. Together these works belong to a transitional phase in Tamil religious and cultural traditions. Standing on the threshold of a new form of poetry, that is, the *bhakti* hymns, the *Paripāṭal* shows evidence of Vedic, Upaniṣadic, and Purāṇic influence, and as has been admirably shown by Friedhelm Hardy's study[4] of emotional Kṛṣṇa *bhakti*, reveals the meeting point of northern Sanskritic devotional themes with the *akam* (interior/love) as well as *puṟam* (exterior/war) themes of Cankam literature. It marks a new synthesis and leads to the intensely powerful emotional *bhakti* in Āḻvār poetry, which derives its principal motifs from the Māl (Viṣṇu) hymns of the *Paripāṭal*.

Bhakti as a concept may also be recognized in another late Cankam text, the *Tirumurukāṟṟuppaṭai* (guide to Murukan), which speaks in exaltation of the idea in relation to the worship of Murukan. Like the *Paripāṭal*, it also speaks of the specific association of a place/places and shrines for the deity. Significantly, Śiva, one of the central deities of the Purāṇic religion, receives only marginal attention and is grouped as one of the five great gods in the *Kalittokai*,[5] none of them being the pre-eminent one. Śiva, it may be pointed out, was not one of the *tiṇai* deities of the Cankam, as Māl and Murukan were of the *mullai* (forest) and *kuṟiñci* (hilly) *tiṇai*s or eco-zones.

The *Paripāṭal* and *Tirumurukāṟṟuppaṭai* would thus seem to represent the transition from the worship of tribal or folk deities of the anthologies to the universalization of godhead and the evolution of formal religious systems, which under the Pallavas and Pāṇṭiyas of the seventh–ninth centuries AD became crystallized as the Purāṇic Vaiṣṇava and Śaiva religions. It was a new regional synthesis of Purāṇic forms in which the northern Sanskritic elements assumed a dominant position while the local or folk cults and their deities either got completely merged or remained major components of the Purāṇic pantheon. The concept of *bhakti*, drawing largely upon the *akam* or love theme of Cankam poetry, was systematically developed initially by the Āḻvārs and subsequently by the Nāyanārs to carry these Purāṇic forms to the Tamil masses in their own idiom, namely an 'intensely human religious awareness'[6] and in the vernacular, namely Tamil.

The idea of the temple as the focus of this devotional cult emerges in the above two works, but is again crystallized and promoted in the *bhakti* hymns. This is not to say that shrines or centres of worship were unknown to the Cankam Tamils. Such cult centres did exist, as is known from the references to *kōyil* and *nakar*, apart from the *kantu* (pillar) and *potiyil* (commonplace)[7] for purposes of worship. What was absent was the institutionalization of such centres for the promotion of a formal religious system.

Āḻvār and Nāyanār *bhakti* brings several strands together, the typical Cankam Tamil humanism, anthropocentric religion, emotional and sensual character of worship, and the northern Brahmanic/Sanskritic concept of a transcendental absolute (monotheism), together with several mythological structures. The *Purāṇa*s and *Āgama*s would seem to have provided the major myths and iconographic forms that find constant mention in the hymns. Under sectarian Purāṇic influence, the Brahmanical religion became polarized into the Vaiṣṇava and Śaiva. While Viṣṇu, the first major deity of this religion was the Māl/Māyōn of the Cankam milieu, Śiva, as has been pointed out, was only of marginal importance in the same milieu and is not even mentioned in the *Tolakāppiyam*, the earliest known grammar, which systematically explicates all important concepts and symbols. It was Murukan, the god of love and war of the Cankam *kuṟiñci tiṇai*, who provided a major component to the Śaiva pantheon, as the son of Śiva. With Koṟṟavi, the deity of the *pālai tiṇai* (arid zone) being identified with Durgā and as the consort of Śiva, the basic elements in Purāṇic Śaivism had become established in the Tamil region by the seventh century AD.

Bhakti thus arose as a sophisticated expression, that is, in singing the praise of god and as an emotional seeking of union with the absolute, symbolized by the temple image. The development of this concept is traceable through various stages in Āḻvār poetry, dominated by emotional Kṛṣṇa *bhakti*. The three early Āḻvārs who have been dated in the pre-seventh-century period, that is, about fifth to sixth centuries AD, express a simple form of devotion[8] and appear to be more preoccupied with the intellectual than the emotional aspects of *bhakti*. The early Āḻvār *bhakti* has also been characterized as a special form of theistic yoga derived from the *Bhagavad Gītā*,[9] a relatively calm expression of adoration, service, and loyalty; a personal experience of intimacy with and dependence on god. The three early Āḻvārs seem to follow the *āṟṟuppaṭai* (guide) poems of the Cankam, which praise the patron by describing his country, applying the nature landscape—the beauty of the temple and its environment—to the praise of god. While the temple is the centre of their religion in a generic sense, they refer to Vēnkaṭam (Tirupati), Mallai (Māmallapuram), and Tirukkōvalūr as three important locales of Viṣṇu worship.[10] Their geographical environment is thus confined to northern Tamiḻakam, with Vēnkaṭam as the spiritual centre.

The development of *bhakti* reaches its culmination in Nammāḻvār (seventh century AD), in whose hymns the intensely powerful emotional *bhakti* supersedes all other religious attitudes and methods.[11] The notion of complete trust and surrender (*prapatti*) clearly emanates from Nammāḻvār, although it is more fully developed only in the Śrīvaiṣṇava theology of the twelfth to thirteenth centuries.[12] With Tirumankai Āḻvār (eighth century) *bhakti* acquires yet another meaning, through the concept of pilgrimage (*tīrthayātra*), which, it has been suggested, was intended to help in resolving emotional tensions. It also signifies the change from the poetic landscape to the landscape of the South Indian temple through the concept of pilgrimage.[13] It is only in the *Tirumaṭals* of Tirumankai that something like a systematic theory of *bhakti* has been recognized.[14]

Bhakti acquires yet another meaning, namely devotion to the true *bhaktas* and becomes more complex with Tirumankai and others like Kulacēkara and Toṇṭaraṭippoṭi, who followed him.[15] These Āḻvārs claim to be devotees of true *bhaktas*, 'carry' them on their heads, or claim to be the 'dust of the feet of the devotees' (*Toṇṭar-aṭi-p-poṭi*). Mathurakavi, who also belongs to the later phase of the Āḻvār movement, emphasizes 'reverence to the ideal *bhaktas*'. Thus the notion of a community of *bhaktas* would seem to emerge along with the concept of pilgrimage.

Periyāḻvār or Viṣṇucitta (ninth century AD) creates a whole series of mythical folk songs through which *bhakti* is brought home, in a variety of ways, into the day-to-day existence of the people. In the poems of the mother and child likened to Yasoda and Kṛṣṇa,[16] composed by this *brāhmaṇa* Āḻvār, folk art and sentiment become interwoven with *bhakti*. In the hymns of Āṇṭāḷ, his foster daughter and the only lady saint among the Āḻvārs, the eroticism of Kṛṣṇa *bhakti* attains a new intensity in her love for Kṛṣṇa and her 'marriage' to god Ranganātha of Śrīrangam as expressed in the *Tiruppāvai* and the 'dream' poem *Nācciyār Tirumoḻi*.[17]

The idea of temple service as hereditary and professional recurs in the hymns of both Viṣṇucitta and Toṇṭaraṭippoṭi,[18] echoing the Āḻvār concept of service to god/temple. In the hymns of Kulacēkara, *bhakti* itself becomes an ideal and an institution. In these later Āḻvār hymns Śrīrangam emerges as the new geographical and spiritual centre in the lower Kaveri valley[19] and continues so through the period of the later *ācāryas* of Śrīvaiṣṇavism to this day.

The *Bhāgavata Purāṇa* of the late-ninth and early-tenth centuries AD[20] marks the culmination of the *bhakti* ideal in its emotional form and renders in Sanskrit the religion of the Āḻvār.[21] It integrates all the different strands, Tamil and Sanskrit, but preserves its southern character as it derives its content and mythology from the vernacular sources, namely Āḻvār *bhakti* poetry, although it adopts the Purāṇic literary structure. This text even adopts the *Advaita* position, probably in response to the non-dualism of Śankarācārya, to reconcile *bhakti* with Brahmanical orthodoxy.[22] Thus, it is said, the Āḻvār religion was finally made available to the rest of the Indian subcontinent through this *mahāpurāṇa*.[23] It also stands at the very beginning of a millennium of intensive speculation on Vaiṣṇava *bhakti* and the different schools of monistic and dualistic philosophies that arose in various parts of South India, and even Bengal and Mathura.[24]

The *bhakti* of the Śaiva Nāyanārs, like that of the Āḻvārs, derives from both the religious humanism of the Cankam works and the influence of the northern Sanskritic traditions. However, there is no evidence in their hymns of a systematic development of the concept, as in the Āḻvār hymns. Theirs, indeed, is a given or received tradition, secondary, and derivative,[25] equally emotional but less erotic than the Kṛṣṇa *bhakti* of the Āḻvārs, particularly of Nammāḻvār and Āṇṭāḷ. Like the *Divyaprabandham* (sacred collection) of the Āḻvārs, the *Tēvāram* of the Nāyanārs also represents a new synthesis of northern Brahmanical traditions and regional Tamil traditions.[26] It also derives its theism, image worship, and temple-centred religion from the *Purāṇa*s and *Āgama*s.

The meaning of the word *tēvāram* has proved elusive, and varied interpretations have been provided with no single interpretation being entirely satisfactory. It is derived from *Devagṛha* or god's house, and from *vāram* as a song addressed to a deity, hence *tēvāram*. It is also said to mean 'private ritual worship',[27] and is applied to the hymns because of their association with temple worship. Significantly, the word has also been used in a Jain context in a ninth-tenth century inscription, which refers to a niche (a shrine in sculpted relief) on a rock enshrining a Pārśvanātha image.[28]

Like the Āḻvār hymns, the *Tēvāram* adopts both the *akam* and *puṟam* structures, although it has been pointed out that it has affinities with the *puṟam*[29] rather than *akam*, for as *puṟam* or 'public poetry' it is used to praise a god manifesting himself in particular places and to celebrate a particular community. As heir to the *puṟam* tradition, the *Tēvāram* hymnists are said to describe the heroic deeds of Śīva, locate them in specific centres (the *aṭṭavīraṭṭānam* for eight heroic deeds), and then transfer the Cankam idea of the king with sacred power to the deity in the temple for example, *iṟaivan* and *perumān*, or lord in the *kōyil* or temple. Śiva thus becomes the local hero to fit into the indigenous concept of the divine. Śiva sometimes even manifests himself at a shrine to protect it from major catastrophes like the cosmic flood.[30] While, in general, the *akam* conventions are less relevant to Śiva *bhakti* vis-à-vis the *bhakti* of the lover-god Kṛṣṇa, Māṇikkavācakar, the fourth important Śaiva saint, incorporates *akam* themes in his *Tirukkōvaiyār*.[31]

Campantar's hymns (seventh to eighth centuries AD) are considered the most successful from the *bhakti* point of view,[32] as they, apart from their emotional significance, also establish Śiva as the local god and the transcendent deity. Campantar's hymns are also significant as extolling the idea of pilgrimage. On his peregrinations to various Śaiva shrines composing melodious Tamil hymns, he is said to have been accompanied by crowds of fellow devotees. A *pāṇar* or musician called Tirunīlakaṇṭa Yāḷppāṇar set his hymns to music (*paṇ*) and accompanied him on his journeys. Campantar also visited many Śiva shrines with his elder contemporary Tirunāvukkaracar (Appar), both of them drawing a large following of devotees.[33]

II

There has been a general assumption among historians and sociologists that the concept of *bhakti*, as expressed in the Āḻvār and Nāyanār hymns, initiated a movement of protest and reform particularly aimed at caste hierarchy and *brāhmaṇa* exclusiveness in Tamil society. This view represents an inadequate understanding of the hymns, the chronological position of the hymnists, both Vaiṣṇava and Śaiva, and the later hagiographical accounts about the hymnists and other *bhakti* saints, some of whose historicity is not beyond doubt. It also points to a lack of clear perspectives of the historical processes that made *bhakti* a major ideological force in the restructuring of economy and society with the Brahmanical temple as its focus.

There was, admittedly, an element of protest or dissent in the Āḻvār and Nāyanār poetry, representing an attempt to provide avenues of social acceptance and even mobility to less privileged castes and economic groups. A certain reformatory zeal characterizes some of the *bhakti* saints like Tirunāvukkaracar and Nammāḻvār, and the later *ācārya*s or religious teachers like Rāmānuja, who followed them. Yet, the movement itself does not reflect a popular character or a broad social base till at least the twelfth century AD. A related question is whether social reform was indeed the end result of the movement, and, if so, what kind of social change was achieved. An answer should be sought in the very contents of the *bhakti* hymns, the social groups propagating them, their objectives and, above all, the ideological implications of *bhakti* for the ruling families. Hence, if the hymns are read as registering a protest, it is important to see what they were protesting against or dissenting from. The hymns themselves provide ample evidence of the nature of protest or dissent, the social background of the hymnists who expounded *bhakti*, and their attitude to caste hierarchy.

The *bhakti* hymns are dominated by three major themes. Foremost among them is the idea of devotion to a personal god, that is, *bhakti*, which has been discussed above. The second is a protest against orthodox Vedic Brāhmaṇism and the exclusiveness of the *brāhmaṇa*s in their access to divine grace and salvation, that is, an elitism in the religious sphere. The third is a vehement denunciation of the Jains and Buddhists as nonbelievers, heretics, and hence as 'heterodox'. It is the second theme, namely protest against orthodox Vedic Brāhmaṇism, that needs to be examined from the point of view of the social base sought by the exponents of *bhakti*. Hints of the struggle between the Tamil hymnists and orthodox Vedic *brāhmaṇa*s are found in the poetry of Nammāḻvār, Toṇṭaraṭippoṭi, and Mathurakavi, and in the hagiography of the twelfth to thirteenth centuries, as, for example, in the story of Tiruppāṇāḻvār.[34]

In Toṇṭaraṭippoṭi, the antagonism to the Caturvedins (*brāhmaṇa*s well versed in the four *Veda*s), who represented the *brāhmaṇa* establishment controlling the temple, is expressed in the following verse:

> You [=Viṣṇu] manifestly like
> those 'servants' who express their love for your feet,
> though they may be born as outcastes, more than
> the Caturvedins who are strangers and without
> allegiance to your service.
>
> [*Tirumālai*, 42]

Mathurakavi (ninth century) says that the Caturvedins, the lords of the four *Veda*s, regarded him as vile and that he accepted only Nammāḻvār (a *Śūdra*), whose hymns represent a Tamil rendering of the *Veda*s, as his lord/teacher.[35] These are expressions of the solidarity of the *bhakta* community with their Tamil *Veda* against the orthodox Vedic *brāhmaṇa*s. Hence, the opposition seems to be against orthodox religious attitudes. It stemmed primarily from the need to defend the *bhakti* tradition not by denying the superiority claimed by orthodox *brāhmaṇa*s but by hailing the devotee's status as higher than even that of the *brāhmaṇa*.[36] In other words, to be a *bhakta* was more important than being a *brāhmaṇa*. Toṇṭaraṭippoṭi states emphatically that even those who recite the *Veda*s and know the six *anga*s, if they speak ill of the devotee of Viṣṇu, are equal to the *pulaiyar* (outcastes). He further holds that even the Caturvedins become slaves if they are not devotees of Viṣṇu, whereas even those actually born among the *kuṭi*s, who work on the lands of others, are better than the *brāhmaṇa*s (if they are *bhakta*s).[37] A similar idea is expressed much more directly in a hymn of Nammāḻvār, which says:

> The four castes uphold all clans
> go down, far down to the lowliest outcastes of outcastes [*caṇḍāla*]
> if they are the intimate henchmen of our lord
> with the wheel in his right hand,
> his body as dark as blue sapphire
> then even the slaves of their slaves are
> our masters.
>
> [*Tiruvāymoḻi*, III, 7.9]

The *Bhāgavata Purāṇa* only reiterates this position when it says that even a *caṇḍāla* or a *svapaca* (dog-eater), who is a true devotee, is better than a 'virtuous' *brāhmaṇa* who has turned away from Viṣṇu's feet.[38]

The story of Pāṇāḷvār, a minstrel of low caste, being carried to the temple by a *brāhmaṇa* (*munivāhana*) implies such a struggle between the hymnists and the Brahmanical temple establishment. The relation between the *bhakta*s and the *varṇa* system is represented here as one of tension, and its resolution lay not in the negation of caste but in an attempted synthesis as narrated in the hagiography.[39] If anything like a direct rejection of caste can be recognized in the Śaiva hymns, it is only in the hymns of Tirunāvukkaracar, popularly known as Appar, as in the following verse:

> O rogues who quote the Law Books:
> Of what use are your *gotra* and *kula* [clan]
> Just bow to Māṟpēru's lord as your sole refuge.
>
> [*Tirumāṟpēru*, V. 2.3]

Appar would worship even the 'leper with rotting limbs, the outcaste, even the foul *pulaiyan* who skins and eats cows, even these men, if they are servants of him who shelters the Ganges in his long hair' (Poem 211 in I. V. Peterson, 1991, p. 263).

Working on the early historical Tamil classics, Hart has pointed out that there were several kinds of *brāhmaṇa*s in the Tamil area, each showing varying degrees of assimilation of the indigenous culture.[40] This is also reflected in the rivalry shown by the *bhakti* saints, some of whom are *brāhmaṇa*s, against the Caturvedins or Vedic scholars and the *brāhmaṇa*s who were temple authorities. That the Smārta *brāhmaṇa*s (Vedic scholars and performers of Vedic sacrifices) are treated as superior to the Ādi Śaivas or Śaiva *brāhmaṇa*s and *gurukkaḷ*s or temple priests[41] is a well-known fact of Tamil society, and this may be traced to the process of acculturation and assimilation referred to by Hart and clearly recognizable in the *bhakti* hymns.

A major aspect of this process of acculturation relates to the creation of temples at various centres by royal and chiefly patrons, which meant, apart from new shrines, also the conversion of local cult centres into shrines of Śiva. The priests of such local cult shrines were evidently integrated into the new order of worship based on the *Āgamas* and the priestly group called Śiva-*brāhmaṇas* in the ninth to twelfth centuries would seem to be such newly initiated temple priests.[42] This class of temple priests later came to be distinguished from the more orthodox Smārta *brāhmaṇas* and Vaḍamas, that is, followers of Vedic and Smṛti rites, with an inferior rank among the *brāhmaṇa* sub-castes.

The caste and occupational background of the *bhakti* saints, if examined closely, would provide a useful insight into the nature of the 'movement'. The first three or early Āḻvārs (fifth to sixth centuries), whose historicity is uncertain, would seem to be elitist or scholarly and may be described as the Cāṉṟōr of the early Tamil texts. They were the first to come under northern, Sanskritic influences. Nammāḻvār, who stands between them and the later Āḻvārs of the eighth to ninth centuries AD was of *Vēḷāḷa* community and hence a *Sudra*.[43] Along with Tiruppāṇāḻvār, the low-caste minstrel, he represents the two non-*brāhmaṇa* saints whose hymns register protest against caste stratification in matters of worship and salvation. The stories of their birth are deliberately camouflaged in the later hagiographies, and hence their *Vēḷāḷa* and Pāṇa associations might well represent a conscious attempt to provide a low-caste background and to create the myth of the social/religious revolt, when the *varṇa* system had become well-established or consolidated.[44] The birth of Tirumalisai Āḻvār is associated with the sage Bhārgava and an *apsara*, and being born as a mass of flesh he is said to have been abandoned in a bush, but due to the grace of Viṣṇu he was revived and brought up by a *Vēḷāḷa*. Tirumankai was a chieftain of the Kaḷvar (robber) clan, Kulacēkara was a Cēra king, while Periyāḻvār, his foster-daughter Āṇṭāḷ, Toṇṭaraṭippoṭi, and Mathurakavi were *brāhmaṇas*. Even Nāthamuni (late tenth century), the first of the *ācāryas*, who 'discovered' the hymns through Nammāḻvār's *Tiruvāymoḻi* was a *brāhmaṇa*.[45]

The Śaiva *bhakti* saints, whose number came to be fixed at sixty-three by the twelfth century AD, were drawn from various social strata, from the *brāhmaṇa* to the *paṟaiya*. However, it is necessary to distinguish between those saints who composed devotional hymns propagating the *bhakti* cult and those who came to be canonized and included in the hagiographical works of the eleventh to twelfth centuries, namely *Tiruttoṇṭar tiruvantāti* and the *Periya purāṇam*. Even as early as the ninth century AD, the *Tiruttoṇṭattokai* of Cuntarar, one of the *Tēvāram* trio, lists all the sixty-two Nāyanār before him. Some of them are known even to the first two hymnists, as, for example, Kannappa, the hunter (Appar, VI, 310; Campantar, III, 327), Caṇṭīśa (Appar, V. 73.5), Kōccenkaṇ, the Cōḷa king (Appar, IV. 40–65; Campantar, VII. 9, III. 276, 277; Cuntarar, VII. 98, and even Tirumankai, *Periya Tirumoḻi*, 6.6.8), Kulacciṟai, the Pāṇṭiya minister (Campantar, III. 378), and Tirunāḷaippōvār, the outcaste (Cuntarar, VII. 39.3), and others.

Only seven of the sixty-three Nāyanārs are credited with hymns, the most important among them being the *Tēvāram* trio. Appar, Campantar, and Cuntarar (seventh to ninth centuries) and Māṇikkavācakar, along with whom they constitute the group of four or Camayakkuravar Nālvar. Campantar and Cuntarar were *brāhmaṇa*s and Appar, a *Vēḷāḷa*.[46] Māṇikkavācakar was a philosopher, an Ādi Śaiva *brāhmaṇa*, and the son of a minister at the Pāṇṭiya court in the ninth century AD. His avowed aim was to discredit Buddhism.

The Śaiva canon (*Tirumuṟai*) includes hymns composed by Kāraikkāl Ammaiyār, the lady saint (fifth to sixth centuries AD), by the Cōḷa king Gaṇḍarāditya (tenth century), and Karuvūr Tēvar, the royal preceptor of the Cōḷa Rājarāja I (eleventh century) apart from Cēramān Perumāḷ (ninth century), a Cēra king and friend of Cuntarar. However, their hymns do not form a regular part of the ritual singing in the temples. Only the hymns of Appar, Campantar, Cuntarar, and Māṇikkavācakar were assigned a special ritual status in the temples even as early as the tenth century AD. These four were the first to be apotheosized and worshipped from the tenth to eleventh centuries.[47] The rest came to be canonized only in the twelfth-century hagiographical work *Periya Purāṇam*. Thus, with the exception of the seven hymnists and Kōccenkaṇ, a pre-imperial Cōḷa king, the other canonized saints are of doubtful historicity and the chronological muddle that surrounds them would lead to the suspicion that many of them were fictitious[48] and were added to make the number sixty-three, the number being directly borrowed from the sixty-three Salākapuruṣas of the Jain *Purāṇa*s. Significantly, the historicity of even Tirumūlar, the greatest of the Tamil Siddhas, whose work *Tirumantiram* serves as the basis of the entire *Śaiva Siddhānta* canon, and whose canonization in the *Periya Purāṇam* was crucial in integrating the Siddhas into Śaiva tradition, cannot be established. The curious story of his origin making him a northern Siddha who came to south India and became a cowherd through an act of transmigration, may be taken as a pointer to the anxiety of the hagiographers to include people of low origins among the sixty-three Nāyanārs. This is true also of the stories of Kaṇṇappar, the hunter, and Nantan, the untouchable, apart from the potter, the washerman, the weaver, and others of a similar social background who figure among the Nāyanārs.[49]

Those who collected the hymns and composed the hagiographies belonged to the *brāhmaṇa* caste, upper strata, and ruling families. Nambi Āṇḍār Nambi who collected the Śaiva hymns under the royal patronage of Cōḷa Rājarāja I[50] was an Ādi Śaiva *brāhmaṇa* and Cēkkiḻar, the author of the *Periya Purāṇam,* was a *Vēḷāḷa* and a minister in the court of Kulottunga II.[51] The propagators came primarily from the upper strata or castes, but the movement acquired a popular character with the canonization of members of the lower castes, untouchables, and unprivileged social groups. Interestingly, the *brāhmaṇa* remained the only medium through whom initiation into religion and salvation could be effected, as is revealed by the story of Nantan, the untouchable, whose purification through Brahmanical rituals was necessary before salvation.

The third major theme in the bhakti hymns is their opposition to the Jain and Buddhist religions. The Āḻvār hymns express a profound reaction to the Jain and Buddhist ideologies, a feature much more pronounced in the hymns of the Nāyanārs, some of whom give vent to their animosity in unequivocal terms. Tirumankai's hymns, in which a systematic theory of *bhakti* can be recognized, reveal clear indications of the rejection of the Jain way of life and perception of the uselessness of their austere penance and self-mortification as a means of attaining salvation.[52] Tirumankai's *Periya Tirumaṭal* (7–9) says:

But we know only from hearsay that person
X at such and such a time obtained exactly

this [*mokṣa*], by eating rotten fruit and dry leaves
by torturing his body...by exposing himself to
the heat of the sun.... We shall not correct
such people with stupid small minds who say
these things without being able to prove them.

[Trans. F. Hary, 1983]

Toṇṭaraṭippoṭi expresses this opposition more directly by saying that it should be the duty of a devotee to chop off the 'heads' of the Jains and Buddhists if they speak ill of the lord (Viṣṇu). [*Tirumālai*, 8.]

Appar, one of the *Tēvāram* trio, laments his past associations with the Jains and expresses his gratitude to Śiva for having redeemed him from the sin of such association (IV, 39—Tiruvaiyāṟu; 100.1—Kacci Ēkampam; 102—Tiruvārūr). He says that the Jains are wicked, full of wiles, and do not understand the truth, that is, greatness of Śiva. To his persecution by the Jains and by their royal patron, identified with the Pallava Mahendravarman I,[53] Appar responded in several hymns, among which the following oft-quoted lines are significant:

We are slaves to no man
nor do we fear death
Hell holds no torment for us
We know no deceit
We rejoice, we are strangers to disease
We bow to none.

[V. 312.1, trans., I. V. Peterson, 1991]

Campantar was a crusader, and his denunciation of the Jains and Buddhists was instrumental in bringing about their decline at the royal court of the Pāṇṭiyas. He constantly refers to 'the false doctrines of the heretic Jain and Buddhist monks' (I, 75.10). The Jains, as also the Buddhists, are 'worthless, wily rogues, scantily clad, wicked' (I, 69; 130). At the Pāṇṭiya court, claims Campantar boastfully, the fire that the Jains aimed against him was instead directed by his prayer to afflict the Pāṇṭiya king as a disease, and by curing the king he established the superiority of Śaivism (III. 1. 309; II. 11.202). Campantar ridicules Jain names ending with the suffixes 'Sena' and 'Nandi' (III.4), and their habits of plucking out their hair, eating food standing, mutilating the good Sanskrit of the *Āgama* and *Mantra*, loudly declaiming (them) in the corrupt Prakrit tongue (III. 2.297). Every tenth verse of his *patikam* (=*padya*) systematically abuses the Jains and the Buddhists. In Cuntarar's view, god condemned the stupid Jains and the stinking Buddhist monks to ignorance (VII. 90.0). The metaphor of the human body as the temple (Appar, IV. 76.4) and the emphasis on the use of the senses in the apprehension of the divine through acts of devotion also provided the much-needed justification of human existence, as against the Jain idea of self-mortification for salvation.

Thus the enemy was not Brahmanical or Purāṇic religion but Buddhism and Jainism, 'alien' to Tamil culture. Hence, it is represented in their hymns that kings who had been seduced by the false doctrines of the Jains and Buddhists were being rescued and brought back to the fold of the true religion.[54]

The *bhakti* hymnists were, at the same time, not negating the importance of the *Veda*s as scriptures. On the contrary, they were trying to provide the status of the *Veda*s to the Tamil hymns. This is nowhere as clearly stated as in the hymns of the most celebrated Śaiva saints Appar and Campantar. To Appar, Śiva was Sanskrit of the north and southern Tamil (VI. 301.1), and it was he who gave the four *Veda*s to the world (I. 100.9). To Campantar, Śiva was the *Veda* and the sacred word (II. 148.1), the *brāhmaṇa*, who knew the four *Veda*s (II. 147.1) and the six sacred sciences. It was through Śiva's grace that the *Veda*s were revealed to the young Campantar (I. 75.11) who, hence, became well versed in them (I. 4.11). Appar and Campantar hail as sacred the places where the *brāhmaṇa*s lived, performed Vedic sacrifices; places which were filled with Vedic chants and the smoke of sacrifice (Appar, V. 157; VI. 216; Campantar, 312.1). Śiva chose such places as his abode, that is, the temple. Several such settlements on the banks of the Kaveri are thus praised by Appar and Campantar; places which acquired temples to Śiva at various points of time under the Cōḷas between late ninth and twelfth centuries AD.[55]

The idea, hence, was to establish the Tamil hymns, both Vaiṣṇava and Śaiva, as scriptures, that is, *maṟali*, equal to the

Vedas, to invest the hymns with authority. In this respect, the Śrīvaiṣṇava teachers (*ācāryas*) were more successful in relating the Sanskrit Vedic tradition to Tamil Vaiṣṇava doctrine and practice[56] than the Tamil Śaivas. The latter could not directly relate their tradition to the Vedic Śruti or revealed literature. However, it has been shown that the Śaiva *patikam* exhibit a close similarity with the Sanskrit *stotra* or poems of praise, and their affinities with early Sanskrit litanies have been stressed (Campantar, II, 148.1). The 'Śatarudrīya' hymn in the *Yajur Veda* is said to be the most influential model of the *patikam*.[57]

It is significant that no commentaries were written on the *Tēvāram*, although the theologies of the Śaiva Siddhānta treated it as scripture and looked up to the Āgamic tradition rather than orthodox Vedic tradition as their metaphysical source.[58] The Śrīvaiṣṇava philosophers, on the other hand, not only wrote in Sanskrit but also evolved a scriptural tradition, in which both Āḻvār *bhakti* hymns (as *Drāviḍa Veda*) and their own philosophical formulations based on the *Vedānta* were related through powerful arguments, and thereby established the authority of the *Divyaprabandham*. The philosophy thus evolved by them represents the *ubhaya Vedānta*, that is, both the Sanskrit and Tamil philosophical traditions.[59]

The sense of a community evolving around a sectarian theistic cult comes through strongly in both the Vaiṣṇava and Śaiva hymns. In the Śaiva context, the image of a community supersedes that of social hierarchy, the members of the community sharing their love/devotion for Śiva and his sacred shrines. Through ritual singing of hymns (*pāmālai* or garland of verses), ecstatic dancing, 'seeing' (*darśana*), and helping fellow devotees to gain Śiva's grace, it is said, the sense of community[60] increasingly binds or brings together people of varying social backgrounds. In the *puṟam* tradition, the hymns are regarded as public poems[61] calling the community to witness, giving a public dimension to the ways in which participation in this experience is made possible for all. Śiva is looked upon as a close kin, father, mother, uncle, aunt, lord, family, friend, etc. (Appar, VI. 309.1).

The concept of pilgrimage added to the movement's growing strength by chalking out the sacred, cultural geography of that community dotted by Śaiva shrines. The Tamil countryside, the Tamil *paṇ* or music, communal singing and dancing derived from the early indigenous rituals of worship at Murukan shrines (*Paripāṭal*, 19), add a regional dimension to the movement. It has been mentioned earlier that the Tamil god Murukan gets a place of primacy in the Śaiva pantheon.

The emphasis in *bhakti* literature on ritual worship as highly meritorious and the temple as the house of god and the iconographic descriptions of the Purāṇic deities (Śiva and Viṣṇu) are closely related to the teaching and ethos of the *Āgama* and *Tantra*, which laid stress on temple and image worship.[62] It was not always a case of the hymnist 'seeing' an icon or sculpture in a specific locale and describing it in his poems,[63] but the reverse is true of many sculptural representations, which seem to be inspired by the hymns. The hymns were meant to popularize Śiva's forms either through complete descriptions or episodic allusions to Śiva's feats, thereby paving the way for introducing them in the temples, which were built subsequent to the hymnal compositions from the tenth to thirteenth centuries.

The most notable iconographic forms of Śiva constantly referred to in the *Tēvāram* are Śiva as a Yogi, that is, Dakṣiṇāmūrti, Naṭarāja, Bhikṣāṭana, and Rāvaṇānugraha (humbling of Rāvaṇa), and above all Lingodbhava.[64] The last one was particularly useful in establishing the cosmic character of Śiva, as the cosmic pillar or column of light, that is, the *linga*, the beginning (head) and end (feet) of which could not be discovered even by Brahma and Viṣṇu, a theme which also at once subordinated the other two of the Brahmanical trinity, Brahma and Viṣṇu, to Śiva.

On the basis of the *brāhmaṇa* and *Vēḷāḷa* background of the hymnists, it has been suggested that the hymns indicate the closeness of the *brāhmaṇa* and *Vēḷāḷa*.[65] Undoubtedly, such an interpretation draws its inspiration from Burton Stein's theory of a *brāhmaṇa–Vēḷāḷa* alliance to demonstrate the peasant basis of society and polity (state) in medieval South India.[66] Further supportive evidence of this relationship is located in the cult leadership and the Śaiva sect's core constituency which were provided by the *Vēḷāḷa*s or non-*brāhmaṇa* agricultural community and in the fact that although the Śaiva hymns and the *Śaiva Siddhānta* canon were composed and compiled by *Vēḷāḷas* and *brāhmaṇas*, the heads of the sectarian Śaiva *maṭhas* were invariably *Vēḷāḷas*.[67] Even the language of Śaiva scriptures, that is, Tamil and of the Vaiṣṇava scriptures, that is, Tamil, Sanskrit, and Maṇipravāḷa, are said to closely relate to the differences that developed in the cultural milieu and caste orientation after the period of the *bhakti* saints, the Śaivas becoming predominantly *Vēḷāḷa* and the Vaiṣṇavas predominantly *brāhmaṇa*.[68] Such a view ignores the developments in Vaiṣṇavism, especially after Rāmānuja, when the social base of Śrīvaiṣṇavism was widened to allow *Sudra* participation in temple rituals and administration after the reforms introduced by him in major Vaiṣṇava centres.[69] It also fails to see the parallel growth of a Smārta tradition after Śankarācārya, the *Advaita* philosopher, leading to the evolution of a *maṭha* organization in which the cult leadership was confined to the *brāhmaṇa* caste, particularly of the orthodox Vedic scholars.

Śankara's *Advaita*, or non-dualism, had its roots in *Vedānta* or Upaniṣadic philosophy and represents a Brahmanical philosophic thrust to the opposition to 'heterodoxy'.[70] His attempts to root out Buddhism and to establish Smārta *maṭhas*, particularly the one at Kāñcīpuram, were more in the nature of an emphasis on the importance of the Sanskritic/normative aspects of the Brahmanical order and the upholding of the Smṛti tradition.

Śankara looked upon Śaiva and Vaiṣṇava worship as two equally important aspects of Brahmanical religion. In a limited sense, his supreme *Brahman*, the universal soul, could be seen in either of the supreme godheads—Śiva or Viṣṇu. Indeed, Śankara scarcely addressed himself to the masses, his following being generally confined to the higher castes and the intellectual elite. Hence, temple worship played a secondary role in his scheme of religious experience. Monastic organization and preservation of Sanskrit scriptures were the two major aspects of the Śankara school, and although, according to tradition, these organizational efforts date from the time of Śankara himself, that is, ninth century AD, there is hardly any reference to them in the more authentic epigraphic records till the post-thirteenth-century period,[71] that is, the fourteenth century onwards, in which a fresh wave of Sanskritization took place in South India, including Tamil

Nadu, which may well be associated with the expansion of Vijayanagar authority.

Philosophical systems, such as that of Śankara, were successfully challenged by the 'institutional coherence and synthesis' attained by the *bhakti* tradition due to organized and collective action on the part of the ruling and landed elite of the Cōḷa period. These philosophical schools worked on a different plane, that is, metaphysical theory and Sanskritic orientation, whereas the *bhakti* tradition worked at a popular level, with a local Tamil orientation.

The *Vēḷāḷa–brāhmaṇa* base of the Śaiva movement should not be seen as a mere caste phenomenon, and this may be perceived in the elitist character of the *Vēḷāḷa* landowners, that is, agriculturally dominant *Vēḷāḷa*s, who alone gained control over the temple and *maṭha* administration and landed property from the twelfth century, as against their sharing of a part of the control over temple lands and administration with the *brāhmaṇa*s in the pre-twelfth-century period, that is, tenth to twelfth centuries. As landowning members of the *Sabhā* of the *brahmadeya*, the *brāhmaṇa*s played a predominant role in the period from the seventh to ninth centuries AD till the temple superseded the *brahmadeya* as an instrument of agrarian expansion and integration.[72]

The twelfth-century situation was one in which the *Vēḷāḷa*s and other non-*brāhmaṇa* castes were gaining social importance vis-à-vis the *brāhmaṇa*s, and hence the *Vēḷāḷa*s achieved greater control over the temple and the *maṭha* by giving a popular character to the Śaiva *bhakti* movement through the hagiographical tradition incorporating all lower castes into the Nāyanār list and thereby acquiring a wider popular base vis-à-vis other sects. It was this tendency that brought into Śaiva temple ritual and pantheon a series of local, popular, and folk forms in the post-twelfth-century temple tradition, the apotheosis of all the sixty-three Nāyanār being of central importance. The lower categories of agricultural classes and craftsmen, who were professionally and socially differentiated from the higher agricultural groups even among the non-*brāhmaṇa*s, retained their earlier association with the 'subsidiary' elements in the Brahmanical, particularly the Śaiva, pantheon. Hence, the lower castes among the non-*brāhmaṇa*s, who professed allegiance to Śaivism, still continued to follow rituals and worship centring on local and tutelary deities rather than major Purāṇic gods. Evidence on this point, which is crucial to an understanding of later-day Śaivism, is scanty, indirect, and largely inferential, based on later social developments and the fact that temples for the goddesses and 'minor' deities increasingly received patronage and centrality in the post-Cōḷa period.[73]

The notion of temple service manifesting itself in the Āḻvār and Nāyanār hymns is often likened to a feudal relationship,[74] that is, between the god and the devotee, which is perceived as deriving from the chieftain–bard or patron–client relationship of Cankam society, and which is said to provide the model for the landlord–tenant or labourer, king–subject and the lord–servant relationships. Further, the references to *attāṇicēvakam* (royal service) in the later Āḻvār poetry are taken to indicate a court model underlying temple ritual and the old meaning of *bhakti*, namely loyalty.[75] The idea of Śiva as patron-king permeates the verses of Cuntarar, the Śaiva poet (VII, 34). The term *aṭiyār*, constantly used in the hymns to denote the servants of the temple, may also imply the idea of service and loyalty.

However, neither the theory of the *brāhmaṇa–Vēḷāḷa* alliance as the basis of a peasant society nor that of the feudal basis of Tamil society explains the complex processes through which resource mobilization and redistribution were achieved in early medieval Tamiḻakam, in which the temple enabled royal and chiefly families to establish their political presence and social dominance by intruding into the peasant regions known as *nāḍus*. The temple, as the house of god, was of central importance not only for the development of the cult but its equation with the palace (*kōyil*) was also of crucial institutional significance in assisting the process of the simultaneous expansion of divine and royal authority by establishing the symbolism of the cosmos/ temple/territory.[76]

III

Bhakti, it has been shown, is a crucial element in the evolution and spread of Purāṇic religion, which emerged by the sixth century

AD as a universal and formal system in the Indian subcontinent as a whole. In the Tamil region, as elsewhere in South India, the expansion of Purāṇic religion is intrinsically linked with local and popular traditions and their interaction with Brahmanical religion in a two-way process. It was a synchronic and at times diachronic evolution, which it would be too simplistic or facile to explain as the interaction between the 'Great' and 'Little' traditions, and one requiring a multidimensional model for correct explication.[77] It is the beginning of such a process that is seen in the *Paripāṭal* and *Tirumurkāṟṟuppaṭai* and reflected more fully in the *bhakti* hymns, in which the concept of *bhakti* progresses and simultaneously the Vaiṣṇava and Śaiva pantheons emerge.

The growth of *bhakti* into a dominant ideology may be historically demonstrated through the Pallava-Pāṇṭiya (seventh to ninth centuries) and Cōḷa periods (ninth to thirteenth centuries). The first two major Brahmanical ruling families of the Pallavas and Pāṇṭiyas adopted Purāṇic religion, the northern normative Sanskrit tradition, and together with their *brāhmaṇa* ideologues established the Purāṇic religion as the vehicle of propagating a 'cosmological world-view'. To some extent, the three early Āḻvārs, who belonged to the Tirupati, Kāñcīpuram, and Māmallapuram regions, would seem to have inspired the Purāṇic temples, both rock-cut and structural, and their narrative sculptures which the Pallavas executed in their capital Kāñcīpuram and port-city Māmallapuram. Rājasiṃha's *magnum opus*, the Kailāsanātha temple, at Kāñcīpuram, derives most of its iconographic forms directly from the Śaiva *Āgamas*.[78] However, the most remarkable iconographic form, which they seem to have innovated, is the Somāskanda image, which appears as the cult object in the principal shrine, which combines Śiva with Murukan and Koṟṟavai (Durgā), the Cankam *tiṇai* deities. Their land grants[79] to the *brāhmaṇas* (*brahmadeya*) and the temples they built for Śiva and Viṣṇu, were directly inspired by the northern *Dharma Śāstras* and Purāṇic and Āgamic forms of ritual and worship. It is significant that no canonical temples, with the exception of the Parameśvara Viṇṇagaram in Kāñcīpuram,[80] owe their existence to the Pallavas or Pāṇṭiyas till the ninth century AD. In other words, no such temple was built in the centres 'sung' by the hymnists, and the vernacular *bhakti* hymns did not inspire their temples of the seventh and eighth centuries.

The hymnists were propagating *bhakti* in a situation of conflict and rivalry with non-orthodox sects like the Jains and Buddhists whose influence and dominance in royal and urban centres had been established in the pre-seventh-century period. This is attested to by the epics *Cilappatikāram* and *Maṇimēkalai*[81] (fifth–sixth centuries) and early archaeological evidence from Puhār or Kāvērippaṭṭiṇam.[82] The establishment of a Jain Saṅgha, known as the Drāviḍa Sangha, at Madurai in AD 470[83] and the patronage presumably extended to the Jain and Buddhist sects by the Kaḷabhras, who are believed to have subverted the early historical Tamil polities of the Cēra–Cōḷa–Pāṇṭiya ruling families,[84] also point to their ascendancy. These two sects drew their followers and support in the early historical period primarily from the merchant and artisan communities, and the general decline in trade by the third to fourth centuries AD, particularly maritime trade, would seem to have forced these sects to turn to other avenues of material support. The acquisition of landed property by the Jains and Buddhists is recorded in the early Paḷḷankōyil copper plates[85] (AD 550) of the Pallavas and also indirectly attested to by the references to *paḷḷiccandam* lands in early medieval Brahmanical records, which exclude them from the land grants made to the 'orthodox' sects. More importantly, the Pāṇṭiya copper plates of the eighth century[86] record the restoration of lands to *brāhmaṇa*s from those who 'appropriated' those lands. The Kaḷabhras, who presumably patronized these sects and made land gifts to them, are referred to in these records as *kali* or evil kings. *Bhakti* would, therefore, seem to have emanated and spread in a context of rivalry for social dominance and royal patronage as seen in Kāñcīpuram and Madurai, which were the centres of such conflict and change. Presumably, *bhakti*, by throwing open the path of salvation to all, irrespective of caste and social hierarchy, imbibed the ideals of the non-orthodox creeds, namely birth and caste as no obstacles to salvation, and thereby succeeded in rooting out 'heretical' sects. Hence, the seventh–eighth-century religious developments are depicted in Brahmanical records as well as in the hymns as a revival of orthodox forms which inevitably led to serious sectarian rivalry, particularly in royal and urban centres. Royal 'conversion' was the symbol of this change and hence central to this conflict. The stories of conflict and persecution leading to royal conversions and change in patronage are referred to in the *bhakti* hymns, and more systematically narrated in the hagiographical literature of the eleventh and twelfth centuries. Epigraphic evidence as well as sculptural and architectural evidence have been cited to prove that the consequent changes led to the conversion of Jain into Śaiva temples under royal patronage.[87] Of the two non-orthodox sects, Buddhism declined, leaving very few traces behind in certain urban centres (Kāñcīpuram),[88] while Jainism became subordinate to Purāṇic religions. Yet, Jainism survived as a significant factor in South Indian religion, and hence repeatedly evoked strong reaction among the Purāṇic sects. Its survival may be attributed to its adoption of the institutional and ritual forms of the Purāṇic religion, namely temple worship.

The second major impact of *bhakti* ideology was more significant as it induced messianic expectations among the lower orders of *varṇa*-based society, presumably by providing a delusion of equality among the low castes, which in reality remained beyond their access even in the ritual area as revealed by the story of Nantan, the untouchable. With its messianic appeal, *bhakti* also became amplified into an ethical (moral) system capable of sanctioning and integrating new values, which the older, particularly northern/Sanskritic norms, could not provide, into a coherent and viable synthesis. Correspondingly, it led to the expansion of the temple's role in restructuring society and economy, and facilitating the advance of those branches of knowledge concerned with ritual display, namely the sciences of architecture, sculpture, painting, the fine arts such as music, dance, and allied crafts—in short iconography, religious and political, and art as efficient ideological apparatuses.

The temple-based *bhakti* was also capable of developing into a transcendental norm and hence acquired a centrality providing a focus for the achievement of uniformity among various sects, given their differences. Several non-conformist elements and religious sects observing extreme forms of rites could also be integrated through the *bhakti* ideology. Through the *maṭha* organization attached to temples from the ninth century AD, the Kālāmukha–Pāśupata sects became an integral part of Śaiva temple religion.[89] They are believed to be anti-Vedic and anti-caste in origin, a fact known even to the Vaiṣṇava teachers of the eleventh and twelfth centuries such as Yāmunācārya and Rāmānuja. However, epigraphic evidence indicates that they favoured the study of the *Veda*s and *Varṇāśrama* in defence of social orthodoxy.[90] The Virasaiva sect, which seems to have been a reformist schism of the Kālāmukha sect in Karnataka,[91] was undoubtedly influenced by the Tamil Śaiva *bhakti*. Vīrśaivism originated both as a counter to Jain ascendancy and also as an anti-caste movement in Karnataka.[92]

Another dimension of the progress of the movement is the interaction of the *bhakti* tradition with the Siddha philosophers, which became a mutually beneficial influence. The Siddhas were an unorganized group of wandering mendicants who generally preferred the seclusion of hills and the periphery of civilization. Although the Tamil Siddha school represents an important and interesting offshoot of the pan-Indian Tāntric-yoga movement, Tamil Siddhism shows features such as anti-Brāhmaṇism and even anti-ritualism.[93] Tirumūlar, one of the canonized *bhakti* saints, was the greatest of the Tamil Siddhas, who laid emphasis on the importance of Śiva and Murukan worship, the latter being the Tamil deity par excellence. His canonization has, therefore, a special significance in the integration of the Siddha element into *bhakti* tradition. His analogy of the human body and the temple of god, and the idea of the body as a fit instrument for the soul (=icon=god) in pursuit of self-discipline and quest for god, provided a convenient alternative to the icon in the temple. His canonization took place in the twelfth century as a part of the attempts to resolve the societal and ideological crisis of the times due to the claims for greater non-*brāhmaṇa* participation in temple ritual and temple administration consequent upon the enhancement of economic status among some artisanal and craft groups, particularly weavers. It was a successful attempt of the twelfth-century Śaiva protagonists to include an important anti-Brahmanical and non-orthodox element in the traditional Śaiva order.

It has been shown earlier that both the Vaiṣṇava and Śaiva saints shared a common animosity aimed at the rooting out of the Jain and Buddhist sects. They however remained exponents of a parallel movement throughout. This is indeed established beyond doubt by the deliberate choice of Śaivism by the Cōḷas after Parāntaka I (907–55), for Śaivism proved to be a more efficacious instrument of acculturating for acquisition of a wider popular base both during the period of the Nāyanārs and subsequently due to royal patronage of the cult of the *linga*, which was of central importance in the process of acculturation. The incorporation of Murukan, Durga, and the equation of the phallic symbol or the aniconic *linga* with the folk worship of the pillar and tree were the most significant factors in the elaboration of the popular base of Śaivism. Śaiva iconogaphy evolved in direct relation to the specific requirements of the ideological needs of Cōḷa power.

Cōḷa royal measures to adopt and propagate *bhakti* were significantly directed towards the expansion of agrarian order, its integration and the restructuring of economy and society, and enhancement of political power. The building of canonical temples from the ninth century AD by the late Pallavas and the early Cōḷas, the sacred geography of the hymns, and the pattern of distribution of *bhakti* centres with temples would indicate that while both the Vaiṣṇava and Śaiva temples were built uniformly in the different sub-regions of the Tamil macro-region, the Śaiva temples superseded both in number and importance the Vaiṣṇava ones from the latter half of the tenth century AD. The sacred geography of the *Tēvāram* and *Divyaprabandham*[94] shows the following pattern of distribution of the Vaiṣṇava and Śaiva temples. Vaiṣṇavism had its major centres in Toṇḍaināḍu and Pāṇḍināḍu, with a few centres including Śrīrangam in Cōḷanāḍu. On the contrary, Śaiva centres had their greatest concentration in the Cōḷa region (Kaveri valley) and in and around the Pallava and Pāṇṭiya capitals of Kāñcīpuram and Madurai. The total number of Vaiṣṇava centres would scarcely be a third of the total number of religious centres that emerged in early medieval Tamilakam, that is, between the seventh and thirteenth centuries AD. The temple and its proliferation indicate the spatial and chronological spread of agrarian settlements and the emergence of urban nuclei.

The collection and organization of the hymns and the ritual of hymn-singing in temples were also made under direct royal initiative and patronage. The Vaiṣṇava hymns were collected in the late tenth century AD by Nāthamuni. The Śaiva hagiology received particular attention in the periods of Rājarāja I (985–1014) and Kulottunga II (1133–50). Closely linked with the collection of hymns was the apotheosis of the Śaiva hymnists and the installation of their images in Śiva temples from the period of Rājarāja I. Some of the remarkable Cōḷa frescoes at Tanjavur depict the stories of two of the Nāyanārs, while the *Periya Purāṇam* stories are sculpted in the narrative panels of the twelfth-century Śiva temple at Dārāsuram.[95] With the exception of Tirumankai, their Vaiṣṇava counterparts remained unrepresented in Cōḷa art. The deification and inclusion of the Āḻvārs in Vaiṣṇava temple worship was a later development and the direct result and more positive expression of the later Śrīvaiṣṇava movement founded by Rāmānuja in the twelfth century AD, when Vaiṣṇava hagiologies also began to be composed. Thus the Śaiva movement was intensified and consolidated even at the expense of Vaiṣṇavism.

The shift in favour of Śaivism under the Cōḷas led to either a neglect of Vaiṣṇava institutions or a more active persecution of the latter under Kulottunga II. In the twelfth century it led to a societal crisis unsettling the existing social structure considerably. It is against this background that the reformatory zeal and activities of Rāmānuja may be viewed. Rāmānuja, a teacher–reformer, spent his formative years in Kāñcīpuram, and subsequently shifted to Śrīrangam, Tirupati, and Melkōṭe (Karnataka). His liberal measures to widen the social base of Vaiṣṇavism involved a reorganization of rituals and incorporation of non-*brāhmaṇa* elements into Vaiṣṇava worship, thus creating avenues of status enhancement for the artisanal groups, including weavers (*kaikkōḷas*), who were among the principal beneficiaries.

Stories of the persecution of Rāmānuja by a Cōḷa king (Kṛmikaṇṭha identified with Kulottunga II) and attempts to eliminate Vaiṣṇava worship from the Chidambaram temple[96] may also be interpreted as evidence of this crisis, when sectarian ideology and rivalry seem to have taken a violent turn in the twelfth century AD. Śaiva ideology was in crisis and an anxiety to re-establish Śaiva supremacy is implied in these developments. The Śaiva religious network seems to have viewed as a serious threat the Vaiṣṇava attempts at extending their social base and assigning greater participation to *Sudras* in temple worship.

The twelfth century represents a crucial period for both the Śaiva and Vaiṣṇava sectarian movements, for we find them constantly drawing upon the *bhakti* tradition of the hymns of the Nāyanārs and Āḻvārs to strengthen their hold. In a sense, the composition of the monumental hagiological work, namely the *Periya Purāṇam* by Cēkkiḻār, a minister of Kulottunga, was indeed an attempt to revitalize the Śaiva *bhakti* tradition by harking back to the earlier *bhakti* hymnists, although the ostensible purpose of the hagiography, as claimed by the Śaivas, was to supersede the Jain *Jīvakacintāmaṇi*. The Śaiva–Vaiṣṇava sectarian rivalry, together with the remnants of Jain influence, would explain the special care with which the Śaiva hagiological works and the *Śaiva Siddhānta* canon came to be codified between the twelfth and thirteenth centuries with royal support. The Śaiva protagonists also resorted to the organization of a monastic network, the *maṭhas* emerging as the custodians of *bhakti* literature and the *Śaiva Siddhānta* canon. *Maṭhas* proliferated all over the Tamil country and emerged primarily in weaving and trading centres and received royal patronage, merchant endowments, and also gifts from the newly emerging trading and craft organizations.[97] The non-*brāhmaṇa* Śaiva lineages of the Mudaliyār Santāna[98] emerged as a direct consequence of this ideological crisis. Monasteries henceforth became a decisive force in the forging of an institutional base for the Śaiva religion, and post-Cōḷa dynasties, particularly Vijayanagar and their military chiefs, had to come to terms with this new force in establishing authority relationships.

Another important development that may be seen as a consequence of this societal crisis is the emergence and crystallization of the vertical division of Right and Left Hand castes which became a paradigm[99] for providing space within the traditional hierarchical order for the various craft groups and lower agricultural orders. Once again it was the *bhakti* tradition which was evoked to provide norms of validation to the newly emerging economic groups. In the medieval South Indian context, all the emergent institutions and urban forms, including the *nagaram*, merchant 'guilds', and craft organizations, were merged into a single systemic relationship. Diverse economic and ethnic groups were thereby accommodated as a substantial component within the same structure, that is, the temple society, by seeking validation within the norms of the traditional order of ritual ranking. Claims to an enhanced ritual status by economically more powerful craft groups such as the weavers (*kaikkōḷa*s) were also met by the expanding temple ritual and even participation in the gift giving and administrative functions of the temple.[100] Thus Tamil society emerged in the form of a tripartite division of *brāhmaṇa*s, *Vēḷāḷa*s, and the Right and Left Hand castes.

Notes and References

1. In this essay, 'dominant ideology' is used strictly in its dictionary sense/meaning.

2. See A. K. Ramanujan and Norman Cutler in Bardwell L. Smith (eds), *Essays on Gupta Culture*, Delhi, 1983, pp. 177–214.

3. The chronology for Early Tamil Classics adopted in this essay is based on the following works:

Kamil V. Zvelebil, *The Smile of Murugan: On Tamil Literature of South India*, Leiden, 1973; Idem., *Tamil Literature, A History of Indian Literature*; Jan Gonda, vol. x, Wiesbaden, 1974; George L. Hart III, *The Poems of Ancient Tamil: Their Milieu and Their Sanskrit Counterparts*, Berkeley, 1975; Friedhelm Hardy, *Viraha-Bhakti: The Early History of Kṛṣṇa Devotion in South India*, Oxford, 1983.

4. Friedhelm Hardy, 1983.

5 *Kalittokai*, vs. 26 and 94. See R. Champakalakshmi, *Vaiṣṇava Iconography in the Tamil Country*, New Delhi, 1981, p. 42.

6. F. Hardy, 1983, pt III.

7. *Paṭṭinappālai*, 49, 57; *Puṟanāṉūṟu*, 51, 78.

8. K. A. Nilakantha Sastri, *Development of Religion in South India*, Madras, 1963, p. 45.

9. F. Hardy, 1983, pp. 282ff.

10. The three early Āḻvārs were born in Kāñcipuram (Poykai), Māmallapuram (Pūtam), and Mayilai (Pēy), and their hymns are devoted to the three Vaiṣṇava centres Vēnkaṭam, Māmallapuram, and Tirukkōyilūr. See R. Champakalakshmi, 1981, ch. 12 and the three Antātis of the first three Āḻvārs in the *Divyaprabandham*.

11. F. Hardy, 1983, pp. 309ff. On *bhakti* in general and Nammāḻvār's *bhakti* in particular, see A. K. Ramanujan, 'Afterword', in his *Hymns for the Drowning: Poems for Viṣṇu by Nammāḻvār*, Princeton, 1981, pp. 103ff.

12. N. Jagadeesan, *History of Srivaishnavism in the Tamil Country (Post-Rāmānuja)*, Madurai, 1977, chs III and IV.

13. F. Hardy, 1983, p. 400.

14. Ibid., p. 388.

15. Ibid., pp. 371ff.

16. *Periyāḻvār Tirumoḻi*, II and III.

17. *Tiruppāvai* expresses the girl's desire to win Kṛṣṇa's favour and *Nācciyār Tirumoḻi* describes her (Āṇṭāḷ's) marriage with Viṣṇu as Ranganātha.

18. *Tiruppallāṇṭu*, 8.1, and *Tiruppaḷḷiyeḻucci*.

19. F. Hardy, 1983, p. 441.

20. R. Champakalakshmi, 1981, p. 41; F. Hardy, 1983, pp. 48ff; for different dates taking it back to fifth century AD, see T. S. Rukmani, *A Critical Study of the Bhāgavata Purāṇa* (with special reference to *bhakti*), vol. LXXVII, Varanasi, 1970, pp. 9–14.

21. R. Champakalakshmi, 1981, chs 3 and 6.

22. Krishna Sharma, *Bhakti and Bhakti Movement: A New Perspective*, Delhi, 1987, pp. 131ff.

23. F. Hardy, 1983, pt V—*Bhāgavata Purāṇa*.

24. Krishna Sharma, 1987, pp. 296ff.

25. R. Champakalakshmi, 'Urbanisation in Medieval South India: The Role of Ideology and Polity', Presidential Address, Ancient India Section, 47th Session of Indian History Congress, Srinagar, 1986.

26. Indira Viswanathan Peterson, *Poems to Śiva: The Hymns of the Tamil Saints*, Delhi, 1991, p. 5.

27. See Francois Gros, Introduction ('Towards Reading the Tevaram'), in T. V. Gopal Iyer (ed.), *Tevaram, Hymnes Sivaites du Pays tamoul*, vol. I, Pondicherry, 1984, p. xxxix; Dorai Rangaswamy, *Religion and Philosophy of the Tevaram*, I, Madras, 1958, pp. 27–35.

28. R. Champakalakshmi, 'An Unnoticed Jain Cavern near Madurantakam', *Journal of the Madras University*), XLI, 1, 2 (January–July 1969): 111–13.

29. I. V. Peterson, 1991, pp. 24, 34–6.

30. See David Shulman, *Tamil Temple Myths: Sacrifice and Divine Marriage in the South Indian Saiva Tradition*, Princeton, 1980, for myths relating to Śiva temples.

31. *Tirukkōvaiyār*, 352–400. On the theme of 'Separation on Account of a Prostitute'.

32. I. V. Peterson, 1991, pp. 38–9.

33. The stories of the Śaiva saints used in this chapter are from K. Vellaivaranan, *Panniṟu Tirumuṟai Varalāṟu*, 2 vols, Annamalainagar, 1972 and 1980.

34. F. Hardy, 1983, pp. 436–8.

35. *Kaṇṇi-nuṇ-Ciṟu-t-tāmpu*, 4, 8.

36. F. Hardy, 1983, p. 493.

37. *Tirumālai*, pp. 39 and 43.

38. *Bhāgavata Purāṇa*, VII. 9 and 10; X. 23.

39. K. Zvelebil, 1973, pp. 190–9; F. Hardy, 1983, p. 478.

40. G. L. Hart III, 1975, pp. 51–8.

41. C. J. Fuller, *Servants of the Goddess: The Priests of a South Indian Temple*, Cambridge, 1984, ch. 3.

42. R. Champakalakshmi, 'Ideology and the State in Medieval South India', Mamidipudi Venkatarangiah Memorial Lecture, Andhra Pradesh History Congress, Srisailam, 1989.

43. F. Hardy. 'The Tamil Veda of a Śūdra Saint: The Śrīvaiṣṇava Interpretation of Nammāḻvār', in Gopal Krishna (ed.), *Contributions to South Asian Studies*, vol. I, New Delhi, 1979, pp. 42–114.

44. K. Zvelebil, 1973, 190–9; F. Hardy, 1983, p. 478.

45. F. Hardy, 1983, pt 4.

46. Campantar was a *brāhmaṇa* of Kauṇḍinya *gotra* from Sīrkāḻi (I.8.11), Cuntarar, a *brāhmaṇa* from Tirunāvalūr, calls himself the servant of the servants of the *Brāhmaṇa*s of Tillai (VII. 9.1), and Appar was a *Vēḷaḷā* from Tiruvāmūr. See K. Zvelebil, 1975, pp. 138–44.

47. Rājarāja I's inscriptions in Tanjavur refer to the making of the images of Śaiva saints. See *South Indian Inscriptions*, vol. II. The *Tirumuṟaikaṇṭa Purāṇam*, dealing with the discovery of the hymns, associates a Cōḷa ruler, identified with Rājarāja I, with the apotheosis of the three saints, Appar, Campantar, and Cuntarar. See K. Vellaivaranan, vol. I, 1972.

48. There are references to former sages and devotees as those 'who seek the lord's feet' and those 'who sing only of Śiva', etc. who are shadowy figures.

49. Vellaivaranan, vol. 2, 1980; K. Zvelebil, 1973, pp. 192–3.

50. K. A. Nilakantha Sastri, *Cōḷas*, Madras, 1975, rpt, p. 637.

51. Ibid., p. 676.

52. F. Hardy, 1983, p. 389.

53. I. V. Peterson, 1991, pp. 292–3.

54. Campantar, II. 202–11, on the Pāṇṭiya king; I. V. Peterson, 1991, p. 12.

55. See S. R. Balasubramaniam, *Early Cōḷa Temples*, Delhi, 1971; *Middle Cōḷa Temples*, Delhi, 1975; *Later Cōḷa Temples*, Faridabad, 1979.

56. K. K. A. Venkatachari, *The Maṇipravāḷa Literature of the Śrīvaiṣṇava Acāryas: 12th–15th Century* AD, III, Bombay, 1980.

57. I. V. Peterson, 1991, p. 26; for the *Śatarudrīya*, see C. Sivaramamurti, *Śatarudrīya: Vibhūti in Śaiva Iconography*, Delhi, 1986.

58. I. V. Peterson, 1991, pp. 53, 90; also Jean Filliozat, 'The Role of the Śaivāgamas in the Śaiva Ritual System', in Fred W. Clothey and J. Bruce Long (eds), *Experiencing Śiva: Encounters with a Hindu Deity*, Columbia, 1983.

59. F. Hardy, 1983, p. 480.

60. I. V. Peterson, 1991, pp. 44–5; 'Communitas' is Victor Turner's term in *The Ritual Process: Structure and Anti-Structure*, Chicago, 1969.

61. A. K. Ramanujan, 'Form in Classical Tamil Poetry', in *Symposium on Dravidian Civilisation*, ed. Andrée F. Sjoberg, pub. no 1, Asian Series, Austin, 1971, p. 97; also A. K. Ramanujan and N. Cutler, 1983.

62. Jean Filliozat, 1983.

63. I. V. Peterson, 1991, pp. 95–6.

64. *Tēvāram* Appar, V. 209; Campantar, I. 100.9; I. 132.1.

65. I. V. Peterson, 1991, p. 44.

66. *See* B. Stein, *Peasant, State, and Society in Medieval South India*, New Delhi, 1980.

67. M. Rajamanickam, *Śaiva Samaya Vaḷarchchi*, Madras, 1972 (2nd edn), chs 9, 11; R. Champakalakshmi, 'Growth of Urban Centres in South India: Kuḍamūkku Paḻaiyāṟai, the Twin City of the Cōḷas', *Studies in History*, I, 1 (1979), 15 (note 94) and 20.

68. I. V. Peterson, 1991, p. 54.

69. B. Stein, 'Social Mobility and Medieval South Indian Hindu Sects', in J. Silverberg (ed.), *Social Mobility and the Caste System in India: An Interdisciplinary Symposium*, Paris, 1966, pp. 78–94.

70. See David N. Lorenzen, 'The Life of Śankarācārya', in F. Reynolds and D. Capps (eds), *The Biographical Process*, Paris, pp. 87–107.

71. R. Champakalakshmi, 1979, pp. 14–15.

72. R. Champakalakshmi, 1986.

73. B. Stein, 'Temples in Tamil Country, AD 1300–1750', in B. Stein (ed.), *South Indian Temples: An Analytical Reconsideration*, New Delhi, 1978, pp. 11–46.

74. M. G. S. Narayanan and Veluthat Kesavan, 'Bhakti Movement in

South India', in D. N. Jha (ed.), *Feudal Social Formation in Early India*, pp. 347–75.

75. F. Hardy, 1983, p. 460.

76. R. Champakalakshmi, 1986.

77. F. Hardy, 1983, p. 11.

78. R. Nagaswamy, *Kailāsanātha Temple at Kāñcīpuram*, Madras.

79. T. N. Subramanian, *Thirty Pallava Copper Plates*, Madras, 1966.

80. Tirumankai Āḻvār refers to Parameśvara Viṇṇakaram in his hymns (*Periya Tirumoḻi*, II. 9). On the basis of the chronology of the canonical temples, i.e., 9th century onwards, B. G. L. Swamy dates the *Tēvāram* trio to the 10th century AD. See B. G. L. Swamy, 'The Dates of the Tevaram Trio An Analysis and Reappraisal', *Bulletin of the Institute of Traditional Cultures*, Madras, 1975, pp. 119–79.

81. These two works, written by a Jain and a Buddhist respectively, refer to the cities of early Tamiḻakam as teeming with Jain and Buddhist followers and monasteries.

82. 'Kāvērippūmpaṭṭiṇam Excavations', reported in *Indian Archaeology: A Review*, 1961–2, 1963–4; Clarence Maloney, 'Archaeology in South India—Accomplishments and Prospects', in B. Stein (ed.), *Essays on South India*, New Delhi, 1976, pp. 1–40.

83. P. B. Desai, *Jainism in South India and Some Jaina Epigraphs*, Sholapur, 1957.

84. N. Subrahmanian, *Sangam Polity: The Administration and Social Life of the Sangam Tamils*, Madras, 1966, p. 29.

85. T. N. Subramanian, 'Pallankoyil Copper Plate', in *Transactions of the Archaeological Society of South India*, Madras, 1958–9.

86. T. N. Subramanian, *Ten Pandya Copper Plates*, Madras, 1967.

87. K. R. Srinivasan, 'South India', in A. Ghosh (ed.), *Jaina Art and Architecture*, vol. II, New Delhi, 1975; R. Champakalakshmi, 'Religious Conflict in the Tamil Country: A Reappraisal of Epigraphic Evidence', *Journal of the Epigrahical Society of India*, IV (1978); also C. V. Narayana Ayyar, *Origin and Early History of Saivism in South India*, Madras, 1974 (rpt).

88. R. Champakalakshmi, 'Urban Configurations of Tondaimandalam: The Kāñcīpuram and Madras Regions 600–1300 AD', *School of Social Sciences Series*, no. 2, New Delhi, 1988 (in print).

89. These sects are known to the hymnists. See Appar IV. 20 and 21 (Tiruvārūr).

90. Romila Thapar, 'Renunciation: The Making of a Counter Culture', in *Ancient Indian Social History: Some Interpretations*, New Delhi, 1978, p. 75; David N. Lorenzen, *The Kāpālikas and Kālāmukhas: Two Lost Śaivite Sects*, 2nd rev. edn, Delhi, 1991, pp. 148–9.

91. David N. Lorenzen, 'The Kālāmukha Background to Vīraśaivism', in S. K. Maity, *et al.* (eds), *Studies in Orientology*, Agra, 1988, pp. 278–93.

92. See A. K. Ramanujan, *Speaking of Śiva*, Baltimore, 1973; see C. N. Venugopal, 'Lingayat Ideology of Salvation: An Enquiry into Some of its Social Dimensions', *Religion and Society*, xxix, 4 (December 1982); K. Ishwaran, *Religion and Society among the Lingayats of South India*, New Delhi, 1982.

93. Kamil Zvelebil, *The Poets of the Powers*, London, 1973; David Shulman, 'The Enemy within; Idealism and Dissent in South Indian Hinduism', in S. N. Eisenstadt, Reuven Kahane, and David Shulman (eds), *Orthodoxy, Heterodoxy, and Dissent in India*, Berlin, 1984, pp. 32–6.

94. George W. Spencer, 'The Sacred Geography of the Tamil Śaiva Hymns', *Numen* 17 (December 1970): 232–44; F. Hardy, 1983, pp. 256–61.

95. R. Champakalakshmi, 'New Light on the Cōḷa Frescoes at Tanjore', *Journal of Indian History*, Golden Jubilee Number (1973): 349–60; J. R. Marr, 'Periya Purāṇam Frieze in Tārācuram: Episodes in the Lives of the Tamil Śaiva Saints', *Bulletin of the School of Oriental and African Studies*, XLII, 2 (1979): 268–89.

96. K. A. Nilakantha Sastri, 1975, pp. 644–5.

97. R. Champakalakshmi, 1988.

98. Ibid., 1979, p. 15.

99. Arjun Appadurai, 'Right and Left Hand Castes in South India', *Indian Economic and Social History Review*, 11, 2–3 (June–September 1974): 216–59.

100. Vijaya Ramaswamy, *Textiles and Weavers in Medieval South India*, New Delhi, 1985, pp. 58–9.

2

Social Mobility and Medieval South Indian Hindu Sects*

Burton Stein

Medieval India and Social Mobility

This symposium on social mobility in the Indian caste system offers the historian a stimulating and challenging opportunity. The problem of social mobility is not one to which historians of India have given much attention, though there is much evidence that this social process may have been extremely important through much of the ancient and medieval periods of Indian history. The discussion below is limited and tentative; too little attention has been directed to the phenomenon of mobility in medieval India, and the previous study of Hindu sects has been restricted largely to doctrinal, literary, and intellectual issues while almost excluding social ones.

* From James Silverberg (ed.), *Social Mobility and the Caste System in India: An Interdisciplinary Symposium* (The Hague, 1968), pp. 78–94.

Medieval Indian history appears to present widespread and persistent examples of social mobility. It is known that members of lower rank ethnic units assumed roles and statuses which were usually reserved for higher units and with the consent of such higher units. It may be argued that this was one of the most important, and as yet underrated, dynamic elements in medieval Indian history.

The very identification of a 'medieval period' in Indian history stems in part from the establishment of Muslim military and political power in much of northern, central, and southern India, which in time produced social change of such magnitude as to permit historians to speak of a great new historical period. And certainly one aspect of the disjunctive change marking this new historical period was the opportunity of countless Hindu warriors, traders, and peasants to realize new roles and higher rank through conversion to Islam over a period of five centuries.

Of equal significance with the movement out of Hinduism was the rise of many warriors within Hindu society from low social rank to high rank as these warriors achieved power which permitted them to assert claims of higher birth. Evidence which exists at present with respect to the mobility of warriors within Hindu society suggests the ironic proposition that during the medieval period of Indian history, when the rank of persons was in theory rigorously ascribed according to the 'purity' of the birth group, the political units of India were probably ruled most often by men of very low birth. This generalization applies to South Indian warriors and may be equally applicable for many clans of 'Rajputs' in northern India. The capacity of both ancient and medieval Indian society to ascribe to its actual rulers, frequently men of low social origins, a 'clean' or 'Kshatriya' (high-caste warrior) rank may afford one of the explanations for the durability and longevity of the unique civilization of India.

While it is possible to identify social mobility as a significant dynamic element in ancient and medieval Indian society, this mobility cannot be generally characterized as corporate mobility in the sense that most modern mobility movements are corporate. It is usually difficult to identify specific and effective ethnic aggregates—for example, jatis (endogamous units in Indian caste organization)—in the materials with which the medieval historian must work. This is not to suggest that there was no corporate mobility; however, it seems appropriate to point out that neither the facilities nor the need for corporate mobility of the contemporary sort existed during the medieval period.

Modern corporate mobility movements often appear to require facilities which have come to exist only in the recent past, such as the printing press and other improved forms of social communication and, more recently, the concrete rewards of a political system which is often based locally upon caste organization. Perhaps a more cogent reason for what may have been a low order of corporate mobility during the medieval period was that there was little need for it: the opportunities for individual family mobility were great. During the medieval period, there remained, in many parts of India, large tracts of marginally settled lands suitable for cultivation which permitted the establishment of new settlements and even new regional societies. This set limits on the amount of tribute, in the form of agricultural surplus, which local warriors could extract from peasant villages under their control, as well as on the other forms of arbitrariness. It is fairly clear that where sufficient causes arose for individual families or groups of families to leave a settlement or a locality—floods, drought, excessive tribute demands, or the denial of existing or claimed privileges—there were settlements in more remote parts to which they could and did go. Different branches of the Vellala community of Tamil-speaking South India, a respected and powerful cultivating caste, seem to have developed in this manner. This 'looseness' in the agrarian order of medieval South India has been noted by historians, but there has been no systematic study of it. If a developing social system, characterized by such 'openness', is seen as typical in many parts of South India during the medieval period, then the model of the contemporary competition of ethnic units for enhanced rank within a narrow, localized ranking system appears inappropriate for understanding the process of mobility in an earlier period. Much of the evidence we have on the nature of the medieval social order indicates that there was considerable opportunity for individual mobility in most parts of India.

There are thus two general assumptions bearing upon the process of social mobility in medieval Hindu India: (1) the widespread and generally functional (that is, structurally and culturally supportive) character of the process, especially as related to Hindu warriors, and (2) the essentially individual, as opposed to corporate, nature of the process.

These assumptions prompt a realistic examination of the conditions and ranking of low-caste persons in medieval India. By low caste, I mean the traditional social category of Sudra. As expressed in the traditional ranking system of India, the varna system, Sudras are the lowest category of Hindu humanity; they are the servants of the three higher varna categories: priests (Brahmans), warriors (Kshatriyas), and broadly speaking, merchants (Vaishyas). If mobility is taken to mean the adoption of higher roles and statuses by low-caste Hindus, a test should be made as to whether and to what extent this was a formal and legitimate social process during the medieval period. Testing this raises obvious difficulties, for upward mobility (particularly the assumption of Kshatriya rank by Sudra families) was well disguised, involving surreptitious legitimation by cooperative Brahman priests and genealogists. Given the ascriptive nature of rank as a persistent norm in the Indian caste system, an open mobility process can hardly be expected. A test of mobility is suggested by the place of low-caste Hindus in the religious sect structure of medieval South India and, in particular, their participation in the Hindu bhakti (devotional) sects which were of such central importance in the general development of South Indian culture during the medieval period.

The bhakti movement in medieval Hinduism, as much as any other cultural element in medieval Indian society, textured and shaped the culture of the time. In its textual aspects, its devotional hymns and commentaries, the bhakti movement stands opposed to the restrictive structure of Hindu society that is expressed in the legal and social texts of the age. The central characteristic of the bhakti movement, in textual terms, is its openness, its universal appeal without regard to caste.

Historians have fully accepted the significance of the impact of bhakti Hinduism upon medieval and modern Indian society.

The richness and variety of Hindu theism have received careful attention from a line of estimable scholars from R. G. Bhandarkar onward. The progress of the devotional emphasis in Hinduism from the early vernacular hymnists through the philosophical elaborations and commentaries by various systematic thinkers is quite clear. However, one essential gap remains in the study of bhakti Hinduism and that is the last and perhaps the most important phase in the development: the emergence of bhakti sects. Bhakti Hinduism has been and remains essentially a sect organized religion, and scholarly work on these sects and cults, though some has been done, still produces in the researcher 'the thrill of excitement' that results from examining a new field of knowledge, as Deleury states in the preface of his study of a bhakti sect in western India.[1]

The emergence and development of the bhakti sects help to delineate the medieval period of Indian history as much as does the establishment of Muslim control. The devotional sects were, first of all, popular—even, more appropriately, ecumenical—in doctrine and appeal. The doctrine of salvation through love and devotion excluded no one, and a substantial part of the teaching and ritual was carried out in vernacular languages. Intimately associated with the devotional sects was the temple institution which came increasingly to be the principal site for sect activity, and temples were provided with generous support and protection by South Indian warriors. The displacement of earlier centres of religious activity—the villages inhabited and controlled by Brahmans, and the isolated forest or hill shrines—by temples involving a large and diverse body of functionaries, with substantial pilgrim participation, was an institutional change of the greatest importance.

However, the question of Sudra participation in the devotional sects of medieval South India is not an abstract one of how far the catholicity of bhakti principles could be reconciled with the traditional and formal disabilities which the Sudra carried within Hinduism; rather, the question is whether a powerful and populous part of Hindu society was to enjoy a ritual rank commensurate with its ranking in other aspects of South Indian life. For the Sudras appear to have exerted a profound influence upon medieval society, enjoying a rank and social power which was far greater than that accorded them by the legal and social texts of the period.

To appreciate the actualities of Sudra rank and power in medieval times, it is necessary to make a preliminary distinction between the two principal sources of evidence on south Indian society: the literary and the inscriptional. Literary sources are the older and better known, and these materials formed the basis for early Indological research. Two classes of literary evidence have been most important: legal treatises (smriti) and versified commentaries on social morals and custom (dharmashastra).

Medieval commentaries, both legal and social, tend to accept and reaffirm the disabilities under which the Sudra was to live in society that had been expressed in ancient times. Among such disabilities were very limited access to sacred learning and ritual; differential and harsh punishment for criminal acts; the polluting effect of physical contact for higher-caste persons; and very limited access to administrative or judicial office. As in the ancient period, medieval social and legal texts were prepared by Brahmans in Sanskrit, and they continued to reflect the view that Sudra participation in society was sharply limited by their inherent impurity inasmuch as the social order was ranked according to the principle of ascribed ritual purity.

In contrast, and even in contradiction, to the literary evidence in legal and social texts stand the vast number of stone and metal inscriptions of medieval South India. According to this diffuse and diverse body of evidence, Sudras were an extremely important and active part of the population of even those portions of South India where the most powerful centres of Brahman influence flourished, such as the Brahman village (*brahmadeya*) and the Brahmanical temple. During the tenth to thirteenth centuries, under the Cola rulers, with their comparatively benign use of military power, each Brahman village was the centre of a largely autonomous local system of settlements: each served the religious, political, and social requirements of satellite Sudra villages; each such relatively independent, self-sustaining sociocultural system was separated from similar Brahman-centred units by tracts of forests and hills peopled by those outside the pale of Hindu society. Even in the areas of great Brahmin influence, there are numerous inscriptions which describe the vigour of Sudra-dominated assemblies, capable of not only taking care of their own affairs, but extending their concern and protection over Brahman villages and temples as well as important trading guilds. Beyond these areas of most dense Brahman control and influence, the stone and metal inscriptions, which are always an expression of the literate and sacred presence of the Brahman, tend to become more scarce; in such places it is difficult to document the significance of Sudra activities, though such activities would become more, not less, important there.

Sudra Participation in the Srivaishnava Sect

The impact of the medieval bhakti sects on the Sudras may be examined with advantage among the Srivaishnavas. The sect was founded by Rāmānuja (b. AD 1017), one of the great religious and philosophical figures of medieval India. Rāmānuja left an impressive body of writings, and he gave many years to the practical problems of sect organization, particularly at the great Vishnu temple of Srirangam in south India. The sect which acknowledges his leadership was, and remains, one of the great sects of southern India. Finally, because the sect became associated with the Srirangam temple and another great south Indian temple, the Tiruveṃgaḍam temple at Tirupati, there is a considerable body of information relating to sect affairs covering much of the medieval period.

As with other bhakti sects of India, the Srivaishnavas of south India based an essential part of their religious position upon the hymns, or devotional songs, in the vernacular of the region, Tamil. These hymns expressed the central ethos of the bhakti faith: divine and redemptive grace conferred by a merciful god upon a loving devotee. The hymns also strongly emphasize the fundamental irrelevance of caste in the attainment of grace. '...people who are my [the deity Raṃganātha at Srirangam] real devotees must be treated with respect by you [Brahmans] even if they are of low birth; teach them things that you know and learn from them things that they know…', or, 'If we descend below the four castes and come to the chaṇḍāḷas [untouchables or men without caste] who, however lacking in virtue are true worshippers of… [Vishnu], their servant's servants are my masters and their feet are mine to worship'.[2]

Participation of Sudras in the Srivaishnava sect is explored in an imperfect way in the medieval literature of the sect. The great expounders of the Vaishnava doctrine—Rāmānuja, Vedānta Deśika, and Piḷḷai Lokācārya—developed their views within the framework of the *Paṃcarātra* agama, a collection of ritual principles and mythology related to the worship of the Hindu deity Vishnu, which dates from the first millennium BC, and is the most important guide to ritual for the sect. By medieval times, over one hundred systematic handbooks of ritual on Vishnu worship had come to be prepared from the *Paṃcarātra* agama and this ritual tradition had become the basis for many, if not most, of the South Indian temples devoted to Vishnu, replacing the other major ritual tradition among Vishnu worshippers, the *Vaikhānasa* agama.

The relationship between these two ritual traditions of Vishnu worship has important social as well as religious implications. The *Vaikhānasa* tradition was one in which Brahman ritual functionaries dominated worship and in which Sanskrit was the exclusive language of ritual. Within this restrictive and esoteric tradition, there was little scope for the devotional colour and popular participation which characterized the bhakti faith of the medieval period, with its public singing of vernacular hymns. There is evidence of serious conflict among various branches of Vishnu worshippers over the restrictive nature of the *Vaikhānasa* tradition, and Rāmānuja's career as a sectarian is identified with the establishment of the more liberal *Paṃcarātra* form in many south Indian temples. Even at Tirupati and Trivandrum, two great Vishnu temples in the south which resisted the pressure to change to the liberal ritual forms, the substance of Rāmānuja's reforms was introduced: the more complete participation of Vishnu worshippers of all social levels was realized despite the formal retention of the *Vaikhānasa* form and the actual presence of Brahman functionaries of the *Vaikhānasa* tradition.

The effects of such reform on Sudra ritual participation received some specific attention in the *Paramasaṃhitā*, one of the more important handbooks on *Paṃcarātra* ritual and one that was well known in the eleventh century when the Srivaishnava sect began. Here it was stated that initiation into the Srivaishnava sect was open to high-caste persons ('the twice-born') and to Sudras 'of good birth, of good character, and possessed of good qualities'. It was further stated that, after proper training—a period of twelve years is specified—a Sudra might be admitted to all aspects of sect worship, excluding only the fire-rites (pari-homa or *agnikārya*), which remained the exclusive right of Brahman sectarians.

By the fourteenth century, however, a split of the Srivaishnavas into two subsects—the 'Northern School' (*Vaḍagalai*) and the 'Southern School' (*Teṃgalai*)—had become well established, a division that had significant implications for the participation of low-caste sect members. Vedānta Deśika (b. AD 1269), recognized in the fourteenth century as a great Srivaishnava teacher and leader, was regarded by the Northern School as the successor to Rāmānuja in being guru (preceptor) of the entire sect. His writings contain many references to caste and caste duty (varnashrama dharma), and the implication of these references appears to be that the traditional ranking and duties of persons within the sect should not be modified by sect membership. There are, in Vedānta Deśika, signs of concern that the universalistic social values of the Srivaishnava sect, which were expressed firmly in the early hymnists and reinforced by the *Paṃcarātra* ritual tradition as spread by Rāmānuja, would weaken the caste identity and obligations of low-caste sect members to the detriment of the social order. Vedānta Deśika's position is stated by his biographer, S. Singh, in the following way: 'His attitude might have meant some setback to the universalism of the Ālvars' [early hymnists'] religion and the liberalism of Rāmānuja's religious culture, but, nevertheless, it went a great way to strengthening the spirit of Hinduism, in those troubled times....'[3] To be sure, this great Srivaishnava teacher's position contrasts with the almost casual manner in which the *Paramasaṃhitā* accepted the place of the low-ranking Sudras as Srivaishnava sect participants.

The issue of Sudra participation was reflected in medieval Srivaishnava sect literature in two ways.

(1) One of these was the degree and kind of preparation necessary for the salvation of the bhakta (devotee), or, as expressed in the sect literature, the nature of *prapatti* and its relationship to bhakti. As seen by Rāmānuja, whose teachings are followed by both subsects of Srivaishnavas, bhakti, the loving devotee's complete subservience to a merciful and saviour deity, and bhakti-yoga, the way of the devotee to god, represented the final stages in the attainment of divine grace; karma-yoga (the way of ritual action) and jnana-yoga (the way of intellect) are prior stages. For Rāmānuja, bhakti represented the ritual and intellectual aspects of religious experience simultaneously and *prapatti*—'surrendering to' or 'taking refuge in' god—was a condition implied in bhakti.

By the fourteenth century, however, a critical issue dividing the two subsects was the meaning of *prapatti*. The Northern School leader, Vedānta Deśika, appeared to understand *prapatti* to be one of several ways of a devotee to god, and, in any case, it involved deliberate human initiative and effort to achieve the condition of *prapatti*. The chief spokesman for the Southern School, Piḷḷai Lokācārya (b. AD 1264), appeared to regard the complete surrender of the devotee as the only way to god and to consider that this way involved no effort by the devotee who merely received the redemptive grace of god. By this Southern School interpretation, Sudras would be as fully qualified to grace as members of higher castes and also as fully qualified to sect membership and participation, for *prapatti* depended on the spontaneous grace of god, requiring no initiative on the part of the devotee such as would require Vedic learning that was accessible only to high-caste Hindus. On the other hand, the Northern School understood *prapatti* to be a state initiated by the devotee through preparation with a guru. The place of the guru, particularly the Brahman guru, and even guru worship, was a vital part of the teachings of Vedānta Deśika.

(2) The medieval Srivaishnava subsects were divided also on the relative importance of the Tamil devotional hymns. These hymns (the *nālāyira prabandam*) have little doctrinal importance

except as they emphasize the experience of *prapatti* as a mystical and emotional condition of bhakti, but these devotional songs were recognized as important by Rāmānuja and his successors, including Vedānta Deśika, as a vital expression of the deep theism of South Indian Hinduism. There was controversy, however, regarding the relationship of the Tamil hymns to the Sanskrit–Vedic scriptural materials. The Southern School placed greater stress upon the Tamil hymns as an adequate scripture upon which to base ritual, while the Northern School, without denying the significance of the Tamil hymns, regarded the traditional Vedic scriptures as the primary foundation for sect initiation and ritual. By the Southern School view that the Tamil scripture was sufficient, and that all had access to this scripture regardless of caste rank, Sudras were or could have been qualified as full participants. The Northern School, in maintaining the equality, if not the supremacy, of the Sanskrit–Vedic scripture, which was accessible only to the high-caste Hindu (and fully only to the Brahman), limited the potential participation of Sudras in sect practices.

The medieval literature of the Srivaishnava sect, as briefly discussed above, makes it appear that from the time of Rāmānuja, in the eleventh century, through the time of Vedānta Deśika, in the late fourteenth century, doctrinal issues came to be related quite directly to the place of Sudras in the sect. The issue of caste as an aspect of sect participation was raised by Vedānta Deśika. And, in the division of the sect into its Northern and Southern Schools, the issues of *prapatti* and the adequacy of the Tamil scripture bore upon the place of Sudras in Srivaishnava devotional activity. While both subsects were under the control of Brahmans, the question of Sudra participation had become a serious one within the sect. This becomes clearer on examination of the actual position of Sudras at two major centres of sect activity in medieval times.

The temples of Srirangam (Tiruchirapalli, Madras State) and Tirupati (Chittoor, Andhra State) have been among the great centres of Vishnu worship in India; both have been important centres of the Srivaishnava sect since early medieval times. Rāmānuja, the founder of the sect, was associated with Śrīrangam through much of his career, and that temple was identified by Vishnu worshippers simply as 'the Temple (*koyil*)'. The Tirupati temple achieved the status of a great temple only in the fifteenth century after a long history as a sacred pilgrimage place. During the sixteenth century, the Tiruveṃgaḍam temple at Tirupati was regarded as the greatest temple in South India. From Srirangam we have one of the most famous of the temple chronicles in the *Kōil Olugu* and from the Tirupati temple we have one of the longest consecutive series of temple inscriptions of any Indian temple. The evidence from these sources permits the following brief examination of actual sect participation by low-caste persons for several centuries at two prominent Srivaishnava centres.

At Srirangam, the organization of temple affairs was based upon a code established by the sect progenitor, Rāmānuja. This code covered aspects of ritual and management for almost three centuries. Under Rāmānuja, the temple accountant (*koyil kaṇakkan*) was a member of the dominant Sudra agricultural community of Tamil country, the Vellalas, and the ritually pregnant task of offering coconut to the deity was given to a member of the low-caste weaver community (Kaikkoḷar). An important ritual role was granted to a category of Sudra functionaries called *sāttādamudalis* (lit. 'a holy man or teacher who does not wear the sacred thread'), who are described as 'outsiders'—meaning that they were introduced into temple service by Rāmānuja—and also described as ascetics, detached from family obligations (that is, sannyasis). There was also a group of Sudra householders, permanently attached to the Temple, who, while carrying on their traditional artistic, artisan, and personal services, also had ritual functions that were as much honours as responsibilities. The important ritual roles of Sudras at Srirangam were maintained according to the code of Rāmānuja—until the Temple was desecrated by Muslims in AD 1323, when the major image was hidden and all services ceased. Ritual at the Temple was restored when it was rescued from Muslim control in the 1370s by the expanding power of Vijayanagar, Hindu warriors from the northern portion of South India. Under officials appointed by the Vijayanagar rulers, the code of Rāmānuja was abandoned, according to the Srirangam chronicle, and this undermined the rights and privileges of Sudra functionaries.

The ritual position of low-caste (Sudra) members of the Srivaishnava sect at Srirangam for three centuries following the establishment of Rāmānuja's code was an upwardly mobile one. This reflected the apparent liberalism of Rāmānuja in his capacity as sect organizer and leader, despite the ambiguity which his writings express on the matter of Sudras. His code gave an important place to low-caste initiates in the sect; after his death, his code and the place of Sudras were protected by the relatively liberal disposition of the leaders of the Southern School, such as Naṃpiḷḷai and Maṇavāḷa. Naṃpiḷḷai, in the early thirteenth century, and Alagai Maṇavāḷa, in the middle of the fourteenth century, both emphasized the importance of sect teachings and religious devotion over caste membership in sect affairs, and the importance of Tamil as a ritual language. Unfortunately, after the disruption of temple organization by Muslim warriors, and the subsequent management of the Srirangam temple by Vijayanagar officials, it is not possible to trace the later position of Sudra sect members beyond noting that the Srirangam chronicle suggests a decline in their rank.

The other centre of the Srivaishnava sect was the Tiruveṃgaḍam temple at Tirupati. Long a sacred pilgrimage place in southern India, the simple shrine in the hills over the town of Tirupati was under the custodianship of Brahmans of the restrictive and esoteric *Vaikhānasa* school. In the fifteenth century, this shrine had become the nucleus for a great temple complex. Indeed, from the middle of the fifteenth century to the middle of the sixteenth, when the Vijayanagar empire was at its height, the Tirupati temple was probably the greatest temple in South India; considering the circumstances of Muslim rule over most of India at the time, it may have been one of the great temples in all of India.

The spectacular rise of the Temple was based in part on its ancient sacred character, in part on a traditional relationship with Rāmānuja, who is credited with founding the town of Tirupati, but most importantly with the support of a great Telugu warrior, Sāḷuva Narasiṃha, whose headquarters was near

Tirupati. Under his patronage, substantial wealth was granted to the Temple for establishing temple buildings and elaborate ritual, thus enhancing its attractiveness as a pilgrimage centre. The agency through which an important part of the transformation of the Tirupati temple took place in the fifteenth century was a Srivaishnava sect leader, invested with gifts and with authority at the Temple by Sāḷuva Narasiṃha.

The nature of Temple leadership during the fifty years of intensive transformation, and the kinds of changes which were introduced, make it appear as if an attempt was being made to bring the Temple under the control of Southern School Srivaishnavas. Until the fifteenth century, the Tirupati temple seemed poised between the two subsects. In fact, the *Vaikhānasa* ritual form was maintained, with its bias for Sanskrit ritual carried on by an esoteric priestly group, even though the shrine was acknowledged as a Srivaishnava centre from the time of Rāmānuja. In the late fourteenth century, a seminary (math) following Northern School teachings, said to have been established by the son of Vedānta Deśika at this Temple, failed and was removed to the more hospitable centre of Kanchipuram (Chingleput, Madras State).

Sāḷuva Narasiṃha's agent, a functionary of decisive power within the Temple organization during the fifteenth century and author of most of the changes which occurred then, was a follower of the leading contemporary Southern School teacher, Maṇavāḷa. Some twenty inscriptions, covering almost fifty years, illuminate his career. Under his influence, much of the ritual and organizational structure of the bhakti temple worship found earlier at Srirangam was transplanted to Tirupati, including the place and rank of Sudras. According to some evidence, he may himself have been a Sudra!

As at Srirangam, where they were called *sāttādamudalis*, there was established at Tirupati an order of celibate and detached Sudras, called *sāttāda ekāki* Srivaishnavas. During the fifteenth century, this order of Sudra ascetics carried on important ritual service.

In addition to the celibate order of Sudras, however, there was introduced into Tirupati a group of Sudra families—sixteen households are mentioned—which were special disciples of the innovating agent of Sāḷuva Narasiṃha. They were especially identified with the many new festivals established at the Temple during the fifteenth century and modelled after those of older Srivaishnava temples that were following *Paṃcarātra* ritual procedures. These families, called *sāttāda* Srivaishnavas, lived in a block of houses on a street near the Temple named after their patron. They performed vital ritual functions in connection with daily worship, recited the Tamil devotional hymns on an equal basis with Brahman functionaries, received regular emoluments for the services they performed, and even were additionally rewarded by specific endowments on their behalf. These Sudra functionaries, in short, appeared to be fully integrated into the regular high ritual at Tirupati.

In the course of the sixteenth century, following the death of Sāḷuva Narasiṃha and his agent at Tirupati, the rank and privileges of Sudras declined. References to the families of *sāttāda* Srivaishnavas no longer associated them with temple ritual service; their functions at the Temple were relegated to tending flower gardens used to produce garlands for ritual service. The ascetic order of Sudras, the *sāttāda ekākis*, ceased to exist as a separate order. Though Sudra ascetics continued to be active at the Temple, they functioned within ascetic orders, comprising dedicated men of all castes. The ritual functions which had previously been carried out by Sudras were retained as part of temple service, but they were executed by Brahman Srivaishnavas.

Though the evidence on the position of Sudras at the two Srivaishnava centres of Srirangam and Tirupati is fragmentary and leaves many issues unclear, it has been possible to reconstruct the general outlines of their position. Certainly, enough is known to assert that within the Srivaishnava sect, high ritual positions were attained by Sudras at Srirangam and Tirupati. However, it is clear from the Srirangam chronicle and the Tirupati inscriptions that these positions were no longer held in the later Vijayanagar period, after the sixteenth century. These changes in position for low-caste Hindus within the context of an important South Indian sect may be examined according to whether they offer a test, however limited, of the mobility process within Hindu sects during the medieval period.

The *sāttādamudalis* at Srirangam and the *sāttāda ekākis* at Tirupati, both Sudra categories, cannot be considered as tests of mobility because, as ascetics and detached men, they were no longer subject to the ordinary restrictions of Sudras. They were fully qualified and initiated sannyasis for whom all normal caste duties, privileges, and restrictions were removed, leaving only the duties and responsibilities appropriate to their orders. However, it is interesting to notice that, in both cases, the Sudra ascetics retained their identity as Sudras (that is, *sāttāda*s) and were not, until quite late at Tirupati, integrated into ascetic orders whose members were not identified in terms of caste origin.

The group of Sudra householders, the *sāttāda* Srivaïshnavas, officiating at Tirupati for about fifty years, would come closest to providing a test of mobility. If the readiness of the *bhakti* sect to accept Sudras as active and significant participants is to be tested, a good case is found in these Tirupati Sudra family households which participated in high sacred ritual together with Brahman functionaries and who enjoyed very high rank. Indeed, these families merit much closer examination than the primarily artisan Sudras at Srirangam, who were also householders, precisely because the Tirupati Sudra householders were performing roles that were priestly in the fullest sense. It is significant that their high rank and their ritual co-participation with Brahmans were achieved *as Sudras*; while the roles and rank positions of these families had altered from those of Sudras in general, they continued to be identified as Sudras. One scholar of Srivaishnavism has suggested that among Southern School Srivaishnavas there was a readiness to admit to Brahman status those Sudras, such as the *sāttāda* Srivaishnavas at Tirupati, whose ritual skills and roles were high, and that certain Southern School 'Brahmans' can still be identified as former Sudras from their names and customs. However, this position is not generally held by scholars of Srivaishnavism. Most tend to argue that, even with the more liberal and universalistic values of the Southern School, Sudras did not actually enjoy full privileges as sect members, either in medieval times or more recently, and that

Southern School Brahmans most certainly did not assent to any claims by Sudras to Brahman identity. In any event, the ultimate rejection by high-caste Srivaishnavas at Tirupati of the place achieved by Sudra families for a time—the fact that the *sāttāda* householders were divested of ritual functions in temple service and reduced to flower garden attendants—marked this episode as a failure in mobility.

Conclusions

At the outset of this paper it was pointed out that, while social mobility in medieval India was widespread, it was not corporate—not the movement of an entire jati or entire jati section from one varna identification to another; rather, it was a matter of movement by individual families. It was also suggested that low-caste participation in medieval religious sects would test whether the assumption of higher roles and statuses by some low-caste Sudras was a formal and legitimate process, whether their ritual rank could match their actual social power and secular rank (superior to what was accorded them in legal and social texts).

Important evidence (for example, the stone and metal inscriptions cited earlier) has attested to the fact that Sudras occupied a significant place as respected and integrated members of Hindu society in medieval South India, unlike the untouchables at the very bottom of that society or the excluded forest people. Indeed, some individual Sudra families seem to have gained Kshatriya identification through their successful assumption of roles as warrior leaders during the period of greatest martial activity (thirteenth through sixteenth centuries). Then, the agrarian order of South India was fundamentally changing; the interstitial forest and hill communities at the margins of Hindu society were being brought under warrior control at a greatly accelerated rate and linked to the older, more stable, and orderly agrarian communities. Enhanced state power was brought much more directly into the control and management of local communities, mobilizing human and material resources over enormous regions to create the greatest warlike state in south Indian history. And this more total control by the Vijayanagar political system, that culminated in the martialization of South India, was achieved in part at the expense of some of the previous largely autonomous power of landed Brahmans. The new warrior state did not perpetuate subservience to the Brahmin control of local communities.

At the same time, the Brahmin villages were partly displaced as the centres of religious activity by the rise of sect-managed temples and by challenges to exclusive Brahman control over religion and ritual. The development of the Srivaishnava bhakti movement, with its universal appeal to all men in the name of devotional faith, particularly in the several centuries that immediately followed Rāmānuja's leadership, seemed to promise vital sect participation for some Sudras in the form of highly ranked ritual roles, so much so as to threaten the traditional Brahman monopoly of leadership in ritual affairs. The bhakti movement implicitly undermined one principle upon which caste hierarchy was based, 'differential purity by birth', to the extent that it tended to measure or validate 'purity' in terms of ritual activities for all participants. Furthermore, the Southern School interpretation of the meaning of *prapatti* and of the place of Tamil scripture in devotional observances, as described earlier, threatened such important Brahman prerogatives as their recitation of Sanskrit scripture and their roles as gurus. As we have seen, then, in such a context, for several centuries some Sudra families did assume significantly high ritual roles at the two great centres of the sect, Srirangam and Tirupati.

The factors involved in the failure of the Sudra Srivaishnavas to maintain their improved ritual position at either Srirangam or Tirupati are difficult to identify. Within other bhakti sects of a somewhat later period, Sudras were apparently more successful in retaining important places in sect activities. Two factors appear to have contributed to the failure of Sudras within the Srivaishnava sect: both represent pressures that favoured Brahman-dominated Hindu orthodoxy, one being largely internal to the sect and the other primarily external.

The most determinative factor relates to the development of the sect itself. The rejection of Sudra participants in the sacred rites of the sect at two major centres may be understood as an internal adjustment necessary for consolidation, perhaps to prevent full division between the Southern and Northern Schools of the sect. By the time of Alagai Maṇavāḷa, the Southern School leader of the fifteenth century, the division between the two subsects was deep enough for endogamy to be normative within them, at least for Brahmans. Maṇavāḷa had to establish seven new lineages (*gotras*) among the Kaṃdāḍai Aiyaṃgār Brahmans who had been converted to the Southern School, so that they could avoid marriage with Northern School members of their caste, according to Southern School genealogical and biographical records (*guruparaṃparās*). In addition, there were disputes between the two Srivaishnava subsects over which of them were to control ritual at Srirangam and at temples in Kanchipuram, and we have seen how they vied at Tirupati in this respect.

To some extent, at least, the deepening division within the sect reflected doctrinal and organizational differences involving the ritual roles of Sudras. At Tirupati, during the fifteenth century, when *sāttāda* Srivaishnava households could play very highly ranked participants' roles under the innovating agent of Sāḷuva Narasiṃha, a crisis may have been reached regarding Sudra participation. The crisis would have been generated not only by the high place of Sudras within the Temple organization, but also by the probability, supported by some available evidence, that Sāḷuva's innovating agent may have been a Sudra himself. That the agent was a Southern School sectarian is certain from the inscriptions. In order to perceive the nature of this crisis, it must be recognized that the leadership and primary membership of both subsects were Brahman. Hence, the growing authority and influence of Sudras at Tirupati, under what may have been a Sudra guru, may have been seen as a direct challenge to Brahman leadership in the sect.

The issue of Sudra participation is also connected to a problem which reached back to the founding days of the sect when Rāmānuja was engaged in establishing the more liberal, popular, bhakti-oriented *Pamcarātra* over the more restrictive form of the *Vaikhānasa*. Involved in this tension between *Paṃcarātra* and *Vaikhānasa* are a number of issues ranging from the principles of Sanskrit exclusiveness as the language of ritual and a simple shrine for a single worshipped deity, to such material issues as the livelihood of the *Vaikhānasa* priests. The relevance of this tension within the *Vaikhānasa* sect for Sudra participation is that, despite Rāmānuja's great prestige, there remained within the sect a strong commitment to the *Vaikhānasa* form of simple Sanskrit ritual carried on by Brahmans alone. Evidence of this persistence may be seen in the failure of *Paṃcarātra* to be established in some sect temples, including the important ones of Tirupati and Trivandrum, where *Vaikhānasa* procedures, albeit in altered form, continued as the recognized tradition.

The elimination of significant Sudra influence at Srirangam and Tirupati may therefore be understood as an internal sect adjustment which reduced the tension between Northern and Southern School followers and between the proponents of *Paṃcarātra* and *Vaikhānasa*, through consensus on the continued significance of Sanskrit learning and the dominance of properly prepared Brahmans in sect leadership and control.

In addition to, and supportive of, the pressure inside the sect by the sixteenth century to reinforce Brahman control of the performance and staffing of ritual roles, there was a primarily external determinant: Vijayanagar espousal of an orthodox Hindu ideology. These rulers identified and justified their own power in terms of the protection of Hindu institutions from Islam. The maintenance of proper caste duties and relationships (varnashrama dharma) was frequently cited as an objective of state policy in Vijayanagar inscriptions. The new warriors, then, did come to terms with the Brahman elite of South India. On the basis of their continued support of Brahman religious prerogatives and high ritual rank—though not support of the earlier almost complete socio-political autonomy of landed Brahman communities—they won recognition from the Brahmans for their own ascendant military and political power. This ideological posture of the Vijayanagar rulers of South India in general—perhaps with temporary exceptions, such a Sāḷuva Narasiṃha—could have contributed to the failure of Sudras to extend or even to maintain their prominent place in the Srivaishnava sect.

The question may be asked as to why Sudras were apparently more successful in achieving and maintaining significant ritual roles in bhakti sects in other times and places in India. In this connection, more research is required to verify the degree and conditions of upward mobility by Sudra sect participants, since examination of bhakti sect literature alone—as would be the case for the Srivaishnava sect literature—may give a misleading impression of enduringly successful Sudra participation. However, another factor is that in no other part of India was the Brahman community so powerful, not only in religious matters, but also in social and political aspects of life—even after the emergence and decline of Vijayanagar state power. The long exercise of Brahman religious, social, and political power in South India is reflected not only in the extraordinary maintenance of traditional Brahmanical institutions on a broad regional basis in the south, but in the significant anti-Brahman political movements and attitudes of the present century.

A number of crucial aspects of the roles of Sudras in the Srivaishnava sect of medieval South India remain obscure and the explanations of their failure to maintain a once achieved high place in the sect are tentative. Much more work deserves to be done on the general problem of social mobility in medieval India and on the particular aspects of mobility within the bhakti sects.[4]

Notes and References

1. G. A. Deleury, *The Cult of Viṭhobā* (Poona, 1960).

2. K. Rangachari, *The Sri Vaishnava Brahmans* (*Madras Government Museum Bulletin, No.* 2) (Madras, 1931).

3. Satyavrata Singh, *Vedānta Deśika; His Life, Works, and Philosophy: A Study* (Varanasi, 1958).

4. In addition to the references already cited, the following works were of particular pertinence in preparing this paper: S. Krisnaswami Aiyangar (ed. and transl.), *Paramasaṃhitā* [*of the Paṃcarātra*] (*Gaekwad's Oriental Series,* No. 86) (Baroda, 1940); V. N. Hari Rao (ed.), *Kōil Olugu: The Chronicle of the Srirangam Temple with Historical Notes* (Madras, 1961); Sadhu S. Sastri (ed.), Tirumalai-Tirupati Epigraphical Series, *Report on the Inscriptions of the Devasthanam Collection with Illustrations* (Madras, 1930); Tirumalai-Tirupati Epigraphical Series, *Inscriptions of Saluva Narasinha's Time; from* AD *1445 to 1504* (*Texts and Translations*, vol. II) (Madras, 1933); J. A. B. Van Buitenen, *Rāmānuja on the Bhagavadgītā* ('s-Gravenhage, 1953).

II
Conversion to Islam

3

Approaches to the Study of Conversion to Islam in India*

Richard M. Eaton

The expansion of Islam east of the Middle East has been, apart from a few notable exceptions, a relatively understudied subject. This is especially remarkable when one recalls that, by far, the world's greatest number of Muslims reside east of Karachi. The reasons for this neglect of scholarship, however, are not far to find. First is the identification of the Arab Middle East with the historical heartland of Islam, which makes it the natural object of study of classicists whose scholastic concerns often focus on the formation of cultural traditions. Second, despite its universalist claims and its undeniable status as a world religion, Islam is related to Arab ethnicity, language, and culture in complex ways that have always somehow made the study of Arab Islam a more legitimate or proper field on the Islamist's agenda than 'Eastern' or sub-Saharan Islam. And third, for at least a century, severe methodological problems have prevented scholars from explaining the formation, through conversion, of the majority of the

* From Richard C. Martin (ed.), *Approaches to Islam in Religious Studies* (Tucson, 1985), pp. 106–26.

world's Muslim population living beyond the Middle East. There have appeared few convincing answers to such basic questions as: What is conversion per se? Can conversion to Islam fit within a larger conceptual category, or must it be considered unique? By what indices can it be measured? What forces favour or hinder its progress?

Nonetheless, scholars of various persuasions have recently taken a lively interest in the study of Muslim conversion movements. It is the aim of this paper to explore some of the approaches to this topic as it concerns one important area of the Islamic world—South Asia—with a view to isolating some of the problems encountered in previous studies and to suggesting a more comprehensive hypothesis explaining the phenomenon.

Theories of Conversion to Islam in India

Most explanations of conversions to Islam in India can be reduced to three basic, and in my view inadequate, theories. The oldest of these is the 'religion of the sword' theory. As a theme in the Western historiography of Islam, it has a long and weary history that dates from the time of the Crusades; and for Indian Islam, too, it has always had its advocates. Yet as Peter Hardy has recently observed, those who argue that Indian Muslims were forcibly converted generally failed to define either 'force' or 'conversion',[1] leaving us to presume that a society can and will change its religious identity simply because it has a sword at its neck. Precisely how this mechanism worked either in theoretical or practical terms, however, is seldom spelled out. Moreover, proponents of this theory seem to have confused conversion to Islam with the extension of Turko-Iranian rule in North India between AD 1200 and 1765, a confusion probably originating in a too literal translation of primary Persian accounts narrating the 'Islamic' conquest of India.[2]

But the most serious problem with this theory is its incongruence with the geography of Muslim conversions in South Asia. A glance at the geographical distribution of Muslims in the subcontinent (see map on p. 107) reveals an *inverse* relationship between the degree of Muslim political penetration and the degree of conversion to Islam. If conversion to Islam had ever been a function of military or political force (however these might have been expressed), one would expect that those areas of heaviest conversion would correspond to those areas of South Asia exposed most intensely and over the longest period to rule by Muslim dynasties. Yet the opposite is the case: those regions of the most dramatic conversion of the population such as Eastern

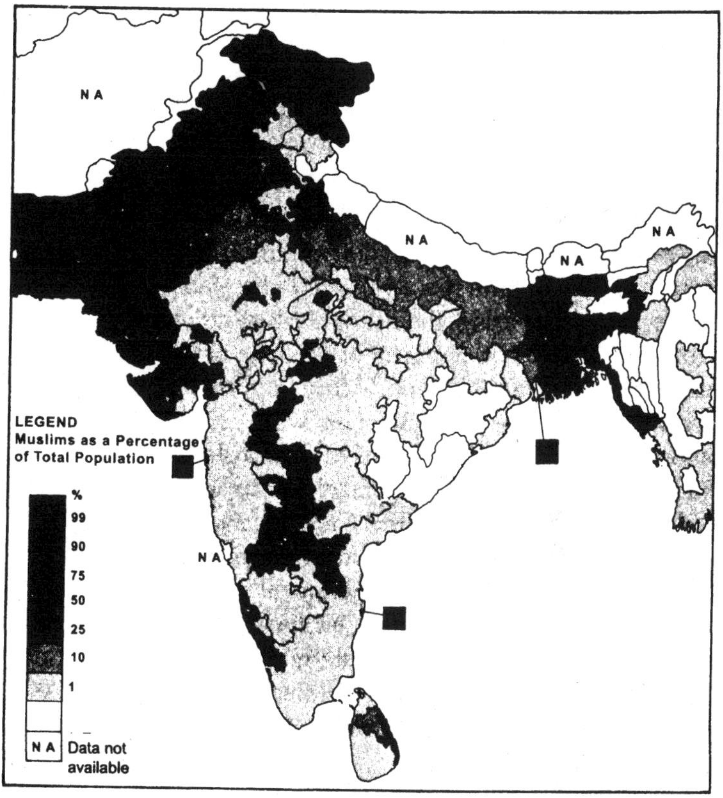

Geographical distribution of South Asian Muslim population. [Adapted from J. Schwartzberg (ed.), *A Historical Atlas of South Asia* (Chicago and London, 1978), p. 94.]

Bengal or Western Punjab, lay on the fringes of Indo-Muslim rule, whereas the heartland of that rule, the upper Gangetic Plain, saw a much lower incidence of conversion.[3]

A second theory commonly advanced to explain the conversions of Indians to Islam is the 'political patronage' theory, or the view that Indians of the medieval period converted in order to receive some non-religious favours from the ruling class—relief from taxes, promotion in the bureaucracy, and so forth. In the early fourteenth century, for example, Ibn Battuta reported that Indians presented themselves as new converts to the Khalaji sultans who in turn rewarded them with robes of honour according to their rank.[4] But individual conversion for political gain frequently lacked conviction, as witnessed by the more spectacular cases of apostasy: Khusrau Khan, a fourteenth-century usurper of the Delhi Sultanate; or Harihara and Bukka, the co-founders of the Vijayanagar empire. Then, too, nineteenth-century census reports speak of landholding families of medieval Upper India declaring themselves Muslims either to escape imprisonment for non-payment of revenue, or to preserve ancestral lands in the family name.[5] More important examples of the 'political patronage' phenomenon were the cases of groups coming into the employment of Muslim rulers and in this way gradually acculturating themselves to Indian Islam. The Kayasthas and Khatris of the Gangetic Plain, the Parasnis of Maharashtra, and the Amils of Sind all cultivated Muslim culture by virtue of their filling the government's great need for clerks and administrative servants at all levels, which Aziz Ahmad compared with the later 'westernization' process.[6] Finally, the acculturation of captured soldiers or slaves, severed as these men were from their families, formed another dimension of this process.

Adequate though the patronage thesis may be in accounting for the relatively light incidence of Islamization in the political heartland, it cannot explain the massive conversions to Islam that took place along the political fringe—especially in the Punjab and Bengal. For political patronage, like the influence of the sword, decreases rather than increases as one moves away from the Delhi heartland toward the periphery.

What is needed is some theory that would explain the phenomenon of mass conversion to Islam on India's periphery and not just in the heartland, and among India's millions of peasant cultivators and not just among urban elites. To this end, a third theory is frequently invoked, one which has for long been the most popular explanation of the phenomenon—the 'religion of social liberation' theory. Elaborated by British ethnographers, Pakistani nationals, and Indian Muslims among many others, the substance of the theory is that the Hindu caste system is a rigidly discriminatory form of social organization and that the lowest and most degraded castes, recognizing in Islam an ideology of social equality, converted to it en masse in order to escape Brahmanical oppression.

This theory, too, has serious problems. The first is that it commits the fallacy of reading the values of the present into the peoples or events of the past. Are we to assume that before their contact with Muslims, the untouchables of India possessed, as though they were familiar with the writings of Rousseau or Jefferson, some innate notion of the fundamental equality of all men denied them by an oppressive Brahmanical tyranny? To the contrary, it seems that Hindu society of medieval India was more influenced by what Louis Dumont calls the principle of *homo hierarchicus*, or of institutionalized inequality, than by the principle of *homo equalis*.[7] Beyond that, a careful reading of Persian primary sources suggests that in their presentation of Islam to Indians, Muslim intellectuals did not stress the Islamic ideal of social equality as opposed to Hindu castes, but rather Islamic monotheism as opposed to Hindu polytheism.[8] Moreover, even if it were true that Islam had been presented as an ideology of social equality, there is abundant evidence that former Hindu communities failed upon conversion to improve their status in the social hierarchy and that, on the contrary, they simply carried over into Muslim society the same practice of birth-ascribed rank that they had had in Hindu society.[9]

But the most damaging problem with the 'liberation theory', as with the two others discussed above, appears when we return to the map (p. 107) and observe the geographical distribution of the South Asian Muslim population. Before the dislocations consequent upon the Partition of 1947, the areas with the highest percentage of Muslims were Eastern Bengal, Western Punjab, Northwest Frontier, and Baluchistan. Now from both historical evidence and anthropological studies we know that the bulk of the population in Baluchistan and the Northwest Frontier were not converted communities at all, but descendants of the immigrants from the Iranian Plateau. This leaves East Bengal and West Punjab as the two areas of the subcontinent possessing the highest incidence of Muslim conversion among the local population. What is striking about those areas, however, is that they lay not only far from the centre of Muslim political power, as noted, but that their indigenous populations had not, at the time of their contact with Islam, been integrated into the Hindu social system. In Bengal, Muslim converts were drawn mainly from Rajbansi, Pod, Chandal, Koch, or other indigenous groups which had had but the lightest contact with the Hindu religious or caste structure, and in the Punjab the same was true for the various Jat clans that came to form the bulk of the Muslim community. Since the greatest incidence of Muslim conversions occurred among groups that were not fully Hindu in the first place, for the vast majority of South Asian Muslims, the question of 'liberation' from the 'oppressive' Hindu social order was simply not an issue.

Towards a New Theory of Conversion: Accretion and Reform

Much more in keeping with the geography and chronology of Muslim conversions in India would be, I would suggest, an understanding of mass conversion as a process whereby preliterate peoples on the ecological and political frontier of an expanding agrarian society became absorbed into the religious ideology of that society. Proceeding from the theoretical work of Nehemia Levtzion, and before him of A. D. Nock,[10] I would further divide this process into two sub-processes, that of accretion and that of reform. Whereas the simplest model of a conversion movement would be one beginning with accretion and ending with reform, we should not see this process as any necessary or irreversible march from the first to the second. A closer examination of individual cases of Muslim conversion movements in India reveals more complex patterns—some, for example, oscillating back and forth between accretion and reform, other stuck on accretion indefinitely, remaining unaffected even by the powerful reform currents of the nineteenth century.

What precisely characterizes these processes? In a cognitive sense, the accretion aspect of conversion sees a people either adding new deities or superhuman agencies to their existing cosmological stock, or identifying new deities or agencies with existing entities in their cosmology. Accordingly, the supernatural agencies, Allah, khizr [the Qur'ānic *Khidr*] or the swarms of *jinns*, for example, may either be grafted onto an already dense cosmological universe, or identified, by name, with existing agencies. But in either case the original cosmology is essentially retained. In the reform dimension of the process, on the other hand, Islamic supernatural agencies are not only distinguished from the pre-existing cosmological structure, but the latter is firmly repudiated. This is accompanied by greater attention given to the all-encompassing power of one Islamic agency in particular, the supreme god Allah, who assumes the function and powers of all other agencies in the former pantheon. In a history of religions, framework, this corresponds to what Max Weber has called the process of religious rationalization, that is, the absorption of many lesser beings by one universal, supreme god.[11]

In terms of social organization, the accretion aspect of conversion entails no Muslim communal exclusiveness or even distinctiveness. Persons will identify themselves as Muslim inasmuch as they worship Allah, for example, or refrain from eating pork—two attributes which in this aspect of the conversion process might be loosely understood as the defining features of Islam. But this by no means prevents them from participating in village propitiation of a local goddess to ward off smallpox or in joining village devotions to an *avatar* of Krishna. Social integration is sustained by other than ritual means, too. A recent study of the Meo community of Rajasthan, a community which for many centuries has adhered somewhat loosely to Islam without responding to reformist pressures, shows that while their practices relating to personal life cycles are Islamic (for example, practising circumcision, burying their dead), their institutions respecting relations with their Hindu neighbours are non-Islamic (for example, marriages are clan exogamous and not cross-cousin; inheritance follows local, not Muslim practice).[12] In strictly social terms, in other words, they are still a relatively indistinct community.

In the reform dimension of the conversion process, however, the community perceives itself as socially distinct and consciously acts upon that perception. Accordingly, the group not only resists participation in non-Muslim rituals, but will, for example, adopt Islamic inheritance customs for daughters as well as for sons, a practice which decisively separates the Muslim community from its neighbours. Or, even more decisively, it might adopt cross-cousin marriage patterns, regarded by many Hindus as simply incestuous. Such practices become more prevalent to the same extent that the Muslim community becomes conscious of its adherence to a single model for social and ritual action, a model whose source of authority stands wholly outside of one's ancestral locality.

Finally, one can distinguish between accretion and reform in terms of the overall socio-political environment in which each process takes place. For mass conversions, anyway, the earlier phase of the process generally accompanied integration into the outer fringes of one of the expanding Indo-Muslim states which, from the twelfth century on, pushed ever outward from the Delhi Doab heartland in the north-central region of the subcontinent. What is critical here (and I will return to this theme of political/ecological integration at the end of this paper) is that this integration always took place in a *regional* context (a region in India) whether one speaks of the expansion of Tughluq power into fourteenth-century Punjab, of the Bahamani kingdom into fifteenth-century Deccan, or of the Mughal empire into sixteenth-century Bengal. In these circumstances whatever Muslim elements were added onto the existing stock of beliefs and practices, they were not perceived as representing a 'world' religion, but only the particular beliefs and practices associated with a local saint, a local *qāḍī* (Muslim judge) or the spiritual power of a local shrine. On the other hand, the context of reform was always a worldwide one, inspired by a vision of Islam as a world religion—or rather, *the* world religion, with Mecca as its geo-spiritual hub. Reform movements, or the reform aspect of the conversion process, are typically initiated by someone freshly returned from the purifying experience of a pilgrimage to Mecca, an experience which, among other things, heightens one's awareness of the universal truth of Islam as opposed to the local and very particularized idioms in which it may be expressed.

Yet the questions remain: how can we measure the growth of a conversion movement, and what are the agents stimulating or shaping it? If we understand religion as 'an institution consisting of culturally patterned interaction with culturally postulated superhuman beings',[13] it can be argued that three sets of symbols, or names, mark such interaction as distinctively Muslim as opposed, for example, to Hindu or Christian. One set of symbols refers to man's identity in relation to the superhuman beings, for example, names of persons such as 'Abd al-Rahman', 'slave of God'.[14] A second set of symbols refers to the identity of superhuman beings in relation to man, that is, man's names for the gods, such as 'Allah' instead of 'Iswara'. A third set of symbols refers to the identity of the sacred place in which the interaction takes place, as in mosques instead of, say, Vaisnavite temples or shrines devoted to the mother goddess.

Although these three sets of symbols will not tell us why a conversion movement took place, they can be used as indices by which we can plot the geographical and chronological expansion of Islam in India, or elsewhere for that matter. For example, the naming pattern of a single Punjabi Jat group, the Sials, suggests that from the thirteenth to the early nineteenth century, the Muslim self-identity of this group proceeded at a very slow rate indeed.[15] In the early fifteenth century, 10 per cent of recorded Sial males had Muslim names; for the mid-seventeenth century, 56 per cent; for the mid-eighteenth century, 75 per cent, and for the early nineteenth century, 100 per cent. This is, I think, a most revealing index of the gradual process of group identity formation.

Just as socio-religious identity is reflected in changes of personal names, it is also reflected in changes in the names of those

TABLE 1: Mosque Construction in Bengal, 1200–1800

Years	Ordinary Mosques	Jami Mosques	Total Mosques
1200–50	1	0	1
1250–1300	2	0	2
1300–50	1	0	1
1350–1400	1	1	2
1400–50	4	0	4
1450–1500	46	7	53
1500–50	21	18	39
1550–1600	11	1	12
1600–50	3	0	3
1650–1700	4	0	4
1700–50	4	0	4
1750–1800	2	0	2

Source: From Shamsud-din Ahmed (ed. and trans.), *Inscriptions of Bengal* (Rajshahi, 1960), vol. 4, pp. 317–38.

superhuman agencies with whom people interact. It is this index, moreover, that most dramatically distinguishes the accretion aspect from the reform aspect of the conversion process. Turning from the medieval Punjab to medieval Bengal, consider the names that local Muslim poets used to denote the one, supreme god of the Qur'ān. The sixteenth-century poet, Haji Muhammad, referred to him as Allah, Khuda ('God' in Persian), and Gosain ('master of the herds'), adding that he assumes limitless forms. The late sixteenth-century poet Sayyid Sultan referred to him as Iśvara (Supreme god, 'lord'), adding that he resided in every entity. Shaykh Mansur (fl. 1703) named him Khuda and Prabhu ('master'), Niranjan (Supreme God, lit. 'without stain'). The eighteenth-century poet Ali Riza referred to him as Iśvara, Allah Yagat Iśvar ('lord of the world'), Niranjan, and Kartar ('creator').[16] In a land where the cult of the mother goddess had great popularity, the sixteenth-century Bengali poet Sayyid Murtaza addressed Fatima as 'the mother of the world' (*jagat-janani*).[17] Similarly, Sayyid Sultan identified the Prophet as a manifestation (*avatar*) of God.[18] What these poets were doing, of course, was laying the intellectual foundations for their readers' adhesion to

Islam; that is, by matching up the cognitive categories drawn from Islam with those drawn from local traditions, they were making possible the process of identification, which is one of the hallmarks of the accretion aspect of conversion.

A third index of growing Islamization consists in changes in the identity of the sacred place in which religious interaction takes place. Table 1 is an abbreviated list showing the chronology of mosque construction in Bengal between AD 1200 and 1800. It is true that the construction of mosques, especially small, private mosques, may reflect only a patron's desire to perform a meritorious act and may not necessarily indicate the expression of popular piety. On the other hand, the appearance of congregational (*jāmi'*) mosques, intended as they are to accommodate the religious needs of entire populations of towns or villages, does give some idea of the chronology, and also the geography, of the growth of the Muslim community. The table, for example, certainly suggests that although Muslim *rule* in Bengal dates from the thirteenth century, Muslim *society* cannot be said to have emerged there until two centuries later.

If the above data provide some of the indices of conversion, what are its agents? Some writers have focused on the Muslim merchant who, interested in economic profit, thrived best under conditions of internal stability. While evangelism was not his aim, the social contacts resulting from the expansion of commerce and the condition of mutual trust in which commerce thrives, created favourable conditions for social accommodation and, to some extent, acculturation. Generally speaking, this process was, then, more typical along India's coasts—from Gujarat down to Malabar and Coromandel, and up to Bengal—than it was in the Muslim states of the interior.

Along the Konkan and Malabar coasts, accordingly, we find the earliest Muslim mercantile communities, which have thrived over a thousand years. In the early tenth century, the Arab traveller Mas'udi noted that an Arab trading community along the Konkan coast, which had been granted autonomy and protection by the local rajah, had intermarried considerably with the local population.[19] The children of such marriages, brought up formally with the father's religion, yet carrying over many cultural traits of the non-Muslim mother, contributed to an expanding community which was richly described by Ibn Battuta in the early fourteenth century.[20] But by virtue of this community's close commercial contacts with Arabia, reflected in religious terms by its adherence to the Shafi'i legal tradition, the foreign aspect of the community was always present and made social integration with the Hindu community difficult.[21] In the last analysis, then, while it is true that Muslim merchants founded important mercantile enclaves and by intermarriage expanded the Muslim population, they do not appear to have been important in provoking religious change among the local population.

A far more influential agent in the conversion process was the village Qadi or judge, one of the key figures that accompanied the establishment of Muslim regimes as local powers. Although a thorough study of the role of the medieval Indian Ulama (*'ulamā'*), and especially the Qadi, has yet to be written, preliminary evidence points to the central and continuing role that local judges played in establishing a measure of uniformity among the various rural folk who, for various reasons, adhered informally to Islam. Qadis were appointed by central and provincial authorities to apply Islamic law in all towns or villages having a Muslim population. And while Qadis theoretically applied Muslim religious law (*sharī'a*) only to those criminal and civil cases involving Muslims, they also settled cases involving Muslims and non-Muslims, thereby drawing the latter into the legal and social orbit of Islam. In this way all manner of disparate groups would have had some of their most important affairs decided by men who, in theory at least, represented a single religious and legal tradition. With reference to the late nineteenth century, district gazetteers repeatedly reported that while particular Muslim 'castes' were lax, avoided beef, kept Hindu festivals, or worshipped Hindu deities, they at the very least respected the Qadi and used him to officiate at their marriages and funerals.[22] Qadis thus stood not only as representatives of the court among peasants, but also as models of their religion before the semi-Muslim folk of the countryside.

What is more, the Qadis represented above all the *literate* aspect of Islam, as living reminders that Islam in the last analysis is a religion of the Book. Recent anthropological research has drawn attention to the great importance of the literacy of an incoming religion as a variable that explains the appeal of that religion to pre-literate societies.[23] The point is that the Qur'ān, as the unchanging Word of God, possessed immense power, and consequently appeal, among pre-literate peoples whose previous cults had not been stabilized by the influence of literacy. Thus, in the history of Islam in India, one important reason that Islam sank such deep roots in areas such as East Bengal or West Punjab was that the native populations of those regions were far less integrated into the literate tradition of the Brahmans than were the peoples of upper India. Although upper India had been for centuries the centre of Muslim administration, the incidence of conversion to Islam there was as a consequence relatively low.

The agent of conversion that has, however, received the most attention is the Sufi. There is an enormous literature on this theme, commencing with Thomas Arnold's fervent portrayal of Sufis as Islamic 'missionaries' among non-Muslims.[24] A close reading of the primary sources, however, would not support this portrayal. In their own writings and in the contemporary biographical accounts of them, Sufis do not appear to have been concerned with conversion. In fact, the sort of self-conscious, highly organized effort along the lines of a Christian missionary society, implicit in Arnold's writing, is at variance with the social roles actually played by medieval Indian Sufis.[25]

If a living Sufi had only minimal influence in the religious life of non-Muslim Indians, a deceased Sufi, especially one blessed with sainthood by the local population, could literally work miracles. This was because the charisma or *baraka* of a spiritually saturated Sufi saint became, with time, transferred to his tomb. And since brick and mortar shrines have much greater longevity than flesh and bone Sufis, self-sustaining centres of religious power were able in this way to grow and span many centuries. Moreover, a saint's *baraka* also adheres to those of his family descendants who inherit spiritual authority associated with the shrine, which also extends the longevity of *baraka*. For example, both the grandson and the shrine of Baba Farid in Pakpattan,

Punjab, became so thoroughly identified with Baba Farid the saint, who died in AD 1265, that when Ibn Battuta visited Pakpattan in AD 1334 he actually wrote of meeting Baba Farid himself. In fact, the living person whom the famous world traveller met was the grandson who had inherited the spiritual and temporal leadership of the shrine complex.[26] An even more dramatic example of a saint's *baraka* growing after his death is seen in the faith common people had in the Chishti Sufi, Sayyid Muhammad Husayni Gisudaraz Bandanawaz, who died in AD 1422. Writing in AD 1609, the historian Firishta could observe that 'the people of the Deccan have such respect for the saint that a Deccany, on being asked whom he considered the greatest personage, the Prophet Mahomed or the Syud [Sayyid Muhammad], replied, with some surprise at the question, that although the Prophet was undoubtedly a great man, yet Syud Mahomed Geesoo-duraz was a far superior order of being'.[27]

It was faith like this that explains the tremendous growth of hundreds of shrines all over the subcontinent, each providing a localized focus of votive worship. These shrines differed a good deal from each other, some specializing in terms of the community to whom they administered, and others in terms of the ailment or complaint the devotees would bring to them.[28] But they all shared in common a mediating capacity between the devotee and Allah, thereby not only softening the theological chasm between man and God, but also presenting God in a locally accessible idiom.

If it is true that the Qadi and the saint's tomb were the most important agents in the Islamization process, we are still confronted with the vexing problem of the geography of conversion. I have argued that the theories of the 'religion of the sword', 'political patronage', and 'religion of social liberation' all fail to account for the exceptionally high incidence of conversion on the political peripheries of medieval India and the relatively low incidence of the heartland. Yet if the agents I have identified as most crucial to the conversion process—the Qadi and the Sufi shrine—were scattered throughout the subcontinent, how can their agency help explain the geography of the issue? As noted, one variable in explaining this is the degree of integration of a region into a literate tradition—in this case Brahmanical Hinduism—prior to its contact with Islam. Also important are those elements of the social and ecological situation within a region that enabled Qadis or Sufis to have greater effect in patterning religious change on the frontiers than in the heartland. As a rule, India's most extensive conversion occurred not in the great agricultural plains but in the pastoral plains or forested regions—areas, in other words, where religious patterns had not yet been stabilized by literacy as represented and sustained by Brahmans. For it was not Hindus who most readily converted to Islam, but non-agrarian forest or pastoral peoples whose contact with Brahmanism and caste stratification had been either casual or non-existent. The process of the absorption of these peoples into Islam was, in fact, similar to the integration of aboriginal peoples into the Hindu caste and ritual structure that had taken place earlier in Indian history. As D. D. Kosambi wrote with reference to that earlier movement, 'The major historical change in ancient India was not between dynasties but in the advance of agrarian village settlements over tribal lands, metamorphosing tribesmen into peasant cultivators, or guild craftsmen'.[29]

It is of the utmost significance, then, that those areas of the most massive conversion to Islam, such as East Bengal or West Punjab, were fringe areas both from the point of view of the socio-ecological frontier of Hindu agrarian society, and also from the point of view of the political frontier of the Muslim state. The consistent aim of the latter—and here reference is mainly to the Delhi Sultanate (twelfth to sixteenth centuries) and its successor the Mughal empire (sixteenth to eighteenth centuries)—was to push its ecological and political frontiers even outwards from the Delhi Doab heartland into Punjab, Kashmir, Gujarat, Deccan, or Bengal. In areas where local Hindu rajahs had already established an agrarian infrastructure by which to extract the surplus wealth of the land, the problem was a political one. Here, the state endeavoured to capture the agrarian structure for its own ends by occupying urban centres, establishing garrisons, and perhaps demoting the rajah to a tribute-paying underling (*zamindar*). As the peasantry in such areas was usually already absorbed into the Hindu social and religious order, conversion to Islam was not normally forthcoming, at least on a mass basis. But as the state expanded its power into regions whose agrarian infrastructure was not well-developed—into unirrigated plains or uncleared forest regions—the expansion of the state was ecological and religious as well as political. Here, the religious ideology of the state, Islam, became adopted bit by bit as one aspect of a larger transformation among pre-literate inhabitants of lands newly made arable. In a word, indigenous non-Hindu non-agriculturalists were, between the twelfth and seventeenth centuries, gradually transformed into Muslim agriculturalists. To the extent that this was the case, Islam, in India at least, may properly be termed more a religion of the plough than a religion of the sword, as formerly conceived.

Data drawn from both the Punjab and Bengal would sustain this argument. As for the former area, what one finds is, from the thirteenth century, the appearance of huge Sufi shrines, such as those of Farid al-Din Shakargunj in Pakpattan or Baha al-Haqq Zakaria in Multan, becoming the objects of popular devotion by non-Hindu Jat pastoralists as they migrated northward from Sind. By the sixteenth century the Mughal government realized the political potential of these shrines and used them as intermediaries by which to control the turbulent Jat groups. Moreover, it was about this time that these same groups began settling down in the Punjab and taking to agriculture, a development much in line with the Mughal interest in maximizing the revenue-generating capacity of the land. Technologically, this development was made possible by the extension of the Persian wheel into the arid plains of the Punjab in the medieval period. Throughout this period, the Jat groups retained their devotional focus on the shrines, gradually becoming ever more closely integrated with their ritual structure. For these groups, then, adhesion to Islam effectively meant adhesion to one of these shrines.[30]

In Bengal, an essentially opposite process had the same effect: instead of the people migrating to the land, the arable land migrated to the people. For many centuries, the Ganges River had emptied into the Bay of Bengal down the western side of the province so that that area became both the (Hindu) spiritual and agricultural heartland of the region, with the aboriginals in the forests of East Bengal remaining somewhat beyond the pale and only lightly exposed to Brahmanical Hinduism. In the sixteenth century, however, the river silted up its old channels and pushed eastwards, opening up huge areas of East Bengal for rice cultivation. River shifts also made possible land reclamation along the lower and eastern delta next to the sea. As these riverine shifts occurred roughly simultaneously with the Mughal conquest of Bengal, many of the colonists moving into the east were Muslim from North India. Significantly, a good many of the saints of East Bengal who had accompanied this colonization are associated with the pioneering of agriculture, and especially with land reclamation in the active delta. In the process, indigenous Bengali peoples who had formerly practised hunting, fishing, or a crude form of forest agriculture, became gradually transformed into rice farmers. So firmly was rice cultivation identified with Islam, that today, in the value system of peasants inhabiting rural Bangladesh, God is believed to have allowed Adam to exercise his mastery over the earth by farming it; being a good Muslim is closely associated with being a good farmer.[31]

If this was the underlying mechanism of the accretion process, it is clear that the result was far from 'total' conversion to Islam. For centuries Punjabis and Bengalis alike had clung to former religious habits and retained long-established social groupings. Basing his observations on nineteenth-century district gazetteers, Mohammed Mujeeb wrote that Punjabi Muslims 'were spiritually dependent on miracles and magic to a degree incompatible with genuine belief in any omnipotent God',[32] while the 1901 Census of India reported Bengali Muslims joining in the Durga Puja, worshipping Sitala and Rakshya Kali when disease was present, and making use of Hindu astrologers and almanacs in their everyday life.[33] For peoples of both provinces, as also in other regions of India, Islam was regarded as one technique among many for tapping a 'power' which, with the performance of the proper rites known to some local expert, could alleviate one's problems or promote one's mundane concerns.

But this nominal commitment to Islam, made possible by a political and ecological integration into a regional Indo-Muslim state, was followed in many areas of India by a reform made possible by a second order of integration, an integration with the Muslim world. This integration was neither political nor ecological in nature, of course, but affective, as more and more putative Muslims of India became aware of the normative unity of Islam. While members of the ulama and some groups of Sufis had urged this unitary reformist vision at all times of the Indo-Muslim history, sporadic reformist movements appeared in various parts of India or among various communities with visible frequency only from the seventeenth century.[34] It was during the nineteenth century, when vastly improved world transportation systems brought masses of Indians in direct touch with Mecca, that such movements became most widespread of all. These reform movements generally witnessed a Qur'ānic literalism that assumed an increasing sense of urgency as more and more Indian Muslims became aware of the gap between the commands of the Book and the actual practices passing for Islam in their native villages. It was at this point that persons began taking the meaning of their names—for example, 'Abdallah', 'slave of God'—more seriously, if not literally. Finally, insistence on a jealous God to the exclusion of all other superhuman agencies was paralleled by movements for social exclusiveness.

The reform dimension of the conversion process, in India at least, carried with it at least two other important implications, one political, one cultural. The first of these was the demand for a separate Muslim state upon the departure of the British in 1947. In one sense, of course, this was but a logical extension of the reform aspect of the conversion process, which stressed social exclusiveness. The Pakistan movement thus represented a modern reenactment of the Prophet's departure from Mecca and his establishment of a distinct community at Medina; it was a 're-creation' of Medina. The other implication of the reform process was its self-conscious adoption of Arab culture. Here one confronts a central paradox of the reform process. The emphasis upon Islamic unity and universalism as a theoretical model was simultaneously accompanied by an emphasis upon Arab culture and language as a practical model, so that while reform movements sought to lift the focus of religious activity above the Indian regional context, they frequently landed it once again in the Arab cultural context. Accordingly, in the early nineteenth century, Bengalis were urged to eat grasshoppers on the grounds that Arabs ate locusts.[35] And in the 1890s, a brilliant Bengali writer, Ameer Ali, championed the Islamic reform movement in Bengal by writing such books as *The Spirit of Islam*, glorifying Arab culture and history. From a religious viewpoint, these political and cultural developments may be seen as efforts to perfect a process of conversion having roots deep in the history of the subcontinent.

To conclude, I must emphasize that this essay by no means attempts to explore all the various processes by which peoples of the subcontinent became drawn into the Muslim community. Clearly this is a complex phenomenon involving a number of distinguishable processes, some of which did not concern conversion at all. There was, for example, the immigration of many thousands of Turks, Afghans, and Iranians into the subcontinent from the thirteenth century onwards, and the slow growth of Muslim communities as a result of intermarriages between Muslim men and non-Muslim women. Even when discussing conversion itself, this essay has passed over the discussion of the conversion of Hindu elites (Brahmans or Kayasthas) in places like Allahabad, Kashmir, or Lucknow. Similarly, a comprehensive study of the conversion of Indians to Islam would have to mention examples of rationally planned, organized conversion efforts such as those of the Shi'i *da'wa*, which successfully integrated trading and agricultural castes of Sind and Gujarat into the Muslim community.[36]

Rather, the thrust of this essay has been to draw attention to a dimension of the conversion question not heretofore generally addressed: mass Islamization of the geographical periphery of the Indo-Muslim state and the relationship of ecological change to religious change. I maintain that for India, at least, mass conversion to Islam was a very gradual process involving two discernible aspects, accretion and reform. In a way, these aspects of conversion movements are comparable with Clifford Geertz's 'model of' and 'model for' dimensions of religious behaviour.[37]

That is, for those Indians who adhered to Islam, the symbols, rituals, and practices of local religion served as 'models of' or descriptions of the social order and its religious life. Thus a Punjabi Sufi might legitimize an ancient, pre-Muslim practice simply by calling it Islamic, and that would be that.[38] In its reform aspect, however, Islam was viewed as a unified set of absolute norms, beliefs, and practices to which one must bend oneself and one's fellows if one is to be saved. Here, as Geertz observed, Islam functioned as a 'model for' behaviour, and was significant not because it described the social order, but because it shaped it.[39]

In the more vulgar language of social science, religious behaviour in the accretion aspect of conversion is a dependent variable since it is a function of socio-political change. It was the migration of Jats into the Punjab and the extension of Delhi's authority there which, along with the introduction of the Persian wheel, attached Jat groups to Sufi shrines and transformed them into agriculturalists. Similarly, it was the migration of the Ganges River eastwards that caused the ecological transformation of East Bengal, making the aboriginal peoples of the area receptive to a 'religion of the plough'. In both cases new centres of political and religious authority (local shrines) acquired influence because of changed socio-economic circumstances, and Islamic ritual and belief systems acquired an unconscious foothold in the countryside without necessarily displacing earlier systems.

To stop here would merely reaffirm the Durkheimian position that religion is a reflection of the social order; yet this does not go far enough. For in the reform process, it is Islam that is the independent variable inasmuch as it can, and did, cause change in the social and political realms. The political geography of South Asia in the second half of the twentieth century would quite obviously not be what it is if conversion in its reform aspect did not have this capacity to shape the social order. By viewing the double role of Islam as a dependent and independent variable, then, we can see the conversion process as a constantly evolving, dynamic interaction between religion and society.

Notes and References

1. Peter Hardy, 'Modern European and Muslim Explanation of Conversion to Islam in South Asia: A Preliminary Survey of the Literature,' in *Conversion to Islam*, ed. Nehemia Levtzion (New York: Holmes and Meier, 1979), p. 78.

2. In these accounts one frequently meets with such ambiguous phrases as *ita'at-i islam numudand* or *dar ita'at-i islam amadanda* ('they submitted to Islam' or 'they came under submission to Islam'), in which 'Islam' might mean either the religion, the Muslim state, or more crudely, the 'army of Islam.' A contextual reading of such passages usually favours one of the latter two interpretations. See Y. Friedmann, 'A contribution to the early history of Islam in India,' in *Studies in Memory of Gaston Wiet*, ed. Myrian Rosen-Ayalon (Jerusalem: Institute of Asian and African Studies, 1977), p. 322.

3. The first accurate census reports, those of the late nineteenth century, put the Muslims of East Bengal and West Punjab at between 70 per cent and 90 per cent of the total, and of the upper Gangetic Plain at around 10 to 15 per cent. Regarding the lack of conversions in the heartland, two sociologists have argued that Mughal persecution of the Meo community of Rajasthan, far from strengthening the Islamic identity of the nominally converted community, reinforced their resistance to Islamic influence. See S. L. Sharma and R. N. Srivastava, 'Institutional Resistance to Induced Islamization in a Convert Community—An Empiric Study in Sociology of Religion,' *Sociological Bulletin* 16/1 (March, 1967): 77.

4. Agha Mahdi Husain, ed. and trans., *The Rehla of Ibn Batuta* (Baroda: Oriental Institute, 1953), p. 46.

5. Hardy, 'Modern European and Muslim Explanations,' pp. 80–1.

6. Aziz Ahmad, *Studies in Islamic Culture in the Indian Environment* (Oxford, 1964), p. 105.

7. See Louis Dumont, *Homo Hierarchicus: An Essay on the Caste System*, trans. Mark Sainsbury (Chicago, 1970).

8. Yohanan Friedmann, 'Medieval Muslim Views of Indian Religions.' *Journal of the American Oriental Society*, 95 (1975): 214–21.

9. See, for example, Imtiaz Ahmed, ed., *Caste and Social Stratification among the Muslims* (Delhi, 1973).

10. See Levtzion, *Conversion to Islam*, pp. 21–3, and Arthur Darby Nock, *Conversion: The Old and the New in Religion from Alexander the Great to Augustine of Hippo* (Oxford, 1933), p. 8.

11. See Max Weber, *The Sociology of Relgion*, trans. Ephraim Fischoff, introd. Talcott Parsons (Boston, 1963), p. 22.

12. Sharma and Srivastava, 'Institutional Resistance,' pp. 73–5.

13. See Spiro Melford, 'Religion: Problems of Definition and Explanation' in *Anthropological Approaches to the Study of Religion*, ed. M. Banton (New York, 1966), p. 96.

14. For a pioneering study of the use of personal names as a correlate of Islamic conversions, see Richard W. Bulliet, *Conversion to Islam in the Medieval Period: An Essay in Quantitative History* (Cambridge, Mass., 1979).

15. Maulavi Nur Muhammad, *Tarikh-i Jhang Sial* (Meerut, 1862), pp. 15–28.

16. Roy Asim, 'Islam in the Environment of Medieval Bengal' (Ph.D. diss., Australian National University, 1970), pp. 189–202, *passim*.

17. Ibid., p. 299.

18. Ibid., p. 300.

19. Al-Mas'udi, *Les prairies d or*, trans. C. Barbier de Meynard and Pavet de Courteille, 9 vols. (Paris, 1891–1917), vol. 2, pp. 85–6.

20. Mahdi Husain, *Rehla*, pp. 176–96.

21. Ibn Battuta observed that although the Muslims of Malabar were the most respected people in the area, 'the natives do not dine with them and do not admit them into their houses,' *Rehla*, p. 183.

22. See *Gazetteer of Bombay Presidency: Bijapur District*, vol. 23 (Bombay, 1884), pp. 282–305.

23. On the significance of literacy for religious conversion in general, see Jack Goody, 'Religion, Social Change and the Sociology of Conversion,' in *Changing Social Structure in Ghana*, ed. Jack Goody (London, 1975), pp. 101 ff. See also J. D. Y. Peel, 'Syncretism and Religious Change,' *Comparative Studies in Society and History* 10 (1967–8): 139–40. Marilyn Waldman's paper, ch. 6 in this volume, discusses the importance of Goody's theory of literacy/non-literacy for Islamic studies.

24. Arnold Thomas Walker, *The Preaching of Islam* (London, 1913), pp. 154–93.

25. See my *Sufis of Bijapur: Social Roles of Sufis in Medieval India* (Princeton, 1978), especially ch. 6.

26. Mahdi Husain, *Rehla*, p. 20.

27. John Briggs, trans., *History of the Rise of the Mahomedan Power in India*, 3 vols. (Calcutta, 1966), vol. 2, pp. 245–6.

28. Data collected in the early twentieth century illustrate this. Shrines of the first category would include that of Hasan Teli of Lahore for oilmen; that of Shaykh Musa for blacksmiths; that of 'Ali Rangrez for dyers; and that of Pir Badar in Chittagong for sailors. The second category would include the tomb of Shah Sufaid in Jhelum district for lepers; the tomb of Miran Nau Bahar for curing hysterical fits; the tomb

of Nizam al-Din in Lahore for warts; that of Pir Bukhari in Quetta for venereal diseases; and that of Shah Mina in Lucknow for legal difficulties. See Thomas Arnold, 'Saints and Martyrs [Muhammadans in India],' *Encyclopaedia of Religion and Ethics*, ed. James Hastings, vol. 11: 70–1.

29. D. D. Kosambi, 'The Basis of Ancient Indian History (I),' *Journal of the American Oriental Society*, 75 (1955): 38.

30. See Richard M. Eaton, 'The Political and Religious Authority of the Shrine of Baba Farid in Pakpattan, Punjab' in *Moral Conduct and Authority: The Place of Adab in South Asian Islam*, ed. Barbara Metcalf (Berkeley, Calif., 1983).

31. John P. Thorp, 'Masters of Earth: Conceptions of Power among Muslims of Rural Bangladesh,' (Ph.D. diss., University of Chicago, 1978), pp. 40–5. This general argument respecting Bengal will be more fully developed in Richard M. Eaton's forthcoming study on Islam in medieval Bengal.

32. Mohammed Mujeeb, *The Indian Muslims* (London, 1967), p. 10.

33. *Census of India*, 1901, vol. 6, p. 176.

34. See, for example, Eaton, *Sufis of Bijapur*, ch. 5.

35. P. M. Holt, *et al.*, eds, *Cambridge History of Islam*, 2 vols. (Cambridge, 1970), vol. 2, p. 77.

36. See Azim Nanji, *The Nizari Isma'ili Tradition in the Indo-Pakistan Subcontinent* (Delmar, NY, 1978).

37. Clifford Geertz, 'Religion as a Cultural System,' in *Anthropological Approaches to the Study of Religion*, ed. M. Banton (New York, 1966), p. 40.

38. This actually occurred in the case of the shrine at Kallar Kahar in Jhelum district, Punjab, an apparently Buddhist shrine which the historical saint Makhdum Jahanian is said to have more or less redefined as the tomb of a Muslim *faqir* or holy man. See *Punjab District Gazetteers: Jhelam District* (Lahore, 1883–4), p. 63.

39. Geertz, 'Religion as a Cultural System,' pp. 35–6.

4

The Rishi Movement as a Social Force in Medieval Kashmir*

Mohammad Ishaq Khan

In Kashmir the transition to Islam between the fifteenth and the eighteenth centuries was the result of a spirited response to the advent of Sufi missionaries from Central Asia and Persia after the establishment of the Sultanate in AD 1320. The response was manifested at the popular level in the founding of an indigenous mystic order, the *Silsilah-i Rishiyyān*, by Shaikh Nūruuddīn Rishī (AD 1379–1442). The Rishis did not marry, abstained from meat, and subsisted on wild vegetables, avoided injury to all living creatures including insects and wild animals, planted trees, and secluded themselves in forest and cave for certain periods of time, and above all proved to be stable upholders of the *Sharī'a*.[1] Notwithstanding the ascetic orientation of the Rishi order, its adherents, under the inspiring leadership of Nūruddīn, launched a bold protest against the cherished notions

* From Muzaffar Alam *et al.* (eds), *The Making of Indo-Persian Culture: Indian and French Studies* (New Delhi, 2000), pp. 129–47.

of Brahmanic supremacy based on caste. Modern scholarship has mainly focused on the asceticism of the Rishis against the background of exaggerated perceptions of the influence of local mystic practices on Islam, and this explains why certain stereotypes continue to distort our vision of the historical role of the Rishis in shaping the contours of Kashmīrī society. Thus, the seemingly syncretic behaviour of the Rishis has been overemphasized as the most important element in the evolution of medieval Kashmīrī society.

Islamic Egalitarianism *versus* Brahmanism in Syncretic Perspective

While I have elsewhere shown that syncretism is less the culmination than an important stage in the development of Muslim societies,[2] it will here suffice to say that the infatuation of the historians with the syncretic model has relegated many crucial issues of social significance to the background. Take for example one little emphasized dimension of expanding Islam in medieval India, its egalitarianism in contrast to Brahmanic ethnocentrism. A related question that therefore still awaits a satisfactory answer is, did Islam emerge as a vehicle of social protest in the evolution of Muslim societies in the subcontinent?

Although Mohammad Habib, S. M. Ikram, and A. B. M. Habibullah were deeply conscious of the role of Islam as a revolutionary force confronting the caste-ridden social and legal structures of medieval India, they did not produce sufficient evidence to substantiate their general statements. Irfan Habib therefore remarks 'there is no evidence of assault from the Muslims upon the caste system; nor even any revolt from within'.[3] Richard Maxwell Eaton totally rejects the theory of 'social liberation' on the ground that it is a 'fallacy' to read 'the values of the present into the peoples or events of the past'.[4] He further asks in somewhat hubristic terms, if we are to assume that, before Muslim contact, 'the untouchables of India possessed, as though they were familiar with the writings of Jean-Jacques Rousseau or Thomas Jefferson, some innate notion of the fundamental equality of all men denied them by a Brahmanical tyranny'.[5]

On the other hand, Eaton is at pains to emphasize 'self-conscious adoption of Arab Culture' as 'a central paradox' of the reform process.[6] His thesis about 'adhesion' and 'reform'[7] actually points to the dichotomy between two constantly interacting forces which Annemarie Schimmel calls 'mystico-syncretistic' and 'Prophetic separatistic'.[8] The underlying thesis is that it is not the so-called 'formal Islam', but the 'aura of holiness' acquired by the Sufis in the Hindu environment that attracted Indians. This idea characterizes work written under the influence of J. Spencer Trimingham.[9]

My paper is addressed to the current debate in Indian historiography concerning the nature of response to Islam in the subcontinent. It must, however, be clarified at the outset that although the empirical base of our research is the Valley of Kashmir, it transcends the limits of a region, nation, or even a particular period, considering the historical significance and emergence of the Rishi movement as a synthesis of universally accepted human values in the face of Brahmanic ethnocentrism. Although the movement was essentially rooted in local tradition, it became an important dimension of Islamic civilization consequent on the process of adoption by the masses of cultural traits or social patterns of Muslim immigrants—Sufis, *'Ulamā'*, artisans—from Central Asia and Persia.[10]

Emergence of *Sharī'a*-oriented Popular Protest

Viewed in the context of Robert Redfield's definition,[11] the so-called Little Tradition of Kashmīrī peasant society seems to have linked itself with the Great Tradition of Islam through Nūruddīn Rishī, who, in his numerous mystical verses, established channels of communication between the two traditions and set standards of mutual reference and influence. But the dichotomy between these two traditions should not divert our attention from the objective fact that, as a result of its gradual assimilation and absorption in the wider system of Islam, the so-called Little Tradition of the peasant society assumed the form of popular culture oriented towards the *Sharī'a* of Muhammad.[12] The development of this historical phenomenon was determined by spontaneous and changing consciousness, expressed, under the influence of Islam, in the peoples' mode of existence, daily life, and collective behaviour. It would seem, then, that any separation of the Great Tradition or High Culture from the Little Tradition or Popular Culture is meaningless considering that it was under the influence of the Great Tradition that the Little Tradition became a vehicle of protest. Protest was directed against certain unethical norms and practices. This is reflected not only in the social protests of Nūruddīn, but also, to a great extent, in explicit anger against Brahmans, exhibited in hagiographic accounts. It was in this sense that the Rishi movement was, in essence, a popular expression of mounting disagreement, disaffection, tension, and conflict generated in the course of time by a particular social order when it was drawn within the orbit of Islamic civilization.

Socio-religious Milieu

Several factors seem to have contributed to the emergence of the movement as a social force. First, Lal Ded, a fourteenth-century Shaivite woman mystic, under the possible influence of Islam, vehemently attacked caste, idol worship, and rituals evolved by the Brahmans. So great was the social impact of Lal Ded's courageous protest that in the *tazkira* literature, Nūruddīn Rishī has been described as her spiritual offspring. On his part Nūruddīn in one of his popular verses acknowledges his debt to Lal Ded by describing her as an *avatāra*[13] of Kashmīrīs.

That Lalla of Padmanpore,[14]
who had drunk the fill of nectar,
She was an *avatāra* of ours.
O God, grant me the same spiritual power.[15]

Modern scholarly attempts at resuscitating Lal Ded as an exponent of Shaivism tend to side-track the crucial question why she was disowned by the *Ahl-i qalam*[16] for the greater part of Kashmīrī history. We may also ask why she was elevated to the second Rābi'a (*Rābi'a Ṣānī*), *Maryam-i Makānī*, *'Ārifa-i majzūba*, *Majnūn-i 'āqila*[17] and so on in the *tazkira* literature. A prominent

Suharwadī Sufi of the Valley, Bābā Dāūd Khākī, eulogized Lal Ded in these verses:

> Passion for God set fire to all she had,
> And from her heart rose clouds of smoke.
> Having had a draught of *ahad-i alast*,[18]
> Intoxicated and drunk with joy was she.
> One cup of this God-intoxicating drink shatters reason into bits,
> A little drowsiness from it is headier than intoxication from a hundred jars of wine.[19]

Curiously, Lal Ded's name is not mentioned either in Sanskrit chronicles or the commentaries on Shaivism of the fifteenth to the eighteenth centuries. Although Bīrbal Kāchrū (fl. 1819–46) in the nineteenth century was the first Brahman chronicler to mention her, his information is based on earlier Persian sources.[20] The fact is that Lal Ded was a rebel against Brahmanism; and a strong tradition of her association with the earliest Kubrawī Sufi in Kashmir, Saiyid Ḥusain Simnānī (d. 1390), needs to be probed in conjunction with the conversion to Islam of Nūruddīn's father, Salāt Sanz, at the behest of the Sufi. This focuses our attention on the emergence of Sufism as a social force in Kashmir.

The earliest documentary evidence regarding the conversion of a non-Muslim to Islam in Kashmir pertains to Rīnchanā (d. AD 1323), a fugitive Buddhist prince from Ladakh. He became the ruler of Kashmir in AD 1320 and soon after approached a Brahman priest of Srinagar, Devāsvāmī, for initiation in to Shaivism. His request was turned down on the grounds of caste.[21] Thereupon Rīnchanā embraced Islam at the behest of Saiyid Sharafuddīn (popularly known as Bulbul Shāh in the Valley), the first Sufi missionary to reach Kashmir from Turkistan.[22] Although Rīnchanā assumed the name Ṣadruddīn and styled himself 'Sulṭan', and founded a mosque, a *khānqāh*, and a kitchen for his spiritual mentor, this did not bring about any radical social transformation in Kashmir. Until the advent of Mīr Saiyid 'Ali Hamadānī in the AD 1380s from Persia, the Sultanate of Kashmir was a successful compromise between the need for political stability emphasized by the Sultans and the demands of the Brahmans for supremacy in local politics and administration. Syncretism was therefore noticeable in the form of ritual observances and beliefs, so much so that the tiny minority of Muslim converts regularly visited a temple in Srinagar in the company of their Sultan.[23] The Sultan's advisers were Brahmans, and he even took part in some Brahmanical ceremonies like *yajñas*, understandably for propitiating the politically active Brahmans rather than to reconcile Hinduism and Islam. While in the capital Brahmans managed to maintain a semblance of authority through their ties with the government, in rural Kashmir there was seething social discontent. Lal Ded's popular songs against Brahmanic rituals and ceremonies, animal sacrifice, idols, and corrupt practices and caste hierarchies also need to be studied in the context of the scant respect that the Brahmans had for the spiritual and ethical values of Hinduism. Lal Ded had no alternative but to seek the company of the Kubrawī Sufi, Saiyid Ḥusain Simnānī, who had settled in the village of Kulgam during the reign of Sultan Shihābuddīn (AD 1354–73).

Lal Ded's association with Saiyid Ḥusain Simnānī must be placed in its socio-historical context. While she was a wandering mystic, Simnānī was on a philanthropic mission in Kulgam. A considerable number of people visited his *k͟hānqāh* and public kitchen, maintained on the revenues of a *jāgīr* granted by the state. Although Simnānī seems to have exercised considerable social influence through his philanthropic activities, hagiographers only refer to the conversion of a lower-caste man, Salāt Sanz, at his behest. Salāt Sanz was a village watchman (*pāsbān*) who now came to be known as Shaik͟h Sālāruddīn. Understandably, he is reverentially mentioned in the *taẕkira* literature not only for his spiritual attainments, but more importantly, for giving birth to a posthumous son, Nand Sanz, who later distinguished himself as Nūruddīn Rishī.

According to a tradition quoted in several hagiographies, for three days after his birth in AD 779/AD 1379, Nūruddīn did not take milk from his mother. But then, Lal Ded visited the house of the deceased convert to Islam and addressed his son: 'Thou wast not ashamed of being born;/Why then art thou ashamed of sucking (at your mother's breast)?'[24]

The baby began suckling and thereafter Lal Ded's visits to the parental house of Nūruddīn continued. It was Lal Ded, indeed, who was the earliest source of inspiration for Nūruddīin. Through her influence Nūruddīn imbibed the spirit of folk Shaivism. In fact, Lal Ded did not give a systematic exposé of Shaivism on the lines laid down by the theologians who preceded her. Instead her songs illustrate 'a picture of the actual hopes and fears of the common folk that nominally followed the teachings of those men whom they had accepted as their guides'.[25]

Keeping in view the historical fact that Islam in the Valley is predominantly associated with Lal Ded and Nūruddīn Rishī, certain misconceptions need to be dispelled so as to clarify the forces behind the evolution of Kashmīrī Muslim society. It has been argued that Lal Ded's verses, in view of their Sanskritized form, belie the influence of Islam on her thought. But to talk in such terms is tantamount to uprooting her from her social environment which was undoubtedly exposed to Islamic influences centuries before the establishment of the Sultanate in AD 1320.[26] One wonders how a wandering mystic like Lal Ded, who did not have a closed mind, could have shut her eyes to the presence of contemporaries like Saiyid Husain Simnāmī, Saiyid Tājuddīin, and Saiyid ʿAlī Hamadānī.[27] A woman ostracized by caste-conscious Brahmans had but three options: to embrace Islam, or reform Hindu society, or revolt against the caste-ridden social order. Concerning the first option, hagiographers and chroniclers do not furnish us with any conclusive evidence;[28] the presumption that she wanted to reform Hindu society flounders on the fact of her association with Islam rather than Shaivism. There is, however, considerable evidence to show that a 'protestant' trend in Lal Ded's verses against the social and spiritual pretensions of the Brahmans set in motion new forces rejecting the latter's cherished idea that social status was determined by caste. An important development in this direction was the flowering of the idea of the dignity and fundamental equality of man, so trenchantly espoused by her younger contemporary, Nūruddīn Rishī.

It would therefore be unreasonable to suggest that Lal Ded remained immune from Islamic influence. From Islam, at least, she imbibed a critical attitude towards the manifold abuses of the caste-ridden social order. It may be true that Islam did not directly contribute to her thought, but it certainly proved to be an important influence in her mode of expression. Her verses against Brahmanic supremacy, in particular, uttered under provocative conditions and worthy of emulation, seem to have been comprehended by Hindus and Buddhists of the Valley, who were undergoing a process of Islamic acculturation, as 'conversion' to Islam. This is attested by strong documentary evidence. So deep was the influence of Lal Ded's conversion in folk consciousness that even Nūruddīn Rishī's verses affirming his faith in Islam were attributed to her.

The popular tradition about Lal Ded's guidance to Nūruddīn, though enveloped in legendary material, contains a kernel of historical truth. It not only conveys some information about her early influence on Nūruddīn's mind, but also imposes a dynamic relationship, a creative tension, between the local and the Islamic mystic traditions. Our examination of Nūruddīn's mystical poetry, widely quoted in the *tazkira* literature, points to the naïveté of the bald assertion that the Rishi movement was not an integral component of Islam, and that it was a dimension of 'folk Islam'.[29] Nor would it be correct to describe the Rishis as marginal Muslims, or compare their movement with that of Bhakti.[30] In fact, such views are based on a superficial examination of some similarities in the social behaviour of the Muslim and Hindu mystics which always tends to create an erroneous impression that syncretism was the dominant characteristic of the Rishi order.[31] Our study shows that the similarities between the Rishi and the Bhakti movements are deceptive and that 'Rishi devotional language', unlike the Bhakti, did not lead to the emergence of religious sects in Kashmir; on the other hand, Nūruddīn Rishī's pervasive mystical poetry was one of the finest expositions of a world-view in the context of a regional manifestation of Islam. What is therefore remarkable about the role of Nūruddīn's poetry and his place as a Sufi missionary is that, in spite of being an outstanding apostle of Hindu-Muslim unity, he did not fail to visualize the risk of Islam being swamped by the ancient syncretistic religion of the Kashmīrīs; he took special care to urge them to mould their life in accordance with the *Sharī'a* of Muhammad.[32] The fact is that Nūruddīn's poetry served as a guide in the personal ethics of Kashmīrīs experiencing acculturation into the Islamic world.

Hindu-Muslim Synthesis

Although during the early stage of his mystical career[33] certain elements in Nūruddin's verses are compatible with the Shaivite aspiration for self-identification with God, such evidence indicates that under the influence of Lal Ded, he gave meaning to the lives of ordinary Kashmīrīs and provided the framework of a culture that drew its vitality from a conflict, a division, a torment, and a struggle created within the individual psyche. Nūruddīn, indeed, does not draw formal and verbal parallels between Hindu and Muslim ideas of unitive experience,[34] but he fully elaborates the spirit that animates the mystical movements in Hinduism and Islam.

What qualities hast thou found in the world,
To allow Thy body a free, loose rope?
The Musalman and Hindu sail in the same boat.
Have thy play and let us go home.[35]

Transcending the barriers of theological orthodoxy, Nūruddīn remarks:

Among brothers of the same parents,
Why did you create a barrier?
Muslims and Hindus are one.
When will God be kind to His servants?[36]

What is unique about the social role of Nūruddīn (and so far least analysed) is his intuitive ability to make profuse and profound use of idiom and vocabulary not only from the Qur'ān, but more significantly from traditional Hindu sources, the Vedas and Upanishads. However, he contrived their use in such a way as to recast their thought-content and make them carriers of Islamic values and contents.

Nirguna, manifest Thyself unto me,
Thy name (alone) have I been chanting,
Lord, help me reach the acme of
  my spiritual desires,
I do remember (with gratitude) how kind Thou art.
Thou removed all veils between Thyself and the Prophet,
  And Thou revealed Qur'ān unto him.

Lord, the one (Prophet) who remained
steadfast in Thy way,
I do remember (with gratitude), how kind Thou art.[37]

According to the Shaivite philosophy of Kashmir, God is Formless (*nirguṇa*) as well as a Qualified Being (*saguṇa*). That Nūruddīn preferred to chose the former term testifies to the profundity of his thought in creating Tauhidic consciousness in a subtle manner. He addresses Kashmīrī Brahmans as brothers and nowhere as infidels (*kāfir*) or heretics (*mushrikīn*).

O Pandit, the brother, O Pandits,
How long will you remain wedded to the worship of
stones and springs?
Your thoughtless search did not bear any fruit.
Submit yourself to the Lord and the Prophet,
Aren't you solicitous of (spiritual and worldly) success?[38]

And criticizing the hypocrisy of the Brahmans:

O Pandits, O believers in *Triguṇa*,[39]
Past and future are linked through the present
O pestering Pandits, whom do you want to deify,
Merge your mind in your vital breath.[40]

True, Nūruddīn became a conscious missionary[41] after coming in contact with the Sufis of the Kubrawī order, but this did not authorize him to 'uproot infidels' from the Valley.[42] By the affirming personal link founded on love that joins the worshipper to God,[43] he created a favourable climate for absorbing the religion of the masses into his mystic order.

In all directions, at all gatherings,
Thou art worshipped by all,
I, a seeker of thine, beseech Thy help.
I remember (with gratitude) how kind Thou art.[44]

I discuss the creative role of the Kubrawī Sufis elsewhere;[45] suffice it to say here that an invocatory prayer,[46] composed by Mīr Saiyid 'Alī Hamadānī especially for his disciples and for Kashmīrīs, itself provides an important source for the above verses. The following verses, translated from the Arabic text of the long prayer recited loudly and daily in the mosques of the Valley, are worthy of note:

> There is no God but Allah who is worshipped everywhere.
> There is no God but Allah who is on
> the tip of every tongue.[47]

The Uniqueness of Islam in Kashmir

Obviously the Rishi movement could not become a doctrine or cult like Bhakti. True, through the conversion of Brahman ascetics, Islam in Kashmir incorporated different spiritual insights; yet in the process of assimilation these were transformed and given a uniquely Islamic orientation. And although the Rishis were gifted with inward illumination, they never attempted to reduce intense personal experience to levels of abstract thought wherein misconceptions, misunderstandings, and misinterpretations become inevitable. So impressed were the Kubrawīs, Suharwardīs, and Naqshbandīs by the *Sharī'a*-oriented asceticism of the Rishis that they perceived the Rishi movement to be a powerful instrument for change, essentially from within, on the basis of Islamic teachings.[48] The synthesis of the Rishis and exogenous Islamic mystic traditions, in fact, created conditions for the gradual eclipse of local Hindu–Buddhist practices in the Valley. By the end of the eighteenth century, we hear very little about Rishis practising celibacy, abstinence from meat, or seclusion in caves, forests, or mountain-tops. Thus the Rishi movement is one of the most subtle phenomena that have inspired and continue to stimulate a subliminal sense of Islam in a particular socio-historical context. The particular social role of the Rishis may be viewed as the product of its relations and contrasts with other roles (Brahmanic, folk Shaivism represented by Lal Ded, Hindu and Buddhist asceticism, Sufism, '*ulamā*' reactions), and maybe that is why a distinguished Suharwardī Sufi of the seventeenth century, Bābā Naṣībuddīn Ghāzī, encapsulates their abiding contribution to Kashmir in the following verses:

> The candle of religion is lit by the Rishis,
> They are the pioneers of the path of belief.
> The heart-warming quality of humble souls

Emanates from the inner purity of
 the hearts of the Rishis.
This vale of Kashmir that you call a paradise,
Owes a lot of its charm to the traditions
 set in vogue by the Rishis.[49]

The implications of the forgoing argument are that Islam is not a set of dogmas but a huge historical movement that identifies seemingly varied, but essentially interacting, relations of practice, representation, symbol, concept, and Tauhidic worldview within the same society and between different societies. There are no fixed patterns in these relations considering changing social patterns over time. However, what is of significance is that Islam in its historical manifestations has moved societies into egalitarian assertiveness. Little wonder that, in the context of our study, the notion of caste versus egalitarianism determines the choice of what events to record, the significance attached to them, and what to delete.

Social Reaction against Brahmanic Ethnocentrism

While Brahmanic chroniclers make a self-conscious attempt at perpetuating the highly venerated tradition of their community's opposition to Islam, they rarely give proof of their ability to realize that their social order had failed to create institutions based on a sound religious philosophy which could have worked as a bulwark against the forces of Islamic egalitarianism. Medieval Kashmīrī society was undergoing a crisis of what may be described as Tauhidic universalism against Brahmanic particularism. And while the most important dimension of this change was the affirmation of the Brahmanic culture within its own realm, at the same time Lal Ded and Nūruddīn asserted the rights of the under-privileged. This may be seen as a reaction against a monopolistic and hegemonic assertion of a single culture. It is not to be wondered, therefore, that the Brahmans also testified to the historical absurdity of their claims: they maintain a baffling and intriguing silence about the two great Kashmīrī mystics in their chronicles. This calls in question the value of eye-witness accounts or so-called authorities on history,[50] nonetheless folk eulogies of Nūruddīn as upholder of the banner of Kashmir (*'Alamdār-i Kashmir*) and leader of the world (*Shaikh al-'Alam*) provide us useful clues as to the complexity of what is missing.

It follows that since the establishment of the Sultanate, Kashmīrī Brahmans were not as much concerned with the revival of the ethical and spiritual values of Hinduism as the preservation of their distinctiveness. This is further evident from our attempt to bring crude historical realism and 'legends' into an effective relationship, claiming them both as indistinguishable aspects of a single experience. We can hardly make sense of history by an outright rejection of legends and folklore, the 'lungs' of rural culture. These, recorded in various *Rishī-nāmas*,[51] can be rendered meaningful only through judicious reference to the socio-historical context.

The story of a well-known Brahman ascetic, Bhūm Sādh, converted to Islam by Nūruddīn Rishī after a great deal of discussion, is illuminating. Long before the outbreak of militancy in the Valley, I visited the tomb of Bābā Bāmuddīn Rishī in the village of Bumzu, district Anantnag (popularly known as Islamabad). The structure of the tomb retains certain features of the temple in which Bāmuddīn lived as an ascetic before his conversion. While the earliest extant Persian chronicle[52] of Kashmir attributes his conversion to a supernatural spell cast by Nūruddīn over him, in the later hagiographies, embroideries of the simple fact of individual conversion point to persistent social discontent against Brahmanic supremacy. Such interpolations are crucial to our understanding of the role 'converts' themselves played in perpetuating the memory of the greatness of Nūruddīn, singling him out as saviour of the downtrodden.

Popular Perception of Nūruddīn Shāh

In popular perception and in particular in the *Rishī-nāmas* of Chrar-i Sharif, Nūruddīn is not only a venerated Sufi but also a champion of the sentiments of commoners, including sweepers and tanners, who prominently figure in the discussion with Bhūm Sādh. It is not unlikely that many lower-caste Hindus must have been attracted to Islam, though by degrees, through open dialogues between Nūruddīn and Brahman ascetics among the folk. What is of further significance is that while contributing to the process of Islamic acculturation, through the repetition of these dialogues at village gatherings, the so-called low-born village dancers and acrobats (*bhand* and *dambel maet*) or *faqīrs*, who were themselves influenced by the wave of Islamic acculturation, played a significant role as transmitters of the values of their 'patron saints' in tradition rural society.

The authors of later *Rishī-nāmas* of Chrar-i Sharif furnish useful details regarding the social impact of Bhūm Sādh's conversion. As a matter of fact, they were in a position of authority to record the oral traditions about the reaction of various strata of Kashmīrī society to Nūruddīn's reformatory role. A meeting of about 1200 Brahmans under the leadership of Tulī Raina with the Shaikh in the wake of the conversion of this prominent saint therefore covered several questions of metaphysical nature. But the outcome of the long discussion concerning the beliefs of Brahmans and those of Islam must have been a gradual assimilation of the folk into the Rishi tradition rather than a 'conversion' in the strict sense as claimed by the *Rishī-nāmas* of the eighteenth and the early nineteenth centuries. It is in this context that Nūruddīn's exhortations to people not to follow polytheistic practices in contravention of what he calls the *Sharī'a* of Muhammad needs to be understood. Significantly, his conception of the *Sharī'a* is purely ethical. For him the *Sharī'a* exists to promote social harmony, tolerance, and equitable justice.[53]

Impact of Nūruddīn's Social Teachings on the Brahmans

Brahman response to Nūruddīn's social teachings was generally to ask how a member of a low caste like him could recognize God and profess to be a Rishi. Such an argument, nevertheless, reveals the particular paradox and tension that Kashmīrī society experienced as a result of Nūruddīn's advocacy of self-imposed poverty, identification with the poor and the downtrodden, and above all, opposition to the caste system. It is significant that on several occasions, Nūruddīn sought to explain the abstract and deep spiritual meaning of God's reality through concrete and material forms.

On one occasion, the founder of the Rishi order sought to humble the pride of certain die-hard Brahmans by way of analogy to a kind of grass abhorrent to cows, horses, sheep, and donkeys. Notwithstanding the worthlessness of the grass in the eyes of the animals, the gardener tied a bouquet of flowers with the same grass for use at the king's palace. What enhanced the value of the grass was not merely the gardener's practice, but more importantly, the social usefulness of an apparently despicable material:

> The grass of a lower stock,
> Not swallowed by devouring animals,
> See, it reaches (even) the head of the King!
> How can animals recognize its true worth?[54]

It follows from Nūruddīn's mystical interpretation of even insignificant material objects that he wanted his followers to adopt a melioristic or pragmatic attitude towards the problems of his society. For him it was not birth but a man's actions that were of supreme importance in determining his social status. How this persuasive mystico-social philosophy of Nūruddīin influenced even men of piety among Brahman families has been discussed elsewhere;[55] it would, however, be worthwhile to emphasize the significance of Nūruddīn's verses in the diffusion of fundamental Islamic precepts about the dignity of labour among Kashmīrī artisans and peasants. In some verses he talks about his experience of understanding (*ma'rifat*) God at the potter's house.[56]

It is little wonder that the town of Chrar-i Sharif was once famous for its excellent pottery. What is more, the town is still known for the best quality products in *kāngrī*.[57]

The Significance of Agricultural Service to God

Nūruddīn Rishī's verses in praise of manual work should be studied against the Kashmīrī Brahmanic tradition which still looks down on all forms of labour as servile in contrast to purely intellectual activities. As to the specific question about the spiritual value of working the land, he admired the idyllic quality of rural life as against the corruption and artificiality of urban civilization. In his long and popular poem *Gongal-nāma*, he comes near to describing the toilers of the soil as the 'chosen' of God, since in his view their activities are not only necessary for a sound social order but also embody certain spiritual truths for the thoughtful. There is little doubt that the rudiments of Islamic rituals were learnt by unlettered people through mystical verses contained in the *Gongal-nāma*. The following was addressed to the cultivators:

The Prophet will plead on your behalf,
Entrust your case to Him.
(For) Nund Rishī fully know the
worth of the cultivators' labour.
One who realizes early will (surely) strive (in His way).[58]

Thus Nūruddīn's view was that if the world is to bear fruit, it must be cultivated. It would not be incorrect to say that in the *Gongal-nāma*, Nūruddīn 'recrystallized the ancient Mesopotamian principle of agricultural service to God as the general transformation of the earth into the orchard wherein Man is to have his nourishment and pleasure'.[59] Although conscious of the transience of the world, he attempted to make villagers aware of its splendour and glory. So strong is his rejection of world-denial in conformity with the ethical limits set by the *Sharī'a* for its realization that it would be worthwhile to reproduce below a few more verses to reject the misconception that self-solace was the only goal of the founder of the Rishi order:

Perform your duties from *Zeth*,[60]
Bearing in mind (the sequel to) the Autumn.
Māgh[61] is the period of fecundity; be thoughtful.
One who realizes early will (surely)
strive (in His way).

Realize early that Spring bubbles over,
'Make hay while the sun shines'.
Beware of falling behind, Spring is a
trap (for the thoughtless).
One who realizes early will (surely)
strive (in His way).

The value of crops will be determined on ripening,
And each product will be named according to its quality.
The fate of the depraved will be sealed.
One who realizes early will (surely)
strive (in His way).

Life has come to its ultimate end stealthily,
Realize, O thoughtless, the (sad)
end of your life,
While exploiting (others) see,
you (actually) robbed yourself.
One who realizes early will (surely)
strive (in His way).

Don't be enchanted by palatial houses,
You will be answerable there (for robbing others).
Is an ignoramus ready enough to heed the warning?
(But) one who realizes early will (surely)
strive (in His way)....

Notes

1. I have used the term *Sharī'a* in the sense in which it was understood by the great Sufis: the moral law, given by Allah and determining the duties of man in relation to God and his fellow beings, not only in congruence with the Qur'ān, but also with the *Sunna*. The *Sharī'a* also comprises the judicial and political obligations as codified in the four schools of Sunni theology.

2. See M. I. Khan, *Kashmir's Transition to Islam: The Role of Muslim Rishis (Fifteenth to Eighteenth Centuries)*, New Delhi, 1994, revised edn, 1997.

3. See I. Habib, 'Economic History of the Delhi Sultanate', *The Indian Historical Review*, IV, 2 (1978): 297.

4. See R. M. Eaton, *Sufis of Bijapur, 1300–1700: Social Role of Sufis in Medieval India*, Princeton, 1978, idem; 'Sufi Folk Literature and the Expansion of Indian Islam', *History of Religions*, XIV, 2 (1974): 117–27.

5. See Eaton, 'Approaches to the Study of Conversion', in R. C. Martin (ed.), *Approaches to Islam in Religious Studies*, Tucson, 1985, p. 110.

6. Ibid.

7. Eaton's view about the assimilation of Indian traditions by the Indian Muslims on the non-urban level and the preservation of Arab identity by the *'Ulamā* lends weight to the Orientalist misconception which dramatized polarity between the so-called Great Tradition of the *'Ulamā* and the Little Tradition of 'Indian Islam'.

8. See A. Schimmel, 'Reflections on Popular Muslim Poetry', *Contributions to Asian Studies* XVII (1982): 18.

9. See J. S. Trimingham. *The Sufi Orders in Islam*, Oxford, 1971, p. 22. On the dichotomy between Islam and Sufism: 'We have shown that Sufism could never be fully accommodated into the Islamic prophetical structure but was allowed to exist parallel to it', p. 143.

10. See Khan, 'Persian Influences in Kashmir in the Sultanate Period, 1320–1586', *Islamic Culture*, LI, 1 (1977): 1–9.

11. See Khan, 'The Impact of Islam on Kashmir in the Sultanate Period, 1320–1586', *The Indian Economic and Social History Review*, XXIII, 2 (1986): 187–205. See also R. Redfield, *Peasant Society and Culture*, Chicago, 1956, p. 72.

12. See Khan, 1997, p. 43.

13. For a detailed discussion on the concept of *avatāra* in socio-historical context, ibid., p. 77.

14. Padmanpore is the ancient name of the modern town of Pampore, famous for saffron cultivation in the Valley.

15. See Nūruddīn Rishī, *Kullīyat-i Shaikh al-'Alam*, ed. M. L. Sāqī, Srinagar, new edn, 1985, p. 21.

16. The Kashmīrī Brahmans adopted this title for themselves on account of the widespread illiteracy among their Muslim compatriots.

17. See Mullā Alī Raina, *Tazkirat al-'Ārifin*, Srinagar, MS. no. 592, fols. 37a–38a.

18. *'Alastu birabbikum, qālū balā*? ('Am I not your Lord?' asked Allah, 'yes, answered they'). For the covenant between Allah and human souls, see Qur'āns, VII, v. 172.

19. See Jayalal Kaul, *Lal Ded*, New Delhi, 1973, pp. 1–2.

20. For a detailed discussion, see Khan, 1997, pp. 73ff.

21. Ibid., p. 62.

22. Ibid., pp. 62–3.

23. See Saiyid 'Alī, *Tārīkh-i Kashmīr*, Srinagar, MS. no. 739, fol. 4b and 'Abdu'l Wahhāb Nūrī, *Fathāt-i Kubrawīyya*, Srinagar, MS. no. 50, fol. 115a.

24. See Bahāuddīn Mattū, *Rishī-nāma* (eds), Muhammad Asadullāh Wānī and Mas'ūd Sāmu, Srinagar, 1982, p. 73.

25. See G. Grierson and L. D. Barnett, *Lalla-Vakyani*, London, 1920, Preface.

26. See Khan, 1986.

27. For a new analysis of Saiyid 'Alī Hamadānī's role, see Khan, 1997, pp. 73ff.

28. The supposed grave of Lal Ded in the town of Bijbehara is of doubtful origin, considering Persian hagiographers' silence about her tomb.

29. See B. Lawrence, 'Lectures on Sufism', *Studies in Islam*, XVIII, 3–4 (1981): 139; 'Islam in India: The Function of Institutional Sufism in the Islamization of Rajasthan, Gujarat, and Kashmir', *Contributions to Asian Studies*, XVII (1982).

30. Ibid.

31. For a critique of such views, see Khan, 1997, p. 50.

32. Ibid.

33. See Khan, 'The Mystical Career and Poetry of Nur al-Din Rishi Kashmiri; Socio-Historical Dimensions', *Studies in Islam*, XIX, 1–2 (1982): 99–124.

34. For a review article on the misuse of *Waḥdat al-wujūd*, Khan, 'Sufism in Indian History', in C. W. Troll (ed.), *Muslim Shrines in India: Their Character, History, and Significance*, New Delhi, 1989, pp. 275–91.

35. See B. N. Parimoo, *Nund Rishi: Unity and Diversity*, Srinagar, 1984, p. 90.

36. Translated by the author from Nūruddīn, *Kullīyāt-i Shaikh al-'Alam* (in 2 vols), vol. II, Srinagar, 1981, pp. 33–4.

37. Translated by the author from the verses as quoted in *Shams al-'Ārifīn*, Srinagar, Seminar Proceedings of Cultural Academy, 1978, pp. 67–8.

38. Translated by the author from Nūruddīn, 1985, pp. 109–10.

39. *Triguṇa*, the three qualities or constituents of nature.

40. See Nūruddīn, *Kullīyāt-i Shaikh al-'Ālam* (in 2 vols), vol. I, Srinagar, 1979, p. 116.

41. In my preliminary research article 'The Impact of Islam on Kashmir...', Nūruddīn does not emerge as a conscious missionary of Islam. However, a very wide range of Persian and Kashmīrī sources I have consulted since 1986 cast serious doubts on my earlier assumption.

42. S. A. A. Rizvi's view that the main mission of the Kubrawī Saiyids was to 'uproot infidelity' from Kashmir is based on an uncritical examination of Persian sources. Both Rizvi (*A History of Sufism in India*, New Delhi, vol. I, 1978, vol. II, 1983) and A. Q. Rafiqi (*Sufism in Kashmir, from the Fourteenth to the Sixteenth Century*, Varanasi, n.d.) make the Kubrawīs and the Rishis somewhat mysterious by labelling them 'orthodox' or 'liberal'. For details, Khan, 1997, ch. VI, especially, pp. 161–5.

43. Innumerable verses can be quoted from the *Kullīyat-i Shaikh al-'Ālam*, to support the thesis that Nūruddīn presented the *Sharī'a* in terms of good conduct, universal love, and exemplary and inspired action (*iḥsān*).

44. Translated by the author from Nūruddīn, vol. II, 1981, p. 14.

45. See Khan, 1997, ch. VI, pp. 161–5.

46. See Khan, 'A Study of Ritual Behaviour and its Impact on the Evolution of Kashmiri Muslim Society', *Islam and Christian-Muslim Relations*, Birmingham, vol. V, no. 1, 1994, pp. 23–33.

47. See Mīr Saiyid 'Alī Hamadānī, *Aurād-i Fatḥiyya*, Srinagar, 1962, p. 9.

48. See Khan, 1997, ch. VI.

49. See Bābā Naṣībuddīn Ghāzī, *Nūr-nāma*; the long poem in praise of the Rishis appears at the end of a brittled manuscript (Bābā Naṣīb, *Nūr-nāma*, Srinagar, Research and Publication Department, MS. no. 3125). The manuscript is not foliated. My translation of the poem first appears in 'The Impact of Islam on Kashmir in the Sultanate Period, 1320–1586', p. 202.

50. See Khan, 1997, pp. 8–10.

51. *Rishī-nāmas* are biographical accounts of the Rishis written during the seventeenth–nineteenth centuries. In particular, the *Rishī-nāmas* written by the Rishis of Chrar-i Sharif in the nineteenth century are rich in details regarding legends and folklore.

52. See Saiyid 'Alī, fols. 38a–38b.

53. For greater details on Nūruddiin's concept of Islamic ethics, see Khan, 1997, ch. V.

54. I have translated from the original verses first produced in Bābā Naṣībuddīn, fols. 59b–60a.

55. See Khan, *Kashmir's Transition to Islam…*, p. 187.

56. See Nūruddīn, *Kullīyāt-i Shaikh al-'Ālam*, 1985, p. 131.

57. A small portable brazier in which coal is burnt. It is carried under garments during winter months.

58. The translation of this and the following verses has been reproduced from Khan, *Kashmir's Transition to Islam…*, pp. 132–3.

59. See I. R. al-Faruqi, *Tawhid: Its Implications for Thought and Life*, Pennsylvania, 1982, p. 96.

60. *Zeth* (Sanskrit, *jyeṣṭha*, Hindi, *jeṭh*), the second month of the Hindu calendar (May–June).

61. *Māgh*, the tenth month of the Hindu calendar (January–February)

References

I. Arabic, Persian, and Kashmīrī Texts

'Abdu'l Wahhāb Nūrī. *Fatḥāt-i Kubrawīyya*, Srinagar, MS., no. 50.

Bābā Naṣībuddiin Ghāzī. *Nūr-nāma*, Srinagar, MS. no. 3125.

Bahāuddīn Mattū, Mullā. *Rishī-nāma*. Srinagar, MS. no. 48 and (eds), Muhammad Asadullāh Wānī and Masūd Sāmū, Srinagar, 1982.

Mīr Saiyid 'Alī Hamadānī. 1962. *Aurād-i Fatḥiyya*, Srinagar.
Mullā 'Ali Raina. *Tazkirat al-'Ārifin*. Srinagar, MS. no. 592.
Nūruddīn Rishī. *Kullīyāt-i Shaikh al-'Ālam* (ed.), Motī Lāl Sāqī, Srinagar, 2 vols., vol. I, 1979, vol. II, 1981; new edn in 1 vol., Srinagar, 1985.
———. 1978. *Shams al-'Arifin*. Srinagar.
Saiyid 'Alī, *Tarikh-i Kashmir*, Srinagar, MS. no. 739.

II. Secondary References

al-Faruqi, Ismail Raji. 1982. *Tawhid: Its Implications for Thought and Life*, Pennsylvania.
Eaton, Richard Maxwell. 1974. 'Sufi Folk Literature and Expansion of Indian Islam', *History of Religions*, XIV, 2: 117–27.
———. 1978. *Sufis of Bijapur, 1300–1700: Social Role of Sufis in Medieval India*. Princeton.
———. 1985 'Approaches to the Study of the Conversion', in Richard C. Martin (ed.), *Approaches to Islam in Religious Studies*. Tucson.
Grierson, George and Lionel D. Barnett. 1920. *Lalla-Vakyani*. London.
Habib, Irfan. 1978. 'Economic History of the Delhi Sultanate', *The Indian Historical Review*, IV, 2: 287–303.
Kaul, Jayalal. 1973. *Lal Ded*. New Delhi.
Khan, Mohammad Ishaq. 1977. 'Persian Influences in Kashmir in the Sultanate Period, 1320–1586', *Islamic Culture*, LI, 1: 1–9.
———. 1982. 'The Mystical Career and Poetry of Nur al-Din Rishi Kashmiri: Socio-Historical Dimensions', *Studies in Islam*, XIX, 1–2: 99–124.
———. 1986. 'The Impact of Islam on Kashmir in the Sultanate Period, 1320–1586', *The Indian Economic and Social History Review*, XXIII. 2: 187–205.
———. 1989. 'Sufism in Indian History', in Christian W. Troll (ed.), *Muslim Shrines in India: Their Character, History, and Significance*, New Delhi, pp. 275–91.
———. 1994. 'A Study of Ritual Behaviour and its Impact on the Evolution of Kashmiri Muslim Society', *Islam and Christian-Muslim Relations*, Birmingham, V, 1: 23–33.
———. 1997. *Kashmir's Transition to Islam: The Role of Muslim Rishis (Fifteenth to Eighteenth Centuries)*. New Delhi, revd 1994, edn 1997.
Lawrence, Bruce. 1981. 'Lectures on Sufism', *Studies in Islam*, XVIII, 3–4: 119–52.
———. 1982. 'Islam in India: The Function of Institutional Sufism in the Islamization of Rajasthan, Gujarat, and Kashmir', *Contributions to Asian Studies*, XVII: 27–43.

Parimoo, B. N. 1984. *Nund Rishi: Unity and Diversity*. Srinagar.
Rafiqi, A. Q. 1971. *Sufism in Kashmir, from the Fourteenth to the Sixteenth Centuries*. Varanasi.
Redfield, Robert. 1956. *Peasant Society and Culture*. Chicago.
Rizvi, S. Athar Abbas. 1978 and 1983. *A History of Sufism in India*. New Delhi, 2 vols.
Schimmel, Annemarie. 1982. 'Reflections on Popular Muslim Poetry', *Contributions to Asian Studies*, XVII, 17–26.
Trimingham, J. Spencer. 1971. *The Sufi Orders in Islam*. Oxford.

III

Rama and the Muslims

5

Rāmāyaṇa and Political Imagination in India*

Sheldon Pollock

From December 1992 through January 1993, more than 3000 people were killed in 'communal' rioting across India, from Surat to Calcutta, from Kanpur to Bangalore. The likes of this rioting had not been seen for generations; in Bombay, for example, more than 600 people died, and the city was brought to a standstill for a week and a half. These recent events were related to but exceeded even the gruesome slaughters that took place in the last quarter of 1990, when a communal 'frenzy' took hold that was then viewed as unprecedented in post-Partition India (Engineer 1991a, cf. 1991b).

* *The Journal of Asian Studies* 52, 2 (May 1993): 261–97.

In different incarnations during 1991, this paper was presented before challenging audiences at the University of Hyderabad, Collège de France, University of Chicago, University of Washington, and the Joint Committee of South Asia of SSRC/ACLS and the South Asian Institute, University of Heidelberg, all of which I would like to thank. Some of the data in this paper appear in preliminary form in *U.P. Shah Memorial Volume* (Baroda, forthcoming).

It is impossible, even irresponsible, to generalize about the causes of what were very disparate acts of violence, unquestionably inflected by local factors that usually had little or nothing to do with antagonism between Hindu and Muslim communities. Yet however complex the causal nexus of these events may be, the occasion and excuse—the symbolic nexus—are simple.

This nexus was first announced in the act that precipitated the earlier violence, the 'Chariot Procession' (*rathyātra*) undertaken by the then-president of the Bhartiya Janata Party ('Indian People's Party', BJP), L. K. Advani, in October 1990. In a Toyota truck turned into an epic chariot, Advani travelled from Somnath in Gujarat to Ayodhyā in north India, the putative birthplace of the hero-god Rāma. As court documents submitted subsequently by the BJP's ally, the Vishva Hindu Parishad ('World Hindu Council', VHP), put it, Rāma is an immemorial object of worship basic to Hinduism, and this worship was being impeded by the presence of a mosque built on the site of his birthplace temple ([Vishva Hindu Parishad] 1991: 4, 70). It was this *yātra* that led, with the force of logic, to the event that inaugurated the most recent riots, the actual demolition of the mosque on 6 December 1992, not by a mob but by what appears to have been a trained group of Hindu militants. Far from damaging the BJP, this most dangerous symbolic act since Partition has only served to enhance its stature; it is now thinkable that this organization—which calls for, among other things, the immediate 'nuclearization' of India's war capability—may become the next ruling party of the country.

It is the symbology of these events that I want to examine in what follows. For whatever ideological cohesion the BJP secured, and the primary impetus for political mobilization—in the name of a Hindu theocratic politics and against the Muslim population—derived in large part from the invocation of a specific set of symbols: the figure of the warrior-god Rāma, his birthplace temple in Ayodhyā, and the liberation of this sacred site.

The ready availability to reactionary Indian politics of central cultural icons like the Rāmāyana text has proved challenging to understand and explain. It seems incomprehensible that a divisive contemporary political discourse is so accessible to, or may be shaped by, what is commonly viewed as a narrative of the divine presence and care for the world. It seems improbable that a heroic tale of love, loss, and recovery from the classical past should be invoked to empower and give substance to the politics of the present. It seems perverse that what have usually been taken to be the utopian impulses of social harmony resonating in the symbol Rāma and his dominion should be directed and directable toward dystopian, indeed, homicidal ends as happened in late 1990 and again in late 1992.

There is a long history to the relationship between Rāmayaṇa and political symbology. From an early period, the story supplied, continuously and readily, if in a highly differentiated way, a repertory of imaginative instruments for articulating a range of political discourses. In fact, it may be doubted whether any other text in South Asia has ever supplied an idiom or vocabulary for political imagination remotely comparable in longevity, frequency of deployment, and effectivity. This is a history, however, that for pre-modern India, at least, remains largely unwritten.

About the earliest course of the political life of the Rāmāyaṇa theme, especially its genetic history in contrast to its receptive history, we know little at present, in part because our sources are so few, but also because the sources we do possess have never been read mytho-politically. Little systematic research has been devoted to the politics of the narrative in the thousand-year period from the putative origins of the Sanskrit version to the flowering of the regional-language treatments of the tale (Kamban, Kīrtibās, Tulsi Dās, etc.). Nor have we learned much about the specific historical locations of this vernacular language production itself. We know, for example, that a large number of dramas and other forms of narrative based on the Rāma theme in Sanskrit, Prakrit, and regional languages were commissioned by, performed before, or indeed composed by kings over a thousand-year period: from the court of the Vākāṭaka (less likely Kashmiri) king Pravarasena in the fifth century (*Setubandha*), to that of Yaśovarman of Kanauj in the seventh (*Rāmābhyudaya*), Bhīmaṭa of Kālañjara in the eighth (*Svapnadaśānana*), Bhoja of Dhārā in the eleventh (*Campūrāmāyaṇa*), to that of Śivājī in the seventeenth (the *Rāmāyaṇa* of Rāmdās). But of the social and political ontologies of most of these texts, we understand little to date beyond the fact that they occupy a central position in elite forms of cultural activity.[1]

The gaps in our present knowledge about the political life of the Rāmāyaṇa theme, then make it risky to talk of sudden, discontinuous revaluation or appropriation. Yet that is what I think happened. For I believe I can show that at a particular historical juncture, a Rāmāyaṇa imaginary came more centrally and dramatically to inhabit a public political space, as opposed to simply a literary space, than it ever had done before, while at the same time its social and political valences were endowed with a more concrete referentiality than ever before. In fact, after tracing the trajectory of the historical effectivity of the Rāmāyaṇa mytheme—tracing, that is, the penetration of its specific narrative into the realms of public discourse of post-epic India, in temple remains, 'political' inscriptions, and those historical narratives that are available—it is possible to specify with some accuracy the particular historical circumstances under which the Rāmāyaṇa was first deployed as a central organizing trope in the political imagination of India.

I should make clear that when I speak of 'Rāmāyaṇa' in the context of north India and the Deccan in the middle period, I am referring to the basic structure of the story as transmitted in Vālmīki's poem. This is the text that lies at the heart of all the material I discuss below, from the external frieze on the central shrine of Vijayanagar, the Rāmacandra temple, to Jayānaka's great biography of Pṛthvīrāja III. One may readily concur that the Rāmāyaṇa can interestingly be viewed not as a fixed text but as a 'multi-voiced entity, encompassing tellings of the Rāma story that vary according to historical period, regional literary tradition, religious affiliation, genre, and political context' (Richman 1991:16). But these tellings are always *retellings of a text everyone knows*. Moreover, it is hard to find evidence of effectivity in the realm of literary, let alone public, discourse of these 'many' Rāmāyaṇas in Rajasthan, Gujarat, or the Deccan in middle-period India. (This holds true for the highly 'oppositional' Jain versions, which were something of a local specialty.) In short, the foundational version, the version everyone knows in AD 1000–1400 and for the whole millennium preceding this period, is that of Vālmīki and his epigones, where the Rāma presented is *kodaṇḍarāma, dharmabhṛtāṃ varaḥ*, 'Rāma with the curved bow, the chief of the righteous', and Rāvaṇa is always *lokarāvaṇa, sarvalokabhayāvaha*, 'He who makes the world weep, who fills all the world with terror.' It is the political valences of this version, which I detail later in this article, that are its most important distinguishing feature.

Unquestionably, the discourse of the epic had already intersected with, or reprocessed, or perhaps even provided an idiom for, the ideologies of early Indian imperial polities, especially that of Aśoka (Pollock 1986: 9–24). Yet if one actually plots a history of the Rāmāyaṇa in the two realms of the political and literary imaginations, one finds a stark disparity. For a thousand years from at least the fourth century AD the literary imagination of India received undiminished stimulation from the Rāma legend, even to the point of hypertrophy (as many later poets themselves came to recognize, for example, *Ullāgharāghava* 2; *Hammīramadamardana* 1.8). This begins as early as the second or third century with Bhāsa, continues with Kālidāsa and Kumāradāsa in the fourth and fifth, extends through to Bhavabhūti, Bhaṭṭi, Murāri, Rājaśekhara in the seventh to ninth centuries, and onward into the next millennium—the list is almost endless and seems at times an entire library of Sanskrit literature. In striking contrast to this, however, the political imagination during the first thousand years of the life of the Rāmāyaṇa is only superficially affected by its existence. The epic may have inflected or embellished the political imagination, supplying an epithetical paradigm of, or argument for, royal sovereignty and indeed royal divinity; it certainly does not shape this imagination. But something very different happens early in the next millennium; at that moment the tale comes alive in the political sphere and for the first time, perhaps, kings *become* Rāma. Although the logic of my argument might entail that these political–cultural processes of middle-period India should themselves recuperate, indeed imitate, earlier ones, all my evidence suggests that this is not the case; the tradition of invention—of inventing the king as Rāma—begins in the twelfth century.

It is this historical moment and its cultural representations that provide the starting point for this article. Initially, I was interested only to discover when, in what circumstances, and with what significations the Rāmāyaṇa entered the arena of political discourse in South Asia, to become a language in which the political imagination expresses itself. But the materials and the historical specificity they reveal became intriguing in their own right. They also raised questions that were larger and more puzzling, questions for cultural theory generally and for our theorization of forms of Indian culture, and to some extent even for the self-understanding and sense of purpose of critical-historical Indian studies.

One of these questions is the problem of what may be termed historical imitation. What concerns me under this rubric is why and how it is that people seem to bring to consciousness or even enact world-historical events only or especially through a revivification of a cultural past; why 'revolution', in the sense of profound and sudden social–political change, is often conceptualized by its agents as a kind of repetition. A second and more specific question relates to the Rāmāyaṇa narrative itself. Can we identify any conceptual or imaginative resources it may provide that made this narrative in particular the representational instrument of choice for figuring forth the historical events that are at issue here? More difficult still is the question of what, if anything, this evidence suggests for our understanding of the modalities of relations between communities in western and central India in the eleventh to fourteenth centuries. Finally, since all historical work is informed by, if not an argument about, the present, what difference does knowing this past make in comprehending the present-day redeployment of Rāmāyaṇa symbology, let alone in addressing the current crisis? What critical value can attach to historiography, and what are the possibilities of historicist intervention in the social–political world of the present, especially given the role of objectivist history in creating that world? In short, why should we want any longer to be historical?

I suggest in what follows that the Rāmāyaṇa came alive in the realm of public political discourse in western and central India in the eleventh to fourteenth centuries in a dramatic and unparalleled way. I believe the text offers unique imaginative instruments—in fact, two linked instruments—whereby, on the one hand, a divine political order can be conceptualized, narrated, and historically grounded, and, on the other, a fully demonized Other can be categorized, counterposed, and condemned. The makers of elite culture in medieval South Asia chose these instruments for the work of divinization and demonization at this historical moment because of the emergence of two enabling conditions. One was the peculiar salience that a far older political theology now seems to have achieved in the service of the legitimation or enhancement or perhaps just self-understanding of kingship. The other was the appearance of Others who—whether, in fact, they presented an unprecedented unassimilability or could opportunistically be represented as such—were especially vulnerable to the demonizing formulation the Rāmāyaṇa made available. All this I feel reasonably confident in arguing. What remains far less easy to figure out is how this material is to be interpreted in understanding community interaction and what pertinence this kind of genealogy has with respect to the problems of the present. The proper and critical task of history here may be not what 'really happened' but how people come to believe what happened. The symbolic meaning system of a political culture is constructed, and perhaps knowing the processes of construction is a way to control it.

Rāma in the World: Temple Cult

The cult of Rāma, its role in the ideology of kingship, and the expression of this doctrine in temple worship have not been mapped for the subcontinent in any historical detail. What I present here, consequently, will no doubt bear supplementation as this mapping takes place, but I doubt that the main conclusions will be seriously affected: The Rāma cult in South Asia is almost totally non-existent until at the earliest the eleventh, or more likely the twelfth century, and the growth of this cult took place in virtual synchrony with a set of particular historical events.[2]

It is many years since R. G. Bhandarkar first made the point that, while the divinity of Rāma was known from quite early on, the temple cult of Rāma was very slow to develop (Bhandarkar 1913: 47). Yet just how limited this development was prior to the twelfth century and, what is more significant, the conditions under which it was initiated after that date have been little explored.

Early evidence for cultic practice devoted to Rāma is sparse, as we can now judge, thanks to Hans Bakker's careful work. There is inscriptional testimony for the founding of a Śārṅgadhara temple during the early Gupta period (Skandagupta), and were this in Ayodhyā (and, more, were it a Rāma temple) it might suggest a royal cult of Rāma in the late fifth century. But there is really little reason to believe that it was or to accept the hypothesis of a relocation of the Gupta court to Ayodhyā (cf. Bakker 1986: 24ff.). Aside from this instance, itself dubious, the evidence prior to the twelfth century that Rāma may have been the object of worship is scanty indeed. There is a well-known fifth century charter issued by the Vākāṭaka queen Prabhāvatīgupta from 'Rāmagirisvāmipādamūlāt' (recalling Kālidāsa's *raghupatipāda*, *Meghadūta* 9), which is taken to be 'Nandivardhana' in northern Maharashtra. But even if this were to be accepted as a Rāma shrine (there are problems here, too, which I notice below), this remains a single instance, in a very limited geographical area and narrow temporal frame (ca. AD 400–65; Bakker 1986: 62). From that point on for the next 700 years, we hear nothing anywhere of Rāma sanctuaries.

This is not, of course, to say that we do not encounter in temples throughout this period scenes from the Rāmāyaṇa and occasional sculptural representations of Rāma. In Andhra Pradesh, for example, reliefs bearing Rāmāyaṇa themes are found in the rock-cut caves at Undavalli (10 kilometres from Vijayawada in coastal Andhra) that may reach back to Viṣṇukūṇḍin times (fourth to fifth centuries AD; Rajendra Prasad 1980: 72). Yet no epigraphical testimony attesting to any temple explicitly dedicated to Rāma is found in Andhra until far later. Throughout the Deccan, the same situation presents itself. From the seventh century on, substantial interest in the Rāmāyaṇa tale is attested, as in the Cāḷukya temples of Virūpākṣa and Pāpanāth at Pattadakal, which are among the first to attempt any kind of systematic narration (some even provide identifying labels in Prākrit), or in the great frieze on the *vimāna* of the Rāṣṭrakūṭa temple of Kailāsanātha at Ellora, A.D. 757–72 (Nagarajarao 1978: 306; Sivaramamurti 1980: 638). From around this period individual scenes also begin to appear in the east and south of the subcontinent—in the late seventh century Paraśurāma temple at Bhubaneswar; the eighth century Kailāsanātha temple at Kāñcī; and the Olakkaneśvara temple at Mahaballipuram (Nagaswamy 1980: 409ff.). Yet nothing in all this indicates dedication to or a cultic significance of Rāma. On the contrary, all these temples are Śaiva, and the majority of Rāmāyaṇa scenes selected for representation are likewise Śaiva in character (the ubiquitous Rāvaṇa-shaking-Kailāsa, for example).

In the north, so far as I can tell, the situation is no different. Again, we find Rāmāyaṇa representations from an early period but nothing to suggest a Rāma cult. The well-known Viṣṇu shrine at Deogarh (ca. AD 500), for example, has some eight Rāmāyaṇa panels; similarly embellished is the recently discovered Viṣṇu temple at Aphṣaḍ, 30 kilometres north-east of Nawadah in the Nawadah district, Bihar, which arguably was erected by the Gupta king Ādityasena in the seventh century (cf. Simha 1968: 216ff.; *CII* 3: 202ff.). But the Deogarh temple has many other Viṣṇu motifs, and in view of the fact that a large Varāha image was also found in Aphṣaḍ, it is likely that this, too, was a standard *daśāvatāra* temple. The same is true in the west. Throughout the vast Gurjara-Pratihāra empire (ca. 725–1000), for example, which at its height extended out from Rajasthan beyond Kanauj in the east and south to the Vindhyas, there are no Rāma temples to be found.

By the mid-twelfth century, however, the situation began to change, with a sudden onset of activity of building temples to Rāma, which intensified over the next 200 years. Among early examples of temples dedicated to Rāma are two built under the Kalachuris of Ratnapur (Raipur district, Madhya Pradesh), a first one at Rājim in AD 1145 by a minister of King Pṛthvīdeva II, and a second (in Rewa near Makundpur) in AD 1193, by a feudatory of Vijayasiṃha of the later Kalachuri dynasty ruling at Tripurī. The first bears an inscription that, although obscure in places, helps us begin to situate the politics of the Rāma cult as it develops in this period: 'Through fear of [this King Jagapāla], the formidable foes—the Māyūrikas and the valiant Sāvantas—the lords of *maṇḍala*s completely submittea to him. Just as the *kṣatriya* Rāma, (best of) warriors, destroyed the families [sc., of the demons; or: families of bowmen], even so did this [King Jagapāla] kill the forces of his enemies with multitudes of arrows.... Reciting all [works] such as the *Rāmāyaṇa*, [being] the support of living beings, self-respecting, conferring gifts on Brahman families for their learning—such is Jagapāla. He has caused this beautiful temple to be constructed for manifesting the splendour of Rāma.' Although the identification of the enemy is unclear here, what is important to register is the explicit comparison of the king with Rāma and the establishment of a cult to celebrate, if not operationalize, their relationship (Mirashi 1955: 450ff.; the temple was originally built as a temple to Viṣṇu, 451 n.2; 346ff.; Bakker 1986: 64–5).

It is around this same time—between the mid-eleventh and the end of the twelfth centuries—that the Gāhaḍavāla dynasty begins to develop Ayodhyā as a major Vaiṣṇava centre by way of a substantial temple-building programme. Unfortunately, the inscriptional record here is very disappointing, but it seems likely that a Rāma temple was constructed at the Svargadvāra ghat, probably by Chandradeva. (And was a birthplace temple built by the last Gāhaḍavāla king, Jayacandra? Cf. Bakker 1986: 51ff., 1987: 17ff.; contrast Sharma 1990: 10).

At the end of the thirteenth and the beginning of the fourteenth centuries, several major cultic centres devoted to Rāma are created or reinvigorated. I will look at only two of these, rather different in character but, I think, identical in their mytho-politics, the Rāma complex at Rāmtek (Rāmatekdi, 'Rāma's Hill', 45 kilometres north-east of Nagpur) and the Rāmacandra shrine at Vijayanagar.

According to 'local legend' recorded by Henry Cousens, Rāmtek is the place Rāma executed the outcaste ascetic, Śaṃbūka. 'Afterwards one Hemāḍpant (some say a Rākshasa, and other a Brāhman) built the following five temples on the Rāmtek hill: one dedicated to Rāma, and containing images of Rāma and Sītā;

one dedicated to Lakshmaṇasvāmi; one to Hanumān; one temple dedicated to the goddess 'Ekādaśī'; and a temple of Lakshmī–Nārāyaṇa' (Cousens 1897: 7ff.; this is what is known as a *pañcāyatana* complex). The site has recently been studied in much greater detail by A. P. Jamkhedkar and by Bakker (Jamkhedkar 1986; Bakker 1989a). There are perhaps as many as five structures dating from Vākāṭaka times on Rāmtek, and a Cāḷukyan-era temple, in addition to the several Yādava structures. None of these Vākāṭaka temples, although Vaiṣṇava, gives iconographic or inscriptional indication of dedication to Rāma (they are dedicated instead to Narasiṃha, Varāha, Bhagavān); those associated with Rāma are of the Hemāḍpant style, and we have little reason to believe these replace any earlier Rāma structures.

Since Cousens time, an undated inscription, unfortunately in a state of decomposition, found on the *garbhagṛha* of the Lakṣmaṇasvāmi temple has been published (*EI* 25: 7ff.; cf. Bakker 1989b). The identity of the ruling house hinted at by the mention of *yādavo vaṃśaḥ* and, further on, of 'Siṃhana', is made clear in line 17, where we find the name of 'King Śrī Rāmacandra, who made [the subordinate official in question] the repository of a royalty brilliant with the prosperity of empire'. The record is referring to the Yādava king of Devagiri, Rāmacandra (great-grandson of Siṃhana), who ascended the throne in AD 1271. Among the records of this king we read elsewhere, 'How is this Rāma to be described...who freed Vārāṇasi from the *mleccha* horde, and built there a golden temple of Śārṅgadhara.'[3] Although he is said to be a *mahāmāheśvara* or 'great devotee of Siva', who 'anoints eight icons of Śambhu with the milk of his fame', he is also called *rāyanārāyaṇa*, 'a very Nārāyaṇa among kings', while his minister is described as a descendant of Vasiṣṭha, the family priest of Rāma and the whole Raghu clan (*EI* 25: 199ff. vs. 18ff.; *IA* 14: 314ff., lines 47, 58).

Now, while there is no contemporary archaeological evidence, the textual sources cited above—Rāmtek and Rāmagiri (of the Vākāṭaka grant) being identical—could suggest that Rāmtek was a site of Rāma worship prior to the time of this grant. What is in any case indisputable on the evidence of this praise-poem (*praśasti*) is that King Rāmcandra empowered his viceroy substantially to embellish the Rāma cult there. And the fact that some major investment in the site took place near the end of the Yādava dynasty is a historical conjuncture unlikely to be coincidental.

There will be occasion below to return to this Yādava king, but before leaving the question of the Rāmtek centre, I want to tie up the loose end in Cousens's report of the figure named Hemāḍpant. There is no doubt that this name—associated with other temple projects dating from the Yādava period (although not with other Rāma temples, since none exist in the area; see Verma 1973)—refers to the celebrated Hemādri Pandit, the *mantrin* of the Yādva king Rāmacandra and his father. It is to him that we owe a text (a *dharmanibandha* or 'law code') that provides liturgical instructions for worshipping Rāma as an incarnation, and describes a ceremony connected with his birth, the *rāghavadvādaśīvrata* (*Caturvargacintāmaṇi*, Vratakāṇḍa: 1034–5). Hemādri also produces a part of the *Agastyasaṃhitā*, the first work to treat of the most important festival associated with Rāma, the *rāmanavamī*, and which itself cannot be dated before the twelfth century. It is Hemādri's 'law code' that provides the cult of Rāma with Brahmanical sanction for the first time (Kane 1962–75, vol. 5: 84–8; Bakker 1986: 153ff., 1987: 15).

The apogee of the growth of a royal cult of Rāma suggested by the foregoing material is reached in the middle (or end) of the fourteenth century with the founding of the Vijayanagar empire in the Deccan. Prior to this, Rāma temples in the region of northern Karnataka or Andhra Pradesh are as rare as they are in other parts of the subcontinent. The earliest I can locate dates from Guntur district in the Kākatīya period, with an inscription of *śaka* 1245 (*ca.* AD 1323) declaring that the inhabitants agreed to give to the temples of Varada Gopinātha and Rāma-Lakṣmaṇa a portion of their incomes for the merit of Pratāpa Rudradeva (*SII* 10: 288).

With the establishment of Vijayanagara, however—at a site, 'Kiṣkindhā' and Lake Pampā, permeated by Rāmāyaṇa lore—we find incorporated into the very structure of the imperial city a temple devoted to Rāma. Situated at the nucleus of the royal centre, the Rāmacandra temple (before AD 1450, cf. Fritz *et al.*

1984a: 62), probably the 'state chapel', is at the same time the focal point of a spatially articulated political theology. First noticed by A. H. Longhurst in 1917, the political–theological code of the city has been analysed by John Fritz. He argues that urban form itself—such features as the movement dictated by the plan of the city, with the Rāma temple as the destination of the 'sacred way' orienting the city, and the mythological associations of the site itself—was designed to establish a homology of the king and the divine hero-king Rāma and a congruence between the terrestrial realm of the king and that of the god. 'The king's actions were a manifestation of Rāma's and he participated in the sanctity of the deity.' As an inscription of AD 1379 puts it, 'In that same city (Vijayanagar) did (King) Harihara dwell as in former times Rāma dwelled in the city of Ayodhyā' (Fritz 1986: 53, 1985: 266; Fritz *et al.* 1984a: 146–54).[4] In the subsequent Vijayanagar/Nāyaka period separate temples with Rāma as the main deity become somewhat more common, but are still strikingly few (two important examples are the Rāmasvāmi temple in Kumbakonam built by Raghunātha Nāyaka in the sixteenth century, and the Bhadrācalam temple on the Godāvarī in Khammam district, Andhra Pradesh, built in the eighteenth century with the end of the Qutb Shahi dynasty, but almost certainly dating back to Kākatīya times).

What may constitute the sole, yet still a minor, exception to what must thus be viewed as a twelfth-century date for the origin of the temple cult of Rāma is found in the early Coḷa realm.[5] Attention is often called to several Coḷa bronzes of Kodaṇḍa Rāma, but these seem to have been highly restricted in both time and place, to tenth-century Thanjavur district and the reign of Āditya, who apparently assumed the title 'Kodaṇḍa Rāma'. Whether these figures were 'made under the influence of Kamban's *Rāma-Kathā*'—or, more interesting, whether the great Tamil poem was composed in that political context—depends on the notoriously uncertain dating of that text; anywhere from the late ninth to the late twelfth century has been suggested, the latter end of this range being most generally accepted. But it certainly remains possible that Āditya prefigured the political instrumentation of the Rāmāyana (Nagaswamy 1983: 7, 154–9).

How far beyond this one case we can go in Tamil country is uncertain. To infer from temples bearing Rāma reliefs that a cult of Rāma existed in the ninth and tenth centuries is not possible; even to attribute a special significance of Rāma for Coḷa kingship is difficult. The positive evidence for such a significance is scant for the early Coḷa domain and weakened by negative comparative evidence: nothing in the epigraphical record of the Bādāmi Cāḷukyas, for example, indicates a political valorization of the Rāmāyaṇa, yet the same area, as already noted, produced some of the earliest plastic representations of the epic. Furthermore, the Rāmāyaṇa competed with a variety of other epic friezes—the *Mahābhārata*, the Kṛṣṇa-cycle—in places like Ellora and indeed in the Coḷa country itself, which certainly seems to diminish the position of centrality some have striven to establish for it (Sanford 1974). The epigraphical remains, too, as I show below, contain little beyond the standard rhetorical ornamentation.

Additional support for the development of the Rāma cult sketched above is provided by the history of Rāma cultic sculpture, that is, works designed for worship and not simply associated with temple narrative panels. This, too, remains largely untraced, but as far as I can see, nothing would contradict the chronology of Rāma-dedicated temples. Such sculpture is extremely rare prior to the twelfth century and, in fact, continues to be rare until long after that date.[6] Bruno Dagens findings for western Andhra may be somewhat atypical—this is admittedly a strongly Saivite region—but they confirm in important ways the differential development of the purely decorative and more centrally cultic dimensions of the figure of Rāma: whereas Rāmāyaṇa episodes play a considerable role on the pillars of temples throughout the area between Alampur and Śrīśailam from at least the tenth century on, cultic images of Rāma are found only far later. In this region, in fact, Rāma appears not to have gained full autonomy as a major god until perhaps as late as the eighteenth century (Dagens 1984: 614–15; cf. 63 and 174–5).

I am not asserting, then, that Rāma was never the object of cultic worship prior to the period with which I am concerned here. Even less am I claiming that the Rāma cult, when it did arise, superseded all others; in Vijayanagar, for example,

Virūpākṣa remained what might be called the *rāṣṭradevatā* ('imperial deity'), whereas many of the kings identifying themselves with Rāma through inscriptions or patronizing his temple cult are thoroughly Śaiva (the Yādava king Rāmacandra already noted, for example, or others I mention below, such as Jayasiṃha Siddharāja, whose most famous architectural achievement is the Sahasraliṅga tank at Aṇahilavaḍa, and Pṛthvīrāja III himself, who is described as a lifelong devotee of Śiva in *Pṛthvīrājavijaya* 11.105). What is certain, however, is that the cult of Rāma has a history. At first extraordinarily restricted in time and space, it exhibits striking efflorescence and assumes a prominent place within the context of a political theology from the end of the twelfth century onwards, achieving in some instances a centrality by the middle of the fourteenth. This development is paralleled in other areas of cultural production as well.

Rāma in the World: Inscriptions

If the architectural remains associated with Rāma have yet to be systematically worked through and synthetically analysed, this is even more the case with the inscriptional materials (beyond those associated with a temple cult) that refer to or invoke the god-king or in one way or another process Rāmāyaṇa themes (Sircar 1980 and Diskelkar 1960 are the sole, unhelpful guides). So here, too, my findings have to be regarded as provisional, but again I would be surprised if further work would require fundamental revision of my conclusion: the Rāmāyaṇa supplies serious material to the political imagination of premodern India as coded in the inscriptional record only from the later medieval period on; references in the first millennium are remarkably few but gain in frequency and complexity especially after the twelfth century. I will glance at the quality of the earlier material, and then go on to examine in more depth a few examples of the very different discourse we encounter later.

Rāma, to be sure, furnishes a standard of comparison (*upamāna*) in hyperbolic inscriptional discourse from an early period, but these are static, formulaic allusions. Their quality may be gauged from what is perhaps the earliest instance, the Sālivāhana *praśasti* at Nasik (ca. AD 150), where Rāma is simply one among a series of heroes: *nābhāga-nahusa-janamejaya-sakara-yayāti-rāma-abarīsa-samatejasa* ('equal in majesty to Nābhāga', etc.). Hardly an exception to such uninteresting formulae in early period is the comparison with Rāma of the Gupta emperor Skandagupta, 'equal to Rāma in his great offensive power' (*CII* 3: 318.5; he is likened to Yudhiṣṭhira in the same line). This is, in fact, the single time Rāmacandra is mentioned in the entire corpus of Gupta inscriptions, and if we knew nothing about the putative move of the Gupta capital to Ayodhyā, the reference would hardly claim our attention at all.[7]

The public discourse of major dynasties for centuries made virtually no appropriation of the Rāma theme. In the records of the Gurjara-Pratihāra empire (ca. AD 725–1000), for example, it seems that reference to Rāma is altogether absent (Puri 1986: 211). There is one exception, however: the ninth-century Gwalior *praśasti* of King Bhoja. This record, commemorating the construction of a domestic Viṣṇu shrine, reads in v. 3, 'In their family [that is, the family of the solar kings], [in which] the lustre [of Viṣṇu, *dhāma*] eventually set foot, Rāma of auspicious birth made a war of destruction and slaughter against the demons...in which Rāvaṇa was killed.' This is followed by a verse on Nāgabhaṭa I that alludes to the campaign of the Arab army of Junaid against Ujjain (ca. AD 725): 'In that family...a shelter of the three worlds, there miraculously appeared the image of the Ancient Sage [Nārāyaṇa] [in the person of] the god-king [*devaḥ*] Nāgabhaṭa. For when crushing the large armies of the powerful *mleccha* king, a destroyer of pious deeds [*sukṛta-*], [Nāgabhaṭa] shone with four arms brilliant with glittering terrible weapons.' This meaning-conjuncture occurs nowhere else in India before the twelfth century; it is a prefigurement, I think, of a political semiotics to come.

Further to the west, among the Śilāhāras, contemporaries of the Pratihāras, Rāma is never mentioned (Mirashi 1977). This is true, too, for the Bādāmi Cāḷukyas (ca. AD 500–750), who, despite their well-attested knowledge of and respect for the Sanskrit epic (for example, *IA* 7: 163.3), make no reference to Rāma in their charters. Among the Gaṅgas, their neighbours to the south-west, a single, pedestrian allusion is found (Ramesh 1984: 196), and only one in the entire extant corpus of inscriptions of the north-central Paramāras (*EI* 2: 15). Besides these cases of simple similes, the most common reference to Rāma in early inscriptions is a minatory verse that begins to appear commonly at the end of land-grants from the early ninth century on, in Rāṣṭrakūṭa regions. 'Common to (all) kings is the dam [*setu*] of *dharma*; you should abide by it moment by moment. Again and again Rāmabhadra [v.1., Rāmacandra] implores all future kings to do this' (the first occurrence is *EI* 23.212, a record of AD 807 of the Rāṣṭrakūṭas of Gujarat). Still, all this presents us with in the end is an image of Rāma as superordinate king, an image the literary texts had already been promulgating for centuries.

More complex in their referentiality are inscriptions that exploit the narrative of the poem with a historicist turn. Although Rāma is otherwise absent from Pallava records, an inscription of King Nandivarman (dated in his 22nd your, that is, AD 753) describes Narasiṃhavarman as surpassing 'the glory of the valour of Rāma by (his) conquest of Laṅkā' (*SII* 2: 348.22), the same boast Rājendra Coḷa I was to make two hundred years later, taunting the Sinhalese with the mytheme when referring to his general's defeat of the king of Laṅkā: Rāma needed the help of monkeys to build his *setu*, and only with great effort could he slay the lord of Laṅkā; 'but my general crossed the ocean in ships and easily destroyed the lord of Laṅkā—and so put Rāma to shame' (*SII* 3: 421, 80, ca. AD 1018; Pṛthivīpati a feudatory of Parāntaka I, is awarded the sobriquet *saṃgrāmarāghava*, 'Battle-Rāma', for his defeat, again, of a Sinhalese king, *SII* 2: 383.10). Considerably more informed by the Rāma tale is the Kanyakumārī inscription of Vīrarājendradeva (ca. AD 1030), which contains a fascinating *praśasti* on the Coḷa dynasty. After praising Rāma in several striking verses, the account goes on to provide a history of the first Coḷa king: while out hunting he is led astray by a magical deer-*rākṣasa* (as Rāma was), to the banks of the Kāverī River. He finds the region to be devoid of Brahmans, relocates many from Aryāvarta southward, and thus establishes the Coḷamaṇḍalam (*EI* 18: 21ff., 37.139ff.).

Not unrelated to the Coḷa discourse is the *praśasti* of the reconstituted Cāḷukyan dynasty of Kalyāṇi (north-east Karnataka) under Vikramāditya V (reigned AD 1008–15): For the first time the dynastic history seeks to establish a connection with the solar kings of Rāma's lineage, describing how, after fifty-nine kings of the Cāḷukya *vaṃśa* had ruled in Ayodhyā, the family emigrated southwards to its present location (*IA* 1887: 15ff.; p. 21.11–12).[8] Vikramāditya VI of the same dynasty comes to be referred to as 'Cāḷukya-Rāma' (*EI* 15: 348ff. vs. 20, Kannaḍa) and, as in the Coḷa records, Rāmāyaṇa narrative elements are used to frame historical events: The first political–historical claim in the narrative of Vikramāditya VI, in a record of AD 1077, is made by means of a complex punning verse on the Rāma story (which beyond the obvious allusion to an alliance with a southern power, no doubt against the Coḷas, is hard to decode): 'He went to seek Lakṣmī [royalty/Sītā] produced by his [her] father (Janaka); along with his brother, the son of Sumitrā, and with a force of monkeys; to the banks of the ocean came the vast royalty of Vibhīṣaṇa (the lord of Draviḍa) out of fear of the Many-headed, and the Cāḷukya-Rāma bowed to him [in compliance with his supplication?]' (*EI* 12.269ff., lines 88ff.).[9]

Yet again, in virtually all the inscriptional materials considered thus far, the semiotic situation is analogous to what we find in the development of temple representations: Rāma and Rāmāyaṇa mythemes function as peripheral rhetorical embellishments, inflecting and texturing a given discourse but not constituting it. Very different are the materials of the succeeding period. Again, I will examine here only a couple of examples, where we can see how the political world comes to be read through—identified with, cognized by—the narrative provided by the epic tale.[10]

The Dabhoi (Darbhavatī) stone inscription of *saṃvat* 1311 (ca. AD 1253), composed by the poet Someśvaradeva, describes, among other members of the Vāghela dynasty of Gujarat, Lavaṇaprasāda, a feudatory and minister of the Caulukya/Solanki king, Bhīma II (AD 1178–1242), who was eventually to establish the Vāghelas as an independent ruling house (*EI* 1: 20ff.; *HIG* 3: 46.6ff.):

> He [sc., Aṃorāja] placed upon his son, Lavaṇaprasāda, the burden of the land of the Gūrjjaras.... While he was ruling this land... was not the Gūrjjara-rājya even greater than *rāmarājya*?[11]...So many the immortal

kings on earth, yet virtually all of them were beside themselves with fear even to hear mention made of the king of the Turuṣkas. When he came for battle in a rage it was [Lavaṇaprasāda] alone (lacuna). [The Turk who] dyed the earth with blood dripping from the severed heads of many kings, even he, when he came before this [King Lavaṇaprasāda], went dry-mouthed in fear. And [Lavaṇaprasāda] defeated him (lacuna) with his pillar-like arm terrible for the sword it held (lacuna). How could he be a mere mortal who defeated the king of the *mleccha*s whom no other mortal could defeat?

A more elaborate variation on this theme is contained in an inscription published by D. R. Bhandarkar in 1912, although never translated and never discussed in later literature with reference to the specific and really quite striking claims of its discourse. The inscription, dated *saṃvat* 1224 (ca. AD 1168), was originally found near Hānsi (appearing as Āsi or Āsika in the inscription), a town in Haryāna of strategic importance for controlling the western approach to Delhi, and an object of struggle since at least the middle of the eleventh century (Sharma 1975: 67). The record is a *praśasti* of the Cāhamāna king Pṛthvīrāja II, which recounts how he put his maternal uncle Kilhana in command of the fort at Hānsi, concerned as he was about an attack of the Turks ('in his belief that the mighty Hammīra warrior was a thorn in the side of all the world', lines 4–5). Kilhaṇa fortifies the stronghold, and checks the advance of the invaders ('You there, Hammīra! Where is your greatness now!' line 7; cf. *EI* 9:77 vs. 34, where Kelhaṇa [sic] is described in a record of the Cāhamānas of Naḍḍula: 'Having soundly defeated the mighty Turuṣka, he built a tower of gold, like a crown of the dwelling of Someśa'). We are then told how Kilhaṇa received a letter from one Vibhīṣaṇa, who reminds him how the two of them once had aided Rāma in the building of the *setu*. Then he declares: *pṛthvīrājo mahārājo rāmo 'sau saṃśayaṃ vinā/hanūmān niścitaṃ vīra bhavān adbhutavikramaḥ//* 'And that Rāma has without doubt become Pṛthvīrāja the great king, and certainly Hanūmān has become you, great hero, a man of miraculous deeds' (line 14). What is implicit in the fragmentary remains of the previous record is here made absolutely clear: the thorough identification (*pace* Bhandarkar 1912: 17) of a historical ruler with the divine king Rāma, and what will become an increasingly explicit demonization—'rākṣasization'—of the agents of the profound historical changes effected during this epoch, the Turkic people from Central and western Asia.

Rāma in the World: Historiography

I want to adduce one last genre of evidence, the historiographical (or 'textualized', or distinguish it from the 'documentary' inscription), in support of the argument I have been making here, that the period of some 200 years starting around the mid-twelfth century witnessed a coding of political reality via Rāmāyaṇa themes such as did not exist—or at least not to anywhere near the same degree—in any previous era. I will cite only two Sanskrit documents, the one a brief episode from a Jain anthology of historical accounts (*prabandha*), the other a full-scale historical poem contemporary with the events it narrates.

In the *Dvyāśrayakāvya* of Hemacandra, a poem that recounts the history of the first patron of this Jain polymath and poet, the Caulukya/Solanki king Jayasiṃha Siddharāja of Gujarat (AD 1094–1143), the king is identified as an incarnation of Rāmacandra (15.56–7), as others have already noticed (Majumdar 1956; note that in his actual inscriptions, like the just-published Bilpank *praśasti*, he is called 'the Supreme Person himself [Viṣṇu] come as avatar to earth', *EI* 40: 27ff., v. 15). We can, however, flesh out the brief allusion of Hemacandra's by means of a passage in Merutuṅga's *Prabandhacintāmaṇi* (AD 1304), the earliest of a new genre of Jain historiographical texts that appears to have come into being in the fourteenth century. The section in question occurs in the *Siddharāja* chapter, and is called the 'Narrative of the Prevention of the Invasion of the Mlecchas':

> While the chiefs of the lord of the *mleccha*s were assembling as a host, the king summoned some spies who had come from Madhyadeśa, gave them secret instructions and dismissed them. On the following day at twilight, when a wind as wild as the wind at the end of time began to blow, the king went off to his assembly hall—like the gods' hall Sudharmā it was—and as he looked on, a pair of Palādas, each carrying a gold brick on his head, descended from the sky. The crowds of people

were overcome with fear on seeing them. The two presented their gift at the footstool of the king, and falling at his feet, they said, 'Today while paying worship to the gods, the great king of Laṅkā, Srī Vibhīṣaṇa, called to mind the one who put him on the throne, the crest-jewel of the Raghu clan, the glorious Srī Rāma. And with his eye of wisdom Vibhīṣaṇa at that moment realized that his own master Rāma had descended into the avatar [°*avatāre 'vatīrṇa-*] of Śrī Siddharāja, crest-jewel of the Caulukya clan. His first thought was how deeply his heart desired to come and pay you homage, but he sent us to inquire whether the lord himself would favour him with a visit. May your Highness indicate your decision through your royal mouth.' [The king declines, presents the golden chain on his own neck as a return gift] and when they asked leave to go he gave them a special message, to the effect that he shouldn't be forgotten by their lord on any other occasion when help was needed. The two *rākṣasas* disappeared into the air. From then on, the *mleccha* chiefs were filled with fear, they lost their courage, and summoned before the king they spoke words laden with devotion for him. They presented to the king appropriate tribute, and then Śrī Siddharāja dismissed them.

(Jinavijaya 1933: 72–3)

This arresting intermixture of fantasy and concrete local particularity, a sort of proto-magical realism that we find elsewhere in Merutuṅga's engaging work, resists easy historical interpretation. But several elements of the new code of interest to me are easily identified: the historical king as incarnation of Rāma—Merutuṅga's Siddharāja cycle ends with the verse, 'Just as Rāma, a treasure of virtues, was born of Daśaratha, so the world-conquering Jayasiṃha was born of him (that is, Karṇa)' (Jinavijaya 1933: 55, v. 88); the threat of the *mleccha*; and the reading of the historical event through the narrative of the old epic poem.

Far more fully developed is this code in the key text for my argument, the long-ignored *Pṛthvīrājavijaya*.[12] A historical *kāvya* by a Kashmiri poet resident at the Ajmer court named Jayānaka (or perhaps Vināyaka Paṇḍita),[13] the *Pṛthvīrājavijaya* deals with the life of the last independent 'Hindu' king of Ajmer. It was written between AD 1178 and 1193—the dates of the defeat of Muhammad bin Ghur by Bhīmadeva of Gujarat (*Pṛthvīrājavijaya* 11.9) and Pṛthvīrāja's own defeat by Muhammad bin Ghur in 1193—and quite likely between the years AD 1191 and 1193, a specificity we can achieve with few other historical poems. Admittedly this was not the first literary-historical text to imagine the career of a king from within a Rāmāyaṇa framework. One important predecessor is the *Rāma[pāla]carita* of Saṃdhyākaranandin (another Pāla text from two centuries earlier, the *Rāmacarita* of Gauḍa Abhinanda, has no recoverable connection with any historical king). The *Rāma[pāla]carita* has nothing to do with Central Asians, but rather concerns political developments in eleventh--twelfth century Bengal; the slot of Rāvaṇa minus demonization, is filled by the Kaivarta king Bhīma (cf. 1.12 and com. ad loc.). But there the epic narrative provides only a rhetorical vehicle, if even that, for the exposition of the life of the Pāla king. Indeed, the very form of double entendre that constitutes the discourse (the work is technically a *śleṣakāvya* or paronomastic poem) serves to establish difference of reference rather than identity. Moreover, the lives of Rāmapāla and Rāmacandra are not presented as parallel, let alone identical. In the political imagination informing Jayānaka's history, by contrast, Pṛthvīrāja III (like his ancestor Pṛthvīrāja II) systematically and throughout the poem *is* Rāma.[14]

The mythopolitical equivalence that informs the entire poem is made clear from the start. After a prelude in which Jayānaka calls Vālmīki's poem 'as true as the Veda' (com. on 1.5), he moves in his apologia to address the king himself before whom he is reciting his work: 'Let him alone who resides in my heart hear me, he who has entered a body consisting of Rāma' (that is, who is Rāma reborn, *jagāma yo rāmamayaṃ śarīraṃ śrotā sa evāstu hṛdi sthito me*, 1.33). In keeping with the actuality of this address, the work is very much a history, a highly referential history, of the present. The *avatāra* of Viṣṇu/Rāma as Pṛthvīrāja is preceded by an account of the pollution by *mleccha*s of the region of Ajayameru, especially the *tīrtha* Puṣkara. Brahmā, as per convention, is represented as beseeching Viṣṇu to descend to earth: in this, the Kali age, Śiva has become indifferent, his bull [here, *dharma*] having only one leg to stand on (1.44); the ascetic Buddha avatar is devoted to peace (1.45); Indra is too weak for lack of sacrificial offerings (1.46); while 'having seen his clan as shocked by the birth of the Buddha as it was energized by the birth of Rāma, the sun doubts his own ancestry now and has lost his glow' (1.48). But at this point the poet departs from formula, to have Brahmā describe what is happening at the most celebrated pilgrimage site in Rajasthan:

With you become an ascetic [i.e., become the Buddha]—with you become a friend of the deer, Viṣṇu—my dwelling place Puṣkara has been overcome with terror of the *mātaṅgas* [='outcastes,' i.e., Turks]. The place where I myself performed the final ablutions after the great sacrifice of world creation, the *mleccha* army now uses to refresh themselves after their violent destruction of temples and Brahman settlements. The place where Sacī forbids even heavenly courtesans to bathe... there now bathe the menstruating wives of these lowest of men. Half dead with thirst from their ride across the desert, those evil men slit their horses' throats and drank their blood. But their thirst was still not slaked, and they now drink the waters only those who feed on nectar should drink.

(1.49–50; 53–4)

The first third of the poem is taken up with an account of Pṛthvīrāja's ancestors, with the immediate genealogy of Pṛthvīrāja given in chapter 6. King Arṇorāja had two wives, one of whom was the daughter of the celebrated king of the Gujarat Caulukya / Solanki dynasty (whom we have already mentioned), Siddharāja Jayasiṃha. This wife gave birth to Someśvara, whose own first son, the astrologers predict, will be an incarnation of Rāma:[15] '[Your] son will be Rāma himself, born [again] in his desire to complete the task he had started' (6.35). The son eventually born is 'the enemy of Rāvaṇa, become an earthly king in the Kali age' (7.6), 'a form of Viṣṇu become a man' (8.10), 'an avatar of Rāma' (*rāmāvatārasyaiva Pṛthvīrājasya*, 8.62), while his ministers, Kadambavāsa and Bhuvanaikamalla, are avatars of Hanumān and Garuḍa, respectively (9.38–9; 86–9). When Pṛthvīrāja becomes king, 'the earth becomes a site of the riches and joys of *rāmarājya* in the very midst of the Kali age' (9.35). In chapter 10, after consolidating his power by the defeat of his regional enemies, Pṛthvīrāja returns to his capital and first hears mention of Muhammad bin Ghur:

The victorious king entered the town, where a wreath about the city tower of Ajmer—a terrible wreath made of his enemies' heads—stopped the Goddess of Royalty from ever leaving. Now, every king in the north-west is as powerful as the wind; but the Lord of Horses had true courage to boot, and so surpassed all others. But even such a king as this had been robbed of rule in Garjani [Ghazni], and rendered empty and light as an autumn cloud by the evil Gori—him who was given to eating foul foods, the enemy [*ari*] of cows [*go-*], from whence he got his very name.[16] They say he strove to become Eclipse itself, to darken the royal fortune of the entire circle of kings.... What more to say? Heedless that the king [Pṛthvīrāja] had vowed to exterminate all demon-men ['*nararakṣasāṃ' mlecchānām*, according to the commentator], he sent an ambassador into the presence of this lion in his den—King Pṛthvīrāja in Ajayameru.

(10.38–42)

The Ghurid ambassador is then described in what may be the first and is certainly the most detailed early representation of a Central Asian in Indian literature, one that provides almost a paradigm of xenophobic differentiation:[17]

His head was so bald and his forehead so broad it was as if God had intentionally made them thus to inscribe [as on a copperplate] the vast number of cows he had slain. The colour of his beard, his eyebrows, his very lashes was yellower than the grapes that grow in his native region [of Ghazni]—it was almost as if even the colour black had shunned him in fear of being stained by his bad reputation. Horrible was his speech, like the cry of wild birds, for it lacked cerebrals; indeed, all his phonemes were impure, impure as his complexion... He had what looked like skin disease, so ghastly white he was, whiter than bleached cloth, whiter than the snow of the Himalayan region where he was born.

(10.43–6)

The poet then summarizes:

Tenfold have these Goris harassed the world and so earned their name: speech they destroy by their faulty language; the directions, waters, eyes, rays of the sun by the clouds of dust raised by their armies; the very heaven and earth by the weight of their crimes; lightning they destroy by [=exceed in] their cruelty, arrows by their attachment to murderous ways [?]; and cows they destroy by slaughtering them.[18] News came that the fort of the Gūrjaras at Naḍvala [Naḍḍula in Marwad] had been overrun by these demons with the bodies of men (*nṛtanubbir asuraiḥ*), who fill to overcrowding the prisons of the God of Death, and drive Him to distraction. And there appeared on Pṛthvīrāja's face a terrible frown—the boundary line of security for the world—announcing it was now the moment to span the bows of war.

(10.49–50)

In the following, penultimate chapter of the extant text, after learning that 'Gori' has been defeated in Gujarat (11.9), Pṛthvīrāja enters his picture gallery (like the Rāma of earlier poets such as Bhavabhūti) to view a full exhibition of scenes of his earlier life as the divine king Rāma (11.24–11.104).

Plotting Against History

Whereas the Rāmāyaṇa may certainly have played a substantial role, in some instances a central role, in the political imagination of earlier India, it comes to be deployed with a fuller and more referentially direct expression—in royal cultic, documentary, and textual representations—from the twelfth century onward. The temporal trajectory of this development, especially plotted against the spatial, suggests compellingly that it was in reaction to the transformative encounter with the polities of Central Asia—with Ghaznavids, Ghurids, Khaljis (and perhaps even earlier, with the Arabs, as the Gwalior *praśasti* cited above suggests)—and the resultant new social and political order instituted by the establishment of the Sultanate that the Rāmāyaṇa lived anew in royal discourse. A minimal correlation of the reasonably secure (and generally well-known) historical record of the invasions with the half-dozen or so important materials adduced above suffices to show this.

In AD 1008 Mahmud of Ghazni defeated at Peshawar a confederacy of kings from the subcontinent under the leadership of the Shāhi Jayapāla, which included the rulers of Ujjain, Gwalior, Kālañjara, Delhi, and Ajmer. Over the following decade Mahmud made repeated raids over the Punjab as far as (but not into) Kashmir and eastern Rajasthan; by September AD 1018 he penetrated east of Delhi and Mathurā; in December of the same year he entered Kanauj; thereafter he moved toward Kālañjara, capital of the Candellas of Bundelkhand, but was repulsed;[19] in AD 1026 he raided the great temple at Somnath-Prabhāsa in Gujarat. Although Mahmud died in AD 1030, Ghaznavid military campaigns continued, and within half a century or so of the death of Mahmud, the Gāhaḍavālas begin to transform Ayodhyā into a major Vaiṣṇava centre, a building programme that was to continue for a century. Within three generations, the first dedicated Rāma sanctuaries are attested just to the south of Kālañjara among the Tripurī Kalachuris, whose own king Jayasiṃha boasted in AD 1167 that by his doing 'the Turuṣka has lost the power of his arms' (*EI* 21: 95-*CII* 4: 327; Jayasiṃha's son Vijayasiṃha repeats the claim in AD 1180, *CII* 4: 649 and n. 3).

Turkic campaigns continued throughout the period from the death of Mahmud to the rise of the Ghurids in the last third of the twelfth century. We have no direct evidence of any military actions in the realm of Jayasiṃha Siddharāja of Gujarat, but Persian sources suggest that the general of the Ghaznavid Bahram Shah may have assembled an army to attack him, and this the *prabandha* material cited above would corroborate (Majumdar 1956: 495–6).[20] His near contemporary, Vigraharāja IV of the Cāhamāna dynasty of Śākaṃbharī (reigned ca. AD 1152–67), fought frequently with the Turks; he is once described as 'the god who made Āryāvarta once again true to its name [that is, making it 'the land of the Aryans (alone)'] by extirpating the *mlecchas*,' and as a king 'of whom no doubt can be entertained that he is the Primal Person' (*śaṅkā vā puruṣottamasya bhavato nāsty eva*, *IA* 19: 218).[21] It was his successor Pṛthvīrāja II who in AD 1168 took the Hansi fort over which Ghaznavids (and Tomaras and Cāhamānas) had fought for some generations. Within a decade, the ascendant power of the Ghurids burst into Gujarat, when Bhīma II (or his brother Mūlarāja II) met in battle and defeated Muhaṃmad bin Ghur in AD 1178, and was himself defeated by Muhammad's viceroy Quṭb al-Din Aibak in AD 1195–6. Bhīma II was the nominal sovereign of Lavaṇaprasāda, and it is likely that the inscription noticed above refers to Lavaṇaprasāda's expulsion of Aibak from Gujarat (*EI* 1:22–3). Further to the east, Muhammad suffered another defeat in AD 1191 at the hands of Pṛthvīrāja III at Tarain (125 kilometres west of Delhi), only to return the following year to crush him and 150 chieftains in his alliance. Within two years, the last king of the Gāhaḍavāla dynasty, Jayacandra, was slain in battle with the Turks, Banaras was raided and, two years later, Kanauj. Malwa and Bundelkhand continued to be targets; in AD 1202 Muhammad bin Bakhtyar Khalji entered Bihar and established himself in Bengal several years later (an inscription from Kanaibarshi, Assam, reads, with annalistic simplicity: 'On the thirteenth day of Chaitra of the Śāka [sic] year 1127 [ca. AD 1205], the Turuṣkas came to Kāmarūpa, and went down to defeat' (*IHQ* 3: 843; *JIH* 15: 175). By AD 1206 almost all of north India from the Ravi River to Assam had come under Turkic military domination.

The last phase of these political events pertinent to my argument begins near the end of the thirteenth century, when Jalaluddin Firuz became the first Khalji sultan of Delhi, followed by his nephew 'Alā al-Dīn. Within a few years (AD 1296–1309), and with spectacular success, 'Alā al-Dīn subjugated the kings of Aṇahilavāḍa (the Caulukya/Solanki Karṇa II), those of present-day Rajasthan and Madhya Pradesh, and, notably, the Yādavas of Devagiri, who as we saw had begun around this time the construction (or substantial reconstruction) of the Rāma sanctuary on Rāmtek, under the patronage of Rāmacandra, the last Yādava king of Devagiri. 'Alā al-Dīn's general Malik Kafur began his campaign against the Kākatīyas of Warangal in AD 1302 and in AD 1309 finally defeated King Pratāparudra, with whom, as I noted earlier, one of the few Rāma sanctuaries in Andhra is associated, and at whose court it is likely that the first major Sanskrit poem on Rāma in Andhra country was composed (the *Udārarāghava* of Śākalyamalla, cf. Venkatacharya 1990: iv ff.). Governors of the Delhi Sultanate were appointed throughout the Deccan, and soon thereafter the Vijayanagar kingdom was established (AD 1346), with a Rāma temple at its city core.[22]

There are cases, let me repeat, where Rāmāyaṇa mythemes in inscription and possibly in temple cult had played a role in texturing the political imagination prior to or outside of the coming of the Turks and the founding of the Sultanate; such may be the case in the early Coḷa realm, for instance. Conversely, this political narrative apparently failed to make an appearance in a number of places where these events had as profound consequences as anywhere else; Bengal is such a case. There is also a disquieting neatness to the concomitance I have drawn between the activation of the political imaginary of the Rāmāyaṇa and the historical events of the eleventh to fourteenth centuries that brings to mind Bacon's 'idols of the tribe' and his admonition that 'the human intellect, from its peculiar nature, easily supposes a greater order and equality in things than it actually finds'. Granting that, the concomitance remains striking and invites some attempt at explanation.

Historical Imitation

One of the most suggestive features of this whole problematic, to my mind, is the very fact that imagining and representing the political present in twelfth-century India enabled by a recuperation of the past. The figures of the Rāmāyaṇa were as fully historical and real for non-modern India as Achilles for the Alexandrians or Brut for the early Britons ('Everything that happened in the [Vālmīki] *Rāmāyaṇa* was absolutely real,' says the sixteenth-century commentator Maheśvaratīrtha [AD 2.41.10 vulg.]). More than this, they seem to play a role for the kings of middle-period Rajasthan, Gujarat, and the Deccan rather similar to that of Cato and other Roman republicans for the French revolutionaries of 1789. In a celebrated passage in *The Eighteenth Brumaire*, Marx ascribes an almost law-like character to this process of historical imitation: with the weight of the dead generations on their brain, the living 'anxiously conjure up the spirits of the past to their service and borrow from them names, battle cries and costumes in order to present the new scene of world history'. This points, in a way, to what I intend by the term 'imaginary', the construction and representation of reality through a more or less systematic historical fantasy. For Marx, further, the 'awakening of the dead' in the French Revolution 'served the purpose of glorifying the new struggles...of magnifying the given task in imagination...of finding once more the spirit of revolution' (Marx 1963:15, 17).

Those who have considered the problem of 'historical revivification' since Marx's formulation have expanded the focus to include more complex questions of intention and self-understanding in human agency. The most acute analysis in this spirit is probably that of Jean-Paul Sartre. In an effort to combat the apriorist economism of 1950s French Marxism and to develop a more nuanced psychosocial conception of agency, Sartre wanted to find in Marx's meditation on the relationship between the 'subjective drama' and the 'real', a 'new idea of human action'. The bourgeois of 1789, says Sartre, both 'pretends to be Cato in order to stop the Revolution by denying History and by substituting virtue for politics', and also 'gives himself a mythical comprehension of an action which he carries out but which escapes him' (Sartre 1963: 45–6; cf. Jameson 1971: 225ff.). I think it may be possible to identify, following Marx, some functional dimensions of the representational gestures based on the Rāma theme, and I suggest two below. One remains troubled, however, by what Sartre persuasively argues is the reduction of 'significations' to 'intentions' that such functionalist analysis invites.

A less risky, though hardly a less complex, question concerns the orientation towards the past that this sort of imaginary comprises, and the wider cultural significance of a historicizing conceptualization of the present. Some suggestive analysis has recently been given of the ways in which, and the degree to which, action especially in moments of historical crisis, presents itself to human consciousness—or may be so represented—as a repetition or return of the past. In reference to 1789, for example, Pierre Vidal-Naquet has explored how the revolution was conceived of as a 'return, with classical antiquity as the privileged instrument of this return...marking the reappearance of the "happy days of Greece and Rome"' (Vidal-Naquet 1990: 215). More generally, Philippe Lacoue-Labarthe and Jean-Luc Nancy have argued that this phenomenon is somehow peculiar to, even constitutive of, the world of modern Europe: 'The fact is...that since the collapse of Christianity a spectre has haunted Europe: the spectre of imitation—which means, above all, the imitation of the ancients. The role played by the classical model (Athens, Sparta, Rome) in the construction of nation-states and of their culture is well known: from the classicism of Louis XIV to the Antique posturing of 1789 or the neoclassicism of the Empire, an entire process of political structuration unfolds, as a national identification and a technical organization (of government, of administration, of hierarchization, of domination, and so on) are simultaneously realized. It is in this sense that it would be necessary to give *historical imitation* the status of a political concept, as Marx, in fact, once thought of doing' (Lacoue-Libarthe and Nancy 1990: 299). I am clearly not prepared to extend the political imitative imaginary of twelfth-century India this far, but something analogous, I think, is taking place, which along with other evidence—from the early Guptas who pretend that they are the Kushans (or Mauryas) to the tenth-century Kannaḍa poets who transform their royal patrons into the heroic figures of the *Mahābhārata*—would prompt us to give historical imitation 'the status of a political concept' in India, too.[23]

But I cannot pursue that question further here, nor those stimulated by Sartre's complex meditation on Marx. I want to push instead on the question implict in all that has gone before, namely, why it is the Rāmāyaṇa in particular that is selected—suddenly selected, as we have seen, and with little precedent—as the privileged instrument for encoding or interpreting the political realties of the twelfth to fourteenth centuries. There were other choices available, not just great martial and dharmic characters from the other epics (I have just alluded to the epic transformations into Arjuna and Bhīma of the patrons of the great poets Pampa and Ranna), but a Vaiṣṇava figure ready-made for an end-of-time narrative of the coming of the barbarians: Kalki, who is found numbered among the Vaiṣṇava incarnations from at least the seventh century, and who is described by an anonymous poet at the court of Ajmer in the middle of the twelfth century as 'the form of Viṣṇu who will come on horseback, spurning Garuḍa; he will carry a black sword in his hand to destroy the Kali age, will join bull with cow, bring back the best of times, the Kṛta age, and put an end to the *mlecchas*' (*EI* 29: 181). It may be argued, of course, that one cannot mobilize political sentiment (assuming for the sake of argument such a necessity in twelfth-century India) on the basis of a future incarnation such as Kalki, no more than one can on the basis of one such as Krishna, the divine child (and quasi-fratricide). But I suggest there are positive, narratological reasons why it was Rāma and no other figure who became the object of cult and the paradigm of royal identity for kings of the period.

Imaginative Resources

The Rāmāyaṇa narrative seems to me to offer special imaginative 'resources', which though perhaps shared to a degree by other mythopolitical narratives, are present in distilled form in this particular story. They are constitutive of it and remain stable, as semiotic slots, however differently interpretive communities will specify their contents. I think these can be categorized under the two broad headings of divinization and demonization. The first points to the fact that, although the political as in so many other Indian texts is at the heart of the narrative, this text offers for the first time a special assessment, or resolution, of the paradox that the political comprises in premodern India. It does this by way of what I think is a new mediation of the religious, that is, the divine or numinous, and the political, by which I mean the nature of life in the human polity. The second heading, the demonization of the Other—a shopworn yet still indispensable phrase—relates to those who stand outside this theologically sanctioned polity. Not only are these two thematics the defining thematics of Vālmīki's epic, they are two of the most powerful conceptions of the social-political imagination. The first proclaims that the order of everyday human life is regulated by the active, immanent presence of the divine; the second, that those who would disturb or destroy that order must be enemies of God and not really human.

Elsewhere I have explored what I take to be the basic set of social questions towards which all early Sanskrit epic literature directs itself—the two great epics as well as many subnarratives within these texts—so I can be sketchy about it here (Pollock 1986: 9–25). Above all, and beyond the admitted profusion of other motifs, the informing problem is that of political power, especially the maintenance and transfer of political power. How does this principal problem—as the *Mahābhārata* puts it, obsessively, in those dreadful moments before the Bhārata war is begun, 'Man is slave to power, but power is slave to no man' (6.41.36, 51, 66, 77)—how does it work itself out in the *Mahābhārata*? As we all know, it is resolved through fratricidal struggle, leading to the death not only of the defeated, but also of the victors: 'We are the living dead,' Yudhiṣṭhira reflects when, after the battle, the brothers return to Indraprastha (15.46.8). In addition to the tragic outcome, there is a tragic dilemma repeatedly suggested throughout the poem: in part the political dilemma is intractable because it results from a fundamental bifurcation of the (hegemonic) spiritual and the political, symbolically coded in the bifurcation of the principal characters (Yudhiṣṭhira, son of *dharma*, here as superordinated 'righteousness', and Arjuna, son of Indra, as representative of the subordinated *dharma*, *kṣatriyadharma*). It is this intractability that the great ninth-century Kashmiri critic, Ānandavardhana, had in mind when arguing that the global meaning of the poem is profound disenchantment with the world (*vairāgya*): 'The great poet himself is explicit on this: "The more the systems of this world fail, and fail miserably, the more transcendent aversion toward them inevitably arises"' [*Mahābhārata* 12.168.4] (*Dhvanyāloka* 4.5).

Presupposing, responding to, and advancing upon the *Mahābhārata*'s tragic aporia, the *Rāmāyaṇa* offers a complex set of solutions. One component of this, I think, is the promulgation of a new form of social and political subordination and hierarchy, whereby the claims of a younger brother—that is to say, divisive political interest—become, in fact, unthinkable. Considerably more important, however, is what appears to be the incorporation in the person of the king of a spiritual moment, whereby he becomes at times sage-like, almost renunciant. In fact, it is more than this: Vālmīki's solution to the political paradox of epic India is the divinized king.

Far from being a later graft—the virtually unchallenged view in the West from the time of Wilhelm von Schlegel onward—the divinity of Rāma is, I have argued, constitutive of the text. Not only is it a theme that nothing in the vast text-critical materials now at our disposal challenges, but a little thought suffices to demonstrate how central Rāma's divinity is to the logic of the narrative. The poem is, in brief—and much of its aesthetic power derives from this—an adaptation of an ancient mytho-poetic morpheme (found in such tales as the birth of Skanda, Nṛsiṃha, and countless others) that requires the existence of a new life-form to destroy extraordinary evil. This must be no simple god or man but an intermediate, combinatory being that draws from and transcends the powers of both realms. The *Rāmāyaṇa* articulates this as clearly as its conceptual and aesthetic constraints allow, at a key moment (key at least in view of the interest that other cultural production, temple sculpture for instance, evinces in it), the death of Vālin: 'It is kings—make no mistake about it—who confer righteous merit, something so hard to acquire, and precious life itself. One must never harm them, never criticize, insult, or oppose them. Kings are gods who walk the earth in the form of men' (4.18.37–8; Pollock 1991: 15–54). The *Rāmāyaṇa* thus presents a very powerful—because direct and unequivocal—imaginative formulation of the divine king as the only being capable of combating evil.

The second feature I want to underscore is precisely the constitution of this evil—what I have called the demonization of the Other. The *Rāmāyaṇa* is profoundly and fundamentally a text of 'othering', if I can use this awkward neologism. Outsiders are made other by being represented as deviant—sexually, dietetically, politically deviant. Rāvaṇa is not only 'other' in his reckless polygyny—'others' always threaten to steal 'our' women—but is presented without question as a tyrant, perhaps even as a kind of 'Oriental despot' constructed by a preform of Orientalism. To appreciate this othering, we need only think how very different it all is from the *Mahābhārata*, where the shared identity of the antagonists is nearly total; not only are they not 'othered', one group from the other, but instead they are 'brothered', whereby the fundamental problem of the story becomes all the more insoluble and terrible.

The question of the demons (*rākṣasas*) of the *Rāmāyaṇa* has tested the interpretative ingenuity of generations of Indian and European scholars. In my view, all the positivistic attempts at concrete identification—with this or that shamanic, tribal, Dravidian, Buddhist group, what have you—are irrelevant to our understanding of their function within the confines of the poem itself. There, as I have argued, one productive way to think of them is from a psychosexual perspective, as representing all that certain traditional Indians—within a Sanskrit cultural formation—might most desire and most fear, concretized both together in a single symbolic form (Pollock 1991: 68–84). However, from the point of the *receptive* history of the *Rāmāyaṇa*, the *rākṣasas*, too, provide a framework for conceptualizing or representing historical political experience.

But what does all this have to do with the world of the twelfth century?

A dominant scholarly opinion holds that ruling elites in the eleventh and following centuries often met the challenge posed by the new political presence in the subcontinent not just by a militarization of the structure of the Hindu realms but also by a renewed emphasis on religious prestige and the legitimation of the ruler via his unique relationship with divinity (Kulke and Rothermund 1986: 196). If this is the case, and if—a bigger if—there is any value to a functionalist analysis of a symbolic system, it is clear the *Rāmāyaṇa* could do powerful ideological work. First, it is the privileged, if not, in fact, the sole South Asian narrative of a hieratic politics. At the heart of the tale, or rather in its logic, is not just a spiritualization of the king, but an ontogenetic argument: the king is a consubstantial entity participating in both the human and divine worlds. The identification of the king with Rāma would thus suggest a wide range of transcendent qualities and powers.[24]

Moreover, the *Rāmāyaṇa*, with its demonizing imaginary, provides, as does no other Indian text, a conceptual instrument for the utter dichotomization of the enemy. True, the Cāḷukyas could imagine the Coḷas as *rākṣasas*, or the Coḷas could thus position the Sinhalese. Conversely, other evidence does show that non-*Rāmāyaṇa* mythemes could on occasion be used to narrate the encounter with the Central Asians.[25] But the peculiar apparatus of othering offered by the *Rāmāyaṇa*, along with the political theology it provided, seems to have been particularly well suited to the political tasks confronting an embattled cultural formation for representing—and perhaps activating—the conflicting agencies of the period.

Communities or Communalism?

Beyond the level of representation and activation, I think, we cannot easily penetrate. It is not possible, that is, to distinguish between representation and reality in the adoption of the demonizing formulation of the Rāmāyaṇa—to separate out some authentic categorical response of otherness from its construction; historical reality only comes to us in forms of textual representation. Even the evidence provided by non-Indian observers themselves, as for example al-Biruni (fl, AD 1030), which seems to be almost a gloss on the political imaginary I have been mapping, does not escape this constitutive equivocation. In the masterpiece on India he wrote at the court of Mahmud of Ghazni, al-Biruni comments in a famous passage:

> In all manners and usages they [that is, the people of 'Hind'] differ from us to such a degree as to frighten their children with us, with our dress, and our ways and customs, and as to declare us to be devil's breed, and our doings as the very opposite of all that is good and proper. [He adds, 'We must confess, in order to be just, that a similar depreciation of foreigners [umam] not only prevails among us and the Hindus [lit., 'them'] but is common to all nations towards each other'].... Mahmud [of Ghazni] utterly ruined the prosperity of the country, and performed there wonderful exploits, by which the Hindus [lit., 'they'] became like atoms of dust scattered in all directions, and like a tale of old in the mouth of the people. Their scattered remains cherish, of course, the most inveterate aversion towards all Muslims.... The antagonism [qati'a, 'division'] between them and all foreigners receives more and more nourishment both from political and religious sources.[26]
>
> (Sachau 1910: 20–2)

Any easy assumption of natural hostility suggested by the beginning of this passage is cancelled by the cultural propagation identified at the end. We cannot, then, take a representation for a 'real'—yet can we say nothing whatever about the reality that informs it? Can we not at least complicate the picture so far projected by 'official' thinking?

The representation of invader as demon and defender as the divine king Rāma, in royal temple cult, documentary inscriptions, and historiographical texts, arising as it seems to do first in the wake of the political events of the eleventh to fourteenth centuries, might suggest to some that it is a response to what was perceived to be a new and special sort of threat. But was it new and special? Surprisingly little, so far as I can see, has been written on the cultural processes of the initial stages in what John Richards nearly twenty years ago properly described as one of the most complex, prolonged cases of 'cultural encounter' to be found in world history (Richards 1974: 91).[27] For this reason, and also because data are devilishly hard to find (in some of what I address below I have been anticipated by Athar Ali 1990), what can be said at present, especially from the perspective of a Sanskritist, has to be tentative indeed. I want to concentrate here on what I will call textual events, certain new kinds of textual practices and the cultural processes they presuppose that may invite wider social inferences.

Despite al-Biruni, there is evidence for long and, as far as we can tell, reasonably peaceful coexistence with Arab communities in the subcontinent from even before the beginning of this period (communities that, to be sure, were likely to have been demographically minute). New ways of life, Arab, Turkic, Parsee, could be accommodated rather comfortably within preexisting conceptual frameworks of culture—by no means were these incommensurable worlds in collision. Some especially suggestive data include a land-grant, of the time of Arjunadeva of the Vāghela dynasty, to one Nuruddin Firuz of Hormuz (*EI* 34: 143–52; Majumdar 1956: 330ff.). He is with effortless reconceptualization incorporated as a 'deeply religious man' (*paramadhārmika*) who 'in accordance with the dictates of his own religious codes' (*svadharmaśāstrābhiprāyena*) wished to build 'a "mosque", that is, place of worship' (*mijigitidharmasthāna*; *mijigiti=masjid*) in 'the Year 662 of the Enlightener-Prophet Mahammada, that is to say, Year 1320 of King Vikrama [ca. AD 1264]' (*bodhakarasulamahaṃmadasaṃvat vikramasaṃvat* [*rasula* < Arabic *rasūl*, 'messenger']). Other evidence shows that attempts at communication were made from the other side, too, even from the seemingly unlikeliest quarter. For example, in AD 1027, near the end of his life, Mahmud of Ghazni had a *dirham* struck at Lahore that carried on the reverse, in *Śāradā* script, a colloquial Sanskrit rendering of the confession of faith, the *kalima*: *avyaktam eka muhammada avatāra nṛpati mahamuda*, 'The Unmanifest is one; Muhammad is [its] incarnation; Mahmud is king' (Deyell 1990: 346, pl. 66; 73–4). Shihabuddīn Ghori also, for a short time, issued bilingual gold coins with images of a seated Lakṣmī (Sircar 1983: 652ff.). The Qutb Minar itself was interpreted simply as another victory pillar (*kīrtistambha* or *jayastambha*) by the workmen who once repaired it, as they wrote, 'during the victorious reign (*vijayarājya*) of Śrī Suratrāṇa ["sultan" as well as "saviour of the gods"] Pherojaśāhi by the grace of Viśvakarma' (Prasad 1990: 3, 19, 34–5). Full-dress Sanskrit *praśasti*s were composed in honour of later sultans such as 'Śrī Hammīra Gayāsadina' (Ghiyāsuddīn Balban, reigned AD 1266–86) and 'Kuddī Alāvadīna' (Alāuddīn Khiljī, reigned AD 1295–1315); regardless of the material motives underlying the discourse, these demonstrate a sustained and largely successful effort at intercultural translation (*JASB* 43: 104–10; Prasad 1990:3ff.; *EI* 12: 23ff.; *JIH* 15: 181–3).

It was an effort, however, in the face of obstacles, as other evidence suggests. The current textbook view of Indian history holds that prior to the medieval invasions, 'Neither religious wars nor other wars involving fundamental principles had ever been waged in India' (Kulke and Rothermund 1986: 166). The question whether the coming of the Central Asians did provoke 'religious wars' or touch on 'fundamental principles' is altogether unclear (as unclear as whether or not such wars antedate this period); in fact, it has proven one of the deeper ideological divides in the historiography of the period. One thing we can say is that these historical events had textual effects in the domain of elite Sanskrit cultural production that were to a degree unprecedented. For instance, whereas India had witnessed earlier immigrations that made lasting impressions in the popular imagination (that of the Partho-Scythians in the first century BC, for instance, or the Ephthalite Huns in the sixth century AD), we have little in literary texts of those earlier periods that is comparable to the ethnically coded representations of difference and visions of martial ferocity found later. We have seen a telling example of this in the tenth chapter of the *Pṛthvīrājavijaya*. Another is provided in a contemporary description of the invasion of Mewar ca. AD 1220 from Act 3 of the *Hammīramadamardana*, 'Crushing the Pride of the Amīr [that is, the Turk]', a drama of the 'historical present' with hardly a precedent in Sanskrit literature for the historical specificity of its violence. By contrast, however—and I would lay stress on this—the *religious* identity of the Central Asians in not once thematized in Sanskrit sources.

In the case of earlier newcomers, moreover, within a generation or two at most, these seem not only to have been assimilated but largely Sanskritized. With the events in western India of the eleventh and following centuries—which in addition marked the first time Islamic culture entered 'Āryāvarta' (the events in Avanti in AD 725 aside), despite a presence on the western border of the subcontinent throughout the previous 300 years—something new was encountered: a cultural force possessed of an apparently secure identity (or, perhaps, in the case of Turkic peoples recently converted to Islam, a particularly assertive identity), largely unassimilating in such crucial areas as linguistic and religious practice. As A. B. M. Habibullah has put it, 'For the first time in her history, India was to reconcile herself to the existence of a separate culture-community' (1961: 53). Again, the discernible textual consequences suggest a sense of destabilization among the elites of the period whose intellectual as well as political dominance was being challenged by an unfamiliar cultural formation, coupled with that kind of self-recognition made possible only by a contrastive Other. It is, for instance, during this period—just in advance of the temporal and spatial progress of the Sultanate—that the *dharmanibandhas*, those great encyclopedic constructions of 'the Hindu way of life', achieved perhaps their first and certainly their most grandiose expression: the *Kṛtyakalpataru* of Lakṣmīdhara at the court of the Gāhaḍavāla king Govindacandra in Kanauj and Banaras (ca. AD 1130); that composed at the court of, or perhaps even by, King Ballālasena of Bengal (ca. AD 1175); the *Caturvargacintāmaṇi* of Hemādri at the Yādava court in Devagiri (ca. AD 1270), and the *Parāśaramādhavīya* of Mādhava at the Vijayanagar court of (probably) Bukka Rāya (ca. AD 1400). Totalizing conceptualizations of the society, one can argue, became possible only by juxtaposition with alternative life-worlds; they became necessary only at the moment when the total form of the society was for the first time believed, by the professional theorists of society, to be threatened.[28] In such a context the threat was easily imagined, or imaged forth, as the threat of an anti-world.

In the face of substantial political uncertainty, then, and consonant with other kinds of cultural representations, the Rāmāyaṇa was repeatedly instrumentalized by the ruling Indian elites of the middle period to provide a theology of politics and a symbology of otherness. One index of such instrumentalization may well be the final textual event I want to notice, the vast vernacularization of the epic. For it is now, from about the thirteenth through the sixteenth centuries, and on the periphery of the Sultanate, that *rāmakathā* first appears in many regional languages, even in those with long antecedent literary histories. In Marathi, for instance, prior to Rāmdās's version ca. AD 1680 we find only the AD 1599 adaptation of Eknātha, which itself has a complex socio-political agenda (Tulpule 1979: 355ff.). The long literary history of Kannaḍa does not produce a vernacular Rāmāyaṇa (beyond the Jain adaptation of 'Abhinava Pampa', ca. AD 1150) until AD 1590, the so-called *Torave-Rāmāyaṇa* of 'Kumāra Vālmīki'. The earliest Rāmāyaṇa in eastern India is the Assamese version of Mādhava Kandalī, composed at the request of the Barāhi king Mahāmāṇikya, ca. AD 1350 (cf. Smith 1988: 27, 35). Like the *dharmanibandhas*, these textual effects followed the trajectory over space and time of political change.

More important than this, however, the valences now formulated and established—of the divine Hindu realm and the demonic 'outsider', a political mythology of efficacious simplicity—acquired a stability unlike any other representations, to be resorted to time and again over the coming centuries. The very fact that earlier powerful groups had deployed them made these symbolic properties all the more ready to hand, and all the more univocal. The identification of the Muslim as *rākṣasa* or *asura*, for instance, begins to find its way into the later commentaries on Vālmīki's *Rāmāyaṇa* itself: when in the third book of the epic the demon Virādha asks to be buried in a pit—for such, says the poet, is 'the immemorial custom with respect to dead *rākṣasas*'—two Decanni commentators of the early eighteenth century note that 'the Yavanas [that is, Muslims] who are the *rākṣasas* of the Kali age still follow this custom' (Pollock 1991: 251). The image becomes almost automatic from the end of our period onwards. In the western Rajasthani narrative *Kānhaḍadeprabandha* of Padmanābha (AD 1455), for example, the poet tells how 'the *asura* stone-breakers climbed up the *śikhara* of the temple [of Somnāth]', and how Kānhaḍade returned home 'after destroying the *asuras*.... He has secured freedom to Lord Śaṅkara from the bonds of the Turks' (Bhatnagar 1991: 10, 28). In the late seventeenth century, Rām Das rewrites the Rāmāyana for Śivājī, king of Mahārāṣṭra, casting Aurangzeb as Rāvaṇa, while Kavī Bhūsan does likewise, although for him, Aurangzeb is the incarnation of Rāvaṇa's gigantic brother, Kumbhakarṇa (Ahmad 1963: 476).

In this light, too, we may wish to view it as an attempt on the part of the Mughals to neutralize by appropriation this meaning system of the *Rāmāyaṇa* when, in the miniatures accompanying the Persian translation of the epic prepared at his court, Akbar is projected as King Rāma and the *rākṣasa*s recorded as Persian *dīv*s. A little later, however, in his letter of AD 1665 to Raja Jaisingh, Śivājī uses just this Persian term to refer to Muslims generally (they are 'demons in the guise of men', *ki dīv ast dar ṣūrat-i ādamī*), and Aurangzeb in particular ('[let us] devise some spells against that mad demon', *fusūnī bar ā dīv-i mast āvorīm*; Sardesai n.d.: 163, 169). And around the same time, Jagat Singh of Mewar AD 1628–52), who traces his lineage from Rāma (*EI* 24: 65 vs. 5), commissions an illustrated *Vālmīki Rāmāyaṇa* of unprecedented grandeur (Andhare 1987: 74ff.; Losty 1978: 3–14).[29] The Mughal revalorization, it would seem, did not go uncontested.

Whatever the 'real' state of affairs, the ruling elites of the period were clearly committed to drawing as keen a dichotomy as they could between a troubled present and an unknown future, and a recreation of the imagined past of the Rāmāyana was the sharpest instrument they could find.

Historicist Interventionism

If the adoption of the Rāmāyaṇa to process the events of the eleventh to fourteenth centuries suggests a complex interplay of culture and political power, equally complex is the problem of the present with which I started, the reappropriation of this imaginary in contemporary India. And, indeed, all that I have recorded seems to have little directly to contribute to this question, to making sense of the display of cultural symbols in the pursuit of political objectives in contemporary India. There are at least two questions here, both difficult to answer: what possible relationships, if any, can be posited between the re-emergence of Rāma—the Rāma of L. K. Advani of the BJP—and an earlier political semiotics of Rāma—the Rāma, say, of Pṛthvīrāja III? And what does it mean to seek to intervene in the present via an archaeology such as I have presented; what is the role of history in the current contention?

Can one argue that, precisely because it had been one of the principal components in a political imaginary repressed or displaced during British colonial rule and the nationalist movement—a non-theocratic movement led by a Westernized elite—the Rāmāyaṇa mytheme has returned with vigour in the post-Independence, or rather post-Partition, period marking the quest for India's political self-understanding?[30] If the Rāmāyaṇa has served for 1000 years as a code in which proto-communalist relations could be activated and theocratic legitimation could be rendered—if it constitutes an imaginary within which the public sphere is not sundered from the religious, and at the same time cannot be conceptualized without a concomitant demonization of some other—it makes sense that it would be through this mytheme par excellence that reactionary politics in India today would find expression in the interests of a theocratization of the state and the creation of an internal enemy as necessary antithesis.

A second thought cautions that it is conceptually impossible even to link these two historical moments. For one thing, the deity Rāma in his abstract (*nirguṇa*) form had intervened, occupying in different degrees and for some four centuries starting with Kabīr, a focal point of almost supra-communal religious devotion. This is a phenomenon difficult to correlate with a communalist coding of the personalized form (*saguṇa*) of Rāmacandra, although I do not think impossibly so (it is not clear that 'Rām' ever means Rāmacandra for Kabir; Vaudeville 1974: 115). A rather stronger reason for caution is that the Rāmāyaṇa—a work whose fluidity and linguistic variability I alluded to at the beginning of this essay but have a priori bracketed—is, to be sure, more than a single text. For some scholars it rather approximates a literary genre, library, or language, added to, reworked, rewritten in every region and every community, and in every century for perhaps the last years; the tradition of the Rāmāyaṇa, it is often argued, has been a tradition of contestation rather than a tradition of canonicity, starting at least with the Jain *Paümacaria* in the fourth or fifth century. For this reason, and because of even the Sanskrit text's instability (often exaggerated, though), some hold that there may no longer exist any such things as *the Rāmāyaṇa*, if ever there did (Rao 1991).

Furthermore, literary meaning is historical, not essential, at the end of the millennium no less than at its beginning; it is generated by interpretive communities not by texts in themselves, and these communities are always changing and repositioning themselves. Beyond all this, the Rāmāyaṇa has been the object of numerous, sustained attempts at reconceptualization. All the reworkings I mentioned are, of course, themselves new interpretations, but the past century has also witnessed new critical reassessments and conscious retargetings of the epic. This might lead to the argument that any notion of a divine political order has already been neutralized for a secular society by such reinterpretations as that of Mohandas Gandhi, for whom 'Rāmrāj means rule of the people. A person like Rām would never wish to rule' (Lutgendorf 1991: 381); or that the Rāmāyaṇa's demonization of the other has been neutralized for a pluralistic society by such reallegorizations as that of Aurobindo, who somewhere asserts that 'the incarnate *rākṣasa*' is the 'huge unbridled force...of the exaggerated ego'.

Yet it seems to me possible to reason otherwise. Consider how the Rāma legend has continuously been subject to a process of canonizing purification. The Ramanand Sagar television version is only the most recent in a long series of attempts, of which Vālmīki's monumental text is doubtless the starting point, to establish a hegemonic version, and it is this, I have contended, all oppositional versions presuppose in their opposition. A similar recirculation of energy seems to be detectable with respect to the narrative's putative communal reading. Medieval codings of the Rāmāyaṇa are an instance of a mytho-political strategy available for recurrent deployment, such as is taking place in India today. This is clear not only in the tactical choice of Ayodhyā itself and the birthplace of Rāma as the site of struggle, but in the attempt on the part of the BJP and VHP to represent Muslims as demonic (Hess 1992; the VHP's *Hindu Vishva*, August 1990: 42ff., reprints the letter of Śivājī noted above).

Yet even if this is all true, it is by no means self-evident what historical analysis of any sort, including the sort I have just made, can add by way of critique to the political conversation of the present. It is rather surprising, actually, to find the question of the relationship of history and cultural critique so rarely posed amid the ever-proliferating historicizations and genealogies of both literary and social texts. At issue are not only complex philosophical and psychosocial questions of the relationship of historical knowledge and political action, although analysis of these questions seems usually to be foreclosed by shibboleths about ignoring and repeating history, or knowing and changing history. There are also equally difficult problems of the public uses of textual forms.

How complex the question of critical interventionism of textual scholarship can be is exemplified by the fate of Salman Rushdie's *The Satanic Verses*. It does little good to try to demonstrate by a close reading of the novel that textually it escapes the charge of blasphemy levelled against it. For, after all, the novel itself—the 'object-text'—has never been the issue; it is an occasion rather than a cause. Those who insist that the novel be banned admit freely that they have not, and would not, read it. 'I do not have to wade through a filthy drain to know what filth is,' Rushdie's main opponent in India famously proclaimed. Similarly, those who have now made Ayodhyā an issue—the BJP and VHP—seem less interested in the text of the history of Ayodhyā than in the divisive politics it can articulate. The scientization of the problem advocated by progressive historians at Jawaharlal Nehru University (JNU) in New Delhi was shown for the misdirection it is when the BJP and VHP indicated their refusal to abide by court adjudication based on 'historical' evidence. In a newspaper advertisement taken out after the demolition of the mosque, the VHP declared, 'We expect others to respect the Hindu faith that Lord Rama was born at the spot where the Ayodhya structure stood. Matters of faith are beyond the jurisdiction of Courts, acceptance by historians, or approval of government agencies.' Thermoluminescence dating of archaeological remains is hardly pertinent here.

It is not easy, then, to sustain a claim for literary-critical or historiographical intervention in the face of problems that are not, in fact, literary-critical or historiographical but something else, whether post-colonial nativism, religious identity crises, political mobilization, or a new phenomenon that awaits categorization. One would think that our target should be the 'denunciation-text' rather than the object-text to which the former refers by what are often most tenuous representations. What, then, grounds the logic of, let alone justifies faith in, critical historiography in such crises?

Not only is the relationship between history and political action problematic, but so is history itself. The very conceptualization of the JNU scholars—of 'the political abuse of history'—ignores the fact that objectivist history has been one of the principal knowledge-forms in which post-Enlightenment politics has expressed itself. The very subject-matter of history is the state, as Hegel put it, which 'involves the production of such history in the very progress of its own being'. It is easier to argue the reverse, in fact, that historical writing itself—I mean historiography with the positivist-objectivist claims of Western science—bears a measure of responsibility for the romantic historicism that has been empowering reactionary politics for the past century, in Europe as well as Asia. Ayodhyā would hardly have assumed the dimensions of the present problem were it not for scientized historicality itself (objectified in such texts as the archaeological reports and colonial gazetteers constantly cited by the parties to the dispute) and the pursuit of origins it delusively inspires. When we consider parallel if more apocalyptic cases such as the role of historicist nostalgia in post-colonial Cambodian politics—the link between modern French historiography of pre-colonial Cambodia and the political programme of the Khmer

Rouge (Barnett 1990)—it is difficult not to wonder how a mode of inquiry partly responsible for the problem can be expected to solve it.

Perhaps it cannot, in fact. As if in desperate acknowledgment of this incapacity, colleagues in India have recently begun to speak of an 'ethics of forgetting', an almost postmodern abandon and 'dememorization' (Lyotard 1973: 303), as if realizing that it is not those who forget, but those who 'remember' the past that are condemned to repeat it. But, alas, forgetting history will never be a matter of ethics. History will always remain a site of struggle since, as Nietzsche said, 'only the beast lives unhistorically'. What seems to me worth considering is how to change the terms of this struggle. Part of the difficulty in confronting a complex and ongoing event like the growth of a multi-cultural society such as India's is the ever-renewed recognition of the aporia of narrative, of finding the one true narrative configuration of facts. There are no grounds free from the politics of the present to determine what story to make this material tell. It is a truism worth repeating that not only do not facts speak for themselves, they are not even facts. The 'documents' of political events of the eleventh to fourteenth centuries in Gujarat, Rajasthan, and the Deccan are themselves representations, constructions, arguments, which offer only as transparent a vision of 'reality' as the contemporary reader wants to attribute to them.

There seem, then, to be cases, not all cases but some like 'Ayodhyā', where wisdom lies in turning from the historical to the meta-historical. Abandoning the dangerous and chimerical quest for the originary in history in favour of charting the ways in which meaning has been created and promulgated in history at least acknowledges the past as something both the objects of our historiography and we its subjects create; the past as something constantly *practised*. This is not brand new programme; Marc Bloch seemed to envision something of this order fifty years ago: 'The [real historiographical] question is no longer whether Jesus was first crucified and then resurrected, but how it came to pass that so many fellow humans today believe in the Crucifixion and Resurrection.'

However unsuccessfully I may have gone about it here, such

a project remains for me compelling. If the grand Rāmāyaṇa continues to be a language of mythopolitics—not because it is inherently such a language but because there is now a history of its doing that specific symbolic work—available for encoding the paired forces of xenophobia and theocracy, one way to begin to neutralize those forces is through analysis of the construction and function of such a meaning system, and of its contemporary redeployment. As their portraits suggest, my two historical moments might be viewed, to return to the great Marxian tropology, as historical repetition: the first time as tragedy, the second as farce. But we have already seen that the first time around may have had less of the tragic about it than is usually supposed. As for the farce, Ernest Gellner warned recently that we should not trust Marx's aphorism too much; the real tragedy may come the second time.

Abbreviations

BI	Bibliotheca Indica
BORI	Bhandarkar Oriental Research Institute
BSOAS	Bulletin of the School of Oriental and African Studies
CII	Corpus Inscriptionum Indicarum
CI	Critical Inquiry
EI	Epigraphia Indica
EPW	Economic and Political Weekly
HIG	Historical Inscriptions of Gujarat
IA	Indian Antiquary
IHQ	Indian Historical Quarterly
JAOS	Journal of the American Oriental Society
JASB	Journal of the Asiatic Society of Bengal
JBORS	Journal of the Bihar and Orissa Research Society
JBRS	Journal of the Bihar Research Society
JIH	Journal of Indian History
JRAS	Journal of the Royal Asiatic Society
JSAS	Journal of South Asian Studies
NLR	New Left Review
SAS	South Asian Studies
SII	South Indian Inscriptions
SS	Social Scientist
WZKSA	Wiener Zeitschrift für die Kunde Südasiens

Notes

1. Note also Kulacekarāḷvār (ca. AD 800, but cf. Dasguta and De 1962: 381n.), a king of the Kongu-Chera line and author of some of the most notable devotional poetry to Rāma, to whom Zvelebil is prepared to ascribe the founding of Rāma worship in Tamil country (Zvelebil 1974: 102).

2. This, I now see, is also the tentative if undeveloped suggestion of Hans Bakker, at least for north India (he cites no evidence from the south), in Bakker 1987: 21–2.

3. Śārṅgadhara Viṣṇu ('Viṣṇu bearing the bow *śārṅga*') likely becomes an allomorph of Rāma in this period, as later (*śār[a]ṇgapāṇi* is an epithet of Rāma in *bhaktamālā*, vs. 55 and 128). The historical context of Rāmacandra's claim to have 'liberated' Banaras is unknown.

4. The narrative followed in the frieze on the central shrine is that of Vālmīki (A. L. Dallapiccola, personal communication, cf. Dallapiccola 1992; this applies to the outer walls of the main shrine. 'A change occurs with the set sculpted on the inner face of the enclosure wall of the same complex,' writes Dallapiccola, for which she suspects the influence of Telugu versions). Stein 1980: 388ff. points to the particular importance attached in the Vijayanagar empire to the Mahānavamī festival, which commemorates Rāma's propitiation of Durgā before marching out to defeat Rāvaṇa. A tenth day commemorating Rāma's victory (*vijayadaśamī*) may actually have been invented in Vijayanagar. The identification between the Vijayanagar king and Rāma will be strengthened in the following century, when the usurper of the Vijayanagar throne, Narasa (AD 1486–1508), is represented in the *Acyutarāyābhyudaya* as 'an avatar of Him who built the bridge over the ocean, and who, perhaps by virtue of powers stored from this former birth, laid down a bridge over the waters of the Sahyajā [=Kāverī] and took the city of Srīraṅga' (1.30).

5. N. P. Unni of the University of Kerala (personal communication) refers to the existence of a Muṣikavaṃśa temple dedicated to Lakṣmaṇa according to an inscription dated AD 920 (the inscription is unavailable to me).

6. The terracottas of the fifth century found in the north-east (Saheth-Maheth, etc.) hardly constitute an exception, given that they almost certainly formed friezes on the walls of buildings. See Pal, 1986–7, vol. 1: 232 (a fifth-century Rāma terracotta bearing a verse of Vālmīki's); cf. also Vogel 1906–8:96 and pl. xxvii, p. 155 (fifth-century Hanumān); Sotheby's *Sale Catalogue* for March 1990, no. 236 (Hanumān speaking to Sītā in the *aśokavana*). But note the prescription in the (ninth century) *Viṣṇudharmottarapurāṇa* for the *svarūpa* of Rāma and Lakṣmaṇa (cited *Caturvargacintāmaṇi*, Vratakāṇḍa: 1035).

7. Pal 1986–7, vol. 1: 74 (cf. 232), asserts that 'Ardent Vaiṣṇavas, the royal Guptas would naturally have chosen to model their standard portrait type on the idealized image of Rāma.' But what evidence do we have that there existed an 'idealized image' of Rāma in Gupta India? The paucity of representations in a recent survey (Williams 1982) implies instead the figure's irrelevance to Gupta-period artists.

8. The impulse to establish this sort of lineage may be as old as the Andhra Ikṣvākus (Sircar 1939: 10ff.). It is found elsewhere in middle-period India, for example among the Pratihāras, who represent themselves as descendants of Lakṣmaṇa, the *pratihāra* or 'door-keeper' of his brother Rāmabhadra (*EI* 18: 95. 4, 107, vss. 3–4). But note that their political discourses, like their ritual practices, are otherwise devoid of Rāma.

9. In the *Vikramāṅkadevacarita* Bilhaṇa describes the father of Vikramāditya VI: 'Then came Āhavamalladeva, also known as Trailokyamalla [Someśvara I].... Because of his purifying history [*pavitracāritratā*] he has been represented by poets as a second Rāma in stories, tales, poems, and plays' (1.87–8).

10. I forgo here detailed consideration of those many inscriptions asserting the identity of the king and Viṣṇu, although I believe, as in the case of the Gāhaḍavālas, these are almost certainly intended as references to Rāma (who is otherwise, strikingly, absent from their records). Cf. *EI* 9: 319ff., v. 16, 'Asked by Hara to protect Vārānasi from the foul Turk warrior [*duṣṭāt turuṣkasubhaṭāt*]—for he alone was able to guard the earth—Hari came into being here, with the illustrious name of Govindacandra'; and the copperplate inscription of his grandson Jayacandra (cited in Bakker 1986: 53, n. 4): 'From him, a man of miraculous power, there arose Jayacandra, lord of kings, who was [in fact] Nārāyaṇa descended to save the earth.'

11. The history of the appropriation of this term in Indian polities has not been traced; as for Gujarat, this is almost, but not quite, the first instance. In a record of Mūlarāja II, dated v.s. 1232 (=ca. AD 1176), we find, in reference to Ajayapāla, that 'he caused *rāmarājya* to descend to earth' (*-avatāritarāmarājya-*, ed. Gadre n.d: 73.9). There is no record of Ajayapāla's having fought with the Central Asians. It may be, however, to his notorious reassertion of Śaiva Brahmanism as against the very public Jainism of his predecessor Kumārapāla that the epithet refers; elsewhere he is said to have 'planted once more the trees of vedic *dharma*' (*bhuvaṃ babhārājayadeva bhūpaḥ/ucchārayan bhūpa-taruprakāṇḍān uvāpa yo naigamadharmavṛkṣān*, *EI* 2.442, v. 21). See further on *rāmarājya* below.

12. The work, already famous by AD 1200 (it is quoted by Jayaratha

on Ruyyaka's *Alaṃkārasarvasva*, Dasgupta and De 1962: 360n.; Sarda 1913: 261), survives in fragmentary form in a single birch-bark manuscript. Serious analysis of this crucial text is non-existent. Besides the superficial notices of Sarda 1913: 259ff.; Sharma 1975: 112, 220, 378; Prabha 1976: 145–78; Lienhard 1984: 219; see Pathak 1996: 98–136, who manages to ignore the mytho-political equivalence that is the central and informing theme of the poem.

13. 'Jayānaka', a Kashmiri poet introduced in the poem itself (12.63, 68), is usually taken as the name of the author. Note, however, that to one Vināyaka Paṇḍita is attributed a striking verse in praise of Pṛthvīrāja found in the *Śārṅgadharapaddhati* (No. 1254): 'I have little relish for paying homage to Śiva, no desire to worship Krishna; I am stiff when it comes to bowing down to Śiva's consort, indifferent to the temple of Brahmā. It was through King Pṛthvīrāja, by his sacred sign upon our face [?] that we were protected from enemy destruction [*asmākaṃ paramardano 'sti vadane nyastena saṃrakṣitaḥ pṛthvīrājanareśvarāt*], and so I worship the very grass on the streets of his capital.' One Kavināyakavināyakabhaṭṭa is credited with completing Bhavabhūti's early Rāma play, *Mahāvīracarita* (ed. Todar Mall, London, 1928, ms. AD 5.46).

14. Such total identification seems not to have been made without some resistance. In both the *Prabandhakośa* of Rājaśekhara (Jinavijaya 1935: 81–2), and the *Purātanaprabandha-saṃgraha* (Jinavijaya 1936: 8–9), the story is told of 'Vikramāditya', who sought to arrogate to himself the title 'Abhinava Rāma'. He is disabused of his arrogance by a display of the power of the real Rāma.

15. Pṛthvīrāja's father Someśvara married the daughter of the Kalachuri king of Tripurī, in whose realm some of the earliest Rāma cultic activities have been traced. (There seem to have been earlier marriage alliances here as well: the fact that the queen of the Kalachuri king Jayasiṃhadeva of Rewa [AD 1167] is named Kelhaṇadevī [*EI* 21: 92], links her with the Ki[e]lhaṇa who was minister to Pṛthvīrāja II.)

16. The reference is, of course, to Muhammad bin Ghur. According to Bosworth's reconstruction, the first major success against Ghazna on the part of the Ghurids, a local family of central Afghanistan (Islamized first by Mahmud of Ghazna), was in late AD 1148 when Saif al-Dīn Sūrī captured the town. For some twelve/fifteen years (perhaps AD 1160–73) Ghazna was then occupied by Oghuz 'military adventurers', until captured by Muhammad bin Ghur, who used the town as a springboard to the Punjab first in AD 1178 (Bosworth 1977: 5, 68–9, 111–29). These Oghuz horsemen, rather than the Ghaznavids, may be the referent of *hayapati* in verse 39 (although this is not, admittedly, a rare epithet of Turkic kings, and is applied to Ghori himself in 11.12). The accession

of Pṛthvīrāja III seems to have taken place by AD 1178 (Sircar in *EI* 32: 299ff., esp. 302), not in AD 1180 (Sharma 1975: 81).

17. In the drama *Lalitavigraharāja* of Somadeva (AD 1153), composed in honour of Vigraharāja IV, two Turuṣka prisoners are introduced at the beginning of the fourth act (they speak Māgadhī but are not described), and later an ambassador from Hammīra, who speaks Sanskrit and, indeed, cites the *purāṇas* ('[no king] is not [in part] Viṣṇu' [read: *nāviṣṇuh pṛthivīpatir ity eva*]), ed. Kielhorn 1901: 10–15. Incidentally, this drama is preserved engraved on stone used by Qutbuddīn Aibak to build a mosque in Ajmer after its capitulation, ca. AD 1200 (*EI* 29: 178).

18. All ten items are possible meanings of the word *gauḥ*, to whom the Turks are 'enemies', *ari*, whence they are called 'Gori' (an etymological scheme found also in v. 40 above).

19. As his father had earlier been; cf. the Candella inscription from Mahoba: 'There appeared [in the Candella dynasty] a blessing for the earth called the illustrious Dhaṅga, who...by the strength of his arms equalled even the powerful Hamvīra [sic], who had proved a heavy burden for the earth' (this may refer to Sabuktagin, cf. *EI* 1:217ff.).

20. It remains uncertain whether the mysterious *rākṣasa* named Barbaraka, whom Jayasiṃha defeated and with whom he is ever associated in legend, is, in fact, to be identified with Bahalim, the viceroy of the Ghaznavid Bahram Shah, AD 1116–57 (cf. also Majumdar 1956: 408–9). Another of Jayasiṃha's contemporaries was the Paramāra chieftain Dhārāvarṣa, who helped defeat Ghori's soldiers at Mount Abu in AD 1178 (Bhatia 1970: 176), and of whom it is said in an Abu inscription of AD 1230, 'Evidently it is the son of Daśaratha [i.e. Rāma] that has been born again on earth as this (prince) of unchecked strength' (*EI* 8:211 v. 37).

21. The pillar text is reproduced in the fourteenth-century poetry anthology from Śākaṃbharī itself, the *Paddhati* of Śārṅgadhara No. 1255–6. In the palace library of this king was a prized manuscript of the Vālmīki *Rāmāyaṇa*, the source of a copy now in Bonn (Katre 1954: 13).

22. J. G. de Caspari and I. W. Mabbett, in referring to the single temple 'foundation (*pratiṣṭhā*) devoted to Rāma as a deity' in Indonesia (recorded in an East Javanese inscription of AD 1486), point to the 'revival of Hinduism' in Vijayanagar at the same time and argue that 'it is likely that there was a direct relation between the developments in South India and eastern Java at a time when both were confronted with the expansion of Islam' (Tarling 1992: 307–8).

23. As, of course, elsewhere in the non-European world. See for example Grabar and Blair 1980:46–55, for epic 'mythification' of the

early Mongol rule in fourteenth-century Iran, and, more generally, Harth and Assmann 1992.

24. The name 'Rāma' and its various homologues become statistically very common among kings during this period. These include Rāmarāya, the last king of the Vijayanagar empire (AD 1564), and Rāmacandra, the local king said to have rescued what could be saved of Gajapati power and restored the Jagannāth cult at Puri around AD 1590.

25. Jaitrasiṃha of Mewar is 'the sage Agastya to the ocean-like armies of the Turuṣkas'; Samara, son of Tejaḥsiṃha, is 'in very person the primal Boar, whose sword was, as it were, his outjutting tusk, and who rescued in an instant the submerged land of Gurjara from the ocean-like Turuṣkas' (cf. *EI* 1: 327 in reference to Trailokyavarman [AD 1203–41] of the Chaṇdella dynasty); Kumbha is 'a Garuḍa in destroying the hordes of the snake-like *mleccha* kings' (*A Collection of... Inscriptions*: 93, vs. 42, 94, v. 46). I find only one Śaiva trope, from eastern India, perhaps late twelfth century: Viśvarūpa Sena was the 'Rudra of the end of Time' to the lineage of the Yavanas of Gargya (= Gharjistan, *JBORS* 1918: 171; Majumdar 1929: 124, v. 21). When it comes to non-Turkic references, *Mahābhārata* or related allusions are found: King Manttata of the Sisodia kings of Chittor, for instance, was a Pārtha to the kings of Malwa (*A Collection... Inscriptions*: 80); Madanavarma of the Chandellas 'defeated the king of Gūrjara as Kṛṣṇa in former times defeated Kaṃsa' (Majumdar 1956: 77).

26. That the 'othering' of the Turks is highly relational becomes evident also in visual representations. In the one attempt I am aware of to explore this question, Hermann Goetz reviews their sculptural representation in Vijayanagar temple panels and concludes that they are viewed as grotesque, rude, awkward, and wild except for those in state service in which case they are presented with the same 'sympathy' as the 'Hindus' (Goetz 1965–6: 199).

27. The ongoing work of André Wink (1990ff.) will fill many of the enormous gaps that now exist at least with respect to the political and economic history of this encounter.

28. I say 'believed... to be threatened' because it is difficult to locate fundamental cultural discontinuity caused by these events. Al-Biruni's well-known remark that 'Hindu sciences have retired far away from those parts of the country conquered by us, and have fled to places which our hand cannot yet reach, to Kashmir, Benares, and other places,' bears more a figurative than a literal interpretation. From what I know at present it certainly seems that various forms of Sanskrit cultural production even in places at the centre of the maelstrom like

Ajmer and Pattan remained largely unimpeded after their absorption into the Sultanate (see, for example, the brief family biography of the court pandits of Ajmer reproduced in *IHQ* 16: 569ff.). This was largely the case in Bengal as well.

29. On Dassehra, as witnessed by Tod, before the Rana of Mewar and his troops, the bards would celebrate 'the glories of the past, the fame of Samra...Sangram, Pratap, Umra, Raj, all descended of the blood of Rama, whose exploits, three thousand five hundred years before, they are met to celebrate' (Tod 1884, vol. 1: 620).

30. Several colleagues (including Jonathan Parry of the London School of Economics) do, however, tell of oral Rāmāyaṇa narratives that projected the colonial administrators as *rākṣasas* (specifically descendants of Mandodarī), and England as Laṅkā. None has been recorded to my knowledge.

References

Ahmad, Aziz. 1963. 'Epic and Counter-Epic in Medieval India', *JAOS* 83: 470–6.

Andhare, Shridhar. 1987. *Chronology of Mewar Paintings*. Delhi.

Athar Ali, M. 1990. 'Encounter and Effloresence: Genesis of the Medieval Civilization', *SS* 20–1, 13–28.

Bakker, Hans. 1986. *Ayodhyā*. Gronigen.

———. 1987. 'Reflections on the Evolution of Rāma Devotion in the Light of Textual and Archaeological Evidence,' *WZKSA* 31, 9–42.

———. 1989a. 'The Antiquities of Ramtek Hill, Maharashtra', *SAS* 5: 79–102.

———. 1989b. 'The Ramtek Inscriptions,' *BSOAS* 52, 467–96.

Barnett, Anthony. 1990. 'Cambodia will Never Disappear', *NLR* 180: 101–25.

Basak, Radhagovinda (ed.). 1969. *Rāma[pāla]carita*, rev. ed., Calcutta.

Belvalkar, S. K. (ed.). 1914ff. *Pṛthvīrāja Vijaya*. Calcutta.

Bhandarkar, R. G. 1912. 'Some Unpublished Inscriptions, 3 Hānsī Stone Inscriptions of *Pṛthvīrāja* [Vikrama-] Saṃvat 1224', *IA*, 17ff.

———. 1913. *Vaiṣṇavism, Śaivism, and Minor Religious Systems*. Repr. ed., Varanasi, 1965.

Bhatia, Pratipal. 1970. *The Paramāras*. New Delhi.

Bhatnagar, V. S., trans. 1991. *Kānhaḍadeprabandha*. New Delhi.

Bosworth, Clifford Edmund. 1977. *The Later Ghaznavids: Splendour and Decay*. New York.

A Collection of Prakrit and Sanskrit Inscriptions [of Kattywar, etc.]. Published by the Bhavnagar Archaeological Department under the Auspices of the Maharaja of Bhavnagar. Bhavnagar. No date [ca. 1896], no editor [introduction by Peter Peterson].

Cousens, Henry. 1897. *List of Antiquarian Remains in the Central Provinces and Berār*. Calcutta.

Dagens, Bruno. 1984. *Entre Alampur et Śrīśailam: Recherches archéologiques en Andhra Pradesh*, Vol. I. Pondicherry.

Dalal, Chimanlal D., ed. 1920. *Hammīramadamardana of Jayasiṃhasuri*. Baroda. Gaekward's Oriental Series 10.

Dallapiccola, Anna Libera. 1992. *The Rāmacandra Temple*. New Delhi.

Dasgupta, S. N., and S. K. De. 1962. *History of Sanskrit Literature, Classical Period*, Vol. I. Calcutta.

Deyell, John S. 1990. *Living without Silver: The Monetary History of Early Medieval North India*. Delhi.

Diskelkar, D. B [sic]. 1960. 'Qualifications and Subjects of Study of Inscriptional Poets', *JIH* 38.2: 553ff.

Engineer, Ali Asghar. 1991a. 'The Bloody Trail: Ramjanmabhoomi and Communal Violence in UP', *EPW*: 155–9.

———. 1991b. 'Remaking Muslim Identity', *EPW*: 1036–8.

Fritz, John. 1985. 'Was Vijayanagar a "Cosmic City"?', in A.-L. Dallapiccola and S. Zingel-Avé Lallement (eds), *Vijayanagar—City and Empire*. Wiesbaden.

———. 1986. 'Vijayanagar: Authority and Meaning of a South Indian Imperial Capital', *American Anthropologist* 88.1.

Fritz, John M. *et al*. 1984a. *Where Kings and Gods Meet: The Royal Centre at Vijayanagara*. Tucson.

———. 1984b. *The Royal Centre at Vijayanagara: Preliminary Report*. Melbourne.

Gadre, A. S. N. d. (ca. 1943). *Important Inscriptions from the Baroda State*. Baroda.

Goetz, Hermann. 1965–6. 'Frühe Darstellungen von Moslems in der Hindu-Kunst', *Oriens* 18–19: 193–9.

Gopal, Sarvapalli *et al*. n.d. 'The Political Abuse of History: Babri Masjid-Rama Janmabhumi Dispute.' New Delhi. Reprinted in *SS* 18 (1990): 76–81.

Grabar, Oleg and Sheila Blair. 1980. *Epic Images and Contemporary History: The Illustrations of the Great Mongol Shahnama*. Chicago.

Habibullah, A. B. M. 1961. *The Foundation of Muslim Rule in India*. Allahabad.

Harth, Dietrich and Jan Assmann. 1992. *Revolution and Mythos*. Frankfurt/Main.

Hess, Linda. 1992. '"I Swear to Rid the Earth of Demons": Uses of the Tulsi Ramayana and Ram-bhakti in the Ram-Janma-bhumi

Movement', Paper presented at the American Academy of Religion annual meeting.

Jameson, Fredric. 1971. *Marxism and Form*. Princeton.

Jamkhedkar, A. P. 1986. 'Ancient Structures', *Marg* 37.1: 25–36.

Jinavijaya, Muni, ed. 1933. *Prabandhacintāmaį*. Śantiniketan.

———. 1935, *Prabandhakośa*. Śantiniketan.

———. 1936. *Purātanaprabandhasaṃgraha*. Calcutta.

Kane, P. V. 1962–75. *History of Dharmaśāstra*. Second edition, Poona.

Katre, S. M. 1954. *Introduction to Indian Textual Criticism*. Poona.

Kielhorn, F., ed. 1901. 'Bruchstücke indischer Schauspiele in Inschriften zu Ajmer.' *Festchrift zur feier des hundertfün fzigjährigen Bestehens der Königl. Gesellschaft der Wissenschaften zu Göttingen*. Berlin.

Krishnamachariar, R. V., ed. 1907. *Acyutarāyābhyudaya*. Srirangam.

Kulke, Hermann and Dietmar Rothermund. 1986. *A History of India*. Totowa, New Jersey.

Lacoue-Labarthe, Philippe and Jean-Luc Nancy. 1990. 'The Nazi Myth,' *CI* 16.2.

Lienhard, Siegfried. 1984. *A History of Classical Poetry*. Wiesbaden.

Losty, J. P. 1978. 'The Jagat Singh *Vālmīki Rāmāyaṇa* Manuscript from Udaipur'. *Bulletin of the International Association of the Vrindavan Research Institute*, 4: 3–14.

Lutgendorf, Philip. 1991. *The Life of a Text: Tulsidās Rāmcaritmānas in Performance*. Berkeley.

Lyotard, Jean-Francois. 1973. *Des dispositifs pulsionnels*. Paris.

Majumdar, Asoke Kumar. 1956. *Chaulukyas of Gujarat*. Bombay.

Majumdar, N. G., ed. 1929. *Inscriptions of Bengal*, vol. 3. Rajshahi.

Marx, Karl. 1963. *The Eighteenth Brumaire of Louis Bonaparte*. New York.

Mirashi, V. V. 1955. 'Inscriptions of the Kalchuri-Chedi Era', Ootacamund. *CII*, vol. 4.

———. 1977. 'Inscriptions of the Śilābāras', *CII*, vol. 6.

Nagarajarao, M. S., ed. 1978. *Calukyas of Badami*. Bangalore.

Nagaswamy, R. 1980. 'Sri Ramayana in Tamilnadu in Art, Thought, and Literature', *in Rāmāyaṇa Traditions in Asia*. Delhi.

———. 1983. *Masterpieces of Early South Indian Bronzes*. New Delhi.

Ojha, Gaurishankar Hirachand and Chandradhar Sharma Guleri, eds. 1941. *The Pṛthvīrājavijaya of Jayānaka*. Ajmer.

Pal, Pratapaditya. 1986–7. *Indian Sculpture*. Los Angeles.

Pathak, V. S. 1966. *Ancient Historians of India: Ä Study in Historical Biographies*. New York.

Pollock, Sheldon. 1986. *The Rāmāyaṇa of Vālmīki, an Epic of Ancient India, vol. 2: Ayodhyākāṇḍa*. Princeton.

———. 1991. *The Rāmāyaṇa of Vālmīki, an Epic of Ancient India, vol. 3: Araṇyakāṇḍa*. Princeton.

Prabha, Chandra. 1976. *Historical Mahākāvyas in Sanskrit*. New Delhi.

Prasad, Pushpa. 1990. *Sanskrit Inscriptions of the Delhi Sultanate*. Delhi.

Puri, B. N. 1986. *The History of the Gurjara-Pratihāras*. Second revised edition. Delhi.

Rajendra Prasad, B. 1980. *Art of South India—Andhra Pradesh*. Delhi.

Rāmdās. 1985. *Śrīrāmdāsāṃce Samagra Graṃtha*. Pune.

Ramesh, K. (ed.). 1984. *Inscriptions of the Western Gangas*. Delhi.

Rao, V. Narayana. 1991. '*Rāmāyaṇa* as Contested Reality: Protest *Rāmāyaṇas* in Telugu', paper presented at the International Conference, '*Rāmāyaṇa*: Texts and Traditions', University of Hyderabad.

Richards, J. F. 1974. 'The Islamic Frontier in the East: Expansion into South Asia', *JSAS* 4: 91–109.

Richman, Paula, ed. 1991. *Many Rāmāyaṇas*. Berkeley.

Sachau, Edward, trans. 1910. *The Chronology of Ancient Nations* (The Āthār al-bāqīyah of al-Biruni). London.

Sandesara, B. J. and Puṇyavijaya, eds. 1961. *Ullāgharāghava of Someśvara*. Baroda.

Sanford, David Theron. 1974. 'Early Temples bearing Rāmāyaṇa Relief Cycles in the Chola Area: A Comparative Study', unpublished diss., UCLA.

Sarda, Har Bilas. 1913. 'The Prithviraja Vijaya', *JRAS*, 259ff.

Sardesai, G. S., ed. N.d. [1927]. *Shivaji Souvenir: Tercentenary Celebration, Bombay: 3 May, 1927*. Bombay.

Sartre, Jean-Paul. 1963. *Search for a Method*. New York.

Sharma, Dasharatha. 1975. *Early Chauhān Dynasties*, Second revised edition. Delhi.

Sharma, R. S. 1990. 'Communalism and India's Past', *SS* 18: 10.

Simha, B. P. 1968. 'Representation of Rāmāyaṇic Scenes on an Old Temple Wall at Aphṣad', *JBRS* 54.

Sircar, D. C. 1939. *The Successors of the Sātavāhanas in Lower Deccan*. Calcutta.

———. 1965. *Select Inscriptions Bearing on Indian History and Civilization*, vol. I. Second edition. Calcutta.

———. 1980. 'Ramayana in Inscriptions', in *Rāmāyaṇa Traditions in Asia*. Delhi.

———. 1983. *Select Inscriptions bearing on Indian History and Civilization*, vol. 2. Delhi.

Sivaramamurti, C. 1980. 'The Ramayana in Indian Sculpture', in *Rāmāyaṇa Traditions in Asia*. Delhi.

Smith, W. L. 1988. *Rāmāyaṇa Traditions in Eastern India*. Stockholm.

Stein, Burton. 1980. *Peasant State and Society in Medieval South India*. Delhi.
Tarling, Nicholas. 1992. *The Cambridge History of Southeast Asia, Volume One: From Early Times to c. 1800*. Cambridge, England.
Tod, James. 1884. *Annals and Antiquities of Rajasthan*. Calcutta.
Tulpule, S. G. 1979. *Classical Marathi Literature*. Wiesbaden.
Vaudeville, Charlotte. 1974. *Kabīr*, vol. I. Oxford.
Venkatacharya, T. 1990. *The Udārarāghava of Śākalyamalla*. Madras.
Verma, Onkar Prasad. 1973. *A Survey of Hemadpanti Temples in Maharashtra*. Nagpur.
Vidal-Naquet, Pierree. 1990. *La Démocratie grecque vue d'ailleurs*. Paris.
[Vishva Hindu Parishad]. 1991. History versus Casuistry: Evidence of the Ramajanmabhoomi Mandir presented by the Vishva Hindu Parishad to the Government of India in December–January 1990–1. New Delhi.
Vogel, J. P. 1906–8. *Archaeological Survey of India Annual Report*.
Williams, Joanna. 1982. *The Art of Gupta India*. Princeton.
Wink, Andre. 1990ff. *Al-Hind, The Making of the Indo-Islamic World*, vol. 1. Leiden-New York.
Zvelebil, Kamil V. 1974. *Tamil Literature*. Wiesbaden.

6

Anachronism of Political Imagination*

Brajadulal Chattopadhyaya

I

In a highly misleading essay, Sheldon Pollock has recently attempted[1] to prove that between the eleventh (but more particularly the twelfth) and the fourteenth centuries, considered by him to be a 'particular historical juncture', 'a *Rāmāyaṇa* imaginary came more centrally and dramatically to inhabit a public political space, as opposed to simply a literary space' (262).** The specific *Rāmāyaṇa* imaginary that Pollock is referring to is that of Rāma as the destroyer of *rākṣasa* Rāvaṇa, Rāvaṇa of this imaginary being the metaphor of the demoniac Turuṣkas whose political power was being established in India on a firm basis between the eleventh and the fourteenth centuries. Pollock thinks that the 'adoption of the *Rāmāyaṇa*'—adoption seemingly connoting a

* From *Representing the Other? Sanskrit Sources and the Muslims* (New Delhi, 1988), pp. 98–115.

** Numerical figures within brackets refer to page numbers in Pollock's essay as originally published.

deliberate, well-thought-out act—'to process the events of the eleventh to fourteenth centuries suggests a complex interplay of culture and political power' (288). Although Pollock talks about the 'reappropriation of this imaginary in contemporary India' (288), the use of the term 'reappropriation' is not really in accord with his thesis which is that '. . . the *Rāmāyaṇa* has served for 1000 years as a code in which proto-communalist relations could be activated and theocratic legitimation could be rendered' (288). In other words, after its 'adoption', the *Rāmāyaṇa* did not need to be re-appropriated, its adoption having determined, once and for all, the direction of inter-community relations in India.

Pollock's article was published in the aftermath of the demolition of the Babri mosque and the most virulent form of communal rioting which swept across the entire country preceding and following the event. Pollock begins his essay with a reference to the events of the early nineties, to the 'symbolic nexus' between 'occasion' and 'excuse', and, in my understanding, without any relevance whatsoever to the possibility of a particular political party becoming 'the next ruling party of the country' (261). Pollock has used the expressions 'historicist interventionism' (288) and 'critical interventionism' (289) in probing into the question 'of the relationship of historical knowledge and cultural critique', and seems to regard 'scientization' of a historical problem as misdirected interventionism (289): 'It is not easy, then, to sustain a claim for literary-critical or historiographical intervention in the face of problems that are not, in fact, literary-critical or historiographical but something else, whether post-colonial nativism, religious identity crises, political mobilization, or a new phenomenon that awaits categorization. One would think that our target should be the "denunciation-text" rather than the object-text to which the former refers by what are often most tenuous representations' (292). Pollock strongly feels that 'Ayodhyā would hardly have assumed the dimensions of the present problem, were it not for scientized historicality itself (objectified in such texts as the archaeological reports and colonial gazetteers constantly cited by the parties to the dispute) and the pursuit of origins it delusively inspires' (292). And yet, it is not only that there is no 'denunciation-text' in Pollock's thesis but, on the other hand, while apparently abandoning the dangerous and chimerical quest for the originary in history' (292), Pollock does in reality take up the question of origins, 'the quest for the originary' in his case being the text of the *Rāmāyaṇa* becoming 'adopted' for 'encoding the paired forces of xenophobia and theocracy' (293). Pollock has not clarified how 'through analysis of the construction and function of such a meaning system' (293) one can, as he claims it can be done, begin to neutralize the forces of xenophobia and theocracy, but from the way he has projected the historical transformation of the text of the *Rāmāyaṇa* as the 'specific symbolic work' of xenophobia and theocracy, one can go about deriving legitimacy for both from his special brand of pursuit of origins.

II

Pollock suggests, and this is a suggestion which has emanated from other authors too, that the text of the *Rāmāyaṇa* has been the most effective text in South Asia for the production of 'an idiom or vocabulary for political imagination' (262) and that 'there is a long history to the relationship between *Rāmāyaṇa* and political symbology' (262). However, in the first 1000 years of its existence, the *Rāmāyaṇa* affected the political imagination of India only superficially; 'but something very different happens early in the next millennium'; '...the tradition of invention—of inventing the king as Rāma—begins in the twelfth century' (263). The two centuries, starting with the twelfth century, are, in Pollock's opinion, crucial for the invention of the king as Rāma and for the growing centrality of the cult of Rāma as enshrined in temples. The historical context for both is provided by the beginning and crystallization of Turkish rule in India; the representation of the king as Rāma and Rāma devotion in the religious sphere are projected as a kind of national response (since it is viewed as 'public') to 'foreign' rule of the Turuṣkas. Since the response is formed by adopting the idiom of the *Rāmāyaṇa*, the image of the Turuṣka embedded in the public, political imagination is that of the demon (*rākṣasa*). The suggested historical causation is not original; it will be seen presently that in tracing the history of Rāma devotion in north India, Hans Bakker too made this causal connection, somewhat casually in the beginning but more firmly later. Pollock's argument, however, goes much beyond making the causal connection; in his construction, Rāma becomes central to a situation of an 'utter dichotomization of the enemy' (283) in the society of early medieval and medieval India.

In substantiating and explaining the invention of the king as Rāma and the growth of Rāma devotion, Pollock has used evidence from architecture, epigraphy (of the variety labelled as 'political inscriptions'), and texts. What we purpose to do now is to take each category of Pollock's evidence and examine its weightage in the light of comparable evidence available for the period. Pollock contends: 'The Rāma cult in South Asia is almost totally non-existent until at the earliest the eleventh, or more likely the twelfth century, and the growth of this cult took place in virtual synchrony with a set of particular historical events' (265). It has already been mentioned that Pollock is not alone in making the causal connection between 'a set of particular historical events' and the growth of the cult of Rāma. Hans Bakker too had postulated the emergence of the worship of Rāma 'in the latest period of independent Hindu rule in north India' and before the firm establishment of Muslim power.[2] Bakker believed that while other *avatāra* cults of Viṣṇu were based on regional, popular, and not specifically Vaiṣṇava traditions, the expansion of the Rāma cult had to wait for '*favourable* historical circumstances' [italics added]: 'This seems to have occurred when Hindus were driven into a defensive position by Muslim power, but this factor would never have led to a cult of such dimensions, impact, and importance, had not a wave of emotional devotion (*bhakti*) of a particular kind completely transformed the outlook and character of Hindu religion, in particular of Vaiṣṇavism.'[3] Although Bakker continued to talk about the 'evolution of emotional devotion of Kṛṣṇa and Rāma into a mass movement' by the Mughal period and about the impact of Sufism and Nātha Yogism on it, historiographically, methodologically, and taken in conjunction with Pollock's position, the following statement of Bakker is significantly different from his earlier statement in that it has moved away from his earlier emphasis on emotional *bhakti*:

When we try to relate the foregoing evidence to the contemporary Sanskrit literature, *we note that the paucity of Rāmaite texts matches the scarcity of Rāma temples* [italics added]. Yet, there are a few texts which endorse the view that the development of Rāma devotion, rather than originating as a popular cult that became accepted by the higher classes of society, was a current within 'higher' Hinduism in which Rāma was substituted for Viṣṇu and conceived of as his supreme embodiment. This movement gained momentum among the members of the ruling class who were evidently supported by a section of the Brāhmaṇical fold. In this connection we should note that the figure of Rāma, the ideal of righteousness (*dharma*), majestic splendour and valour (*kṣatra*), lent itself perfectly to the role of principal deity, a symbol of the desperate Hindu struggle against a new and uncompromising power that threatened to subvert its traditional pattern and values.... It might therefore be more than just coincidence that the archaeological remains of Rāma sanctuaries and epigraphical evidence testifying to Rāma devotion are found in septentrional India, in particular in the mountainous districts of Madhya Pradesh and Mahārashtra that temporarily functioned as a buffer zone between the Muslim advance and traditional Hindu society. The physical character of the terrain, difficult of access and a hindrance to effective control, spared some of the Hindu edifices from total oblivion.[4]

In this ecology of Rāma sanctuaries and the newly accentuated causation, emotional devotion is not even given the benefit of a doubt.

The evidence presented by Pollock, which is taken to contrast with representations of *Rāmāyaṇa* themes in pre-twelfth century temples, consists of inscriptional references of the twelfth century to two temples dedicated to Rāma in kingdom of the Kalacuris of Ratanpur in the Chattisgarh area of Madhya Pradesh, the Rāma complex at Ramtek, and the Rāmacandra shrine at Hampi in the kingdom of Vijayanagara (266–9). Although Pollock talks about 'several major cultic centres devoted to Rāma' being 'created or reinvigorated' at the end of the thirteenth and the beginning of the fourteenth centuries, he does not specify what they were. He is not sure himself what the situation in the Gāhaḍavāla kingdom of Uttar Pradesh was like; he refers to Bakker's work on Ayodhyā to point out that the 'Gāhaḍavāla dynasty begins to develop Ayodhyā as a major Vaiṣṇava centre by way of a substantial temple building programme' (266). Although no definite inscriptional evidence is forthcoming, Pollock would nevertheless like to believe that 'a Rāma temple was constructed at Svargadvara ghat, probably by Chandradeva. (And was a birthplace temple built by the last Gāhaḍavāla king, Jayacandra?)'*

By standards of 'objectivist' history which Pollock derides but to the method of which he has resorted, rather weakly, the evidence, considering the significant growth of temple building activities all over India from the Gupta period onward, is decidedly thin. Whether one takes inscriptional references to the sectarian character of the temples built or the evidence of the temples themselves, it would certainly not require an expert on religious history or on temple architecture to tell us that in the adequate documentation available so far, it is temples of Śiva and Viṣṇu, and comparatively less significantly, those of other deities which would constitute the majority.[5] If numbers do not matter, one wonders in what terms exactly one can establish the growing centrality of the cult of Rāma. Pollock's supposition that 'the apogee of the growth of a royalty cult of Rāma ... is reached in the middle (or end) of the fourteenth century with the founding of the Vijayanagar empire in the Deccan' (267) is again premised on the weight of his elusive 'royal cult of Rāma' in the pre-fourteenth century period. Although the Rāmacandra temple was located in the nucleus of the royal complex at Vijayanagara, Pollock too finds it difficult to consider it as the shrine of the *rāṣṭradevatā* of Vijayanagara, the cult centre repeatedly mentioned in the official epigraphic records of the Vijayanagara kings being

* The correct spelling of the name is Jayaccandra. Gāhaḍavāla rule did not end immediately after Jayaccandra. It may be noted that according to Jaina *Prabandhakośa*, Jayantacandra (Gāhaḍavāla Jayaccandra) lost his kingdom to the Muslim overlord of Takṣaśilā who was invited, by Jayantacandra's concubine, with an offer of a huge amount of gold, to come and destroy Vārāṇasī. See Phyllis Granoff (ed.), *The Clever Adulteress and Other Stories: A Treasury of Jain Literature*, London, 1990, pp. 161–2.

that of Virūpākṣa.[6] In fact, the following is the kind of sacred landscape which a Vijayanagara inscription would present:[7]

He performed various gifts at the Golden Hall (Chidāmbaram), at the shrine of holy Virūpākṣadeva, at the town of the holy lord of Kalahasti, on Veṅkaṭādri, at Kāñchī, at Śrīśaila, at Śoṇaśaila, at sacred (city of) Harihara, at Ahobala, at Saṅgama, at Śrīraṅga, at Kumbhaghoṇa, at the sinless *tīrtha* of Mahānandi (and) Nivṛtti.

Compare this with the landscape of sacred centres in late thirteenth-early fourteenth centuries Andhra.[8]

The land extending from the Southern Ocean to the king of mountains (*Himālayas*) was known as Bhāratavarsha...in that was situated the land of the Andhras, otherwise called Triliṅga-bhūmi by its association with three famous shrines (*liṅgas*), viz. Śrīśaila, Kāleśvara, and Dākṣārāma.... Therein are the five gardens (*ārāmas*) namely Dāksha, Amara, Kshīra, Kumāra, and Prāchya, the sporting grounds of Śiva and the holy rivers such as Gautamī (*Godāvarī*), Krishṇaveṇī, Malapahā, Bhīmarathī, and Tuṅgabhadrā.... On the bank of the river Krishṇā is Śrīkakula, the abode of Vishṇu (Śrīvallabha) for the protection of the three worlds.

Both the Vijayanagara and Andhra inscriptions were written in the heyday of Turuṣka penetration into the Deccan. In fact, there are a number of fourteenth-century inscriptions from Andhra, which portray in vivid colours the predicament of the Andhra people because of Turuṣka invasions and rule, and also the achievements of the local heroes in liberating them.[9] The 'political imagination' which these inscriptions display has no reference to Rāma; their sacred landscape is projected in terms of what had emerged by then as the major sacred sites of the region.

When one considers the royal cults of the early medieval period, in so far as a list of such centres can be prepared on the basis of epigraphy and actual sites, what should strike one as significant is their distinct variety. If Bṛhadīśvara and Gaṅgaikoṇḍacolapuram could be regarded as royal cult centres respectively of Rājarāja and Rājendra among the Colas of Tamil Nadu,[10] then the epigraphs and also the coins of the Kadambas of Goa consistently refer to Śrīsaptakoṭīśvara as their deity;[11] the Śilāhāras of Kolhapur invoked Mahālakṣmī in their inscriptions,[12] the Caulukyas and Vāghelas of Gujarat appear to have considered Somanātha as their most important deity.[13] In Rajasthan, the site of Ekaliṅga was gradually emerging as a major centre of royal cult in the kingdom of the Guhilas of Mewar,[14] in Orissa, the Bhañjas worshipped Śiva and Stambheśvarī,[15] and, as is well known, the cult of Jagannātha with which the entire region came to be later identified exemplified the royal cult par excellence from the time of the Coḍagaṅgas onwards.[16] These are only a few examples, but even so, viewed from this new historical process of the formation of royal and regional cults, which cannot be pinned down to any particular century, the evidence adduced by Bakker and Pollock does not appear extraordinarily significant and may have to be explained in ways other than what they have advocated.

I would like to make two further points before moving on to the next section, one relating to the iconography of the king who is supposed to have been 'invented as Rāma', and the second relating to the iconography of Rāma. Whatever little is available of the iconography of the king in early medieval and medieval art does not indicate the invention of the king as archer Rāma—a development which was expected in terms of Pollock's argument.[17] Pollock's use of two illustrations, one of a contemporary right wing politician as Rāma and the other of Pṛthvīrāja III Cāhamāna[18] is again misleading because of his suggested hint of continuity from the early medieval period. The first is indeed the invention of journalism; the second, of Cāhamāna Pṛthvīrāja III as an archer, belongs to the early nineteenth century and may have nothing to do with Rāma. If the representation of a king as an archer was intended to convey his invariable identity as Rāma, then the Gupta kings figuring as archers on their coins should all surely have to be considered as Rāma.[19] Secondly, regarding the iconography of Rāma in the context of the representation of *Rāmāyaṇa* themes in art, one may cite as a sample, P. Banerjee's work titled *Rāma in Indian Literature, Art, and Thought*.[20] The total number of illustrations included in the work is 286; dated between the early historical period and the nineteenth century, the illustrations do not indicate any preference for a particular kind of icon at any historical stage; on the other hand, they relate to a wide variety of themes in the *Rāmāyaṇa* story. Of the 286 illustrations, seven depict the fight between Rāma and Rāvaṇa;[21] of these six belong to the period between the sixteenth and the nineteenth centuries, although, since they occur alongside representations of different *Rāmāyaṇa* themes, one cannot see how any particular significance can be attached to this.

III

Pollock's second category of evidence consists of inscriptions which, it may be mentioned in the beginning, increase manifoldly in number from the Gupta period onwards and of which thousands are available. Pollock relates the 'public discourse of major dynasties', as articulated in their inscriptions, to the 'appropriation of the Rāma theme' (271) from the twelfth century. He refers to a few inscriptions datable up to the twelfth century and feels that till that stage 'Rāma and *Rāmāyaṇa* mythemes function as peripheral rhetorical embellishments, inflecting and texturing a given discourse but not constituting it' (272). By contrast, 'the later-period' political world comes to be read through—identified with, cognized by—the narrative provided by the epic tale' (272). Two inscriptions are cited to support this supposition about the envisioned political world: (1) the Dabhoi stone inscription (AD 1253) of the Vāghela family of Gujarat, and (2) Hansi inscription of AD 1167, which may be regarded as a *praśasti* of Cāhamāna Pṛthvīrāja II.

The Dabhoi inscription[22] refers to *Gurjjara-rājya*, ruled over by Lavaṇaprasāda, as greater than *Rāmārājya* and to the defeat of the Turuṣka king, dreaded by other kings, by Lavaṇaprasāda, who, the inscription asserts, could not be a mere mortal. However, the 'meaning-conjuncture'—an expression which Pollock has used to point to the identity of the king as victor over the Turuṣkas with Rāma, the slayer of Rāvaṇa—does not take place in this record. Lavaṇaprasāda surely defeated the Turuṣka king, but as his *Gurjjara-rājya* was perceived as greater than the model *Rāmārājya*, he was not being identified as Rāma. Indeed, other details of the record, not mentioned by Pollock, are worth taking note of in this context. The inscription was composed to record the construction, by the reigning king Vīsaladeva, of a temple of Kumāra at Vardhamāna, of several temples of Śiva, of the restoration of a Sun temple called Mūlasthāna, and of another temple which 'resembled a peak of the mountain of Hara'. The record refers to Arṇorāja, founder of the Vāghela line, as imitating the feats of Kṛṣṇa; however, his adversary Raṇasiṃha, slain on battlefield, was like Rāvaṇa. Lavaṇaprasāda, victor over the Turuṣka king, is mentioned as of greater fame than Yudhiṣṭhira, and his son Vīradhavala was 'the image of Daśaratha and Kākustha'. The composer of the record obviously drew upon a repertoire of available motifs from both epics, and the inscription offers no evidence of Pollock's desired 'meaning-conjuncture'.

The Hansi record of AD 1167 from Haryana does institute an identification, through the mediacy of an enigmatic Vibhīṣaṇa, of the Cāhamāna king Pṛthvīrāja with Rāma and of Kilhaṇa,* Pṛthvīrāja's maternal uncle, with Hanumān.[23] One will, however, need to locate the evidence of the Hansi record in the comparable contexts of many other contemporary inscriptions.

It has been mentioned in our text that in the repertoire of divine and legendary figures with whom our heroes are identified, the liberator is usually Viṣṇu or Mahāvarāha who lifts the earth submerged in the ocean of Turuṣka rule; one also comes across Agastya as the swallower of the ocean.[24] However, in the early medieval epigraphs, whether in the context of Yavana raids or outside them, the king as a hero and a ruler has many identities: Indra, Viṣṇu, Viṣṇu Trivikrama, Mahāvarāha, Śiva, Pṛthu, Agastya, Kāma, Revanta, Yudhiṣṭhira, Bhīma, Rāma, and so on. The use of the legendary figure of Rāma and the reference to his ideal rule are a part of a complex of motifs, and there is never any suggestion in the records themselves that a particular motif

* Pollock wrongly identifies (and therefore wrongly discovers a mistake in the spelling of the naṃe (Kelhaṇa) Kilhaṇa who was a Guhilāüta (Guhila) and maternal uncle of Cāhamāna Pṛthvīrāja with Naḍḍūla Cāhamāna Kelhaṇa.

gains precedence over others in a specific context. Let me illustrate this point by juxtaposing extracts from a few early medieval inscriptions:

(1) Miraj Plates of Śilāhāra Mārasiṃha, AD 1058:[25] The king Mārasiṃha resembles Revanta (and) Udayana in respect of excellent horse-riding, and Bhīma by his terrible valour;...he is the god of love in respect of beautiful form,...and by his deeds he resembles Rāma and other primeval (great) kings.'

(2) Machchishahr Copperplate Inscription, AD 1197:[26] 'To whom was born a king called Vijayacandra (son of Gāhaḍavāla Govindacandra) who was capable of destroying the allies of enemy kings; just as Indra is capable of cutting asunder the wings of the (fabulous flying) mountains and who (Indra), had washed off the heat of the terrestrial world with streams of water from the clouds in the shape of the eyes of the Hammīra women, when he was indulging in the sport of subduing the world (?).'

(3) Chaudharapada Stone Inscription of Keśideva II, Śilāhāra king of north Konkan, AD 1240:[27] 'Having seen the mode of administration of him who is a store of immeasurable and holy valour, the divine earth does not remember (with regret) (the ancient) kings such as Rāma.'

(4) Ajaygadh rock inscription of Candella Vīravarman, AD 1261:[28] '...Pṛthvīvarman was king, similar to Pṛthu; and then Madana ruled over the kingdom, a god of love to the opponents. Then came the illustrious king Paramārdin, who, as a leader, even in his youth, struck down opposing heroes.... Then the prince Trailokyavarman ruled the kingdom, a very creator in providing strong places. Like Viṣṇu he was, in lifting up the earth, immersed in the ocean formed by the streams of Turuṣkas. Victorious is his son Vīra, that ruler of the earth of spotless bravery who has delighted the damsels of heaven by sending them, as lovers, the hostile heroes whom he cut down on the field of battle. Victorious (and) to be worshipped by all men is he whom, when he strikes down the wicked (and) disperses crowds of opponents, people gaze at—wondering whether he be Viṣṇu riding on Garuḍa or Śiva on his Bull.'

These few samples should suffice to show that Pollock has arbitrarily isolated Rāma in relation to a specific context from the variegated world of the model divinities and legendary kings as he has isolated one *rākṣasa/asura* by avoiding reference to others.

IV

Pollock's last category of evidence is what he calls 'historiographical' or 'textualized' (273). The evidence is provided by two texts: *Prabandha-cintāmaṇi* of Merutuṅga and *Pṛthvīrāja-vijaya* of Jayānaka (*c.* 1190–2). Both texts consider their respective kings, Jayasiṃha Siddharāja and Pṛthvīrāja III Cāhamāna as incarnations of Rāma, and the text *Pṛthvīrāja-vijaya* in particular dwells at length on the depredations by the Turuṣkas in the region of Ajayameru in Rajasthan. This apparently lends incontestable support to Pollock's supposition of 'mytho-political equivalence' (275).

I have cited enough evidence from inscriptions by now to show that in the early medieval period, there were different ways of making comparisons and that, therefore, there was more than one pattern to the invocation of equivalence. For example, Turuṣka depredations and textual representation of cultural difference, it must be noted, are not unique to *Pṛthvīrāja-vijaya*; the *Madhurā-vijaya* and the Vilasa Grant, cited by us in the text,[29] have comparable details but do not seem to lend support to Pollock's particular brand of 'myth-opolitical equivalence'. This of course is another illustration of Pollock's method, that is, to generalize on the basis of select evidence without bothering to find out whether evidence exists to contradict it. Marginalization of Sandhyākara Nandi's *Rāma-caritam*—which too does not suit his hypothesis—is another example.[30]

A synchronic view of texts, advocated by us, would involve looking for different patterns in disparate material which nevertheless was the product of the same age. A synchronic view of texts—epigraphical and literary—of the early medieval period concerning kings would suggest that the discourse on monarchy was constituted by attempts to construct images of the king:

(a) as hero and conqueror in which the motif of *digvijaya* is significantly present; (b) as an ideal ruler; and (c) as protector. The meanings of individual texts and of the wide range of images in them can appear compatible only with reference to this general discourse. References to concrete historical events elaborated the major points in this discourse; attempts to arrive at a particular 'mytho-political equivalence' through 'a minimal correlation of the reasonably secure (and generally well-known) historical record of the invasions' (277) with select evidence can be made as it has been made by Pollock, by completely ignoring the broad textual meanings of different dimensions of king and monarchy.

It is reference to this general discourse which may be helpful in understanding the growing incorporation of Rāma and his rule in texts which are concerned with monarchy. Instead of focusing on Pollock's rather limited 'imaginary resources' (281) of the *Rāmāyaṇa* as provider of images of 'Divine' and 'Demon', let us examine the relevance of Rāma for a general monarchical discourse:

> Since ancient times the term *Rāma-rājya*, 'The kingship of Rāma' represents the Indian concept of an ideal state. It originates in Vālmīki's *Rāmāyaṇa*, the well-known Sanskrit epic of King Rāma of Ayodhyā. In the course of time the Sanskrit *Rāmāyaṇa* was translated and reworked in a number of other—both south and north Indian—languages. These translations and adaptations of the Sanskrit *Rāmāyaṇa* especially took place in connection with the movement of Bhakti which focused on a personal love of God. Within this context the character of Rāma, the hero of the Sanskrit *Rāmāyaṇa*, underwent a significant change. He was no longer regarded as a human king but came to be viewed as an *avatāra* 'incarnation' of the god Viṣṇu. As a result, Rāma assumed the character of a king/god.[31]

While this rather 'conventional' view effectively suggests that there are historical movements, apart from political events alone, which too can offer insights for 'minimal correlation', the suitability of the *Rāmāyaṇa* in the discourse of monarchy and its textual representation comes out further from the following:

> Both the *Mahābhārata* and the *Rāmāyaṇa* are concerned with abiding problems for kings: palace intrigue, determining the heir to the throne,

and being a good ruler. The *Mahābhārata*, despite all its mythology, is a profoundly realistic work for the modern reader, for its pessimism, in the failure of the righteous Yudhiṣṭhira to reign satisfactorily. Although the *Rāmāyaṇa*, the first *Kāvya*, is considered the elder epic by Indian tradition, it is in fact well on the way to being a court epic, and this not only on account of its more polished style. *Rāmārājya*, Rāma's royal rule, is the perfect political state, in the view of all succeeding ages because Vālmīki, the first poet, set out to make it so.... This shaping, this loss of heroic ruggedness, no doubt explains why subsequent poets often retell the whole *Rāmāyaṇa* but select only single episodes of the *Mahābhārata*.[32]

It was in the logic of historical change in India then that the discourse of monarchy was to hinge largely on the *Rāmāyaṇa*: this was its essential 'imaginative resource'. I have elsewhere tried to argue that the final resolution of the tension between non-monarchical and monarchical systems of governance was resolved during the Gupta period; the pace of the proliferation of local kingly power through the process of local-level state formation; crystallization of regional kingdoms, and the triumph of monarchical ideology were all developments of the post-Gupta period which substantially changed the political landscape of India and underlined the centrality of *varṇāśramadharma* in the monarchical discourse.[33] This spatial expansion of what we have called state society, during the centuries following the Gupta period, was the historical context in which the growing importance of Rāma and the *Rāmāyaṇa* has to be located; in this state society, defined by *varṇāśramadharma*, the Yavanas or the Mlecchas, as social groups, would always be outsiders and would be perceived as others. To link Rāma and the Rāmāyaṇa not to this vision of the ideal state but to invasions alone would be at the cost of sidelining the broad processes of historical change which integrated disparate regions of India through the centuries marked by the emergence of the large regional states of early medieval times.

One final point. There cannot, perhaps, be any disagreement with Pollock that analysis of ways in which meanings are created and promulgated in history is a more worthwhile historical enterprise than attempts at simply unravelling the authenticity, or otherwise, of historical events. But perhaps the historical, objective 'reality' of meanings is as elusive—and dubious—as the reality of historical events themselves. The quality of investigation into meanings will also be contingent upon the contemporary privileged position of the investigator with the particular ideological position he may choose to take or espouse; Pollock has demonstrated how contemporary communal consciousness can be traced back directly to the early medieval phase of Indian history and that a construction of the history of communal consciousness does not have to make any reference to its colonial phase. The past, one cannot help feeling after confronting this 'originary', will ever remain a dumb victim of its wily investigators.

Notes and References

1. 'Ramayana and Political Imagination in India', *The Journal of Asian Studies*, vol. 53, no. 2 (1993), pp. 261–97.

2. Hans Bakker, *Ayodhyā*, pt. I (Groningen, 1986), p. 66.

3. Ibid.

4. Hans Bakker, 'Reflections on the evolution of Rāma devotion in the light of textual and archaeological evidence', *Wiener Zeitschrift für die Kunde Südasiens und Archiv für Indische Philosophie*, Band XXXI (1987), pp. 20–1.

5. For forming an impression about the sectarian affiliations of numerous temples constructed in the early medieval period, it is necessary to wade through a vast mass of epigraphic and architectural evidence. R. K. Chattopadhyaya was kind enough to go through, with me, a number of relevant recent publications on early medieval temples and confirm my initial impressions. For a preliminary idea, the following recent publications may be cited: Krishna Deva, *Temples of India*, vol. I (Text) (Delhi, 1996), *passim*, and Site and Temple Index; M. W. Meister (ed.), *Encyclopaedia of Indian Temple Architecture, South India: Lower Draviḍadeśa* (Delhi, 1983); see also the architectural survey by S. K. Saraswati in R. C. Majumdar (ed.), *The Struggle for Empire (The History and Culture of the Indian People)* (Bombay, 1957), ch. 20.

6. Anila Verghese too underlines the importance of the Rāmacandra temple as a royal temple, but distinguishes it from the guardian deity of the State: 'Pampā Virūpāksha has undoubtedly been the principal deity at the site from before the founding of the empire onwards, and he was adopted as the guardian deity of the Vijayanagara State,' Anila Verghese, *Religious Traditions in Vijayanagara: As Revealed through its*

Monuments (Delhi, 1995), p. 132. Verghese finds no evidence of a Rāma temple at Vijayanagara before the early fifteenth century and associates the growth of Vaiṣṇava cults—those of Rāma and Viṭhala—with vigorous Mādhva and Śrīvaṣṇava activity during the late fifteenth and sixteenth centuries; ibid. The following statement of Pollock therefore is again misleading: 'Governors of the Delhi Sultanate were appointed throughout the Deccan, and soon thereafter the Vijayanagara Kingdom was established (AD 1346), with a Rāma temple at its city core (279).' G. Michell, on the other hand, believes that the nucleus of Vijayanagara's early sacred centre at Hampi consisted of Śaivite shrines; examples of early Vijayanagara shrines in the Telugu zone are: Mādhavarāya temple at Gorantla near Penukonda and Mallikārjuna at Śrīsailam; see G. Michell, 'Architecture and Art of Southern India' (*The New Cambridge History of India* 1:6) (Cambridge, 1995), pp. 31–2.

7. E. Hultzsch, 'Hampi Inscription of Krishnaraya, dated Śaka 1430', *Epigraphia Indica*, I, pp. 361–71.

8. K. H. V. Sarma and T. Krishnamurty, 'Annavarappadu Plates of Kataya Vema Reddy', *Epigraphia Indica*, vol. 36, p. 168.

9. See ch. 2 of this volume.

10. For the Colas, see K. A. Nilakanta Sastri, *The Colas* (Madras, 2nd edn, rpt, 1975), chs. 9, 10.

11. G. M. Moraes, *The Kadamba Kula*, Bombay, 1931.

12. V. V. Mirashi, *Inscriptions of the Śilāhāras*, XLIX, New Delhi, 1977.

13. See, for example, G. Bühler, 'Eleven landgrants of the Chaulukyas of Anhilvad: A contribution to the history of Gujarat', *Indian Antiquary*, vol. 6 (1877), pp. 180–214.

14. Nandini Sinha, 'A Study of State and Cult: The Guhilas, Pasupatas and Ekalingaji in Mewar, seventh to fifteenth centuries AD', *Studies in History*, vol. 9, no. 2 (1993), pp. 162–82.

15. The usual expression in inscriptions is: *Stambheśvarī-labdhavaraprasāda*; see. S. Tripathi, *Inscriptions of Orissa*, vol. 6 (Bhubaneswar, 1974), pp. 66, 73, 79, etc.

16. A. Eschmann, H. Kulke and G. C. Tripathi (eds), *The Cult of Jagannath and the Regional Tradition of Orissa* (Delhi, 1978), *passim*.

17. Royal portrait sculptures are not available in plenty, but even so reference may be made to a few: (1) Rājendra, the Cola ruler, receiving a floral garland of victory from Śiva at Gangaikondacolapuram [G. Michell, *The Hindu Temple: An Introduction to its Meaning and Form* (Chicago, 1988), p. 17]; (2) the Coḍagaṅga ruler at Konarak. Of several representations of Narisiṃha, the Orissan ruler of the thirteenth century at Konark, only one is that of an archer (collections at the National Museum, New Delhi, and the photo-archives of the Archaeological

Survey of India); (3) Candella ruler and his consort as worshippers [Devangana Desai, *The Religious Imagery of Khajuraho* (Mumbai, 1996), p. xxviii]; (4) Kṛṣṇadevarāya: represented as a worshipper at north Gopura at Chidambaram [George Michell, 1995, pp. 158–9, fig. 114].

The observations of Anila Verghese on the iconography of the king and of Rāma at Vijayanagara would be pertinent in this context: 'If the king in Vijayanagara is identified with Rāma, in turn Rāma is also portrayed as a king. This is to be found in certain reliefs in the temples, which is at variance with the traditionally accepted iconographic representations of this god. In these unusual reliefs, Rāma is shown sitting on a throne-like seat, leaning against a cushion or bolster, with one leg crossed over the other, often with one hand raised in the *tarjanī-mudrā* (one finger pointing upwards) and usually with a shawl draped around one arm. He is depicted exactly as the kings are on the enclosure walls of the Rāmachandra temple complex, on the Mahanavami platform, and elsewhere. The only difference is in the headdress: while the god wears the *Kirīṭamukuṭa*, the typical crown worn by Viṣṇu in his diverse manifestations, the kings are bareheaded or wear the *Kullāyi*': Anila Verghese, 1995, p. 51, pls. 19, 20. In the iconography, neither the god nor the king is Kodaṇḍa-Rāma.

18. Pollock, pp. 290, 291 [original version].

19. For Gupta kings as archers, see John Allan, *Catalogue of the Coins of the Gupta Dynasties and of Śaśāṅka, King of Gauḍa* (London, rpt, 1967). pp. 6–7, 24–33, 61–6, etc.

20. P. Banerji, *Rāma in Indian Literature, Art, and Thought*, 2 vols (text and illustrations) (Delhi, 1986).

21. Ibid., nos. 202, 204–9.

22. G. Bühler, 'An Inscription from Dabhoi', *Epigraphia Indica*, I, pp. 20–32.

23. D. R. Bhandarkar, 'Hansi Stone Inscription of Prithvirāja, (Vikrama) Samvat 1224,. *Indian Antiquary*, vol. 41 (1912), pp. 17–19.

24. N. Venkataramanayya and M. Somasekhara Sharma, 'Vilasa Grant', p. 253, fn. 3.

25. V. V. Mirashi, *Inscriptions of the Śilāhāras*, pp. 200ff.

26. P. Prasad, *Sanskrit Inscriptions*, pp. 58–70.

27. V. V. Mirashi, *Inscriptions of the Śilāhāras*, pp. 169–72.

28. F. Kielhorn, 'Two Chandella Stone Inscriptions from Ajaygadh', *Epigraphia Indica*, I, pp. 325–30.

29. See ch. 2 of Chattopadhyaya's book.

30. Cf. Pollock (283): 'True, the Cālukyas could imagine the Colas as *rākṣasas*, or the Colas could thus position the Sinhalese. Conversely, other evidence does show that non-*Rāmāyaṇa* mythemes could on

occasion be used to narrate the encounter with the Central Asians.' It is, however, not enough to refer to the other evidence; one expects to learn how the evidence cited is intelligible in the light of the hypothesis offered or whether it is simply negligible aberration. Similarly, Pollock does not offer to explain how his evidence (285) which may demonstrate a 'sustained and largely successful effort at intercultural translation' can be reconciled with his notion of 'the utter dichotomization of the enemy' (283).

31. A. G. Menon and G. H. Schokker, 'The Concept of Rāmārājya in South and North Indian Literature', in A. W. Van Den Hoek, D. H. A. Kolff, and M. S. Oort (eds), *Ritual, State, and History in South Asia: Essays in Honour of J. C. Heesterman*, Leiden, New York, 1992, p. 615.

32. David Smith, *Ratnākara's Haravijaya: An Introduction to the Sanskrit Court Epic* (Delhi, 1985), pp. 14–15.

33. B. D. Chattopadhyaya, *The Making of Early Medieval India* (Delhi, 1994), chs. 1 and 8. Also idem, 'Historiography, History and Religious Centres: Early Medieval North India, circa AD 700–1200', in Vishakha N. Desai and Darielle Mason (eds), *Gods, Guardians, and Lovers: Temple Sculptures from North India AD 700–1200* (New York and Ahmedabad, 1993), pp. 33–47.

7

The Founding of the Ramanandi Sect*

Richard Burghart

The Ramanandi sect, which is said to have been founded by Swami Ramanand in the fourteenth century, performed a particularly significant role in the development of both Hindu religion and Hindi literature. The ascetics of the Ramanandi sect led a minor social revolution in the Ganges basin by recruiting women and members of servant and untouchable castes into their sect. Moreover, the followers of Swami Ramanand wrote much of their sectarian literature in the vernacular languages of upper India rather than in Sanskrit. The study of modern Hindi literature, as it is taught in the schools and colleges of India today, usually begins with the devotional stories and poems written by such great saints as Tulsi Das, Mira Bai, and Kabir whom the Vaisnavite bards claim were spiritual descendants of Swami Ramanand. Given the historical importance of the Ramanandi sect, it is surprising to find so little information in the sectarian literature on the events which led to the formation of the sect. Drawing upon these sectarian sources, scholars have sought to

* From *Ethnohistory* 25, 2 (Spring 1978): 121–39.

reconstruct the early history of the Ramanandi sect. The facts, however, are meagre and the inferences which scholars have used to interpret these facts are various so that there is some disagreement over the circumstances which actually led Ramanand to found the Ramanandi sect. In this essay I shall apply an anthropological analysis to the information from sectarian sources and propose instead that the reason why the founding of the Ramanandi sect has remained such an enigma to scholars is because Swami Ramanand never did actually found the Ramanandi sect.

I

According to the classical codes of religious law, Hindus who were twice-born, that is to say those who were born from their mother's womb and reborn through sacrifice in the body of a Brahman, a warrior (*Kśatriya*), or a herder or tiller (*Vaiśya*), could renounce the family which assisted at both of their births and follow a discipline which, through the control of their body, speech, and mind, would result in their union with Brahma. Only twice-born Hindus were thought to be endowed with sufficient spiritual energy to discipline themselves in such a way; only twice-born Hindus were thought to possess a body of sufficient purity to make themselves a suitable subject of discipline. Thus, according to the classical codes, servants (Sūdra), untouchables, and women did not possess the right to renounce their family and to become an ascetic.

During the sixteenth century, however, some Hindu ascetics who had been attracted by the new devotional discipline which had come from the Dravidian south, carried the following message across the Ganges basin, 'Do not inquire from anyone his caste or sect; whoever worships the Lord belongs to the Lord.' For those ascetics their Lord and Saviour was Ram Candra who had been born many years ago in the House of Dasrath in Ayodhya and who had defeated in battle Ravana, the demon King of Lanka. Ram Candra was the seventh incarnation of the god Vishnu Narayan, and it was Vishnu Narayan who at the dawn of time spawned this mind-born cosmos. Floating on the Sea of Milk, Vishnu Narayan was stirred by the residual energy of previous creations and his Supreme Soul fragmented. Each fragment of his Soul became embodied in a creature inhabiting this world. To be sure, all creatures are classified into species (*jāti*) and species differ from one another according to their relative spiritual energy and purity of body; nevertheless all creatures are animated by a fraction of the same Supreme Soul. It is desire for this created world which hinders the reunion of the embodied soul and the Supreme Soul and which condemns the embodied soul to be born from diverse wombs over many lifetimes, perpetually suffering the pains of birth and death. Devotion to Ram and the repetition of His name, however, secure the release of the embodied soul from the perpetual cycle of rebirths. Since Ram, as Vishnu Narayan, dwells in all living creatures, then why should not all mankind regardless of caste, sex, or sect have the right to renounce their families and pass the remainder of their lives in the service of Ram? The ascetics who propagated this new message claimed that they heard the teaching from their preceptors. The preceptors were living evidence of the new teaching, for they included not only several Brahmans and a Rajput king, but also a barber, a farmer, a cobbler, a woman, and even a Muslim weaver. The preceptors called themselves Ramanandis, for they, in turn, claimed that they had heard the message from a saint by the name of Ramanand who used to live on the banks of the Ganges in the holy city of Benaras.

Very little is known about Swami Ramanand and the early development of the Ramanandi sect apart from information which is derived from sectarian sources, the purposes of which are not always historical. Most scholars who have written about Swami Ramanand have assumed that Ramanand, sometime after having been initiated into the Sri sect of Ramanuja, founded his own sect known as the Ramanandi or Ramavat sect. Scholars have either considered the sectarian sources to be accurate or they have second-guessed the literature in order to reconstruct the events which led to the founding of the Ramanandi sect. For Farquhar (1967: 324–5) Ramanand was a Ramaite ascetic living among the Sri Vaisnavas in Tamil Nadu who went north to Benaras around AD 1430 preaching the *Adhyatma Ramayana* and Ramanuja's *Sri Bhasya*. According to Ghurye (1964: 165) Ramanand was born in northern India at Prayag in AD 1300. He was initiated as a *Tridandi sannyasi* by Swami Raghavanand who was the abbot of the Sri monastery in Benaras. Wilson (1846: 31–2) claimed that Ramanand was born sometime after AD 1400 and that he was initiated into the Sri sect founded by Ramanuja. Ramanand went on a pilgrimage and when he returned to the Sri monastery, he was denied commensality with his co-disciples because they assumed that during his pilgrimage Ramanand could not have observed the caste and sect rules of commensality. The accusation incensed Ramanand who thereupon quit the Sri monastery and established his own sect. Sinha (1957: 61–4) recounts a similar incident but claims that it was not Ramanand but instead his *guru* Raghavanand who was denied commensality. The incident, however, did not provoke the establishment of any new sect. Instead, it was in the course of his travels that Ramanand fell under the doctrinal influence of Tantrism. This set him apart from his co-disciples in the Sri sect who followed exclusively the devotional doctrine of Ramanuja. Ramanand left the Dravidian south and travelled north not in order to spread the devotional doctrine of Ramanuja but in order to receive the Tantric doctrine of the *nirguna* ascetics who lived in the Ganges basin. Barthwal (1936: 13; 1955: 30), however, found a different reason for the establishment of the Ramanandi sect. According to the *Bhavisya Purana* (4.21.52–3) Ramanand went to Ayodhya where he converted to Hinduism those Hindus who had been previously converted by force to Islam. Barthwal then assumes that Ramanand had been initiated into the Sri sect of Ramanuja and then infers that the acceptance of reconverted Muslims within the Sri sect antagonized the more orthodox elements within the Sri sect and caused a schism which led to the founding of the Ramanandi sect.

These diverse and somewhat contradictory opinions oblige us to acknowledge at the outset that we do not know with any degree of certainty the most basic facts about Swami Ramanand. We do not even know, for example, where he was born, when he was born, and when he died. Nor is the question of his spiritual genealogy beyond dispute. Of the few books and poems written by him, some of them may have, in fact, been written by his followers and then attributed to Ramanand in order to give legitimacy to some doctrinal tendency within the sect. Sectarian sources disagree over the names of several of his disciples, and the saying for which Ramanand is most remembered, 'Do not inquire from anyone his caste or sect; whoever worships the Lord belongs to the Lord,' cannot even be found in any of the writings attributed to Ramanand.[1] The lack of accurate information about Swami Ramanand and his role in the early development of the sect suggests the possibility that he was not a historically important or doctrinally unique enough saint in his own lifetime to have caused others to note his biography. When compared with Sankaracarya, Gorakhnath, and Caitanya who, it is said, also founded important ascetic sects, we know relatively little either about the historical or the legendary Ramanand. Moreover, we know more about Sankaracarya, Gorakhnath, and Caitanya from their sectarian literature than about their direct disciples, but in Priya Dass' commentary on Nabha Ji's *Sri Bhakta Mala*, the account of the life of Ramanand is dwarfed by the accounts of the lives of his disciples.

While scholars have sifted through this poverty of information in order to reconstruct the life of Ramanand and the early history of the sect, they have overlooked one of the most important facts of all, and that is the poverty of information. The one thing which we do know is that we know very little indeed about Swami Ramanand; moreover, for a very long time, our ignorance has been shared by the Ramanandi ascetics themselves. This fact is important, for one feature of the Ramanandi sect which appears unique in comparison with other ascetic sects is its diversity. During the sixteenth and seventeenth centuries, both devotional and Tantric disciplines were attributed to Ramanand; both twice-born Hindus as well as members of the servant and untouchable castes, women, and perhaps even Muslims were recruited into the sect. A number of poems written in the vernacular were attributed to Ramanand; but other important texts attributed to Ramanand were written in Sanskrit and hence were accessible only to disciples of Brahman birth. Some of Ramanand's descendants continued to observe caste rules of commensality within the sect while other descendants abandoned such rules. This diversity during the early period of the sect is not limited to belief and practice; there was also a diversity of Ramanands. For some, Ramanand was a spiritual descendant of Ramanuja. For others Ramanand was only a follower of the doctrine of Ramanuja. Some of Ramanand's followers obviated the historical question of Ramanand's spiritual ancestry by making him an incarnation of Lord Ram. For the *nirguna* ascetics, who worshipped the attributeless Supreme Being, Ramanand was the eternal truth-*guru* (*satguru*). The plethora of Ramanands suggests at least that if more had been known about the historical Ramanand then it would not have been possible to attribute so many diverse doctrines and practices to him. But these diverse images of Ramanand, which serve a devotional purpose for the Hindu ascetic, tell us very little about the life of Ramanand. Why in the early sectarian literature is there such a poverty of biographical information on a saint who was supposed to have caused a social revolution in Hindu asceticism?[2] Could the reason why scholars have found the real Ramanand so elusive be that Swami Ramanand never did personally found a sect of sadhus known as the Ramanandi or Ramavat *sampradaya*?

II

The scholars who have written about Swami Ramanand have assumed that Ramanand founded the Ramanandi sect and then they have searched for information concerning the events which led to the founding of the sect. Rather than make such an assumption, let us use the same information and see what we can deduce about the early history of the sect from a knowledge of its social structure. To become a member of any of the Vaisnavite sects, the candidate approaches a member of the sect and asks to receive the ritual formula, called the *mantra*, of the sect's tutelary deity. The member of the sect who bestows the initiatory *mantra* upon the candidate becomes the candidate's *guru*. The *guru*, in turn, received the *mantra* from his *guru* who received it from his *guru* and so on back to the founder of the sect who heard the *mantra* from his *guru* and so on back through time until one ultimately comes to the dawn of time when the tutelary deity divulged His personal *mantra*. This initiatory and redeeming *mantra* of the tutelary deity is a secret which is jealously guarded by the sect. Only by initiation can one come to know it. It is the basis of the sect's unique historical origin and of its spiritual independence from other sects.

The *mantra* is the link between the *guru* and the disciple which down through the generations forms the segmentary structure of the sect. With their segmentary structure the Ramanandi sect together with the other Hindu ascetic sects appear to us as so many tribes composed of segmentary lineages which perpetuate themselves by spiritual initiation rather than sexual reproduction and which exploit a territory for its alms rather than for its natural wealth. In order to maintain themselves over time, the ascetics of the various Hindu sects acquired access to three important resources: devotees and disciples, pilgrimage routes and pilgrimage centres, and political patronage. The availability of these resources was limited. Although some ascetic sects were founded in the outerlying regions of the subcontinent, nearly all of them, like the Ramanandi sect, eventually spread to the Ganges basin where, given the number of sects operating on that territory, the competition for these three limited resources was very intense. In the competition for devotees and disciples, Ramanand and/or his followers gained a significant advantage over their rival sects. The servant castes, untouchables, women, and former Hindus who had converted by choice or by threat of force to Islam comprised more than three-fourths of the population of the Ganges basin and constituted an immense hitherto unexploited source of devotees and disciples for an ascetic sect. The competition for control over pilgrimage routes and pilgrimage centres led to outright battles between the Ramanandi sect and the Dasnami sect of Sannyasis in which the Ramanandi sect did not fare so well. In the early eighteenth century, the Sannyasis encircled and captured Ayodhya on the very birthday of Lord Ram thereby routing the Ramanandi ascetics from the birthplace of their tutelary deity (Prasad 1930: 42). According to the sectarian bards, the loss of Ayodhya provoked the leaders of the Vaisnavite sects to call the conference at Galata near Jaipur in the course of which the Vaisnavite ascetics organized themselves into militant orders (*akhāṛā*). By the close of the eighteenth century, the militant orders of the Dasnami sect and the Ramanandi sect were engaged in armed combat for the control of pilgrimage centres.[3] In 1760 the Dasnami ascetics captured Hardwar and it was not until the British administered the district that the Ramanandi ascetics were able to return to this pilgrimage centre (Farquhar 1925: 17). In 1789 a battle erupted over the bathing rights at the Kasi Sangam on the Godavri River in which reportedly 12,000 ascetics lost their lives.[4] Political patronage was an important factor in the development of the ascetic sects. As the 'Abode of Compassion' (*karuṇā nidhān*), the king was the supreme court of appeal in the kingdom. Disputes between sects, such as the one over the bathing rights at the Kasi Sangam on the Godavri River, were settled by the king or by his courts. As the 'Lord of the Land' (*bhūpati*), the king was the most significant donor of land in alms within the kingdom. The various ascetic sects fought both military and yogic battles against one another in order to obtain royal patronage. For example, according to legends in the sixteenth century, Taranath, an ascetic of the Gorakhnathi sect, roamed the region north and west of Delhi where he enjoyed the patronage of the local kings. When Taranath was defeated in a yogic battle at Galata by Krisna Das Payahari (Saran 1969: 305) and at Pindori by Bhagawan Ji (Goswamy and Grewal 1969: 5–6), the local rulers saw that the spiritual power of these Ramanandi ascetics was greater than that of the Gorakhnathi ascetic and they shifted their patronage from the Gorakhnathi to the Ramanandi sect. Krisna Das Payahari built his monastery at Galata and Bhagawan Ji built his monastery at Pindori near Simla. In the course of time, both of these monasteries prospered from the munificent royal gifts of land.

The *guru*–disciple succession provides the segmentary structure of the ascetic sect; spiritual genealogies record the names and delineate the relationships of that structure. The *guru*–disciple relationship is personal and irrevocable and, in theory, the spiritual genealogies are as unalterable as the events which they record. A perusal of spiritual genealogies of the Ramanandi sect reveals, however, significant differences in the records of the transmission of the *mantra* from *guru* to disciple. Insofar as the purpose of spiritual genealogies is historical then spiritual genealogies are records of facts and the discrepancies which occur among different spiritual genealogies may be judged according to their truth or falsehood. Insofar as the purpose of spiritual genealogies is political, every falsehood becomes a truth of another kind. That is to say, every genealogy is a record of a strategy in which the sect has reinterpreted its past in order to compete more effectively for the three limited resources which are necessary for its survival in the present. Let us consider four spiritual genealogies of the Ramanandi sect taken from the early fifteenth century, late sixteenth century, early eighteenth, and early twentieth century and analyse them against a backdrop of 600 years of competition among ascetic sects for devotees and disciples, pilgrimage routes and pilgrimage centres, and political patronage.

In *Ramarcanapaddhiti*, a Sanskrit text attributed to Ramanand, the author traces the following spiritual ancestry of Swami Ramanand[5] (Figure 7.1). The *Ramarcanapaddhiti* genealogy is interesting because it includes in the tenth generation the Vaisnavite saint Ramanuja who founded the Sri sect in the Tamil-speaking region of south India during the twelfth century. Let us briefly compare the above spiritual genealogy of the Ramanandi sect with the genealogy of the Sri sect founded by Ramanuja[6] (Figure 7.2). The two genealogies are similar in three respects. First, the *Ramarcanapaddhiti* genealogy is written in Sanskrit, the medium by which Ramanuja and the ascetics of the Sri sect transmitted their doctrine. Second, the Sri genealogy begins with a celestial couple, Vishnu Narayan who gave the *mantra* to Lakshmi; the *Ramarcanapaddhiti* genealogy also begins with a celestial couple, Ram Candra who gave the *mantra* to Sita. Ram Candra was an incarnation of Vishnu Narayan and Sita was an incarnation of Lakshmi. Third, the names in the two genealogies are identical from the third to the tenth generation. The sole difference between the two genealogies is that in the

1. Ram Candra
2. Sita
3. Visvaksen
4. Sathkop
5. Nathmuni
6. Pundrikaksa
7. Ram Misra
8. Yamunacarya
9. Mahapurnacarya
10. Ramanuja
11. Kuresa
12. Madhvacarya
13. Vopadevacarya
14. Devacarya
15. Purusottam
16. Gangadhar
17. Rameswar
18. Dvaranand
19. Devanand
20. Sriyanand
21. Hariyanand
22. Raghavanand
23. Ramanand

FIGURE 7.1: The spiritual genealogy of the Ramanandi sect as recorded in the early fifteenth century.

1. Narayan
2. Lakshmi
3. Visvaksen
4. Sathkop
5. Nathmuni
6. Pundrikaksa
7. Ram Misra
8. Yamunacarya
9. Mahapurnacarya
10. Ramanuja

FIGURE 7.2: The spiritual genealogy of the Sri sect.

Ramarcanapaddhiti genealogy Ram bestows the six-syllable Ram *mantra* upon Sita and in the Sri genealogy Narayan bestows the eight-syllable Narayan *mantra* upon Lakshmi. Inevitably the Ramanandi ascetics, who worship Ram, had to obtain their *mantra* from Lord Ram. If Lord Ram had not been the source of the *mantra* then the *mantra* would have been ineffective in transporting the devotees to the celestial refuge of Lord Ram. The most interesting feature of this early Ramanandi spiritual genealogy, therefore, is its ambiguity. Ramanand is a spiritual descendant of Ramanuja thereby making Ramanand a member of the Sri sect, but Ramanuja received the *mantra* from Ram and Sita, not Narayan and Lakshmi, thereby making Ramanuja a Ramanandi or Ramavat ascetic. The genealogy does not prove that Ramanand was, in fact, a member of the Sri sect, but it does indicate that at the time of its compilation, the author of the genealogy, either Ramanand or one of his followers, found it advantageous for Ramanand to be included as a spiritual descendant of Ramanuja.

Nabha Ji, who was in the fourth generation of Ramanand's descendants, compiled the *Sri Bhakta Mala* in the late sixteenth century. In *chappaya* 29 of this text, Nabha Ji names Ramanuja, Nimbarka, Vishnuswami, and Madhvacarya as the founders of the four main Vaisnavite sects (*catuḥ saṃpradāya*). In Ramanuja's spiritual genealogy (*chappaya* 30) Narayan and Lakshmi are given their rightful place at the top of the list. Nabha Ji, however, neglects to mention the names of Ramanuja's disciples. In *chappaya* 35, however, we learn that Raghavanand lived in Varanasi and saw all Hindus, regardless of their caste, as devotees of the Lord. Raghavanand's disciple was Ramanand who appeared on the terrestrial world and was bold in the doctrines of Ramanuja. Ramanuja is included in Ramanand's spiritual ancestry and in the following *chappaya* Nabha Ji names Ramanand's twelve disciples. The information in the *Sri Bhakta Mala* yields, therefore, the following spiritual genealogy of the Ramanandi sect (Figure 7.3). The *Sri Bhakta Mala* genealogy was compiled during the period of greatest diversity within the Ramanandi sect. The list of disciples includes a weaver (Kabir—it is not specifically mentioned that Kabir is a Muslim), a cobbler (Rai Das), a farmer (Dhana), a barber (Sena), a woman (Padmavati), and a married couple (Sursuranand and Sursuri). Pipa was a Ksatriya who, prior to his discipleship, was the King of Gagraun. The remaining

1. Narayan
2. Lakshmi
3. Visvaksen
4. Sathkop
5. Nathmuni
6. Pundrikaksa
7. Ram Misra
8. Yamunacarya
9. Mahapurnacarya
10. Ramanuja
11. Devanand
12. Hariyanand
13. Raghavanand
14. Ramanand

Anant-anand	Sursur-anand	Sukh-anand	Bhav-anand	Narhar-yanand	Kabir	Dhanna	Sena	Rai Das	Pipa	Sur-suri	Padma-vati

FIGURE 7.3: The spiritual genealogy of the Ramandi sect as recorded in the late sixteenth century.

disciples, Anantanand, Sukhanand, Narharyanand, Bhavanand, plus Sursuranand and his wife, were Brahmans. No doubt Ramanand had more than twelve disciples, but twelve was a sacred number and we find that other famous ascetics who founded sects, such as Gorakhnath, were also known to have had twelve disciples. According to Chaturvedi (1964: 218–52) there is no evidence in the writings of Pipa, Sena, Dhanna, Rai Das, and Kabir which proves that they were, in fact, the disciples of Ramanand. It is possible that Pipa, Sena, Dhanna, Rai Das, and Kabir had attracted followers in their own name who found it advantageous to claim Ramanand as their ancestor. This may explain the unusually long lifespan of either 111 or 148 years which has been attributed to Ramanand by various sectarian sources. To make Ramanand the preceptor of Anantanand, Sukhanand, Pipa, Kabir, Rai Das, and the other disciples, the bards of the sect may have been required to keep the legendary Ramanand alive longer than the historical one. In sum, the position of Ramanand in Nabha Ji's *Sri Bhakta Mala* is still ambiguous. Ramanand is included within the Sri sect, but he is attributed twelve disciple as if he had founded his own sect.

Moreover, these twelve disciples include twice-born Hindus, servants, untouchables, and women in contravention of the social practices of the Sri sect who are said to have recruited only twice-born male Hindus into their sect in upper India.

At the turn of eighteenth century, about ten generations of Hindu ascetics had claimed spiritual descent from Ramanand. At that time, according to the sectarian bards, an important conference of Vaisnavite ascetics was held at Galata in the Kingdom of Jaipur in order to organize the defence of the Vaisnavite ascetics and their pilgrimage centres against the Sannyasis of the Dasnami sect. The militant orders (*akhāṛā*) and armies (*anī*) of the Vaisnavite sects date from this time. It seems, however, that there was a second purpose for which the conference was convoked and which has remained untold by the sectarian bards. Prior to the conference the four main Vaisnavite sects comprised the sects founded by Ramanuja, Nimbarka, Madhvacarya, and Visnuswami. Collectively these four sects were known as the *catuh sampradaya*. The followers of Ramanand were affiliated to the *catuh sampradaya* by virtue of their descent from the Sri sect founded by Ramanuja. At the Galata conference, the Ramanandis displaced the Sri sect and were recognized as the original members of the *catuh sampradaya* together with the sects founded by Nimbarka, Madhvacarya, and Visnuswami. This new arrangement was sealed by the subdivision of the four sects into fifty-two 'doors' (*dvārā*). Each door, or what we might call a spiritual clan, was said to have been established by a prominent Vaisnavite ascetic who was a spiritual descendant of Ramanand, Nimbarka, Madhvacarya, or Visnuswami. All members of the four main Vaisnavite sects traced their spiritual descent back to a founder of a spiritual clan. Anyone who could not trace his descent back to the founder of a spiritual clan was not a member of any of the four sects of the *catuh sampradaya*. Of the fifty-two spiritual clans, thirty-six were founded by Ramanandi ascetics and twelve were founded by Nimbarki ascetics. The remaining four spiritual clans were founded by ascetics of the Madhvacarya and Visnuswami sects. The thirty-six founders of the Ramanandi spiritual clans fall within the first and sixth generations of Ramanand's descendants. Following Nabha Ji's list of twelve disciples, twenty-seven spiritual clans were founded by Anantanand and his descendants; four spiritual clans were founded by Sursuranand and his descendants. Narharyanand, Sukhanand, Bhavanand, and Pipa each founded a spiritual clan.[7] Finally there was an ascetic by the name of Ram Kabir who founded a spiritual clan. Most genealogists of the sect claim that Ram Kabir is unrelated to Kabir, the weaver, and hence is not one of Ramanand's direct disciples.[8] Of Ramanand's twelve disciples Anantanand, Sursuranand, Sukhanand, Narharyanand, Bhavanand, and Pipa were twice-born Hindus. Evidence abounds that in the course of their travels, Kabir, Rai Das, Dhanna, and Sena made many disciples and that there were even sects which were founded in their names (Chaturvedi 1964: 218–52). They were, however, not assigned the honour of being the founder of a spiritual clan. The servant, untouchable, and female disciples of Ramanand were still recognized as having been Ramanandi ascetics, but by virtue of their not being recognized as the founder of a spiritual clan, they lost their role as a transmitter or preceptor of the tradition. From the early eighteenth century until the present day, no Ramanandi ascetic claims his spiritual descent from the servant, untouchable, or female disciples of Ramanand. At the conference at Galata, therefore, the Ramanandi sect was delimited by the following genealogy (Figure 7.4). Other genealogies indicate that male and female Hindus of servant and untouchable birth were still being admitted into the Ramanandi sect, but from

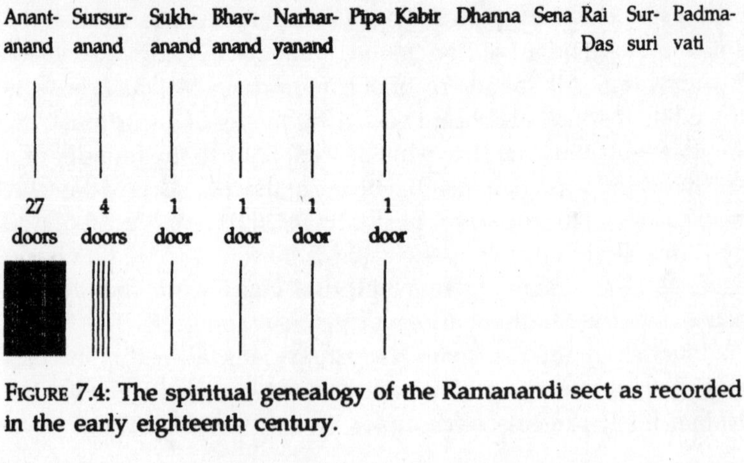

FIGURE 7.4: The spiritual genealogy of the Ramanandi sect as recorded in the early eighteenth century.

the early eighteenth century all Ramanandi ascetics, regardless of their caste or sex, who traced their spiritual descent from the servant, untouchable, and female disciples of Ramanand now found themselves outside the Ramanandi sect.[9]

At the Kumbh festival of 1921 held at Ujjain, the Ramanandi ascetics met in assembly and formally approved the following spiritual genealogy of Swami Ramanand[10] (Figure 7.5). The proponents of this new genealogy argued that, in fact, the genealogy was not new. Rather, it had been found among the writings of Agra Ji who had established the Ramanandi monastery at Raivasa in the Kingdom of Jaipur during the sixteenth century and who was the preceptor of the 'Branch of sentiment' (*rasik saṃpradāya*) within the Ramanandi sect. Although this genealogy may be found as early as the nineteenth century in the literature of the 'Branch of sentiment', it is doubtful if the

1. Ram Candra
2. Sita
3. Hanuman
4. Brahma
5. Vasistha
6. Prasara
7. Vyasdeva
8. Sukadeva
9. Purusottamacarya
10. Gangadharacarya
11. Sadacarya
12. Rameswaracarya
13. Dvaranand
14. Devanand
15. Syamanand
16. Srutanand
17. Cidanand
18. Purnanand
19. Sriyanand
20. Hariyanand
21. Raghavanand
22. Ramanand

FIGURE 7.5: The spiritual genealogy of the Ramanandi sect as recorded in the early twentieth century.

genealogy dates from the time of Agra Ji. In comparing the 1921 spiritual genealogy with the genealogy of the *Ramarcanapaddhiti* in Figure 7.1, one may note two important changes. First, from the third to the fourteenth generations of the *Ramarcanapaddhiti* genealogy, Ramanuja's Dravidian spiritual preceptors and descendants have been replaced by six generations of gods and rishis. Second, from the fifteenth to the twentieth generations of the *Ramarcanapaddhiti* genealogy, the names of five new preceptors have been added thereby extending the generational depth of the 1921 genealogy. In the early twentieth century, therefore, the ascetics and bards of the Ramanandi sect finally affirmed their sectarian independence by claiming the unique historical origin of the sect. The *mantra* was divulged by Ram Candra and was transmitted down though twenty-two generations to Ramanand without passing through any of the Dravidian preceptors of the Sri sect. In sum, approximately 500 years after the time of Swami Ramanand, his followers finally solved the problem of their history. The 1921 genealogy is completely unambiguous with regard to the origin and development of the sect. It should come as no surprise, therefore, that it was also during the early twentieth century with the publication of *Sri Ramanand Natak* and *Srimad Ramanand Digvijaya* that the sectarian literature for the first time treats us to detailed biographical information about the life of Swami Ramanand.

Let us now review the information which I have presented above. Each spiritual genealogy reveals the names of ascetics who were included or excluded from the spiritual ancestry and descent of Ramanand and in this way illuminates the phases in the development of the sect. In the early fifteenth century, according to the *Ramarcanapaddhiti* genealogy, Ramanand was a spiritual descendant of Ramanuja. Ramanuja, however, was a devotee of Ram and Sita rather than of Narayan and Laksmi. The ambiguity suggests that Ramanand and/or his followers were reluctant to detach themselves from the Sri sect and from the preceptorship of Ramanuja. One reason for this reluctance may have been that it was more advantageous for the Ramanandis to profit from the established reputation of the Sri sect and the Sri monastic facilities at the pilgrimage centres than to abrogate this link and to fend for themselves in the competition with other ascetic sects. By the late sixteenth century, according to the *Sri Bhakta Mala* genealogy, devotees and disciples regardless of their caste, sex, or sectarian affiliation were initiated into a Vaisnavite sect by Ramanand. The genealogy reveals the broadening of the criteria for recruitment into a Vaisnavite sect thereby enabling the sect to compete more effectively for devotees and disciples. The spiritual genealogy established by respected Vaisnavite ascetics at Galata at the turn of the eighteenth century reveals that a Vaisnavite sect which was known formally as the *Ramanandi sampradaya* had displaced the Sri sect from the *catuh sampradaya* thereby establishing its separate identity. Moreover, the Ramanandi sect purged itself of the secondary sects which had been founded in the name of Ramanand's disciples of servant caste and untouchable birth.[11] The ascetics of these secondary sects were not known to observe caste rules of commensality and hence they would have been considered untouchable by Hindu householders. The purge of such ascetics from the Ramanandi sect, therefore, enabled the Ramanandi ascetics to compete more effectively for the patronage of householders and, in particular, for the patronage of the Hindu king. According to the spiritual genealogy of the Ramanandi sect which was approved at the Kumbh festival held at Ujjain in 1921, Lord Ram divulged his *mantra* which was transmitted down through twenty-two generations of gods, *rishis*, and saints to Ramanand. The Sri tradition and the Dravidian preceptors were purged from the history of the Ramanandi sect thereby affirming the sectarian independence of the Ramanandi ascetics. Thus we find that the followers of Ramanand passed through four stages in the formation of the sect. In the first stage Ramanand and/or his early followers included themselves within a larger, more established sect. In the second stage ascetics from diverse castes, either sex, and different sectarian affiliations included themselves within the Ramanandi sect. In the third stage, the more influential faction within the sect excluded from its midst the 'impure' spiritual descendants of Ramanand, and in the fourth stage, the more influential faction excluded 'alien' spiritual antecedents of Ramanand from the sect. The four spiritual genealogies, when analysed chronologically, reveal, therefore, that the Ramanandi sect was not established as a separate and independent ascetic sect, but that it became this way after passing through phases of inclusion and exclusion.

This reconstruction of the development of the Ramanandi sect and the proposal that Swami Ramanand did not personally establish the sect is further supported by what we might deduce about the early history of the sect from a knowledge of its social structure. The transmission of the *mantra* from *guru* to disciple perpetuates the sect over time. The fission of the sect into segmentary spiritual lineages is an inherent process of its generational growth. Insofar as succession and fission are continual processes of growth in any segmentary lineage system, each stage of the process is no more a beginning of the succeeding stages than it is an end of the preceding stages. How then could a Hindu ascetic transform his role from a mere transmitter of the *mantra* to the founder of a sect? At the time in which Ramanand lived, the founders of the ascetic sects whose followers resided or travelled in the Ganges basin were usually known as 'preceptors' (*ācārya*). An ascetic became a preceptor by writing a commentary (*bhāṣya*) on a sacred text, such as the *Brahma Sutra* or the *Bhagavad Gita*, and then by propagating a 'teaching' (*updeśa*) and 'spiritual discipline' (*sādhana*) based upon that commentary. There is neither tradition nor evidence, however, that Ramanand ever wrote a commentary on a sacred text; indeed he was known to have used the *Sri Bhasya* written by Ramanuja. We may deduce from this that if Ramanand withdrew from the Sri sect and established the Ramanandi sect, he certainly did not do so in the manner customary to his time, that is to say, in the manner which would have been understood by his contemporaries. Later at the turn of the seventeenth century, when Ramanand was becoming known as the founder of a sect, the sectarian bards avoided the problem caused by the fact that Swami Ramanand had never fulfilled the requirements of a preceptor. In the devotional literature, such as Nabha Ji's *Sri Bhakta Mala*, Ramanand was likened to an incarnation of Ram and in the *nirguna* literature, such as the *Siddhant Patal*, Ramanand was known as a 'truth-*guru*' (*satguru*) or a 'primal *guru*' (*ādiguru*) who has existed since the dawn of time. Both as an incarnation of Ram and as a truth-*guru*, the historical Ramanand was transformed into an eternal Ramanand and removed from the context of the segmentary spiritual lineages created by the transmission of the *mantra*. For the sectarian bards, this must have been a convenient way of avoiding the problem of Ramanand's ancestry and transforming Ramanand into the role of the founder of a sect.

There is, however, another possibility which must be considered. Perhaps Ramanand was ostracized from the Sri sect and then by force of circumstance, he gathered his followers together and established his own sect. From our knowledge of the social structure of the sect, we may doubt that the founding of the sect ever occurred in such a way. No Vaisnavite ascetic, not even one's *guru*, can 'defrock' another Vaisnavite ascetic. If Ramanand had been ostracized by the Sri ascetics, this ostracism could have been effected in only two possible ways. First, Ramanand could have been banished territorially from a rent-receiving Sri monastery by the abbot of that monastery. It is possible, but very improbable, that the influential abbots of the Sri monasteries could have appealed to their king to banish Ramanand from the kingdom. Such banishment was, perforce, local. Ramanand would only have had to travel to another locality where his reputation had not caught up with him in order to begin life anew as a Sri ascetic of good standing. Second, Ramanand could have been ostracized commensally by the ascetics of the Sri sect. Such ostracism would have meant only that Ramanand had become less pure than the Sri ascetics; in other words, the Sri ascetics would no longer have accepted cooked food from Ramanand. Ramanand might still, however, have been able to accept cooked food from the Sri ascetics and hence to benefit from their hospitality. And even if the Sri ascetics in a region denied Ramanand food, fire, and water in the customary manner of excommunication, Ramanand could still have travelled to another region where his status as a member of the Sri sect would have been unquestioned. In sum, the hypothetical ostracism of Ramanand from the Sri sect could not have been very effective. The only effective means of isolating Ramanand from the sect would have been to purge him from the sect historically. A council of respected Sri ascetics could have revised Ramanand's genealogy not in order to show that Ramanand had been excluded from the sect, but rather to show that Ramanand had never been included in the sect.[12] If such a council of respected Sri saints ever met in the lifetime of Ramanand then their revision of Ramanand's ancestry was ineffective because four generations later at the time of Nabhi Ji, the followers of Ramanand still traced their descent from Ramanuja.

III

Monasteries of the Ramanandi sect are found today throughout the states of Bengal, Bihar, Orissa, Madhya Pradesh, Maharashtra, Gujarat, Rajasthan, Punjab, Haryana, and Uttar Pradesh as well as in the Nepal Valley and the Nepalese Tarai. Current census figures are not available, but judging from head counts of ascetics in the processions at the Kumbh festival, the Ramanandi sect vies with the Dasnami sect for the honour of being the largest Hindu ascetic sect (Farquhar 1967: 327–38). The geographical distribution and numerical strength of the Ramanandi sect today is the measure of its success in the competition with the sects founded by Sankar, Gorakhnath, Ramanuja, Nimbarka, Madhvacarya, Visnuswami, Chaitanya, Vallabha, Siva Narayan, Dadu, Swami Narayan, and other Hindu saints over the three limited resources: devotees and disciples, pilgrimage routes and pilgrimage centres, and political patronage. The history of the Ramanandi sect, as it is recounted by the Ramanandi ascetics and the sectarian bards, is as much a product of the success of the sect as it is an account of that success. Until recently, however, the sectarian sources from which one might reconstruct the events surrounding the formation of the Ramanandi sect were meagre and contradictory. Anthropological methods cannot uncover additional facts about those past events, but our knowledge of the sect's segmentary lineage structure and our analysis of the spiritual genealogies as records of strategy rather than records of fact does call into question the assumption underlying previous reconstructions of those events, namely that Ramanand actually founded the Ramanandi sect. The chronological analysis of the four spiritual genealogies suggests that the founding of the Ramanandi sect was not an act initiated by Ramanand himself, but instead an act of the imagination initiated by Ramanand's followers. Swami Ramanand was an important Vaisnavite saint whose teachings acquired renown in the Ganges basin during the fifteenth century. The earliest ambiguous indication that Ramanand founded a sect, however, did not occur until the late sixteenth century when Nabha Ji attributed twelve disciples to Ramanand. The followers of Ramanand grew in number and influence, but it was not until the turn of the eighteenth century when certain impure spiritual descendants were excluded from the sect and the Sri ascetics were displaced from the *catuh sampradaya* that Ramanand became retrospectively and retroactively the founder of the Ramanandi sect.

Notes

1. Nabha Ji's list in the fifteenth *chappaya* of the *Sri Bhakta Mala* contains the following names: Anantanand, Sursuranand, Bhavanand, Narharyanand, Sukhanand, Pipa, Kabir, Sena, Dhanna, Rai Das, Padmavati, and Sursuri. The list of the 'twelve and one-half disciples' in the sixteenth to the nineteenth *sloka* of the *Agasthya Samhita* contains the following names: Anantanand, Sursuranand, Narharyanand, Yoganand, Sukhanand, Bhavanand, Galanand, Kabir, Ram Das, Sena, Pipa, Dhanna, and Padmavati. The famous saying which has been attributed to Ramanand cannot be found in the collection of Ramanand's poetry in the vernacular which has been edited by Pitambar Dutt Barthwal under the title *Ramanand ki Hindi Racnaen*. The saying is in Hindi and hence would not be found in the two Sanskrit texts, *Vaisnabamatabjabhaskar* and *Ramarcanapaddhiti*, which have also been attributed to Ramanand.

2. The recruitment of women and the members of servant and untouchable castes into an ascetic sect was an innovation in Hindu asceticism, but it was not an innovation in South Asian asceticism. The so-called heretical sects, such as the sects founded in the name of Sakyamuni Buddha, were open to all Hindus regardless of their caste or sex status long before the appearance of Swami Ramanand in upper India.

3. During the latter part of the eighteenth century, the Mughal emperor's control over his civil administration slackened and a number of local and regional revenue collectors profited from the situation and

established their own petty kingdoms. During this turbulent period in the administration of upper India, the Dasnami Sannyasis secured a significant share of the trade in light-weight luxury items, such as gold, coral, gems, and musk. The pilgrimage routes doubled as commercial routes and some of the Dasnami monasteries also served as banking institutions. The abbots of these monasteries loaned both troops and money to the petty kings. The battles between the Sannyasi and Ramanandi ascetics usually occurred at pilgrimage centres and were provoked by the competition for precedence in religious processions. The commercial and financial activities of the ascetic sects during this period are not well known, but it is possible that the battles between the ascetic sects were caused by both economic and religious competition. See Sir Jadunath Sarkar, *A History of the Dasnami Naga Sannyasis* and Bernard S. Cohn, 'The Role of the Gosains in the Economy of the Eighteenth and Nineteenth Century Upper India'.

4. The Peshwa court settled the dispute in 1813 by assigning separate bathing places to the two sects. The battle in 1789 is mentioned in the 1813 settlement inscribed on a copperplate, a facsimile of which has been published in *Jagriti*, 10, 4, 1945, pp. 896–7.

5. I have taken this spiritual genealogy from Sinha, *Ram Bhakti men Rasik Sampradaya*, p. 323. Sinha claims that the genealogy is authentic (*pramāṇik*), but he does not provide any detailed information concerning the date and location of the particular manuscript of *Ramarcanapaddhiti* to which he had recourse.

6. This genealogy appears to be the standard north Indian genealogy of this south Indian sect. This particular genealogy was taken from *chappaya* 30 of the *Sri Bhakta Mala* which Nabha Ji wrote during the latter part of the sixteenth century.

7. I have followed Ramanandi sectarian sources here. According to the *Ram Patal*, pp. 111–13, the spiritual clans founded by Anantanand and his spiritual descendants are: (1) Anantanand, (2) Ram Raval, (3) Yoganand, (4) Khoji, (5) Karmacand, (6) Alakh Ram, (7) Raghocetan, (8) Agra Ji, (9) Hathi Narayan Das, (10) Khil Das, (11) Ram Thabhan Das, (12) Nabha Ji, (13) Tila Ji, (14) Ram Ramani, (15) Hanuman Hathila, (16) Jangi Ji, (17) Bhagawan Narayan Das, (18) Tan Tulsi Das, (19) Divrakar, (20) Purna Bairathi, (21) Govind Das, (22) Laharam, (23) Lal Tarangi, (24) Deva Murari, (25) Kalunayana, (26) Maluk Das, and (27) Deva Bharangi. The four spiritual clans founded by Sursuranand and his spiritual descendant include: (1) Sursuranand, (2) Anabhyanand, (3) Kuva, and (4) Damodar Das.

8. The opinion of the genealogists of the sect is also held by Sinha, *Ram Bhakti men Rasik Sampradaya*, p. 329.

9. Ghurye (1964: 182) has written that 'the Dwārā [spiritual clan] affiliation was significant in the past in so far as the Nāgā ascetic [member of a militant order] could establish his identity to the Vaisnavite bairagis through an esoteric formula in which his Dwārā figured.' The genealogists of the Ramanandi sect who operate in Bihar and the Nepalese Tarai were unable to confirm Ghurye's opinion for me, nor could they recall the existence of any esoteric formula. Contrary to Ghurye I suspect that the spiritual clans never had a function. They were merely a genealogical arrangement to purge the sect of impure elements and to attract the patronage of householders. Ḥaving served their purpose, they became at once vestigial organs. At present, membership in a spiritual clan confers no rights and duties upon the Ramanandi ascetic.

10. After the Kumbh festival of 1921, the genealogy was published in Ayodhya as a broadsheet by the Sri Ramanandiya Vaisnab Mandal. The broadsheet has been reprinted in Sinha, *Ram Bhakti men Rasik Sampradaya*, pp. 320–2.

11. The Sri sect of south India was also divided on the issue of the participation of the members of the servant castes in the organization of the sect. Stein (1968: 78–94) describes the events leading to the division of the Dravidian Sri sect into a Southern School and a Northern School and notes the different positions of these two schools on the issue of servant caste participation in the rituals and organization of the sect. Stein goes on to note that during the sixteenth century, the influence of the members of the servant castes waned and the Sri ascetics of Brahman birth performed the more significant roles in the organization of the sect. I have not found any information, however, which links these events in the Dravidian south with the later displacement of the Sri sect from the *catuh sampradaya* by the Ramanandi sect and with the purge of the secondary sects founded in the name of Ramanand's disciples of servant caste, untouchable, or female birth.

12. The Sri ascetics of northern India did eventually take this course of action but at what appears to be a much later date than the lifetime of Swami Ramanand. In a spiritual genealogy published in 1923, the Sri ascetics adapted the subdivision of the *catuh sampradaya* into fifty-two spiritual clans to their own purposes. One finds the names of Ramanand's spiritual descendants (Anantanand, Sukhanand, Pipa, Agra Ji, Khoja Ji, etc.) as the heads of Sri spiritual clans. Ramanujacarya, Sudarsanacarya (Nimbarka), Sri Vallabhacarya, and Madhvacarya are listed as being the preceptors of the four sects of the *catuh sampradaya*. There is no indication in the genealogy that a saint by the name of Ramanand ever existed. The genealogy may be found in Pandit Tikam Das, *Sri Vairagya Kula Karmma Sara Sangrah*, bound between pp. 40 and 41.

References

Barthwal, Pitambar Datt. 1936. *The Nirguna School of Hindi Poetry*. Benaras.

———. 1955. *Ramanand ki Hindi Racnaen*. Kasi.

Bhagavadacarya, Swami. 1967. *Srimad Ramanand Digvijaya*. Ahmedabad (First edition, 1927.)

Chaturvedi, Parasuram. 1964. *Uttari Bharat ki Sant Parampara*. Allahabad.

Cohn, Benard S. 1964. 'The Role of the Gosains in the Economy of the Eighteenth and Nineteenth Century Upper India'. *The Indian Economic and Social History Review* 1: 175–82.

Das, Avadh Kisor. 1935. *Sri Ramanand Natak*. Benaras.

Das, Pandit Tikam. 1927. *Sri Vairagya Kula Karmma Sara Sangrah*. Ajmer.

Farquhar, J. N. 1925. 'The Fighting Ascetics of India', *Bulletin of the John Rylands Library* 9, 2.

———. 1967. *An Outline of the Religious Literature of India*. Delhi (First edition, 1920.)

Ghurye, G. S. 1964. *Indian Sadhus*. Bombay.

Goswamy, B. N. and J. S. Grewal. 1969. *The Mughal and Sikh Rulers and Vaishnavas of Pindori*. Simla.

Nabha Ji. 1969. *Sri Bhakta Mala*. Lucknow.

Prasad, Raghunath. 1930. *Sri Maharaja Charitra*. Ayodhya.

Ramanand (attributed). n.d. *Ram Patal*. Pandit Saryu Das, ed. Benaras.

———. n.d. *Siddhant Patal*. Benaras.

Saran, Sita Ram. 1969. *Bhakti Sudha Svad*. Being a commentary on the Sri Bhakta Mala. See Nabha Ji.

Sarkar, Sir Jadunath. n.d. *A History of the Dasnami Naga Sannyasis*. Allahabad.

Sinha, Bhagawati Prasad. 1957. *Ram Bhakti men Rasik Sampradaya*. Balrampur.

Stein, Burton. 1968. 'Social Mobility and Medieval South Indian Hindu Sects', in *Social Mobility in the Caste System in India*. James Silverberg, ed., pp. 78–94. The Hague.

Wilson, Horace Hyman. 1846. *Sketch of the Religious Sects of the Hindus*. Calcutta.

IV

Kabir and the Sants

8

The Times and their Need*

P. D. Barthwal

Introductory

The soul of India has always yearned for the greater life that extends illimitably beyond the short span of this life. Indians have, as a people, ever listened with absorbing interest, to the voice that exultingly points to the golden chain of love which binds the individual with the universal life. The sources of this current of spiritual tendency flowing in the life of India are hidden in the mists of the remotest antiquity. The current has incessantly flowed unhindered from age to age, of course, accommodating itself to the exigencies of time. In the fifteenth century it took a form which is traditionally, though not very aptly, known as the Nirguṇa School. The object of this work is to deal with the thought represented by this school, which has a bearing on practically all departments of life. Its replica is preserved in the poetic literature of Hindi, which being the people's tongue, was accepted by the teachers of the new school as a proper vehicle for their popular teachings. Many causes—social, religious, political, and the like—combined to give this spiritual movement its characteristic

* From *Traditions of Indian Mysticism based upon Nirguna School of Hindi Poetry* (New Delhi, 1978).

intensity of content and novelty of form. The immediate occasion for it was supplied by the political condition of the country consequent upon the Mohammadan conquest, which brought into contact the two most divergently minded races and had its repercussions in every sphere of life. To understand fully the thought that the school stands for, it is necessary to understand the special conditions that gave rise to it.

India under the Frown of Islam

'In religion,' declared Al Qoran, 'let there be no compulsion. Wil't thou compel men to become believers? No soul can believe but by the persuasion of god.'[1] In spite of this divine injunction, the sword did play the major part in the spread of Islam. The Arabs and, following in their footsteps, other entrants to the Islamic fold, carried death, destruction, and desolation to lands far and wide. India with her untold wealth, exuberant soil, and teeming population did not fail to attract the unscrupulous believers, and that land of ease, plenty, and philosophy, met no different a fate at their hands. Men, women, children, colleges, libraries, monuments of arts—nothing was too sacred to escape destruction. Though the Hindus did not easily give in, and put up a stubborn fight at every step, yet their scorn for dangers, their moral scruples even in the field of battle, and a number of superstitious beliefs served them ill and they had to yield to the humiliation showered on them. Al Beruni, the intelligent historian who came in the train of Mahmūd of Ghazni, wrote of his patron, that he 'utterly ruined the prosperity of the country and performed those wonderful exploits, by which the Hindus became like atoms of dust scattered in all directions and like a tale of old in the mouths of the people.'[2] Besides the large death-toll in actual battle, every conqueror's slaughters and enslavements were numbered at thousands and hundreds of thousands and his plunder was beyond computation. Even the centres of learning and culture were not spared. When Mohammad-bin-Bakhtyār seized the capital of Bihār in AD 1197, he demolished the great Buddhistic college monastery, put to sword all the occupants thereof who could be caught hold of, and put the college library called

Ratnāwali, to flames.[3] And Bakhtyār must not have been single in this destructive aptitude of his. As early a writer as Al Beruni, saw the Hindu sciences 'retire far away from the part of the country conquered by us (Mohammadans) and fly to places, which our (the Mohammadans') hands cannot reach yet.'[4]

Even when the Mohammadans had seen the wisdom of settling down in the country and carving out regular kingdoms for themselves, the policy of fleecing the children of the soil to their utmost and making life practically impossible for them was not abandoned. The Hindu subjects had no right to live except at the sufferance of the Moslem ruler, and they were suffered to live because they were useful to the state as revenue-paying units. This was deemed quite justifiable even by such a conscientious man as Qāzī Mughīsuddīn[5] of Alāuddīn's Court. The taxes levied on the Hindus were not few. During the reign of Alāuddīn they were made to pay as much as 50 per cent of the yield of their sweating labour. Hardly as much was left with the people in these circumstances as would enable them to maintain even a bare hand-to-mouth existence. Even those who were considered wealthy were not able to ride a horse, to find weapons, to get fine clothes or to indulge in betels. Such was the miserable plight of the Hindus that their wives had to go to the houses of the Mohammadans to work for hire.[6]

Of course, the question of religious freedom for the Hindus could not arise. Their faith was treated with express contempt. Wholesale levelling down of temples was indulged in by almost all the Moslem conquerors and rulers, and the broken idols were put to mean uses. Fīroz Śāh (acc. AD 1357–d. AD 1388) caused a Brahman to be burnt alive for practising Hindu rites in public.[7] Feriśtā tells of one Buddhan, a Brahman of Kaithan, who was done to death in the presence of Sikandar Lodī, for having publicly declared that his religion was as good as that of the Prophet. The punishment, it is said, was inflicted in accordance with the verdict of a meeting of the Ulemā, which gave Buddhan a choice between Islam and death; and he, rather than kill his conscience, bravely submitted to being killed.[8]

All the privileges of respectable citizenship were thus denied to the Hindus. Their life was simply a drudgery. There was nothing earthly with them that could instil sweetness into their soured souls. To them the future was all darkness.

The Inequity of *Varṇa*

But Hinduism was as much to be saved from its own tyranny, as from that of the Moslems, which the Hindu-Moslem contact brought to clear light. The Hindu socio-religious system in its anxiety to leave no social or political function to the caprice of the individual, defined every relation between man and man, and their duties by each other. But the *Varṇa* system, a classification based originally on the qualities and vocations of men, gradually came to be determined by birth, and wisely so indeed, because qualities and aptitudes are the results of environments, and environments begin to cast their influence on one from one's very birth. But the Hindus forgot that every rule has exceptions, and what were meant to be beneficial precautionary measures, became in the end perpetrators of inequity and cruelty. The individual was born into definite vocation, and possibilities in other directions were barred for him for ever. The classification of castes, instead of being a system of division and specialization of labour, became a gradation of social order with seniorities and inferiorities attached to them. The Śūdras, who were considered to be of the lowest order, were shut out from all the good that a civilized society could provide. They could not peep into the Vedic and other scriptural literature, and the lowest of them, the *Antyajas*, could not even enter temples. Their touch, even, was considered to pollute a higher-caste man.

Having remained in this condition for centuries together, they had begun to view it as a matter-of-course-thing. But the contact with Mohammadanism awakened them to the reality of their position. In Islam there was no caste system. Among the Moslems, none was considered high or low in the sense in which it was in Hinduism. Being Mohammadans they were all equal. Any one entering the Mohammadan fold could consider himself socially equal to any other Mohammadan. But it was not so in Hinduism. To every right thinking man, the whole situation rose in a great interrogation: what justification is there for such invidious distinctions to be allowed to remain in the Hindu society?

To the low-caste, this was the central problem to which he was awakened every now and then by rude shocks received from the higher-caste people. Nāmadeva has recorded in one of his songs, how he was once turned out of a temple, when people came to know that he was a calico-printer by caste.[9]

Seeking the Divine Shelter

While North India was being convulsed with political cataclysm, the echoes of which were late in reaching the south, the south was full of life and religious activity. The *Advaita* doctrine of Śankarāchārya having failed to fill the void caused in the heart of the people by the Buddhistic non-theistic philosophy, they were once again turning to the ancient Aikāntic Dharma, or religion of single-minded love later termed Bhāgavata Dharma. Gopāl (the cowherd) Krishṇa and Vāsudeva (son of Vasudeva) Krishṇa had blended into one personality to receive absolute homage in this religion of the Pānchrātras. According to Bühler, it dates from a period long anterior to the rise of Jainas, in the eighth century BC (*IA*, XXIII, p. 248). Vāsudeva Krishṇa is mentioned in the pre-Buddhist *Chhāndogya Upanishad* (*EHV*, p. 40), which must be placed before the sixth century BC. It was him again that, 400 years before Christ, Megasthenes referred to as Heracles (*Hari Krishṇa*), the God 'held in especial honour' by the Sourseni, in whose country was situated Methora (Mathurā) and the river Iobares (Yamunā) flows (McCrindle, MA., p. 201). Followed as it was by the Sāttwat tribe, the religion also came to be known as the Sāttwat Dharma. Gradually, Krishṇa began to be identified with Bhagavat-Nārayaṇa and considered an incarnation of Vishṇu, which accounts for the names Bhāgavatism and Vaishṇavism. In 140 BC Heliodoros, the Greek ambassador from the Court of Antialkidas, king of Takshaśilā, at the Court of Bhāga-bhadra, the king of Vidiśā, was a Bhāgavata. From the third century onwards, the Bhāgavatas are usually mentioned in the inscriptions to be found along the basin of the Ganges. The Gupta kings in the third, fourth, and fifth centuries were

Vaishṇavas and styled themselves *Parama Bhāgavatas* in their coins and inscriptions. Inscriptional and other evidence traces its progress to the eighth century, and though Śaivism and other forms of religion replaced it as a prominent force in the religious sphere, it nevertheless was not an extinct religion in the twelfth century and was followed by the Āḷvār saints of the Tamil-land, with whom it was a living passion. It was from these Āḷvārs that Rāmānuja, who placed himself at the head of the regeneration of Vaishṇavism, is said to have taken his cue. Rāmānuja systematized the Vaishṇava thought, and gave it a sound philosophical backing. He became a zealous Vaishṇava missionary. He overthrew his adversaries in disputations; he converted monarchs, built scores of new temples, and his devotional doctrines began to spread.

In course of time, this current of devotional religion was made to overflow the entire land from one end to the other by a galaxy of noble souls within whom blazed the divine spark in its full splendour. Contemporaneously with Rāmānuja, who is said to have flourished in the twelfth century, Nimbārka, himself an inhabitant of South India, preached the Vaishnava bhakti in Brindābana, near Mathurā, in North India.

In Canarese-land and Gujarāt, the great Canarese teacher Madhwa, who flourished roughly between AD 1200 and 1275 (Bhāndārkar: *Vaishṇavism*, p. 59), gave it the support of his dualistic philosophy. Side by side with this proselytizing movement, there sprang up a number of Vaishṇava poets in different parts of the country, in whose sweet and musical verses the noble sentiment of bhakti found adequate expression. In Bengal, Jayadeva (fl. AD 1170) of *Gītagovinda* fame had already given vent to the effusions of his heart in devotional songs of shining glory, the echoes of which were heard in the equally exquisite and dramatic lyrics of Vidyāpati (fl. AD 1400) of Mithilā, who unlike Jayadeva, sang exclusively in the vernacular of his province. In the mouth of Chaitanya (AD 1485–1533) and his little band of devoted disciples, who were incarnations, as it were, of love and renunciation, these songs of Vidyāpati and Jayadeva became very effective means of popularizing the bhakti cult. In the north, again, teachers like Rāghavānanda, and Rāmānanda and

Vallabhāchārya, who preached devotion to Rāma and Krishṇa respectively, made a tremendous effort to popularize the bhakti cult.

The Hindus in North India were just at this time experiencing in their own being the truth of that basic principle of all systems of Indian religious philosophy, according to which the world is but an unalloyed misery. They were in just that condition in which the falsity of the world, of its riches and pleasures, is realized as a natural sequence. And, crushed, tyrannized over, and sunk into misery as they were, they sadly withdrew their eyes from the pleasures of the world and madly plunged into the current of this bhakti cult, sponsored by the Vaishṇavite teachers, which combined in itself religious devotion and philosophic renunciation, to enjoy the full measure of the only joy, to withhold, which does not lie within the competence of any.

This gave them a sort of passive force, which taught how to scorn danger, endure oppression, and survive the most throttling calamities: and a race which, driven to despair, appeared to be fast losing hold on life, became endowed with the vitals that nothing could eat into.

The Meeting Ground being Prepared

But the 'Vaishṇava movement' did not meet the whole situation. The two races, which were brought together by the trend of events were diametrically opposed to each other. Besides the differences that do exist between the conquerors and the conquered, there were the religious differences, which were proving to be ever-new incentives to further ill-treatment and oppression. For, Mohammadan conquest did not simply mean a conquest for the Mohammadan king, but for Mohammad also. The Mohammadan armies were supposed to be on the mission of Mohammad when they were scoring victories for their commanders and conquering kingdoms for their kings. So, it was not only a conflict between the two races but also between the two creeds. The Hindu was an idol-worshipper, the Mohammadan an idol-breaker; the Hindu bowed to many gods, to the Mohammadan owing allegiance to any but the one God, whose only prophet is Mohammad, was sacrilege, was *kufra*; and to slaughter a *kāfir*, one who was guilty of *kufra*, was religiously extolled, so much so that on the slaughterer was bestowed the title of *Ghāzī*, a distinction to which every Moslem aspired. No wonder, therefore, that the persecution of the Hindus by Mohammadans was not on the decrease, and the 'most inveterate aversion'[10] for the Moslems, that Al Beruni had observed in the Hindus, was unabated. There was thus a vast gulf of hatred separating the two races that still needed to be bridged.

Fortunately, there were men in both the races who viewed this state of things with grave concern. They realized that the Moslems had come to stay and that the Hindus could not be made extinct by either conversion or slaughter. That the Hindus and Moslems should remain like good and peaceful neighbours, was clearly the need of the moment and these men of broad vision realized it as clearly. The renunciates of both the races, who were above all race prejudice and looked beyond the immediate gains and losses, pains and pleasures, and sorrows and joys, felt it the most. Some disciple of Gorakhanātha addressed two of his treatises, *Kāfirbodha* and *Avali Salūk*, to Mohammad, a king in an endeavour to press home to him that both the Hindus and the Mohammadans were the servants of the Lord, emphasizing at the same time that the Yogīs made no distinction between the two and thus were not partial to any of them.[11] Half a century later, Rāmānanda, a Vaishṇavite teacher, accepted Kabīr, a Moslem youth, who was destined to be the founder of a great unifying movement and of whom we will presently speak, as his disciple.

Among the Mohammadans themselves, there were the Sufi Faqirs, who were united to the Hindus with nobler ties than those of blood, that is, by those of thought. Their monistic pantheism was a gift from the Hindu philosophy.[12] This affinity of thought naturally drew them to the Hindus. They freely mixed with them and sympathized with them in their miseries. To the uplifted sword of their co-religionists, they cried a halt in their own way. Not to the logic of the brain, but to that of the heart did they appeal. They revealed to their view the Hindu heart in its simple beauty and endeavoured thereby to bring to the surface, the beauty of the Moslem heart. They interpreted to the Moslems the deepest culture of the Hindus by means of touching love stories on the model of Jalāl-uddīn Rumī's *Masnavī*. The origin of these stories that represent the romantic movement in Hindi poetry is lost. Probably, Mullā Dāūd who flourished in about AD 1440, during the reign of Alāuddīn Khiljī, and of whose poem *Nūrak aur Chandā kī Kahānī*, nothing except the name is known, was not the progenitor of the long line of them. In Kutban, the author of '*Mrigāwatī*', the first known work of this type, who wrote in about AD 1500, during the reign of Sikandar Lodi, just the time when the mutual understanding of the clashing cultures was most needed, we find the art of story writing in poetry developed to such an extent, that we cannot take him to be the founder of the line. Following his example Manjhan wrote '*Madhumālatī*,' Jāyasī the '*Padamāvat*', and Usmān '*Chittrāwalī* (AD 1613). The current of these love stories has flown even up to the twentieth century. In these stories, which are slightly veiled allegories, human love pointing towards divine love, the Mohammadan authors appear to be preaching the Hindu philosophy of life. The faithful portraiture of Hindu life to the minutest detail that we find in these stories of the early Mohammadan period evidences the free mixing of these Moslem faqirs in the Hindu society as also their association with the Hindu sādhus. All this bespeaks the sympathy that they felt for the Hindus, which must necessarily have resulted in evoking respect and admiration for them in the hearts of the Hindu laity and their sādhus. It has come to the observation of Pandit Rāmchandra Śukla, the Hindi savant, that the families in which Jāyasī's *Padamāwat* was found have invariably been characterized by tolerance and goodwill (*Jāyasī Granthāwalī*: Intro., p. 6). Thus was being prepared the ground on which both the Hindus and the Moslems could amicably meet.

Meeting the Śūdra Halfway

Wc have seen how the Hindus were seeking the Divine shelter to find solace in their hours of misery. The Śūdra had a double cause to seek it. He was doubly oppressed. He was oppressed by the Moslem for being a Hindu and by his own co-religionists of the regenerate classes for being a Śūdra, and he was seized with a storming passion for godly life.

The religious annals of the medieval period of Indian history are full of names which belong to the Śūdras, but which are still remembered with respect by all castes alike. Śaṭakopa (the Āḷvār), Nāmadeva, Raidās, Sena, and many others, are names to conjure with. But, for this, the Śūdras have not much to thank their orthodox high-caste co-religionists who did in no way facilitate their path. It was rather in spite of the disabilities placed in their way that the above-named low-caste devotees rose so high spiritually. The little that Rāmānanda, of whom we shall presently have to speak, did for them was also resisted by the high-caste people.

In the Tamil-land, the devotional spirit had, long before the advent of the Moslem, brought home to the Śaivite poets and the Vaishṇavite Āḷvār saints, the ancient Vedic ideal of the fatherhood of God and brotherhood of man, which made the injustice of caste exclusiveness dawn upon them, and they became desirous of seeing a change of heart, which would enable men to be just and equitable to each other. Tiru Mular (fl. before AD 1000) said there is one caste and there is only one God;[13] Nammāḷvār declared that caste could not make one high or low. It was only the knowledge of God that could make that distinction,[14] and Pattakiriar, the Śaivite poet, longed for the day when people would cease to brand their own brothers as men of low birth:

> When shall our race be one great brotherhood
> Unbroken by tyranny of caste,
> Which Kapil in early days withstood
> And taught, that men once were in times once passed.[15]

When Tiruppanāḷvār was prevented from entering the temple of Śrīranga because of his low caste, one of the high-caste devotees entered the temple with him on his shoulders.[16]

But the orthodox auspices, under which the regeneration of Vaishṇavism took place, was too much for the infant wish to be equitable. The great southern Āchāryas grudged even the right of devotion to the Śūdra. They wanted to keep them in complete ignorance. Rāmānuja prescribed for them the *Prapatti mārga*, which means complete dependence on God; his path for the high caste being *bhakti*, by which he means intense meditation on God with a view to the realization of His knowledge. Of this sort of *bhakti*, the Śūdra was considered unworthy.

However, when this Vaishṇavism came to the north, the environments there wrought their influence on it. This was first visible in Rāmānanda, who is said to have come of a high Brahman family of Prayāga. He was educated at Benares, his favourite subject being the Śankaran Advaitic philosophy. But he received the orders of renunciation at the hands of Rāghavānanda, a Viśishṭādwaitin saint in the direct descent of Rāmānuja's discipleship, who is said to have saved his life through his occult powers. Tradition represents Rāmānanda to have lived throughout the fourteenth and a decade in the fifteenth century.[16]

He carefully took stock of the facts as he found them. He realized that there had arisen in the hearts of the low caste a genuine yearning for devotional life, to try to repress which would be sinful. He, therefore, threw open the doors of spiritual domain to all, by organizing an order of ascetic sādhus called Bairāgīs, which everybody was free to enter. He engendered that spirit which crystallizd itself in the adage, 'Let nobody inquire of one's caste, whosoever in love remembers God, is His own.' In the spiritual domain, he not only shook off caste distinction, but cast off race prejudice also. Besides some Brahmans of high caste, who kept the current of Rāmite Vaishṇavism, that never crossed the orthodox limits, flowing in its own channels, a Kśatriya king and two ladies of high birth, his disciples included many drawn from the depressed classes. Dhannā was a Jāṭ, Sena a butcher, Raidās a cobbler, and Kabīr a Mohammadan weaver. *Bhavishyapurāṇa* represents him as having gone to the length of taking back into the Hindu fold many people who had been forcibly converted to Islam. These re-converts are called the *Sanyogīs* or the reunited and are found near Ayodhyā. On this occasion Rāmānanda is said to have performed a miracle by which these people found themselves supplied with the rosary and their foreheads marked with white and red frontal marks.[17] This liberal attitude caused a schism in the ranks of the Śri-Vaishṇavas, to which sect Rāmānanda belonged, and it became necessary for him to found a new line of the Śri-Vaishṇavas, which appears to have some difference with the mother-sect, the Rāmānujan Śri-Vaishṇavism, in fundamental principles. But Rāmānanda too, had been brought up in orthodox training, which did not allow him to go far enough to meet the aspirations of the awakened Śūdras. He had taken the robes of renunciation in accordance with the strict rules of *Āśrama* or the life stages of a Hindu and was a Sanyāsin of the three-staffed order (Tridaṇḍī). No doubt, he unstintingly scattered devotional knowledge to all alike through his discourses, still he was not prepared to make a greater departure from the past. In his *Ānand Bhāshya*, in the chapter on Śūdras, he did not recognize the right of a Śūdra to read the Vedas. And in matters of social concern, he could not be expected to cast off the sense of superiority of a Hindu over a Mohammadan and of one belonging to the regenerate classes (*dwijas*) over a Śūdra. It was left to Kabīr, a Moslem disciple of Rāmānanda, in whom the new thought found its full expression.

The Nirguṇa School

Thus medieval India urgently needed a reform movement which would aim at sweeping away all ignorance and superstition that gave rise to Mohammadan bigotry and fanaticism on the one hand and inequitous social fetters on the other, and that stood in the way of communal rapprochement and social equity.

We have seen how the renunciates of both the races were freely mixing with each other and with the laity of the opposing religions, taking pains to awake and promote neighbourly feelings by pleading for goodwill and tolerance. It was in this that the germs of a spiritual upheaval, in which the needs of the times would find their solution, lay hidden; for it was here that one got the training in throwing the searchlight on one's own race and kith and kin as on others, and here that the two opposing creeds peacefully acted on each other. When in due time, after a slow evolutionary process, the upheaval came in the shape of the Nirguṇa School, it was found that not only were the Hindus and the Mohammadans one, being subjected to same pains and pleasures, griefs and joys, and hopes and ambitions, but also that there existed a common ground even in the domain of religious philosophy, which was dividing the two races. It was realized that the points of contact were rather basic and the differences, which were being exaggerated and emphasized, were unessential. Here were the ideas born of the clash of creeds itself that would alleviate the bitterness thereof. The basis for the common ground on which both the Hindus and the Moslems could amicably meet was supplied by the *Vedānta* of the Hindus and the Sufism of the Moslems, the latter being but the former with a passionate colouring.

The new point of view found its full expression in Kabīr, who, though born of Moslem parents, had spent much of his time in the company of the Hindu sādhus and had learnt his lessons in *Vedānta* at the feet of Rāmānanda and those in Sufism in the association of Śaikh Taqī. In him both *Vedānta* and Sufism joined hands to proclaim that God is one and imageless, that He is not to be found in rituals and forms which are but veils of falsehood hiding Him from us, but is to be realized as one with us being enshrined in our own hearts, and forming the substance in all that exists. And bitterness of the preliminary controversies apart, there was nothing in the new thought against which the sense of a Hindu or that of a Moslem could reasonably revolt. That the idol is not God was nothing new to the Hindu, for the highest philosophy that he revered, that is, *Vedānta,* was loudly proclaiming it; and it must have been a particular fascination for the Moslem. Though the monistic philosophy countenanced by the new school was subtler than the Mohammadan monotheism, it did not apparently conflict against it. No doubt, the idea of the unity of God and man was foreign to Moslem notions of Divinity and was considered *Kufra,* entertaining which meant the forfeiture of one's life; still Sufism which may be said to be a Vedāntic commentary on the Qoran had made the Moslems used to it. Hallāj Mansūr who died on the stake for having declaṛed himself to be one with God (*An'l Haq*) and other Sufis by their steadfastness to their views, even in the face of bitterest persecution from bigoted monarchs, demonstrated that their faith was a reality for which one could gladly sacrifice one's life. When therefore the saints of the new school proclaimed 'He I am' (*So'ham*) somewhat in the Upanishadic strain, the Moslem might be expected not to be alarmed thereby. Kābā in this field of common experience became Kāsī and Rāma became Rahīm.[18] All distinctions between man and man were thus stormed away. For being the creatures of one God, all, whether Hindus or Mohammadans or whatever other designations they may be called by, were one. The folly of shedding blood over differences that did not exist was thus made patent.

When the distinction of race and religion, the bitter memories associated with which were still fresh, could be condemned as unwarranted, there was no reason why the distinction of caste should not meet the same fate. To a Vedāntin, who had fully developed the identity-consciousness, the distinctions of caste were based on falsehood. *Bhagwadgītā* tells us that a really wise man is he who makes no distinction between a learned Brahman, a cow, an elephant, a dog, and an outcaste.[19] But this never meant that the Vedāntin had any desire to reform the traditional social system. Even Rāmānanda, that sturdy champion of equality of all men before God, did not go in for social equality as well. The most that he is said to have done in the way of social reform is this. The southern Achāryas preserved not only strict segregation but also perfect privacy in matters of food, for they held that cooked food and food in the process of being cooked was polluted by the sight of a Śūdra falling on it. Rāmānanda slackened this rigour. He did not consider that the sight of a Śūdra polluted the food, and therefore did not regard privacy as an essential rule for the purity of it. But beyond this he did not go. There was distinction in matters of food and social intercourse even among the Brahmans themselves; how could he be expected to abolish it in respect of their relation with the Śūdras?

But when in Kabīr the utter dislike of a Moslem for all caste distinctions combined with the high Vedāntic conceptions, the traditional social system was faced with an unrelenting foe, who condemned it outright and claimed for the Śūdras perfect equality with the other castes.

Thus did the needs of the times find their realization in the Nirguṇa movement initiated by Kabīr. Nānak, Dādū, Prāṇanāth, Malūkdās, Palaṭū, Jagjivan Dās, Śibadayāl, Tulasī Sāhib, and a host of other saints took up his mission from time to time and worked for the propagation of this movement for unity and equality.

Notes

1. Sale, 'Al Qoran', p. 503.
2. Quoted by I. Prasad in 'Medieval India', p. 92.
3. Prasad, 'M. India', p. 127 on the basis of 'Tabaqāt-i-Nāsiri', Raverty, I, p. 552.
4. Vide footnote 2, above.
5. Barani, 'Tārīkh-i-Fīroz Śāhī' *Bibliotheca Indica*, pp. 290–1, Prasad, 'M. India,' pp. 208 and 475; Elliot, p. 184.
6. Ibid., p. 288; ibid., p. 475; ibid., pp. 182–3.
7. Smith, *Students' History of India*, p. 126.
8. I. Prasad, 'Medieval India', pp. 481–2.
9. हँसत खेलत तेरे देहुरे आया, भक्ति करत नामा पकरि उठाया।
   हीनड़ी जाति मेरी जाद भराया, छीपे के जनमि काहे को आया॥

   —"Granth," p. 629.
10. Quoted by Prasad, 'Medieval India', p. 92.
11. हिन्दू मुसलमान खुदाई के बन्दे। हम जोगी न रखें किस ही के छन्दे॥

    —"Kāfir bodha," 9, "Pauri Ms," p. 243
12. The commercial contact between India and Arabia is as old as 1086 BC ('An Outline of the History of Medicine in India', being the Sir George Birdwood Memorial Lecture by Cpt. P. Johnston St. before the Indian Section of the Royal Society of Arts, London. Reproduced in part by the *Hindu University Magazine*, vol. 29, no. 3, p. 230). Buddhism had crossed the bounds of India in the north-west during the reign of Aśoka and the Mahāyānism, its later development which had absorbed much of the Yoga philosophy and Hindu theism in itself, did it before the fifth century AD Fahian saw it in Khutan. Dr Stein's discoveries corroborate him. The conquest of Sindh by the Arabs took place in AD 712. The conquerors took with them not only the spoils of war, but also the best things that India could offer—its culture, its science, its philosophy. And in that very century, Arabia saw the rise of Sufism. The first mention of the term Sufi is found in Abu Hasan, a Syrian Zahid who died in AD 780 (The 'A'wāriful-M'ārif', p. 1). From AD 756 to 806, the Abbiside throne at Baghdād was occupied by cultured Caliphs like Mansūr and Hārūn Rashīd who liberally patronized learning and worked to that end under the advice of their Barāmakā ministers who belonged to an originally Buddhist family (Nadvi, 'Arab aur Bhārat ke sambandha', p. 94) and were naturally drawn towards Indian culture. Yāhiā Barāmakī

who was minister between AD 790 and 810 commissioned a competent man to inquire into and report on the Hindu systems of medicine and religion. Though the report is not now extant yet a summary thereof is preserved in the 'Kitābūl-pheharist' of Ibn Nadīm who wrote seventy or eighty years after the incident (ibid., p. 167). A perusal of it convinces that the author of the report understood the philosophical significance of the Hindu religious beliefs quite well. The Arabs should have been sufficiently well acquainted with the main religious beliefs of the Hindus before they could enter upon a deeper inquiry into the religions of India, and it is a well-known fact that in India religion and philosophy are intertwined. That Sufi thought does not show traces of the Śankaran Vedānta ought not to lead one to the conclusion that Hindu thought has no part in shaping Sufi thought, for even in India Śankarism is a later development of Vedānta. Possibly, Gnosticism and Neo-Platonism might also have influenced Sufism but it is significant that Mr E. Pecocke in his book *India in Greece* sees everything Indian in everything Greek. It is also not justifiable to term as Sufis the group of men who as a protest against the Qoranic injunction, 'No monarchism in Islam' (The 'A'wārif-ul M'ārif', p. 1), joined in AD 623 to lead an ascetic and monastic life, for the charactristic of Sufism is not simply austerities but an intense love of God which breaks all conventionalism. Howsoever that, the later development of Sufism, which came to India with the conquerors from the north-west and which we are directly concerned with here, took shape in Persia, under the influence of Hindu thought, is a proposition past all controversy now.

13. 'Siddhānt Dīpikā' 11, 10 (April, 1911), p. 433; Carpenter, 'Theism in Medieval India', p. 369.
14. 'Tamil Studies', p. 327; Carpenter, *TMI*, p. 382.
15. Ibid., Tr. Gover, p. 159; Carpenter, *TMI*, p. 369.
16. Carpenter, *TMI*, p. 379.
17. म्लेच्छास्ते वैष्णवाश्चासन् रामानन्द प्रभावतः।
    संयोगिनश्च ते ज्ञेया अयोध्यायां बभूविरे॥
    कंठे च तुलसी-माला जिह्वा राममयी कृता।
    भाले त्रिशूल चिह्नं च श्वेतरक्तं तदाभवत्॥
    —*Bhavishya Purāṇa*, pt. 4, ch. 21, coups. 52–3.
18. काबा फिर काशी भया, राम भया रहीम। —"KG," p. 55, 10.
19. विद्या-विनय-संपन्ने ब्राह्मणे गवि हस्तिनि।
    शुनि चैव श्वपाके च पण्डिताः समदर्शिनः॥—V, 18.

9

Kabir's Place in Indian Religious Practice*

Hajariprasad Dvivedi

During the period in which Kabir appeared, an unprecedented event had occurred in the history of India. This event was the arrival of such a well-organized religious tradition as Islam. This event gave a rough jolt to Indian religious doctrine and the social system. The caste system, which was then thought to be unchangeable, for the first time received a strong blow. The whole Indian environment was upset. Many Brahmin intellectuals

* This text is based on ch. 13 (pp. 178–93) of Dvivedi's Hindi book, *Kabir* (Delhi, 1971). This was first published in 1942. Many of the keywords used by Dvivedi have somewhat different senses in different contexts or have no exact English equivalents. A few of these have been left untranslated (e.g., *ras, acar, nirgun, sagun, lil*). In other cases I have used a single English equivalent, even though it may be slightly awkward in certain contexts (e.g., 'religious practice' for *sadhana*). Dvivedi has also often contrasted words that have only one easy equivalent in English (e.g., *dharma* and *mazahab, jap* and *namaz, Bhagavan* and *Khuda*) but in Hindi clearly mark a distinction between Islam and Hinduism. I have sometimes added the adjectives 'Muslim' or 'Hindu' to make the contrast clear in English (Translator's note).

busied themselves in the search for the cause of this turmoil, and as best they could they made an effort to support their society and religious doctrine.

First, it should be understood why this event was unprecedented and what was its novelty. India was not a new country. Various great empires were buried in its dust. Various great religious proclamations had resounded in its atmosphere. Various great civilizations had sprung up and dissolved in its every corner. Lifeless souvenirs of them are still standing, as if the laughing Goddess of Victory had been paralysed by a ray of lightning. From time immemorial, troops of many castes, tribes, races, and roving nomads have kept coming into this country. For some time they upset the country's environment, but in the end they could not remain foreigners. Their deities came to occupy some among the of thrones and seat themselves, and they became objects of devotion like the more ancient deities, sometimes managing to get even more esteem. It is a characteristic of Indian culture that no interference of any sort has been made in the internal social system and religious doctrine of those tribes, races and castes, yet nonetheless they have been made completely Indian. In the *Bhagavata-purana*, a complete list of such castes is given and it is said that once they take refuge in God [Bhagavan], they become pure. Among them are the Kiratas, the Hunas, the Andhras, the Pulindas, the Pukkasas, the Abhiras, the Sungas, the Yavanas, the Khasas, the Sakas, and also certainly many other castes whose names the author of the *Bhagavata* did not enumerate. The reason Indian culture was able to adopt so many guests is this. From the very beginning its religious practice remained individualized. Each individual has a right to separate religious worship. In a festival, people could join together in a group, but none in practising devotion. In this, each individual is himself responsible for what he does. The sign of excellence is not to believe in a certain religious doctrine or do *puja* to a special god. Rather, it is one's purity of proper moral and ritual conduct [*acara*] and one's character [*caritrya*]. If a person is faithful to the religion [*dharma*] professed by his own ancestors, then his character is pure. Not imitating the customs of other castes or individuals, but rather dying in one's own religion is understood to be meritorious. If one is faithful and honest, then he is excellent, whether he belongs to the Abhira lineage or the Pukkasa guild. Family rank is the fruit of the karma of former births. Character is the symbol of the karma of this birth. A deity is not the property of any one caste, he belongs to all and all have a right to worship him. But if the deity himself wants that the medium for worshipping him should be a particular caste or individual, then Indian society has no objection. A Brahmin will perform worship of the goddess Matangi, but by means of [a priest called] a Matanga. What does it matter if the Matanga is a Candala [that is, an untouchable]. If Rahu stipulates that in order propitiate him it is necessary to give charity to the Doms [that is, untouchables], then the Doms it is. The entire Indian society will give charity to the Doms and will thus protect the moon from the harm of the eclipse. In this way Indian culture has accepted all the castes, together with all their characteristics. But up to now, no such religion [*mazahab*] as Islam had arrived at its door. It did not have the power to be able to absorb it.

What is 'religion' [*mazahab*]? A religion is an organized religious doctrine [*dharma-mat*]. Many people believe in a single God. They follow just one set of behavioural rules and religious ritual [*acar*]. And when they assimilate into their own organized group any individual of any race, tribe, or caste, they make him abandon all his cultural characteristics and accept that particular doctrinal position. Here religious practice is not individualized, it is collectivized. Here religious and social regulations are intertwined. Indian society was an intermixture of various castes. An individual of one caste could not change to a different caste, but religion is just the opposite of this. It makes the individual a part of the group. Each caste of Indian society is a group of various individuals, but the individual of any religion is a part of a large group. The individual of one preserves a separate existence but cannot be separate. The individual of the other is separate, but does not preserve a separate existence.

Muslim religion [*dharma*] is a 'religion' [*mazahab*]. Its organization was completely contrary to Indian social organization. Indian society kept a caste-associated character and fostered an individualized religious practice. Islam omitted caste-associated character and fostered a collectivized religious practice. The central point of one was conduct [*caritrya*], that of the other was religious doctrine [*dharma-mat*]. In Indian society it was an accepted fact that whatever one's beliefs might be, if one's conduct was pure, then that individual was excellent, whatever caste he might belong to. The belief of Muslim society was that one who accepts the religious doctrine that Islam fosters has a right to eternal heaven and one who does not believe in this religious doctrine is compelled to go to eternal hell. India would have nothing to do with such a doctrine. It never held the belief that its highest duty was to break the impiety of a caste that did not accept its *acara* and doctrine. That this thing might be the highest duty of any other, even of this it was unaware. For this reason, when the new religious doctrine made the promise to erase the impiety of the entire world and began to employ all sorts of means, then India could not understand this correctly. Therefore, for some time its tolerant mindset became frustrated. It became agitated. But this frustration and agitation did not please the Creator.

Thus it seems that for the first time Indian intellectuals felt the need of fostering a religious *acar* bound to an organization. Before the coming of Islam there was no single name for this great mass of people. Now its name became 'Hindu', Hindu, that is to say, Indian, that is to say, a non-Islamic doctrine. It is clear that in the non-Islamic doctrine, there were several sorts of doctrines, some monistic, some ritualistic, some Saiva, some Vaishnava, some Sakta, some Smarta, and others of other sorts. The thoughts and traditional doctrines of this mass of people was a great jungle that extended for thousands of kilometres and had lasted for thousands of years. To find a path through the great forest of Smrti, Purana, folk customs, and family customs, was a very difficult task. The Smarta pandits took on this difficult business. Throughout the country a search for scriptural texts began to be undertaken. The aim was that there should be extracted from the texts the sort of doctrine that would be esteemed by all, that there should be in force a single set of rules for funerals and marriages, that there should be a single method for the organization of festivals. Having accepted the scriptures of Indian thought as the foundation, the biggest effort was for the solution of its own biggest problem. From Hemadri to Kamalakara and Raghunandana, many pandits, after much effort, made certain determinations that, although not esteemed by all spokesmen, nonetheless were such that without a doubt, by means of the investigation of the statements of scripture, a somewhat mixed and *acar*-oriented religious doctrine was able to be made firm. This was a very big contribution of the legal digests. The first foundations of the thing that is called 'Hindu solidarity' appeared by means of these legal digests. But this was not the solution to the problem.

The biggest weakness of this effort was its orientation towards *acar*. The new religious doctrine that was shaking up the Indian people and society gave no importance at all to *acar*. Its organization was completely the opposite. The legal digests propounded a doctrine of 'one religion' that was grounded on *acar*. At its core operated a doctrine of acceptance of all opinions. Once one reverently accepted all scriptural statements, this was made into the achievement of the impossible. But the rival it had to work with was very zealous for exclusions. In other words, it had vowed to destroy other doctrines mercilessly, and a religious propensity for exclusion was its chief weapon. Although that society was exclusionist in religious form, it was inclusionist in social form, while Hindu society was inclusionist in religious form and exclusionist in social form. Hindu society could accept any religious practice, but it was not the proponent of accepting any single individual into a religious doctrine. On the other hand, Muslim society understood its highest duty to be the inclusion of the individual in its own religious doctrine, but it considered a special religious practice for any of its own individuals to be completely wrong. The legal digests made the Hindu even more Hindu, but they did not indicate any path to assimilate the Muslims.

In this way, together with the arrival of the Muslims, the Hindu religion became chiefly behaviour-oriented. The tradition of pilgrimages, vows, fasts, and oblation rituals became its core. In this period, in the east and north, the most powerful sectarian tradition was that of the Nath Panthi yogis. We earlier saw that these people did not accept scriptural Smarta doctrine, and they were not in agreement with any philosophical ideology based on the *prasthana-trayi* [that is, the Upanishads, the *Brahma-sutra* and the *Bhagavad-gita*]. But they were able to attract the people's attention. By means of various *siddhi*s [magical powers] they became objects of esteem and awe. They were worshippers of a transcendent Siva or a *nirguna* [without attributes] Absolute. Moreover, their worship was by means of meditation or trance. By means of various sorts of bodily religious practices, that they called 'corporal technique', they made efforts to find the highest Absolute. Those among them who were *siddha*s, *sadhak*s, and *avadhut*s [that is, types of Hindu ascetics] were not householders, but among their disciples were many who had fallen from their ascetic life and become householders. They ended up taking the form of a Yogi caste. The Hindu religion did not esteem householders who had fallen from an ascetic life. To the contrary, it looked on them with disdain. These householders fallen from an ascetic life, then, were not Hindu—since they were not in agreement with any doctrine or *acara* of the Hindus; and they were not Muslims—since they had not accepted the Islamic religious doctrine. After being in contact with Islam for some time, they gradually began to move towards the Muslim religious doctrine, but their inherited concepts remained for a long time. While they were passing through this process, Kabir made his appearance.

Here we should mention two other important religious movements. The first current came from the west. This was the religious practice of the Sufis. The religious Muslims could not harm the central core of Hindu religion, they could only shake its outer body. Moreover, the Sufis were not opposed to Indian religious practice. Their noble path of love began to conquer the minds of the Indian people. Even so, they could not attract the *acara*-centred Indian society. The ideology could not be in harmony with *acara*-centred Hindu religion. Here it is necessary to keep in mind that neither Sufi ideology nor the religious practice of the *nirguna* Supreme Truth of the yogic path were able to carry that great burden of asceticism which was established on following the example of the Buddhist community. In the country for the first time, the caste system had to confront an unprecedented situation. Up to now the caste system had no rival. Individuals who had fallen from *acara* were separated from society and created a new caste. In this way, even while continually creating hundreds of castes and sub-castes, the caste system somehow continued functioning. Now it faced a powerful rival society that was ready to assimilate every individual and every caste. Its only condition was this: that he accepts its special sort of religious doctrine. The individual being punished by being exiled from society was no longer helpless. If he wished, he could get the support of a well-organized society. At this time, from the south there arrived a Vedanta-related bhakti that spread from one end of the great Indian subcontinent to the other. Dr Grierson said: 'Like a flash of lightning, a new thing appeared above all the darkness of religious doctrines. This is the Bhakti movement.'[1] It produced self-illumination in two forms: first in the form of *saguna* [with attributes] worship centred on the Puranic avatars and, second, in the form of the religious practice of *nirguna* love-bhakti centred on yogic meditation on the *nirguna* highest-Brahman. The first religious practice sprinkled interior love on the dryness of the external *acara* of the Hindu caste and filled it with *rasa*. The second religious practice made an effort to eliminate completely the dryness of external *acara*. One took the path of compromise, the other that of rebellion. One took the help of the scriptures, the other that of wisdom. One adopted the *saguna* God, the other the *nirguna* God. But love was the path of both. Both rejected dry wisdom. Both were not in agreement with mere external *acara*. Both desired an internal revelation of love. Disinterested bhakti was desirable for both. Self-surrender to God without any conditions was the favourite means to salvation of both. In these things both were one. Their biggest difference was in their thoughts related to *lila* [God's play in the world]. Both had faith in the love-*lila* of God. Both had experienced that God sustains this awakened universe for His *lila*. But the chief difference was this. The devotee who worshipped with *sagun* emotion experienced God by looking at Him from afar, while the devotee who worshipped with *nirgun* emotion considered the highest aim to be to experience God moving within his own soul.

What is *lila*? It is the highest concept of the Indian devotees. We know that God is transcendent, limitless, unconditioned intelligence, without desire. We also know that He is attainable only through experience, only through his own essential form can the seeker experience Him. He cannot be described, He cannot be spoken about. But these are all things of knowledge. The devotees consider God to be unattainable by knowledge, since the power of humans is limited. The range of their intellect is very ordinary. Nonetheless, He is attainable through love: 'Unattainable by knowledge, you are a beggar of love.' Hence knowledge, all things considered, shows us how little we know. But love makes good all mistakes. However many mistakes a son may have made, his mother still clasps him to her breast, because mother-love makes good all deficiencies. The person who loves makes good, through his own love, all that is lacking: 'If one finds the company of the Beloved, then one has no fear even of hell.' Because hell, finally, is the name of certain deficiencies. Pain is merely the absence of pleasure, and there is only one divine weapon for eliminating deficiencies, namely love. Poverty, pain, and deficiency: these are all synonyms. In age after age, poets and sages have had this experience and have said that the only power capable of eliminating all deficiencies is love: 'The bed may be broken; the house may be leaking, but in the pillow of your lover's arm, pleasure is everywhere.' If someone asks why this is so, then no answer can be given. This is the *maya* [magical power] of God. Like God it is full of secrets and thus indescribable. Moreover, it can be asked: 'Why *maya*?' Why did the perfect Supreme Soul need this complex thing, *maya,* to eliminate the deficiencies of His own creation?

This question is difficult to answer. The wise man calls it '*maya*'. The very wise man perhaps calls it 'instinct'. But giving it a name does not solve the problem. Let it be called '*maya*'. In the universe we encounter secrets of this sort that are beyond the power of the intellect to understand. They are beyond the heart. They are *maya*. But we cannot explain why they are. The devotee gives the answer that God consists of Supreme Love and all this is his *lila*. Whatever is seen, whatever happens, and whatever event is possible, all that is the *lila* of Him who consists of Supreme Love. He finds bliss in playing. He makes complete all that is incomplete in the devotee. Therefore He is the essential form of Supreme Love. But why does the devotee love? Because he makes himself complete. What deficiency does God have that He becomes a beggar of love? The devotee says that there is no reason for this. This love business is simply *lila*. Why *lila*? Simply for the sake of *lila*. What is the object for *lila*? *Lila* itself. What is the fruit of *lila*? *Lila* itself: '*Lila* has no purpose, since *lila* is the state of [not] having any purpose.' Whoever does not understand this *lila*, has gone astray. *Lila* is the light of God's essential form of bliss. The Upanishads have said that what exists has been created from bliss. Whatever is seen, whatever has happened, whatever is about to happen is through bliss. If this bliss does not exist, then even if living beings are created they cannot continue to live. Bliss is the basis of life (*Taittiriyopanisad* 3.6). If every corner of space were not filled with bliss, then no one could take a living breath. God consists of bliss, His essential form is *ras* [enjoyment]. He has this characteristic also, that once He gets *ras*, He becomes full of bliss. Even though His own essential form is *ras*, He is a lover of *ras*, and even though His own form is bliss, He does not become blissful until He gets *ras*. This is a paradox, but the claim of the devotees is that they witness this in the form of experience:

> He is indeed *rasa*. Having obtained *rasa*, He becomes bliss-full. Who breathes in and out, if there is no bliss in the air?
>
> (*Taittiriyopanisad* 2.7)

Whoever will want to investigate this by logic, for him this thing will appear mysterious. But he who will look with the vision of love, for him there is no mystery in it, no contradiction, and no inconsistency. For him, this is God's *lila*. He Himself keeps extended the net of this *lila*. Therefore clearly, He is hungry for love. It is useless to ask: 'What is He lacking since He is hungry? Because all this is His *lila*. The truth is that He does not become blissful without getting *ras*'.—' He becomes bliss-full having obtained *ras*.' For the sake of this *lila*, the Lord, the beggar of love, pours His 'colour' over the devotee who walks on His path. Those who are worldly and whose activities are externally oriented, they do not experience the *lila* of that 'colour'. They walk their own paths. But those who have the experience, they become bewildered. They hear a bewildering cry. A lover, after repeated caresses, expels such a cry whose impact is difficult to bear. This cry pierces the whole body. There is no medicine for it, no mantra, no healing herbs. What can the poor doctor do? Whoever gets such an impact becomes overwhelmed. Whether it is a deity or a man, whether a sage or a man walking on a path, whether a Muslim *pir* [teacher] or *auliya* [holy man], once the impact has been received, it becomes difficult to preserve oneself. Kabir Das is a witness. A man who has received the impact of the Lord's 'colour' gets coloured with all colours. Nonetheless, his colour is different from all colours. Kabir Das himself got coloured in this way. He was wounded by this spontaneous cry of love. Bewildered, he went to the True Guru to ask about a curative treatment:

> *Listen O True Guru, the Lord has poured His colour on me.*
> His word has made an impact on my mind. It has pierced my whole body.
> No herb or medicine is any use. What can the poor doctor do?
> Gods, men, sages, devotees, *pirs* and *auliyas*: no one gets to the other shore.
> Lord, Kabir has been coloured with all colours, but his colour is distinct from all other colours.
>
> (*Kabir Sahab ki Sabdavali*, vol. 1, p. 8)[2]

The season of Phagun [February–March] approaches. The devotee gets drenched with the colour poured by the lover and forgets his own self. With bewildered emotion, he begins to think—Alas, will I be able to find that bliss again? Will I meet that charming Lord again? Will I again be joined in the good fortune of receiving the impact of His colour? Who can take me to the lover? Blessed are the devotees who, each joined with the lover, play Holi. Blessed is the devotee who is His sweetheart, and unfortunate is that female companion who has quarrelled with Him. How can one describe the lover's form? How does the female lover mad with love explain Him as separate. She is absorbed in Him. She has become part of Him. Kabir Das experienced the bliss of the *lila* of Holi. On his testimony, we can believe that that Holi is not the ordinary Holi. On this earth there can be no Holi to compare with it. It is not something to speak about. It is something to be experienced. It is an 'un-tellable story'. The experience of this highest pleasure is joined in the destiny of exceptional persons:

The season of Phagun has approached.
Can someone help me meet with the Lover?
She is the beauty who keeps attention to the Lover.
She is the Lover's sweetheart.
Playing Holi, she does not turn aside her body.
She clings to the True Guru.
Playing, some girlfriends arrive at his house.
Some are tied up with their own families.
Some go astray without the Name,
engaging in quarrels.
How can I describe the Lover's form?
I am absorbed in His form.
She, completely coloured with His colour, is intoxicated
with His beauty.
Body, mind, she forgets everything.
Don't think that this is a simple Holi.
This is an un-tellable story.
Kabir says: Listen, brother sadhu.
This goal only an exceptional person knows.

(*Kabir Sahab ki Sabdavali*, vol. 1, p. 13)

This is *lila*. To understand its mystery is difficult, because this is the solution of all mystery. How can there be a solution of the solution? The devotee's claim is that this [*lila*] is achieved through an experience. *Lila* itself is the path of *lila*. *Lila* is the means, *lila* is the end. A seeker who has once tasted its pleasures, he remains drunk the whole day. No, not just the whole day. He extracts and drinks its *ras* forever after. He remains drunk with its intoxication the whole day. He lives his life in the bliss of Brahman. He dwells in the *lila* of God's bliss. For him, to catch the Truth is easy, because he rises above the true and false. The error of his birth and death runs away. He has no fear, no pain. He becomes fearless.

The whole day he stays drunk.
The whole day he drinks himself drunk.

The whole day he remains drunk with intoxication.
  The seeker lives in the bliss of Brahman.
Truth he speaks and truth he grabs.
  He abandons the false and holds on to the true.
Kabir says: Thus the seeker has become fearless.
  The error of birth and death runs away.
(*Kabir Sahab ki Sabdavali,* vol. 1, p. 84)

The bliss-play or love-*lila* of the devotee with God is the core of the religious practice of all devotees of medieval India. To experience this *ras*-filled *lila* with God is the devotee's highest desire. The *lila* that has no purpose, no fruit, no cause, no beginning, no end. About this, the medieval period's great Vaisnava devotee Visvanath Cakravarti said: 'Love is the highest aim of man.' The things that are commonly called the 'aims of man'—namely dharma, *artha* [wealth-and-power], *kama* [sensual enjoyment], and *moksa* [salvation]—have no allure for the devotee. And Kabir Das has said this in a most effective way:

Madly in love with the Name, one gets drunk and satisfied with love.
Mad for the encounter, one has to be forced to request salvation.
(*Kabir vacanavali,* pp. 80–1)

And, announcing the ideal of bhakti, in unambiguous language, he has said:

Without luck, you will not get the bhakti of pure love.
Without love there is no bhakti, the whole world is full of bhakti.
Whatever bhakti is without love, that is one's own hypocritical thought.
Because of filling one's stomach, one's whole life is lost.
(*Satyakabiraki sakhi*, p. 41)

But Kabir Das was somewhat different from the devotee dedicated to *sagun* religious practice of his own epoch. Although the central core of both types of religious practice is the bhakti of love—whether it be called 'play in bliss', 'love', 'bhakti', '*lila* of Love,' etc.—nonetheless in one thing they are completely distinct. We indicated above that Indian sages in that period had joined in researching the law books and Puranas. They dedicated themselves to ancient Indian tradition. In other words, having accepted everything, having shown an emotion of respect to everything, they set out to complete the path they were themselves walking upon. The troop of *sagun* worshipping devotees were completely supporters of the mentality obtained from this ancient tradition. Intelligently considering all the scriptures and sages as their own leaders, they began to force a compatibility of their words to the cause of love. For this, they did not have to make an ordinary labour. In making a meaning based on a bhakti of love for all the scriptures, they had to accept the necessity of having many authorities and many styles of devotional worship. They had to theorize various stages and occasions. They had to theorize styles of devotional worship of devotees of infinitely varied characters and infinitely varied systems, each depending on the distribution of the elements of purity, passion, and ignorance [that is, the three *gunas* of Samkhya ontology]. To all they gave a proper boundary. Although in the end they had to accept the *Bhagavata-purana* as the chief authoritative text, nonetheless they did not neglect or ignore any scriptural text. Their vision remained directed equally to God's form filled with supreme love and His captivating *lila*, but they forced an illogical compatibility on scripture and established in society an unprecedented faith and love of custom.

Kabir Das's path was just the opposite. By luck, he found a favourable moment. As many paths of tradition as there were, they were all mostly closed to him. He, though being a Muslim, was in truth not a Muslim. Though being a Hindu, he was not a Hindu. Though being a sadhu, he was not a sadhu. Though being a Vaisnava, he was not a Vaisnava. Though being a yogi, he was not a yogi. He was made different from all others and was sent from God. He was the human likeness of God's Man-Lion avatar. Like the Man-Lion he had come to earth on the meeting point of various circumstances thought to be impossible. Hiranyakasipu [the evil demon king and father of the pious demon Prahlad] had requested the boons that the being who could kill him was neither man nor beast, that the time of his being killed was neither day nor night, that the place of his being killed was neither on earth nor in the sky, that the weapon for killing him was neither of metal nor stone, etc. Therefore, to be able to kill him was an impossible and miraculous business. The Man-Lion therefore chose a meeting point of various categories. For an impossible business, perhaps God has a wish for a meeting point of such mutually contradictory categories. Kabir Das stood on such a meeting point, a point from where in one direction Hindu-ness emerges and in the other direction Muslim-ness emerges, where in one direction knowledge emerges and in the other direction lack of education, where in one direction the path of Yoga emerges and in the other direction the path of bhakti, from where on one side *nirgun* Reality emerges and in the other direction *sagun* religious practice. He stood on that excellent crossroad. He was able to look in both directions and he saw clearly the faults and virtues of the paths going in mutually opposed directions. This was the God-given good fortune of Kabir Das. He made good use of it.

As was said in the beginning, Kabir Das began his own religious-practice grounded in the bhakti of love from a completely different shore. This starting point was completely the opposite of the starting point of *sagun* seekers. *Sagun* seekers accepted everything. Kabir rejected everything. The greatness of the devotees of the first group is in their tireless labour and absolute steadfastness, and Kabir's greatness is in his fearsome courage. He began to write on white paper [= a blank slate]. He considered bookish learning that teaches one only to carry a load of knowledge to be useless. It makes a man stupid and deprives him of God's love. On God's love his sight was so firmly fixed that he considered this to be the most important thing.

> Continual reading has become stones, continual writing has
> become bricks.
> Kabir says: Not a drop of love is attached.
> Reading and reading books, the world has become dead.
> No one has become learned.
> He who reads the single syllable 'love' is the one who becomes
> learned.

This love is everything, not the Vedas, not the scriptures, not the Koran, not prayer [*jap*], not garlands, not painted images, not temples, not mosques, not avatars, not prophets [*nabi*], not teachers [*pir*], not messengers [*paigambar*]. This love is way beyond the reach of all external *acara*. It is much better than the performance of all life cycle rites. Whatever stands in its path should be avoided.

Kabir completely rejected all vows, fasts, and pilgrimages. He declared his own aim to be affection towards the one untainted Allah, Niranjan. The means to this affection or love is love itself, and he did not accept any intermediate means. Love is the end, and love is the means, not vows, not Muharram [= the month for mourning the death of Husain], not *puja*, not prayer [*namaz*], not hajj, not pilgrimage [*tirtha*].

I have one Niranjan and Allah, I don't belong to the Hindus
or the Turks.
I don't keep vows nor know about Muharram.
I keep in my memory Him who is the prime cause.
I do not do *puja*, nor do I spend time in *namaz*.
I offer homage to the formless one in my heart.
I don't go on hajj, nor do *puja* at sacred bathing places.
I recognize the One, where is the second?
Kabir says: All error has fled, my mind is attached to the one
Niranjan.

(*Kabir granthavali, pad* 338)

The Muslim teachers and messengers, the *qazis* and mullahs, their fasts and prayers, and their bhakti of labour: these are all mistaken. And the Hindu gods and Brahmins, their eleventh day fasts and Diwali festival, and their bhakti of the eastern quarter: those are also all mistaken. Indeed, the God of the Hindus resides in the temple and the God of the Muslims in the mosque, but where there is no temple and no mosque, who exercises divine sovereignty there? Kabir Das did not accept all these things and did not accept those people who are content to walk with their eyes closed. He walks out, making his own soul his companion. He says: O Fakir, Go on your own path. Don't go to the temple and don't face towards the mosque. Why do you fall into quarrels? For you there should be no difference between Ram and Rahim or Kesava and Karima. For you both are one. The one has no second.

Whether He is called Ram, Rahim, Karima, Kesav,
Allah or Ram, for me He is the true.
Having stopped saying 'In the name of Allah',
one can say 'World-supporter.' But He is One.
There is no other.
Of the [Muslims] there are *qazis*, mullahs, *pirs*, messengers,
fasts, prayer towards Mecca in the west.
Of the [Hindus] there are the eastern direction, gods,
Brahmins, puja,
the eleventh day fasts, the Ganges, lamps,
Turks in the mosque, Hindus in the temple.
In both places exists the divine power of Ram.
In the place where there is neither mosque nor temple,
there who has the sovereignty?
The paths of both the Hindus and Turks are broken
and cracked,
Below and above, in all ten directions, here and there,
everywhere king Ram is present.
Kabir Das says: O fakir, go on your own path, brother.
The Creator of the Hindus and Turks is one.
The goal which is He is not seen.

(*Kabir granthavali, pad* 58)

But Kabir did not stop here. If the word 'Allaḥ' represents Muslim religion and the word 'Rama' Hindu culture, then he is ready to pay homage to both. In the end, any word will do. But if Arabic and Persian words remind one of Muslim culture and Sanskrit and Hindi words remind one of Hindu culture, then Kabir Das does not allow this division of intellect to flourish. Going beyond the Vedas and Koran, he says:

There the sky thunders and the rain always falls.
A trumpet is blaring continuously.
There there is no reach of the Vedas and Koran.
Kabir says: There some hero enjoys himself.

(*Kabir Sahab ki sabdavali,* vol. 1, p. 85)

In this way Kabir Das, having shown great courage in rejecting all exterior religious *acar*, appeared on the field of religious practice. Merely to reject is not a thing of importance. Anyone can reject anything. But to reject obstacles that block a great purpose is truly a work of courage. A rebellion without a purpose is destructive, but a rebellion dedicated to a good purpose is the dharma of a hero. With unswerving confidence, he established his own path of love. All his life, he waged war against the great army of conventions and bad concepts. Temptations and setbacks, desire and anger certainly must have stood in his path, but he conquered them with unlimited courage. His only means was the sword of knowledge. He did not allow this wondrous sword to stop even for an instant. It was wielded even-handedly, but he also did not abandon love of virtue. This was his shield. Without pity, he cut the snares of bad concepts, conventions, and external *acar*. Taking his head in his hand, he emerged to face his own fate. Even for an instant, his eyebrows were not furrowed. He did not show displeasure. He waged war like a true hero.

> He wields a sword evenly.
> Some saintly hero endures the game.
> Having conquered the troops of desire, having given blows to anger,
> There in the place of highest pleasure he meets Surati.
> Showing love for virtue, he takes the sword of knowledge.
> He comes into the arena and plays the game.
> Says Kabir: That Sant, devotee and hero,
> He offers his own head, and he makes his move.
> (*Kabir Sahab ki sabdavali*, vol. 1, p. 86)

What do the people who consider Kabir Das to be a reformer who ecumenically harmonized the Hindu and Muslim religions have to say about this? It is hard to imagine. Kabir's path was very straightforward. He was not one who harmonized by bowing down to both. He was a revolutionary who destroyed all the snares of external *acar* and bad concepts. Compromise was not his path. The ability to reject such big snares cannot be found in an ordinary man. A man of weak sinews cannot bear such a heavy burden. Someone who does not have unbroken confidence in his own mission cannot be so remarkably resolute.

Kabir, then, having rejected all external *acara*, carried out a religious practice that seated man on the throne of the common man and God on the throne of the impartial God. What the consequences of this were and whether or not it will be useful in future or not, these questions are not so important. Success is not the only touchstone of greatness. Today, perhaps, this truth is being experienced with intense emotion, namely that having preserved the particular characteristics of all, a common role of human interaction cannot be prepared. Having cut the net of the many particular characteristics related to caste, family, religion, concepts, beliefs, scriptures, and communities, that throne can be prepared where one man can meet another according to their natural human capacities. As long as this does not happen there will be a lack of peace, there will be struggle, there will be violent rivalry. Kabir Das sowed the seed of this great religious practice. What the fruit was, this question is not important. The best poet of the present time, Rabindranath Tagore, has confidently sung that in life *puja*s cannot be fulfilled. I know well that they also have not been lost. The flower that falls to earth before it blooms, the river whose stream gets lost in the desert, I know well that they are not lost. In life, even today, whatever has been left behind, whatever has been unfinished, I know well, even that has not been in vain. Whatever my future is, that which is even now untouched, all these things are being played on the strings of your *vina,* I know well, they have not been lost....

Kabir Das's religious practice also has not disappeared, has not been lost. He was completely confident that the religious practice of whoever is with God and whoever has unbroken confidence in his own aims cannot be moved even if one shakes it for millions of ages.

> Whose mind is confident, is always with the guru.
> Shaken by millions of deaths, even then his intellect is not broken.
> (*Satyakabiraki sakhi,* p. 184)

[Essay translated from Hindi by David N. Lorenzen]

Notes

1. I could not find the original English of this quote and had to translate it back to English from Hindi (Translator's note).

2. The page references given here and elsewhere have been changed, when possible, to correspond to newer editions. The publishing details are noted at the end of this essay (Translator's note).

References

Kabir granthavali, edited Mataprasad Gupta (Allahabad, 1969).
Kabir Sahab ki sabdavali, vol. 1 (Allahabad, 1989).
Kabir vacanavali, edited by Sri Ayodhyasimha Upadhyay (Varanasi, Sam. 2044).
Satyakabiraki sakhi (Bombay, 1984).

V

Historical Overviews

10

Towards a New Perspective*

Krishna Sharma

Rationale

The inquiry which led to this work was initially undertaken to examine the social and political impact of the Bhakti movement. It was prompted by the ambivalence and inconsistencies noticeable in its evaluation in the historical studies on medieval India. All lapses in the assessments made in this regard stem from the accepted unitary approach to the Bhakti movement, which is not viable. A striking disparity exists amongst what are reckoned as the constituents of the Bhakti movement. The ideological differences that mark the positions adopted by the medieval bhaktas are a clear indication of this. Besides, the religious modes and organizational aspects of the sects, the origins of which are attributed to this movement, show a wide range of variations. Hence, what is referred to as the Bhakti movement, was not a unified or homogenous movement as such. The designation, in fact, covers a number of religious movements—each with its own

* From *Bhakti and Bhakti Movement: A New Perspective* (New Delhi, 1987), pp. 1–38.

distinctive features and ethos. Some of them were even antithetical to one another, notwithstanding their common denominator, bhakti.

Since the so-called Bhakti movement was a multiplex phenomenon, the nature of its impact also had many dimensions. But their proper comprehension is hampered because of its treatment as one integrated movement. This monolithic view of the Bhakti movement has given a leeway for general theorizations about its social and political impact, regardless of its many-sided character. Generalizations of this type are arrived at through concentration upon some one particular aspect of the movement in isolation from its other facets. The contrarieties existing within the totality under question are not taken into account in such instances. This tendency is quite evident in the historical writings on the subject. For example, when the Bhakti movement is described as a radical movement aimed at socio-religious reform and new social values, the fact that it included certain fundamentalist and conservative forces as well is either ignored or underplayed. In fact, if the Nirguṇa bhaktas like Kabīr and Nānak had rejected the caste hierarchy and all social conventions based on caste distinctions, Saguṇa bhaktas like Tulsīdās had zealously upheld the sanctity of the caste system and the supremacy of the Brahmins. If the former had championed new social values, the latter had advocated the preservation of the existing social order and socio-religious norms. If the teachings of one group had led to the emergence of new unorthodox and protestant sects, those of others had nourished and reinvigorated the old existent Hindu sects.

Similarly, when the spirit of universalism and belief in the essential unity of all religions is ascribed to the Bhakti movement, contrary factors related therewith, and their consequences in the opposite direction, are overlooked. If Kabīr and Nānak stood for the non-acceptance of the differentiation between Hindus and Muslims, the ideology of the Vaishṇava bhaktas could have but a limited appeal, that is, for the Hindus only. Besides, a strong sense of a separate Hindu identity is sometimes detectable in some of the Vaishṇava bhaktas. Insofar as the final outcome of the Bhakti movement is concerned, instead of the convergence of different religious groups, it had led to the multiplication of religious sects, orthodox as well as unorthodox. An outstanding paradox in this respect can be seen in the rise of Sikhism. The followers of Nānak, a man who had stressed upon the meaninglessness of all sectarian and religious differences, had developed not only a separate sectarian identity, but also a separate religious identity. Whereas Nānak had preached the non-difference of the two major religions of the Indian subcontinent, Hinduism and Islam, the sect founded by him gave shape to a third.

In the context of the contemporary political situation also, certain paradoxical aspects of the impact of the Bhakti movement deserve special attention. The finality of the establishment of the political dominance of one religious community (Muslim) over the other (Hindu), in itself must have necessitated the activization of forces conducive to the peaceful coexistence of the two. Peace was a necessity for both. Perpetual strife was not in the interest of either. The message of universalism and oneness of all religions, as given out by some of the medieval bhaktas, could provide a leverage to both the communities to ensure the required peace and stability: to one, for the consolidation of power and a conscious drive to establish a popular government; to the other, for survival with dignity, and a willing adjustment with the new political structure. One stream of the Bhakti movement, therefore, must have contributed in its own way, towards a political rapprochement and concordance between the two warring communities. Nevertheless, another aspect of this movement could serve as an opposite force that could lead to political confrontations. The religious fervour inspired by the medieval bhaktas had resulted in the galvanization of people into groups with a common ideology and a common code of conduct. Although such groups had emerged in the form of different religious denominations only, they could sometimes assume the nature of communities with a potential for concerted activity. At times, the sense of its definite identity and unity could lead a group into political action to achieve political objectives. Considering the inversions of the impact of the Bhakti movement on the medieval political scene, it is not surprising that references are made to it in altogether contrary contexts. On the one hand,

Akbar's eclectic approach to religion and culture and his state policy of religious tolerance are attributed to the climate of opinion generated by it; on the other, it is invariably recounted in historical works as a contributory factor in the emergence of Maratha and Sikh nationalism, the two forces that conflicted most with the Muslim imperial power.

The aforesaid paradoxical aspects of the Bhakti movement relate to social and political issues that are of great consequence to the historian. As indicated earlier, my original intention was to examine only these issues. However, for the analysis of the social and political content of the Bhakti movement, one was constrained to start with certain basic assumptions. One had to accept what is generally understood by bhakti and the Bhakti movement. In other words, the terms of reference had to be drawn from the existent academic framework. But I became sceptical about the legitimacy of that framework while working on the established lines. The given definition of bhakti seemed not only non-viable, but also erroneous; similarly, the monolithic approach to the Bhakti movement seemed both unwarranted and untenable. Proceeding ahead with the task of examining the social and political impact of the Bhakti movement without questioning these seemed illogical and unsound. I was convinced of the necessity of reviewing the existing terms of reference and of the need for a new perspective for the study of bhakti and the Bhakti movement. *This meant the rejection of the current academic definition of bhakti, which has served as the substratum of all theorizations about the Bhakti movement.*

In all academic works, historical as well as others, bhakti is defined as a monotheism based on devotion to a personal God, and as the opposite pole of the monistic stream of the Hindu religious tradition which advocates belief in an impersonal God. Bhakti is therefore understood as the antithesis of the Advaita Vedānta and its emphasis on jñāna. What is known as the Bhakti movement is interpreted in accordance with these specifications of bhakti. Its inspirational source is therefore fixed in the theologies of the medieval Vaishṇava āchāryas—Rāmānuja, Nimbārka, Madhva, and Vallabha—all of who had upheld the concept of a personal God and had questioned the Advaita or monistic interpretation of the Vedānta. This perspective is generally accompanied by the proposition that the movement was a reaction against the religious ideology of Śaṅkarāchārya, the greatest exponent and systematizer of the Advaita Vedānta. It is argued that the impersonal concept of the God and the path of jñāna, which Śaṅkara had stressed upon, amounted to a purely intellectual approach to religion. Such an intellectualized religion was beyond the comprehension of the common man who needed a simple faith in a personalized God—a God unto whom he could surrender, a God whom he could love, adore, and depend upon. It is further posited that Rāmānuja, Madhva, Nimbārka, and Vallabha fulfilled this need by propagating the 'bhakti cult', the popularity of which led to a countrywide movement of bhakti during the medieval period.

For the examination of the social and political dimensions of the Bhakti movement, therefore, one had to begin with the following assumptions: (a) that bhakti was a religious mode and belief; (b) that the Bhakti movement was an assertion of a 'bhakti religion' against the path of jñāna and the Advaita Vedānta of Śaṅkarāchārya; (c) that this movement had a unitary character since bhakti (as academically defined) was common to all medieval bhaktas; and (d) that the systems of Vedānta propounded by Rāmānuja, Nimbārka, Madhva, and Vallabhāchārya constituted the ideological base of the Bhakti movement. But the validity of all these assumptions seemed questionable. A closer look at the personalities connected with the movement showed an absence of a common ideology in the first place. Besides, the ideology implied in the standardized definition of bhakti could not be applied to them all. The metaphysical foundation of the ideas propounded by bhaktas like Kabīr, Nānak, Dādū, and Raidās, does not conform to the positions taken by Rāmānuja, Nimbārka, Madhva, and Vallabha. On the contrary, their views stand closer to those of Śaṅkarāchārya.

To resolve the inconsistencies observed, it became imperative to have a clearer understanding of the concept of bhakti itself. But a closer look at the main religious texts[1] that are generally cited to uphold the current meaning of bhakti made it all the more difficult to accept it as correct. A comparative study of

Śaṇkara and the four medieval Vaishṇava āchāryas did not help either. It only gave rise to further questions. Besides, the bhakti of the medieval bhaktas did not present any uniform pattern of ideas, beliefs, and practices. Evidently, there was something inherently wrong with both the operative definitions of bhakti and the monolithic view of the Bhakti movement. *I therefore abandoned the existing framework, and made that itself the subject of my inquiry.* It seemed evident that a lot of theorization had taken place about the Bhakti movement in the light of a faulty definition of bhakti, and that an elaborate superstructure had been erected over a set of wrong hypotheses. The resultant errors could not be corrected without questioning the given definition itself. The basic error obviously lay there.

Bhakti is a generic term meaning loving devotion or attachment. It signifies a feeling and a sentiment, that is, an emotive state of mind. Its meaning can get particularized only when the entity towards which it is directed is specified. For example, guru-bhakti is devotion for the preceptor, whatever that may mean or imply in a given situation. Similarly, deśa-bhakti is love and attachment for the country whatever it may involve or require. Accordingly, the word bhakti, when used in the religious context, can acquire particularity only when the name or the notion of the deity to whom it is directed is mentioned along with it. Only then can it indicate a particular theology and religious mode. For example, Vishṇu-bhakti (as well as its variations, that is, Kṛishṇa-bhakti, Rāma-bhakti) and Śiva-bhakti can be legitimately explained in terms of Vaishṇava and Śaiva theologies. By the same token, since bhakti stands particularized here, it can be interpreted in the light of the sectarian thought, practices, and beliefs of the Vaishṇavas and Śaivas respectively. Therefore, even in the religious context, the term bhakti, when used without any prefix, can mean devotion to God only in a general sense, and nothing more. By itself, it does not suggest any doctrinaire or ideational position, nor any particularized concept of God, personal or impersonal. Since the Hindu religious tradition is pluralistic in character in regard to beliefs, ideas, and practices, bhakti (in the sense of religious devotion) cannot be confined to any one part thereof. Nor can it be lent a specific meaning in the light of any particular sectarian theology or religious behaviour.[2] The present academic definition of bhakti, therefore, is erroneous and unwarranted.

A definition is a specification implying or containing a configuration of determinants. The justification and correctness of a given definition, therefore, lie in a valid and uniform configuration of the relevant elements. If one element or factor contained in a definition changes, and all others remain unchanged, the definition tends to lose its validity and exactitude. Continued usage of the same definition cannot then mean or deal with the same thing. If these principles are accepted, the current definition of bhakti cannot be applied to all Hindu expressions of bhakti. Nor can it be applied to the whole of what is known as the Bhakti movement. As stated earlier, the definition under question comprises three factors, namely, the belief in a personal God, a non-monistic view of reality, and the negation of the efficacy of jñāna. Not all Hindu devotional forms conform to these. There are some which rest on a configuration of opposite factors. The same holds true of the medieval devotional movements as well, which are collectively referred to as the Bhakti movement. The personalities connected with them show an uneven combination of these factors. In some, not only is there a total absence of the accepted determinants of the bhakti definition, but also the presence of those totally opposed to them. Although Saguṇa bhaktas like Chaitanya, Tulsīdas, Sūrdas, and Mīrabai uniformly conform to at least one factor, namely, the belief in a personal God, the approach of most of them is flexible with regard to the other two. The teachings of the Nirguṇa bhaktas like Kabīr and Nānak are not in keeping with any one of them. They uphold the impersonal concept of God, the monistic view of the Ultimate Reality, and the importance of jñāna.

Since the medieval period was marked by a regeneration of various religious sects and ideologies, the medieval expressions of bhakti were also varied in nature. What is summed up under the general designation, Bhakti movement, was really an amalgam of a number of devotional movements. A monolithic view of these movements can be taken only if their common denominator, bhakti, is understood in its generic sense. Not otherwise.

The difference and juxtaposition of the Nirguṇa and Saguṇa schools of bhakti (upholding devotion to an impersonal and personal God respectively) are far too clear in the medieval devotional movements. In contravention to the accepted academic definition of bhakti, the former was characterized by monistic thought and the idea of an impersonal God. As indicated earlier, the Nirguṇa bhaktas were in greater agreement with the Advaita Vedānta of Śankarāchārya than with the theologies of the Vaishṇava āchāryas—Rāmānuja, Nimbārka, Madhva, and Vallabha. And yet, even when a distinction is made between the Nirguṇa and Saguṇa streams of bhakti in relation to the medieval period, the convention persists of taking them as parts of a common movement which is traced back to the aforesaid Vaishṇava āchāryas. The result is an academic ambivalence which can at once be attributed to the persistent usage of a fallacious definition of bhakti. The existing ambivalence can be removed only if the generic meaning of bhakti is recognized. In other words, by replacing its present definition which is a '*definition specifica*' with its '*definition generica*'.

The non-acceptance of the current academic definition of bhakti has, therefore, served as the starting point of this inquiry. The rejection of the unitary approach to the Bhakti movement has followed it as its logical corollary. The new position taken in this work draws its maximum validity from the discovery of the fact that the accepted definition is of very recent origin. Evidence found to that effect shows clearly that the modern academic definition of bhakti was, in fact, formulated in the nineteenth century by some Western scholars regardless of the indigenous understanding of it. Having arrived at this conclusion, it was easy to identify the fallacies inherent in the established notions about bhakti and the Bhakti movement. All relevant issues connected with the two themes could be reviewed thereafter in freedom from the accepted terms of reference.

Postulations and Groundwork

It is my contention that the modern definition of bhakti, the basis of all interpretations of the Bhakti movement, was formulated by certain Western Indologists of the nineteenth century. Without belittling their invaluable contribution to Indian studies in general, it must be said that the definition of bhakti was wrongly conceived by them. It was wrongly conceived since it is not corroborated by Hindu evidence. A deeper probing into the relevant Western writings leaves no doubt that it was evolved gradually, and artificially, with the aid of alien standards of judgement. The process of its formulation can be traced back to the identification of the general term bhakti, first with Kṛishṇa-bhakti, and then with Vaishṇavism as a whole. Subsequently, the Western Indologists were able to define bhakti as a religion and doctrine with the help of whatever knowledge they could gain of the history and theology of Vaishṇavism. The differentiation between religion and philosophy, and between monotheism and monism, had served as the major factors in their theorizations. These differentiations were based on the principles that belief in a personal God is a necessary concomitant of theism, and that all impersonal explanations of God constitute part of philosophy and not of religion. Therefore, the scholars who elaborated upon the bhakti theme associated religion and Hindu theism with the worship of the personal deities. They described the impersonal concept of God found in the *Upanishads* and the Advaita Vedānta as pure philosophy. Taking this position, they projected Vaishṇavism as a monotheistic religion since it showed both the presence of a personal concept of God and concentration on the worship of one personal deity, be it Vishṇu or his incarnation, Kṛishṇa. Bhakti (made synonymous with Vaishṇavism) was thus explained as a monotheism and was distinguished from the monism of the Hindu philosophical tradition.

The above standards of judgement were drawn from a totally alien context and had no relevance to Hinduism. They had originated in the West and were a direct result of the theological exercise undertaken by the Christian thinkers from the seventeenth to the nineteenth centuries to safeguard the Christian concept of a personal God. The need for such an exercise had arisen on account of the advent and growth of modern European philosophy during that period. The growing trend towards the impersonalization of God in modern European philosophy had posed a serious threat to Christianity which could be counteracted only through a reiteration of faith in the Biblical God, who was personal in nature, and was different from the God of the philosophers. As a consequence of this, religion and philosophy, which had gone hand in hand till then even in the Western world, were disentangled and rendered apart. This separation of religion and philosophy was accompanied by the growth of a new mode of theology which was the result of intensive Christian intellectual activity. The Christian theologians now made it explicit, as never before, that religion was a matter of faith and emotion, and not of knowledge and reason. Acceptance of the philosophical abstractions regarding God was not to be confused with the true belief in God. Theism, therefore, was technically defined as belief in a personal God. The differentiation between monotheism and monism was an outcome of this definition of theism, and the principle of division between religion and philosophy. Monotheism was defined as belief in *One Personal God*; and the philosophical explanations of the oneness of God in impersonal terms, as either pantheism or monism.

However, the barometers used to arrive at the present definition of bhakti have no validity vis-à-vis Hinduism in which religion and philosophy have always remained interconnected and wherein 'theism' does not necessarily imply belief in a personal God. Besides, the Hindu thinkers never thought of making any distinction between what is understood by monotheism and monism. In other words, the impersonal concept of God (as Brahman or Ātman) has been as much a part of Hindu religious tradition as the worship of numerous personal deities. Disregarding these factors, when the Western scholars applied alien criteria in the analysis of Hinduism, it resulted in a number of misconceptions, including those connected with the bhakti theme.

The whole of the religio-philosophical and sectarian content of Hinduism can be viewed in two broad divisions; namely, the Śruti and Śmṛiti traditions.[3] The same are indicated by the terms Nigama and 'Agama, the former representing the Vedic/ Upanishadic/stream and the latter, the Itihāsic/Purāṇic stream. The two were never taken as exclusive of each other by the

Hindus. In fact, for purposes of synthesis, they were very often referred to in conjunction with each other as Nigamāgama or Śruti-Smṛiti-sammat. Nevertheless, the two traditions are distinguishable. Bhakti as religious devotion, however, is reckoned as a necessary condition for religious pursuit in both. One (the Upanishadic)[4] lays stress on devotion to the Nirguṇa Brahman or an impersonal God; the other (the Purāṇic), on devotion to personal deities.[5] If these two forms of devotion are accepted as Nirguṇa-bhakti and Saguṇa-bhakti, there is continuous evidence of both in Hinduism. Whereas Saguṇa-bhakti can be connected with the various Hindu traditions of the worship of personal deities, the genesis of Nirguṇa-bhakti can be traced back to the Upanishadic speculations about the Nirguṇa Brahman and the monistic view of reality. If the generic meaning of bhakti is taken into account, and if Nirguṇa-bhakti is recognized as a particular form of bhakti, the question of incompatibility between bhakti and the impersonal concept of God can hardly arise. The possibility of bhakti within the framework of the Advaita Vedānta would not seem incongruous then. Similarly, if jñāna is understood in its Vedāntic meaning of knowledge of the Brahman (by the self of the Self in the sense of Self-realization), it would not appear as antithetical to bhakti.

While discussing the errors and limitations of the current theories about bhakti and the Bhakti movement, I have tried to establish Nirguṇa-bhakti as a category separate from that of Saguṇa-bhakti. The contention is that a co-relation between the two is possible—but not essential. They stand corelated when the saguṇa (determinate) or personal concept of God is identified with the nirguṇa (indeterminate) concept of the Brahman or vice versa.[6] Nevertheless, synchronization of the two is a striking characteristic of the Hindu religious tradition. Exceptions to the contrary are extremely rare. But when a definite emphasis is laid on any one of them in particular to the exclusion of the other, the difference between Nirguṇa-bhakti and Saguṇa-bhakti becomes significant. Their difference can then get sharpened to the extent of one cancelling out the other. That is to say, belief in a highly personalized image of God (for example, as Vishṇu or his incarnation Kṛishṇa, etc.) may not leave any room for Nirguṇa-bhakti—and a strict commitment to the belief in the impersonal nature of God may rule out Saguṇa-bhakti altogether. If we take examples from the medieval Bhakti movement, it can be said that the bhakti of Chaitanya represented the former phenomenon; and that of Kabīr and Nānak, the latter. Chaitanya had placed Kṛishṇa-bhakti above every other form of religious devotion. The Chaitanyaite school, therefore, had taken an almost antagonistic position vis-à-vis Nirguṇa-bhakti. Kabīr and Nānak, on the other hand, had condemned outright the worship of personal deities and their idols because of their total observance of Nirguṇa-bhakti. It may be added here that in contrast with the extreme positions adopted by these bhaktas, Tulsīdas had managed to maintain a co-relation between Nirguṇa and Saguṇa bhakti.[7]

Besides underlining the non-applicability of the present academic definition of bhakti to the tradition of Nirguṇa-bhakti, I have also made an attempt towards a reassessment of Hindu theism and monotheism. This is done because the errors involved in the bhakti theories include a misrepresentation of these as well. Reference to bhakti as a monotheism, and to the Bhakti movement as a monotheistic movement, raise the following fundamental questions. Judging entirely from the Hindu viewpoint, can Hindu theism be divorced from Hindu philosophy? And Hindu monotheism, from Hindu monism? Taking into account the Hindu pantheon and the seeming Hindu polytheism, in what way can the existence and nature of Hindu monotheism be correctly determined? Is it justifiable to connect Hindu monotheism with the worship of any *one* personal deity of the Hindu pantheon, like Vishṇu, as suggested in the Bhakti theories? Should it not be sought in the realm of Hindu speculations about the oneness of God? My inquiry into the nature of Hindu theism and monotheism is an attempt to answer these questions. Such an inquiry is very necessary to rectify the long standing errors that the modern definition of bhakti entails.

Since pointing out the lapses and inconsistencies of any well established theory in itself cannot lead to its total negation (for that can well be taken as a matter of a different interpretation only), I have considered it much more important to prove the artificial nature of the bhakti theories. It was imperative to undertake such an exercise. Only this, and this alone, can clear the area of doubt which can arise on account of the new postulations made. A two-way course has been adopted to achieve this. One, by tracing the entire process of their formulation and two, by examining the non-Indian bias that gave them their present shape. The first has led to the recounting of the writings of the Western orientalists responsible for their origin. The second necessitated a branching off to the intellectual history of Europe from the seventeenth to the nineteenth centuries to trace the genesis of the alien conceptual framework and the standards of judgement that shaped the bhakti theories.

While delineating the formulation of the modern definition of bhakti and the related theorizations, I have traced their beginnings to the writings of H. H. Wilson, Albrecht Weber, Lorinser, Monier-Williams, and George A. Grierson. The core idea was provided by Wilson. It was he who first mentioned bhakti as a religion in his *Sketch of the Religious Sects of the Hindus* (1846). Making a stray and casual observation about the Vaishṇavas of Bengal, he wrote that 'their religion' could be summed up in one word 'bhakti'. Wilson was obviously referring to the Kṛishṇa-cult of Gauḍīya Vaishṇavism which had taken shape as a result of the teachings of Chaitanya. He did not define bhakti in general terms. Nor did he connect what he described as the bhakti religion with Vaishṇavism as a whole. Nevertheless, Wilson's reference to bhakti as a religion opened the way in Western scholarship for treating Kṛishṇa-bhakti as the 'bhakti religion', and for the subsequent identification of the 'bhakti religion' with Vaishṇavism in general. The writings of Albrecht Weber and Monier-Williams contributed most in this regard. The in-depth study of the Kṛishṇa-cult undertaken by Weber made the link already established between Kṛishṇa-bhakti and the 'bhakti religion' more firm. Whatever he said about Kṛishṇa-bhakti was taken as an elaboration of the nature of the 'bhakti religion'. This idea was strengthened by Lorinser, a contemporary of Weber, who drew attention to the *Bhagavad Gītā* as its relevant scripture.[8] Subsequently, Monier-Williams used this connection to identify the 'bhakti religion' with Vaishṇavism. As a result, bhakti acquired a wider connotation. It became possible to theorize further upon it in relation to Hinduism as a whole. Monier-Williams now described the Vaishṇava faith (identified with bhakti) as a monotheism, placing it in juxtaposition to the monism (also described as pantheism) of the *Upanishads* and the Advaita Vedānta. For purposes of the analysis of the multidimensional Hindu religious traditions, Monier-Williams categorized its contents under two broad divisions, that is, Brahmanism and Hinduism. He made a distinction between the religion of 'the higher, cultured, and thoughtful classes as Brahmanism'; and 'of the lower, uncultured, and unthinking masses as Hinduism'.[9] He placed the Upanishadic/Vedāntic content under the former, and the cults of the personal deities and the related sects, under the latter. This categorization was, however, an over-simplification of a sort since it ignored the interrelation and the intermixture of the elements placed under the two.[10] But it went a long way in helping Monier-Williams to draw a distinction between Hindu monism and monotheism. In short, bhakti through the writings of Monier-Williams, got more firmly defined as a monotheism in its Western technical sense, that is, as a religion of love and devotion for a personal God, accompanied by a feeling of otherness on the part of man in relation to Him.

Using the broader canvas provided by Monier-Williams, George A. Grierson constructed a historical account of Vaishṇavism and called it the 'ancient monotheistic religion of India' by tracing its antecedents in the religion of the Bhāgavatas, and in the Ekāntika-dharma mentioned in the *Mahābhārata*. Whatever he said in this connection was taken as an elaboration of the nature and history of the 'bhakti religion'. Grierson added yet another factor to the bhakti theme. He linked the medieval Hindi bhakta poets with the ancient religion of bhakti, and described the religious movements led by them as the collective expression of its resurgence during the medieval period. This description of the different devotional currents of that period as the 'Bhakti movement' was followed by further theorization to fix its source of inspiration in the system of Vedāntā evolved by the medieval Vaishṇava āchāryas (Rāmānuja, Nimbārka, Madhva, and Vallabha).

The bhakti theories were constructed, step by step, by the aforesaid authors through: (a) their general works on Hinduism; (b) the articles they contributed to the different learned journals (particularly the *Journal of Royal Asiatic Society*); and (c) the papers they read at various Oriental conferences from time to time. The whole academic process of their artificial formulation was complete by 1909 when the current definition of bhakti in its consolidated form was incorporated in the *Encyclopedia of Religion and Ethics* edited by James Hastings.[11]

The bhakti theories initiated by the Western Orientalists found a ready acceptance amongst the Indian scholars of the nineteenth century. Since the beginnings of the study of Hinduism on modern academic lines were made by Western scholarship, the approach of the early Indian academicians who first used the historical-analytical methods in the study of Hinduism was largely determined by it. Amongst other things, they could not avoid working within the limits of the definition of bhakti as laid down by the Western scholars. R. G. Bhandarkar was the first Indian scholar to write on the bhakti theme. Although he expressed some difference of opinion in regard to the current theories about bhakti, he did not question the basic premise on which they rested. He had differed from his Western contemporaries mainly on the question of the influence of Christianity on the 'Bhakti religion'.[12] Refuting Weber's theory of the Christian influence on bhakti, Bhandarkar managed to prove the remote antiquity of Kṛishṇa-worship and Vaishṇavism by bringing forth literary and epigraphic evidence. But he did not question the Western equation of bhakti with the Kṛishṇa-cult and Vaishṇavism. His writings, therefore, could only add a new dimension to the picture presented—they could not change or replace it. The operative definition of bhakti continued to remain the same. In fact, its acceptance, usage, and elaboration by Bhandarkar made it more firm.

Dealing with the alien bias that runs through the bhakti theories, I have traced the origins of the criteria used for their construction in the history of Western thought. The criteria under question pertain to: (a) the division between religion and philosophy; (b) belief in a personal God as the mark of true theism;

and (c) the differentiation between monotheism and monism. The formulation of these principles, as stated earlier, has a direct link with the conflict between religion and philosophy which began in the West during the seventeenth century, and continued thereafter. The new philosophical viewpoints tended to impersonalize God and explain His oneness through abstractions about the oneness of the Ultimate Reality. The Christian thought tried to neutralize these viewpoints by highlighting the Christian faith in the personal nature of God. These parallel developments finally resulted in the general acceptance of the principles mentioned above. To elucidate this, I have examined the growth of modern European philosophy from Descartes (1596–1650) to Hegel (1770–1831)—and also of Christian thought from Pascal (1623–62) to Schleiermacher (1768–1834). The objective is to focus attention on the exact nature of the challenge posed by the new philosophical thought to Christianity and the factors that determined the Christian responses. The principles under question were the outcome of the latter.

The modern European philosophers on the whole, showed two different trends: (i) to include God in their philosophical systems; and (ii) to keep Him and religion outside the realm of philosophy. Descartes, Spinoza, Leibniz, Berkeley, and Hegel represent the first; Locke, Hume, and Kant, the second. Descartes had placed God in the category of 'innate ideas'. Spinoza described Him as the 'eternal existence'. For Leibniz, He was the 'original simple substance' and the 'sufficient reason' for the 'pre-established harmony of the universe'. Berkeley defined Him as the 'eternal invisible mind'. Hegel explained Him as the 'Absolute', 'Idea', 'Mind', and 'Spirit'. All such explanations were impersonal abstractions, none of which could be truly adjusted with the Christian view of God. Locke's philosophy was not concerned with the nature and existence of God. According to him, there could be no 'idea' outside human experience. Hume subjected religion to philosophical reasoning and said that Christianity could not stand 'the test of reason'. He stated that since religion was only an aspect of human nature, speculations about God could not constitute rational knowledge. According to Emmanuel Kant also, questions pertaining to conventional religion did not fall within the 'legitimate limits' of philosophical investigations. Thus Locke, Hume, and Kant (each in his own way) had kept God outside the realm of philosophy.

The Christian thinkers rejected all explanations of God offered by the philosophers and proclaimed that religion and philosophy were two separate realms. They evolved a new form of Christian theology, through modern modes of reasoning, to establish the validity of the personal concept of God. Sharpening the difference between religion and philosophy, they defined religion strictly in terms of faith in a *personal* God. The conceptual categories of theism, monotheism, pantheism, and monism, as they are understood today, were evolved in accordance with the pattern of Christian theology which took shape after the emergence of modern European philosophy, to serve the Christian purpose. Subsequently, they were commonly used by the Western scholars in studies of other religions as well. No doubt, these categories could be applied with equal justification in the study of revealed religions similar to Christianity.[13] But not to Hinduism. To the extent the Bhakti theories were conceived with the aid of these categories based on alien norms and non-Hindu criteria, they were artificial and contrived.

In order to prove the fallacious character of the bhakti theories further, I have scrutinized the main Hindu religious texts that are cited in their support. They are: the *Bhāgavad Gitā*, the *Bhāgavata Purāṇa*, and the *Bhakti Sūtras* of Nārada and Śāṇḍilya. The *Bhagavad Gitā* was the first that was utilized by the Western Indologists to lend authenticity to their theories. Since they at the very start had identified bhakti with the Kṛishña-cult in particular, the presence of Kṛishṇa in this otherwise philosophical work helped them in interpreting it as the 'Gospel of Bhakti'. Subsequently, they dwelt a great deal on the *Bhāgavata Purāṇa* (which concentrates mainly on Kṛishṇa-worship) to justify their ideas about bhakti. The *Bhakti Sūtras*, however, were put to use at a much later stage of theorization. All these texts have been carefully analysed to show they do not conform to the modern definition of bhakti. Each one of them gives due recognition to the two forms of bhakti, that is, the Nirguṇa and the Saguṇa. That the *Bhāgavad Gitā* should do so is easily understandable since it was, in any case, an attempt at synthesizing the different schools of philosophy and religious beliefs. But even the *Bhāgavata Purāṇa*, which is truly a Vaishṇava text, does the same. The *Bhakti Sūtras* of Nārada and Śāṇḍilya also speak of the two forms of bhakti, although Śāṇḍilya concentrates on Nirguṇa bhakti, and Nārada on Saguṇa. It is significant that even Nārada does not rule out the former. The current academic definition of bhakti, therefore, is not borne out by the texts mentioned above. In none of them is the meaning of bhakti confined to the worship of a personal God. Bhakti is viewed by all in conjunction with jñāna. Furthermore, there is no evidence in these texts of any inherent contradiction between bhakti and jñāna and between bhakti and a monistic view of reality.

After establishing the spurious nature of the Bhakti theories, I have gone into the misconceptions caused by them vis-à-vis the medieval Bhakti movement. In this connection, the discussions on 'Bhakti in the medieval context' in this work are concerned mainly with two issues. Namely, the historical perspective used for the study of the Bhakti movement, and the non-justification of taking a monolithic view of it. While dealing with the first, an attempt is made to nullify the theories that the Bhakti movement was the result of the propagation of bhakti as a religious ideology by Rāmānuja, Nimbārka, Madhva, and Vallabha. Dealing with the second, attention is drawn to the fact that the whole of the Bhakti movement cannot be taken as a reaction against the Advaita Vedānta and the path of jñāna as advocated by Śaṅkarāchārya. The validity of the presuppositions employed to arrive at these conclusions has been duly questioned. The presuppositions are: (i) that Rāmānuja, Nimbārka, Madhva, and Vallabha had put forward a uniform doctrine of bhakti, conformable to its modern academic definition; (ii) that bhakti is absent in Śaṅkara; and (iii) that the main difference between him and the aforesaid āchāryas was that of jñāna and bhakti. Negative evidence has been presented to prove the inexactitude of these assumptions. It is shown that the main difference between Śaṅkara and the medieval āchāryas is rooted in their respective concepts of Nirguṇa and Saguṇa Brahman. Whatever disagreement there is between their interpretations of the Vedānta, in terms of monistic and non-monistic views of reality, is also related to these concepts. The positions of Śaṅkara and the four medieval āchāryas have been examined to show that the latter were Vaishṇavas first and foremost,[14] and that the differences they had with Śaṅkara did not hinge on any 'Bhakti religion' as such, but were caused by their Vaishṇava loyalties. Also, that their systems of Vedānta were in the nature of a Vaishṇava response to the challenge posed by the growing influence of the Advaita Vedānta of Śaṅkarāchārya.[15]

Questioning the correctness of the monolithic approach to the Bhakti movement, the example of Kabīr is taken up as a case study to elucidate the point that all the medieval bhaktas can neither be adjusted with the present definition of bhakti, nor with the theological movements led by Rāmānuja, Nimbārka, Madhva, and Vallabha. This holds true of not just Kabīr, but of all the Nirguṇa bhaktas of the period. The example of Kabīr for a detailed study has not been chosen at random, but for a valid reason. He was the pioneer of the medieval movement of Nirguṇa-bhakti which found a rich expression in the fifteenth and sixteenth centuries. Although his activities were more or less confined to Benaras, the trend set by him led to a number of similar movements in different parts of the country. He preceded Nirguṇa bhaktas such as Nānak, Dādū, Raidās, Dhanā, and Senā, all of whom form a chain of like-minded men. It is true that the followers of each one of them (including those of Kabīr), formed separate sects of their own, but broadly speaking, they all shared many common beliefs. The movements they led gave shape to a new popular cult, namely, that of the Nirguṇa-pantha. The medieval sects of Kabīr-panthīs, the Sikhs, the Dādū-panthīs, the Raidāsīs, the Satnāmīs, etc. fall within this tradition of the Nirguṇa-pantha. This is not to suggest that Kabīr was the harbinger of an altogether new religious ideology. Though there was much that was new in his message, he was very much the product of the religious forces that had been at work long before him. Our inquiry, therefore, does not stop at recognizing the distinctive features of Kabīr's Nirguṇa school; it proceeds further, to pick up those strands from the contemporary context which contributed towards its making.

The religious climate of North India during the early medieval period was characterized by the predominance and popularity of three major factors, namely, the precepts of the Advaita Vedānta, Tāntricism, and yogic practices (with high concentration of Haṭha-yoga). The Advaita Vedānta had acquired a unique status in the eighth century and after. Besides finding general acceptance within the Brahminic fold, its influence had penetrated deep into the Buddhist and Jaina traditions as well. The Tāntrika beliefs and practices were imbibed by Hindu as well as Buddhist groups. Haṭha-yoga had assumed a popular form and had led to the formation of important sects which were predominantly yogic in character. Out of the three factors mentioned above, the first shows continued vitality, whereas the other two show signs of either decline or transformation, caused by some form of extremism or another. The licentiousness that had crept into Tāntricism affected the measure of its popularity, leading to its final decay. Too much emphasis on the physical aspects of yoga caused the need for a reversal to its meditative aspects, and also for the transformation of the yogic sects which had initially concentrated most on Haṭha-yoga. During the later medieval period, the two forces that finally retained their popularity in North India were the ideology of the Advaita Vedānta and the contemplative aspects of the yogic tradition.

A unique and significant development of the medieval period was the meeting of the āstika and the nāstika traditions[16] on a large scale. Kabīr's Nirguṇa school was very much the product of this trend also. Although there had been much interaction between the two earlier, and although there is evidence of mutual assimilation of precepts and practices on both sides, the two had followed separate courses till then, without any instance of one merging or getting transformed into the other. Such a merger and transformation are first seen in the emergence of the Nātha-pantha, and later, in the Nirguṇa school of bhakti. The Nātha-pantha was an offshoot of the nāstika tradition of the Buddhist Siddhās. But it had upheld many āstika values as well. The transformation of the Buddhist Siddha tradition into the Nātha-pantha came about when Gorakshanātha tried to cleanse the former of the Tāntrika elements by replacing them with the yogic. His preference for yoga was coupled with āstika beliefs in the existence of an eternal Reality (which was clearly rejected in Buddhism) and a broad acceptance of the monistic philosophy. Gorakshanātha had also incorporated the cult of Śiva-worship in his sect which brought the Nātha-pantha close to the Śaivite sects. These features of the Nātha-pantha gave it the character of an āstika sect in spite of the fact that it had stemmed from the nāstika Buddhist Siddha tradition. Nevertheless, it had retained certain residues of its nāstika background as well. The heterogeneous character of the Nātha literature is a good indicator of the nature of this sect. On the one hand, we have the Nātha texts in Sanskrit (the orthodox literary medium for religious writing); and on the other, a sizeable number of verses composed in the different vernaculars of the north. The former must have been for the consumption of the Brahmins and for giving the sect an honourable status; the latter were obviously meant for the masses and for popularizing the Nātha teachings.

The Nirguṇa school of Kabīr presents a similar kind of phenomenon of a dynamic combination of the āstika and nāstika elements. His religion was based on monistic ideas and an impersonal concept of God which had been part and parcel of the āstika tradition from the Upanishadic times. But his attitude of questioning the established religious norms and mores, and of rejecting them by the use of reason, shows the influence of the nāstikas. His severe attack on the caste system, idol worship, and ritualism was possible only because of his adoption of the unorthodox spirit of the nāstikas.[17] Similarly, his use of the spoken language for communicating ideas, which were conveyed earlier only through the medium of Sanskrit, was also in keeping with the nāstika tradition.

There is a direct link between the medieval school of Nirguṇa bhakti and the Nātha-pantha. The connecting link is Kabīr. The influence of the Nātha-pantha on Kabīr is a generally recognized fact by now.[18] Nevertheless, further exploration is still required regarding the interconnection between the Buddhist Siddhas and the Nātha-pantha, and between the Nātha-pantha and Kabīr's movement, for determining the antecedents of the one mentioned last. A clearer understanding of the processes of transformation and transmutation of the first two, and of the points of differentiation of all three, is important in this regard. I have not been able to examine these at length. Nevertheless I have made some general observations about them against the total background of the medieval religious situation. One thing seems quite clear. Just as Gorakshanātha had caused the transmutation of the Siddha tradition by cleansing it of its decadent practices by launching a religious movement in a new direction, Kabīr had served a similar purpose in relation to the Nātha-pantha. If the Siddha tradition had lost its vigour because of the preponderance of Tāntrika practices, the Nātha-pantha had faced a similar crisis on account of its extreme emphasis on the Haṭha-yoga. The Nātha-pantha, in its decadent stages, had turned into a sect in which the physical aspects of yoga and the external lifestyle of a yogi had become ends in themselves. Such a development could undermine the importance of the attitude of the mind and heart in religious pursuits. Kabīr replaced the importance of Haṭha-yoga with that of the emotive element of bhakti in his school. Since Kabīr had been under the influence of the Nātha-pantha, he did use the terminology of Haṭha-yoga in his verses.[19] But if a total view is taken of his ideas on yoga; they are related more to the discipline of the mind than that of the body. He concentrates more on the state of dhyāna or constant remembrance, in achieving which the yoga of the body is meant to serve only as a helpmate.[20]

Besides the modification of the Nātha-panthī attitude to Yoga, Kabīr's bhakti had moved more positively towards mysticism. The Advaita Vedānta, when coupled with the practice of the meditative yoga, had always led to the mystic path. But the truly mystic modes had remained more or less confined to the sādhus and sannyāsīs who always stood as a class apart from the common man. Kabīr, through his movement of Nirguṇa-bhakti, gave mysticism the form of a popular religion—open to all. He based his religion not on any particular scripture or doctrine, but on mysticism itself. As a true mystic, he regarded the personal spiritual experience alone as the final truth. The formal philosophical controversies over the questions of the Dvaita (dualistic) and Advaita (non-dualistic) explanations of the Ultimate Reality, and the Nirguṇa and Saguṇa nature of the Brahman were thus totally irrelevant for him.

I have traced the antecedents of the medieval school of Nirguṇa-bhakti on the above lines to invalidate the theory that the inspiration for the whole of the Bhakti movement was provided by the Vaishṇava āchāryas and their systems of Vedānta. Through the example of Kabīr, I have tried to disconnect the Nirguṇa bhaktas not only from the Vaishṇava āchāryas, but also from Vaishṇavism as a whole. Dealing with the question of the link between the Vaishṇava guru Rāmānanda and Kabīr, attention is drawn to the fact that certain Vaishṇava sects had also come under the influence of the Nātha-pantha, and that Rāmānanda belonged to one such Vaishṇava sect. For that matter, living in Kāśī, the citadel of Hindu learning, Kabir must have had contact with various religious men and groups, Vaishṇava as well as others. Belonging to the Muslim community as he did, he could not have gained that deep understanding of the Hindu religious heritage without that.

While examining the antecedents of Kabīr I have not gone into the question of the Sūfī influence on him for the simple reason that his concepts, images, and idioms are predominantly Hindu. They can be understood only against the background of the totality of Hindu religious thought. This is not to suggest he had no knowledge of Sūfīsm, nor that he had no contact with the Sūfīs.[21] Nor is it to say he had not been influenced at all by the Sūfī tradition. If despite his Muslim upbringing,[22] Kabīr could familiarize himself so well with the multifarious nuances of Hindu thought, he must have been familiar with Sūfīsm also. But there are no positive marks of any Sūfī influence in his verses, as against the overwhelming presence of the Hindu. Nor do we have any evidence of his connections with any Sūfī sect. If there are similarities between his ideas and Sūfīsm, those are similarities due to the common factor of mysticism which cuts across the divisions of formal religions distinguishable from each other. Mystics of all religions share certain essentials, namely, the spirit of universalism and the principle that the inner spiritual experience is the most authoritative source of determining and realizing religious truth. But since mysticism in general finds expression in every religion in one form or another, for academic purposes, its nature can be particularized only in the light of its intellectual and verbal expression. That is, the terms of reference used in a particular pattern of mysticism may be in keeping with one definite religious tradition or the other. Judging from this angle, Kabīr's mysticism is very much in line with the Hindu. Furthermore, mysticism had been an integral part of the Hindu religious thought right from the beginning.[23] In contrast with this, in the case of revealed religions like Christianity and Islam, the mystic elements appeared only at a certain point of their history. Chronologically speaking, Islam had its beginnings in the sixth century AD but the Sūfīs or the Muslim mystics are not heard of before the eighth or ninth century. Moreover, they had to struggle long to obtain the approval of the orthodox Muslims before their precepts and practices could be accepted as a part of the Islamic heritage. The rapprochement between Sūfīsm and Muslim orthodox opinion could not be achieved till the twelfth century.[24] In view of this, and the antiquity as well as the continuous existence of Hindu mysticism in India, the possibility of any direct or fundamental borrowing of ideas from Sūfīsm by Nirguṇa bhaktas like Kabīr seems rather remote.

The ideology and antecedents of Kabīr set him apart from the Saguṇa bhaktas of the medieval period. The same can be said about the other Nirguṇa bhaktas as well. The Nirguṇa and the Saguṇa bhaktas did not share a common ideology, nor were the sources of their inspiration the same. They represented very different socio-religious and intellectual currents of the medieval period. A proper evaluation of the different religious movements that constitute the totality signified by the name Bhakti movement can be possible only if the Nirguṇa and Saguṇa bhaktas are taken as two separate groups. The distinction made between them, particularly in literary studies,[25] has not led to a disentanglement of the two groups. The Nirguṇa and Saguṇa bhaktas continue to be taken as parts of a common movement that is traced back to the medieval Vaishṇava āchāryas. The treatment of the Bhakti movement, in historical as well as literary studies, suffers from this lapse.

The Bhakti movement, as said before, was a variegated phenomenon. The unitary approach to it tends to diffuse the ideological differences between the Nirguṇa and the Saguṇa bhaktas. Their differences, however, were not marginal, but fundamental. The Saguṇa bhaktas had strengthened the existent sects, and had supported the established socio-religious norms.[26] As against this, the Nirguṇa bhaktas had taken a radical position, and their teachings had led to the formation of new and unorthodox sects. The Bhakti movement, therefore, embodied the conservative and the liberal, as well as the revivalist and the reformist trends. It contained forces of both conformism and dissent. These different elements can be sifted and judged separately only if the dichotomy presented by the Nirguṇa and Saguṇa bhaktas is faced squarely. The monolithic treatment of the Bhakti movement, and the historical perspective that sustains it, have been questioned in this work to provide a *raison d'être* for the *polarization* of the two groups. This alone can help in ascertaining correctly the impact of the different facets of the Bhakti movement on medieval Indian society and religion.

Some outstanding questions related to the study of the Bhakti movement which have engaged the attention of the historians can be examined afresh, if the Nirguṇa and Saguṇa bhaktas are viewed as two different and independent groups. These questions pertain to the evaluation of the Bhakti movement as a movement of dissent and social reform, the assessment of the impact of Islam on it, and the contribution of this movement towards the improvement of Hindu–Muslim relations and communal harmony. New queries, which should be of equal significance for the historians, can also be posed on the same basis. Queries such as, why was the impact of the Nirguṇa bhaktas felt more in certain regions of the country? Why do the conventionalist and the radical movements, led by the Saguṇa and the Nirguṇa bhaktas respectively, show greater vitality in comparison with each other at different points of time during the medieval period? I have not dealt with these questions since they fall outside the purview of this book, the main objective of which is to establish reasons for abandoning the conventional framework used for the study of the Bhakti movement.

Historians' Approach to the Bhakti Movement: A Critique

The general interpretation and analysis of the Bhakti movement has been pre-eminently the concern of the historian. Whereas sociologists, literary critics, etc. may concentrate on any one aspect thereof and stop there, the historian must look at it in its entirety. Microscopic studies of different parts of a general theme are, of course, of equal importance for the historian. But since the main obligation of the historian is to trace the process of development, he must strike the interconnection between the different facets of a given phenomenon and the different stages of its formation. Therefore, although the Bhakti movement has engaged the attention of scholars belonging to other disciplines as well, the work of interpreting and analysing it as a whole has remained the forte of the historian. Since the perspective for viewing it as an integrated movement is provided by the historian, it is but natural for those belonging to other disciplines to take the lead from him. That is why even when findings of the latter, within the limits of their specific areas of inquiry, reveal disparate factors within the Bhakti movement, they tend not to question its unity. For example, the advance of sociological inquiries into various sectarian movements of the medieval period, which reveal their diversity, have not raised the relevant questions regarding the validity of treating them as parts of a common movement. Similarly, the numerous literary studies in Hindī and other vernaculars on the medieval bhaktas, even when they bring into light sharp differences amongst them, have not led to the denial of a common source of inspiration for them all. Thus the picture presented by the historian is not disturbed in spite of the new facts brought forth through growing scholarship on the subject. A wrong framework, therefore, continues to enjoy academic legitimacy in other disciplines on account of its firm acceptance in historical studies.

Curiously enough, assessment of the Bhakti movement in Indian historical studies had not emerged from the discipline of history itself. It was not shaped by the historian, but by the Indologists. In other words, it was not achieved through the historical analytical method of first examining the facts, taking all the variables into account, and then drawing the conclusion from the total evidence. In contrariety with this, the Indologists had framed the definition and the conceptual theories about bhakti first (and that too with a definite Western bias), and had then applied those theories to the medieval Indian religious situation. Thus a connected account of the Bhakti movement was first conceived by the Indologists. Subsequently, the historians merely incorporated it in their general works on medieval Indian history. Needless to state, while doing so, they also accepted the given definition of bhakti.

A significant fact must be noted in this connection. The Bhakti movement does not find mention in the general works on Indian history written before the crystallization of the Bhakti theories. The earlier works on Indian history do not give any account of the socio-religious phenomenon of the medieval period which is now referred to as the Bhakti movement. However, once the Bhakti movement acquired a place in historical writings on medieval Indian society and culture, new dimensions were added to it by the historians themselves. Fuller accounts of the history of bhakti and the Bhakti movement followed suit but invariably in accordance with the basic definition of bhakti as provided by the Western Indologists. No doubt, this helped a great deal in reconstructing the socio-religious history of medieval India. But not without errors, errors that were inevitable on account of the use of a wrong frame of reference. The results are: (i) investigations in the history of Vaishṇavism are accepted as historical accounts of the 'Bhakti cult' (because of the subtle identification of bhakti with Vaishṇavism) without any controversy; (ii) the Bhakti movement is treated as a monolith (in the light of the given definition of bhakti) despite the variations observable therein; and (iii) because of this monolithic approach, generalizations are made about the Bhakti movement which are not viable. The first two have been discussed already. They do not require any further elaboration. However, the kind of historical writing related with the third deserves a closer attention here. A few examples of these are discussed below.

An important line of generalization based on a monolithic view of the Bhakti movement relates to the question of the role and influence of Islam in bringing it about. The reason for the great concern of the historian with this is obvious, since the ascent of Islam in India had coincided with the flowering of the Bhakti movement. It is argued that the movement was largely inspired by the Islamic ideology. But theorizations in this direction suffer from a number of discrepancies. When Tarachand, Yusuf Hussain, and many others speak about the impact of Islam on the Bhakti movement, they correlate the two on the following grounds. One, that the idea of a personal God, which is the mainstay of Islam, constituted the core of the Bhakti religion also. Two, that emotionalism, simplicity of faith, and the spirit of surrender that characterize Islam, were emphasized by the Bhakti movement also. The fact is overlooked that these similarities, if they can be fixed at all, can have bearing only on one stream of the Bhakti movement (the one represented by the Saguṇa bhaktas), but not on the totality it represents. The Nirguṇa bhaktas on the other hand, attached great importance to the impersonal concept of God, a monistic view of reality, jñāna, and individual spiritual endeavour. While fixing the influence of Islam on the Bhakti movement, silence is maintained with regard to the glaring contradiction between the following facts: (i) that orthodox Islam leaves no scope for the idea of an impersonal God and the principle of non-dualism between God and man; and (ii) that the Nirguṇa bhaktas had emphasized precisely these.

Similarly, the whole of the Bhakti movement is described as a crusade against the caste system and idol worship. This aspect of the movement is attributed to the influence of Islam. And legitimately so, since Islam is an egalitarian religion; and out of all religions, the most intolerant of idol worship. However, the fact cannot be ignored that all the medieval bhaktas had not opposed the caste system and idol worship. Only the Nirguṇa bhaktas had adopted that stance. The caste system and idol worship were not questioned by the Saguṇa bhaktas. It is noteworthy that the Saguṇa bhaktas who preached the religion of surrender and simple faith in a personal God (attributed to the ideological influence of Islam) had done so with a strong commitment to idol worship, a thing which was blatantly contrary to the spirit of Islam. Insofar as the caste system is concerned, but for a very few exceptions like Chaitanya, the Saguṇa bhaktas had not said or done anything to reject it.

The assessment of the Bhakti movement in general as a movement of religious reform and social change is also questionable. Although the movement included a drive towards these, it contained contrary forces as well. No doubt there were many bhaktas who struggled to create public opinion against meaningless rituals, superstitions, and the social inequalities caused by the caste system. Such bhaktas were definitely imbued with a desire to bring about change in contemporary society and religion. But there were the other bhaktas also (they too are reckoned as the leaders of the Bhakti movement), who zealously upheld the ritualistic and conventional forms of religion.[27] The latter showed a positive concern for the sanctity of the caste system and the social supremacy of the Brahmins, to ensure the perpetuation of the existing social order.

The monolithic approach to the Bhakti movement and the adherence to a faulty definition of bhakti continue to serve as the base for all modes of theorizations on the subject, resulting in a multiplication of interpretative errors. The most recent development in this respect can be seen in the writings of the Marxist historians. Using the standardized definition of bhakti and the Marxist idiom simultaneously, some of them suggest that the bhakti religion was an accordant of the medieval feudal order. The argument offered is that the spirit of devotion and surrender it professed in relation to the deity was the same as that which was expected from the serf for his lord. At the same time, the Bhakti movement is described by some others as an expression of the rise and assertion of the lower classes and a manifestation of protest against class exploitation. Thus the 'Bhakti ideology' is interpreted by the Marxist historians as one of submission as well as dissent. These are conflicting points of view conveniently arrived at through the use of Marxian concepts. The intention here is not to enter into any general debate about the Marxist interpretation of history as such. It is only to underline the fact as to how the use of a misconceived definition of bhakti and a unitary approach to the Bhakti movement have led to numerous interpretations, including the Marxist, which are unjustifiable.

D. D. Kosambi was the first Marxist scholar to establish a link between bhakti and feudalism. Observations to that effect were made by him in his book *The Culture and Civilization of Ancient India* and also in a separate essay he wrote on the *Bhagavad Gitā*.[28] He interpreted the 'doctrine of bhakti' as the 'unflinching loyalty' to God similar to the loyalty that linked together 'in a powerful chain, the serf and the retainer to the feudal lord'. According to him, bhakti 'suited the feudal ideology perfectly'.[29] Borrowing Kosambi's views on bhakti in toto, R. S. Sharma describes the medieval Bhakti movement as a reflection of the medieval feudal order. Bhakti, he states, 'reflected the complete dependence of the tenants or semi-serfs on the landowners in the medieval times'. While examining the issue of the transition from ancient to medieval Indian history, he goes to the extent of listing bhakti, along with feudalism, as one of the major characteristics of Indian 'Medievalism'.[30] This line of theorization[31] is obviously based on the academic definition of bhakti which has been questioned throughout this work. However, even if we were to accept the said definition, that is, even if bhakti is taken strictly as devotion to a personal deity, its history had been traced back to the pre-Christian era by the nineteenth-century Indologists themselves, who had framed that definition. Besides, evidence of bhakti for personal deities can be found throughout the religious history of India. Its practice and importance still prevail. How can it then be connected specially with a particular economic pattern or any one stage of economic development, medieval or otherwise? Moreover when R. S. Sharma sees the correlation between medieval bhakti and feudalism, he commits the grave mistake of ignoring the medieval school of Nirguṇa bhakti. The Nirguṇa bhaktas were committed to the belief in an impersonal God and had opposed the worship of personal deities. Besides, their thought shows a strong note of dissent and revolt. The stream of medieval bhakti can hardly be taken as something in keeping with the feudal characteristics of surrender and servitude.

As stated earlier, the Marxist interpretations of the Bhakti movement work in two opposite directions. On the one hand, it is explained as a corollary of the feudal order; on the other, it is viewed as a revolt of the lower classes. In the latter kind of interpretations, caste is easily identified with class. The validity of equating the two remains a moot question. Nevertheless, the caste system being what it is, by and large, the lowest castes did comprise the working classes. It is also a fact that the bhaktas like Kabīr, Dādū, Raidās, and Nāmadev who led a crusade against the caste system came from lower castes and class. But many leading bhaktas belonged to the higher castes as well. For example, Chaitanya, Tulsīdās, and Sūrdās were all Brahmins. So were the four āchāryas (Rāmānuja, Nimbārka, Madhva, and Vallabha) who are accepted by all historians (including the Marxist) as the harbingers of the medieval Bhakti movement. Even the Nirguṇa bhakta Nānak belonged to a high caste. Nānak was a Khatri (or Kshatrīya). So were all the ten Sikh Gurūs who headed the sect founded by him. It does not seem valid therefore to describe the whole of what is known as the Bhakti movement as a movement of the lower castes only.

It will not be out of place to mention here Irfan Habib's reference to the medieval bhaktas in his discussion on the agrarian crisis of the Mughal empire.[32] Pointing out the importance of the 'ties of caste and religious communities' in the peasant uprisings, he lists the names of Kabīr, Dādū, Haridās, and Nānak as leaders of a movement which had led to the formation of new religious communities during the medieval period. His contention is that they 'belonged mostly to lower classes'. It is interesting to note Habib's stratification of their castes. While he mentions that Kabīr was a weaver, Dādū a cotton carder, and Haridās a Jāt, he refers to Nānak as a grain merchant, without mentioning his caste. It seems this omission is due to the intent of projecting the class character of the movement led by bhaktas like Nānak. Neither by birth nor by trade did Nānak (a Khatrī and a grain merchant) belong to a lower caste or class.[33]

Notwithstanding the use of common analytical tools, the Marxist historians have thus come forward with divergent viewpoints about the Bhakti movement. If R. S. Sharma sees the Bhakti movement as a reflection of the contemporary feudal order, Irfan Habib seems inclined to detect in it seeds of a class conflict leading to social mobility. According to Habib, the movement led by bhaktas like Kabīr, Nānak, and Dādū. had opened a new avenue for social mobility for two classes in particular, namely, the artisans and craftsmen in the towns, and the rural peasant groups such as the Jāts in the rural areas.[34] Evidently, if the Bhakti ideology is accepted as feudalistic in character (as done by Kosambi and Sharma), it can hardly be interpreted as a thing which could be helpful in bringing about any kind of social mobility for the artisans and the peasants (as suggested by Habib).

Irfan Habib's postulations about the Bhakti movement need further probing here, since they have conditioned the writings of many other historians. According to him, the Muslim conquest had led to the expansion of the class of artisans and craftsmen in towns. New and greater demand for certain goods by the ruling class had led to the creation of new skills and crafts, and the 'adoption of new professions by members of the indigenous population'. The lower castes readily took to these for they could give them a new dignity in the caste hierarchy. Since this meant the breaking of caste rules, the anti-caste religious movement of Kabīr, Nānak, etc. found a greater following amongst the growing class of these artisans in North India. 'The visible breaches in the walls of the caste system, and the economic temptation to break its rules,' he states, 'lay behind the artisan's fervour' for this movement. Picking up the example of the Jāts from the peasantry, Irfan Habib explains that the Jāts were a pastoral people to begin with, who had later taken to agriculture—a fact that 'demeaned them in relation to other peasant communities'. He goes on to say, 'It was inevitable that they should protest against a social discrimination, which had no material basis any longer; and the contemporary monotheistic movement provided the best and strongest form of such protest. In the guise of a Sikh or Satnāmī, a Jāt peasant would assert a dignity which was previously denied to him. In its turn, the movement itself obtained a far broader support for itself in the region of the Jāts because here it reached beyond the ranks of the artisans into the peasants.' Comparing the support that the Bhakti movement had from the artisans and the peasants, Habib writes: 'Looking at such information as we possess about the social classes affected...we notice that artisan classes are uniformly involved. The involvement of peasantry, on the other hand, does not appear to be universal.'[35]

Since Irfan Habib's views on the Bhakti movement are accompanied by the theory about the expansion of the artisan class after the Muslim conquest, it may be stated here that this theory was first put forth by Muhammad Habib.[36] The latter had advanced that theory to explain the cause of the easy political success of the Muslim invaders in India. According to him, their success was due to the appeal of the new egalitarian ideology (Islam) for the growing class of the artisans in the urban areas (a consequence of the Muslim conquest) who were keen to gain their freedom from the shackles of the caste system. There is a striking similarity in the arguments of Muhammad Habib and Irfan Habib in this regard. The former uses them in the context of the Muslim conquest, and the latter in relation to the Bhakti movement. Taking the aid of Muhammad Habib's theory of the growth of the urban artisan class as a sequel to the Muslim conquest, Irfan Habib states similar reasons to explain the causes of the popularity of the Bhakti movement within this class. This is easily done by substituting the ideology of Islam (used by Muhammad Habib) by that of the Nirguṇa bhaktas like Kabīr, Nānak, Dādū, and Raidās. Irfan Habib's theorization, however, suffers from a serious lacuna. He shows very little concern with the religio-philosophical content of the Bhakti movement. He is therefore unable to relate the teachings of the bhaktas whom he accepts as the leaders of the movement with factors of protest and class struggle. He has to admit in the end that the bhaktas 'did not preach defiance of the existing system of exploitation...'; and also, that they 'were almost Christian in their attitude of submission.... Any appeal that they had was not based on any material redemption they promised to their hearers.'[37]

Linking up the Bhakti movement with urban centres and its artisan class has become a common characteristic of the Marxist writings on the subject. This has led to generalizations that it was an urban movement which drew strength from the 'lower caste urban groups' and 'the urban professional castes'.[38] In keeping with such generalizations, Kabīr and Nānak are sometimes described as men who expressed the sentiments of the urban class in towns, and of the artisans in the villages who were in contact with the towns. An obvious fact is worth noting in this context. The majority of the Indian people have always belonged to the villages and not towns. Undoubtedly, the urban population in the medieval period must have been far smaller than now. How could any movement gain strength and popularity under those circumstances if it expressed the sentiments of the urban classes only? Besides, there seems no reason to doubt that the anti-caste movement of Kabīr and Nānak must have attracted the lower castes everywhere, irrespective of the rural/urban divisions. How else can the fast spread of Sikhism in the whole of rural Punjab be explained?[39] Similarly, how can one account for the small pockets of the living remnants of the Kabīr-pantha in remote villages of North India to this day?

In whichever way the historians may theorize about the Bhakti movement, whether on the Marxist lines or otherwise, they continue to work with a faulty definition of bhakti, and a cohesive view of the Bhakti movement, which is unjustifiable. The distinction between the Nirguṇa and Saguṇa bhaktas, therefore, is never adequately maintained by them. Nor is the convention of linking them both with the medieval Vaishṇava āchāryas abandoned. This gives them the freedom to make generalizations about the Bhakti movement by concentrating upon one set of bhaktas in isolation from the other. The result is, the contradictions and inconsistencies noticeable in them. These become more glaring in the theories that are put forward by taking into account the Nirguṇa bhaktas only. The reason is simple. Whereas the Saguṇa bhaktas can be adjusted with the accepted notions about bhakti and the antecedents of the Bhakti movement, the same cannot be done with respect to the Nirguṇa bhaktas. Observations made on the basis of the study of only the Nirguṇa bhaktas involve certain fundamental questions—those of the validity of (a) interpreting the thought of the Nirguṇa bhaktas in the light of the given definition of bhakti; and (b) correlating them with the Saguṇa bhaktas and the Vaishṇava āchāryas on the ideological plane. These vital issues, however, are generally bypassed in such contexts. Besides, even when awareness is shown of the difference between the Nirguṇa and Saguṇa bhaktas, its significance is lost because of the non-repudiation of the standardized definition of bhakti and the constant reiteration of the fixed theories about the nature of the Bhakti movement and its antecedents.[40]

All errors in the generalizations made about the Bhakti movement in historical writings arise from a wrong set of premises. As long as these premises continue to operate, all theorizations on the subject remain vulnerable. The required correction in the basic frame of reference cannot be achieved without probing deep into the concepts and conceptual categories used in the formulation of those premises. And that is not possible without journeying across from the discipline of history into those of religion and philosophy. The nature of the work in hand has been largely determined by this requirement to achieve the revision of the basic conceptual structure connected with the Bhakti theme.

On the Nature of the Task Ahead

The existing academic framework associated with the study of bhakti and the Bhakti movement has had the sanction of more than 100 years of scholarship. The fundamentals on which it rests have not been questioned till now. Questioning a firmly academic established academic frame of reference is an arduous task—particularly so, when it happens to enjoy a long standing inviolability. Mere statement of errors detected therein cannot prove sufficient for its rejection. Nor is it enough to attempt a nullification of those errors by replacing one theory with another. Such steps can at best lead to an alternate approach which may or may not find general acceptance, leaving scope for the continuation of the old terms of reference. *An accepted frame of reference can be invalidated only by establishing the errors it involves as genuine errors.* And this can be achieved only by tracing the whole process of the formulation of the thought structure responsible for the occurrence and perpetuation of those errors. Only then can the rest of the exercise serve the required purpose, that of the invalidation and rejection of the theorizations based on the use of an erroneous frame of reference. The importance of these considerations has had an overriding influence over the present undertaking.

The endeavour to uproot the deeply entrenched ideas on the subject has proved all the more difficult, since they have been rejected here in entirety and not in parts. There has been a constant need, therefore, to refer back to the ideas that are rejected. It has been necessary to do so all along the line because of operating on two tracks simultaneously, that is, nullifying a whole set of established notions and putting forward new postulations. This has involved certain stylistic difficulties. Being neither a straightforward exposition nor an explanatory narrative, a linear approach with a simplistic structure has not been possible in this work. In a linear treatment of a subject, one can classify the materials more easily by making separate enclosures which may criss-cross the line vertically and yet form a chain and not hamper the linear progression of the theme. A neat structure follows on its own in that case. But in a mode of presentation wherein, for the sake of clarity, one has to spell out at each step what one rejects along with what one has to state, the style tends to be more or less circumambulatory in nature. The structure can then develop only along the circumference. The substructures also do not get interconnected without getting intersected. There is an inherent hazard in adopting such a style of sounding either repetitive or polemical. I have tried to avoid these lapses as far as possible. But in case there are traces of these in my writing, I can only seek the indulgence of the reader to remember the nature of the undertaking and the limitations caused by it.

Yet another encumbering factor has affected my mode of presentation. The subject undertaken falls within the broad spectrum of Hinduism, one of the most complex religious traditions. Although I have touched upon only those aspects of Hinduism which are relevant to this study, it has been necessary at times to make references to it as a whole also. This is done in a limited manner, lest the track of the main theme gets lost. Working within this constraint it has not been possible to elaborate upon the general observations made about Hinduism. One has had to battle against the fear of saying too little or too much in all such contexts. The pluralistic Hindu tradition, in any case, defies attempts at sharp categorization of its different elements. Although its varied components can be separately identified, they can hardly be taken as consistently interdictive of each other. This makes classification of Hindu materials in a definite and equable manner extremely difficult.[41] Nevertheless, I have made some general stipulations about Hinduism at certain places. Such stipulations, however, are made without taking recourse to any conventional methodology for its structural analysis.

As indicated at the very outset, the task in hand was undertaken out of the need felt for a different perspective to arrive at a correct understanding of what is referred to as the Bhakti movement in historical studies. It is, therefore, addressed mainly to historians. Nevertheless, the sum and substance of what is said here might draw the attention of others also who happen to deal with the themes of bhakti and the Bhakti movement within the bounds of their own disciplines. The present undertaking provides reasons for the legitimate rejection of the prevalent definition of bhakti and its application in assessing the nature of the Bhakti movement. The reasons offered rest on the perception of the generic meaning of bhakti and the non-viability of its current academic connotation. An effort is made, therefore, to disengage the term bhakti from the ideological content ascribed to it. Along with this, I have tried to examine the Nirguṇa form of bhakti on its own terms, independent of the accepted notions about bhakti in general. The ultimate objective of the entire exercise is to establish a rationale for the necessary modification in the current approach to the Bhakti movement and the medieval bhaktas. Perhaps the position taken in this work can clear the ground for fresh inquiries into the various socio-religious movements which are collectively designated as the Bhakti movement. It may also help in re-evaluating some of the leading thinkers and religious leaders of medieval India.

Notes

1. The *Bhagavad Gītā*, the *Bhāgavata Purāṇa*, and the *Bhakti Sūtras* of Nārada and Śāṇḍilya.

2. The Hindus never used the term bhakti to denote any *mata* (school of thought), *siddhānta* (doctrine), or *sampradāya* (sect).

3. The *Vedas* are reckoned as Śruti; and the Itihāsas and Purāṇas, as Smṛiti. The *Rāmāyaṇa* and the *Mahābhārata* fall in the category of Itihāsas. There is a multitude of Puraṇas. The more important amongst them are dedicated to personal deities, e.g., the *Vishṇu Purāṇa*, the *Bhāgavata Purāṇa*, and the *Śiva Purāṇa*.

4. I use the word Upanishadic here (and not Vedic) because the Upanishads constitute the speculative part of the Vedas.

5. That is not to say that the Puraṇic did not include within itself the Upanishadic elements. The personal deities eulogized in the *Purāṇas* were very often identified with the Upanishadic Brahman in them. By and large, in the sectarian theologies, personal deities (be it Vishṇu, Rāma, or Kṛishṇa) are explained as Saguṇa Brahman (also termed as Īśvara and Purushottama).

6. This holds good of the Hindu religious texts despite the fact that some do show greater concentration on one or the other. For example, even though Śaṅkarāchārya's works are directed towards establishing the finality of the Nirguṇa Brahman, he does not de-recognize the personal deities. Similarly, a work like the *Bhāgavata Purāṇa*, though concentrating on the deity Kṛishṇa, does not preclude the idea of the Nirguṇa Brahman. If Śaṅkara subsumes the personal concept of God in the impersonal, the reverse example is seen in the *Bhāgavata Purāṇa* in which the impersonal is identified with the deity Kṛishṇa.

7. He was able to do so in his *Rāmacharitamānas* by concentrating on the personality of Rāma on one hand, and by identifying him with the Nirguṇa Brahman, on the other.

8. This assessment of the *Gitā* found easy acceptance mainly because of the importance of Kṛishṇa in it.

9. Monier-Williams, *Brahmanism and Hinduism or Religious Thought and Life in India*, London, 1891, p. xi.

10. What Monier-Williams described as 'Hinduism' has never been free of the influence of what he called 'Brahmanism'. In fact, the latter had always found acceptance within the former in one way or another.

11. See George A. Grierson, 'Bhakti-Marga', *Encyclopaedia of Religion and Ethics* (*ERE*), ed. James Hastings, Edinburgh, 1908–26, vol. II, pp. 539–51.

12. Albrecht Weber and Lorinser had developed the Bhakti theme mainly to point out the similarities between Kṛishṇa-worship and Christianity. Gradually the idea became current that the said religion of Bhakti was a theistic expression of Hinduism comparable with Christian theism.

13. Like Islam and Judaism.

14. They are, therefore, referred to as 'Vaishṇava āchāryas' in this work.

15. This hypothesis is strengthened further by taking into account the Śaiva example. Reactions of similar nature can be seen in the post-Śānkara Śaiva philosophies also.

16. Āstika and nāstika traditions are understood as the theistic and the atheistic. The words āstika and nāstika are derived from the word *asti* (third person singular form) meaning 'to be'. Therefore, *asti iti āstika; nāsti iti nāstika* (Pāṇini, IV.2.60).

The one who believes 'there is' is an āstika; and the one who believes 'there is not' is a nāstika. The categorization of thought and people into āstika and nāstika was the most important division recognized by the ancient Indians. In general, the two words implied belief and non-belief in the existence of the Ultimate Reality, in whatever form it may be conceived (as 'God', as Supreme 'Consciousness', or 'Spirit').

17. Kabīr's condemnation of the caste system, idol-worship, and ritualism also shows the influence of Islam.

18. The credit for establishing this link goes mainly to the Hindi scholars, particularly to Pandit Hazariprasad.

19. This may well be taken as an expression of a particular stage of his religious development. The wide range of religious influences seen in his verses suggest a process of change and progression of his religious views.

20. Terms such as Surati-yoga and Sahaja-yoga are very often used by him to convey this view.

21. Suggestions that Kabīr was greatly influenced by Sūfism are made on the following grounds: (i) his descriptions of God as the beloved and the soul as the lover (as man and woman) which is characteristic of Sūfī poetry; (ii) his allusions to the pain of separation (when one is in love with God); and (iii) his use of the simile of the wine (of love) and of the wine-giver. However, the use of the Sūfī idioms and imagery in Kabīr's poetry (which in any case is occasional), does not indicate any intellectual borrowing from any school of Sūfī philosophy. As against this, there are numerous verses of Kabīr which sound as though they were only simplified expressions of exact passage from certain Hindu religious texts.

We come across the name of only one Muslim saint in the verses of Kabīr, Shaikh Taqī Mīr, who, in all probability, must have been a Sūfī saint. Not only Kabīr, but some other Nirguṇa bhaktas also had close contacts with the Sūfis; Kabīr's contact with them must have been still closer in view of his Muslim background. A mutual understanding between the Sūfis and the Nirguṇa bhaktas was always possible because of the common factor of mysticism which cuts across the divisions of formal religion.

22. The parentage of Kabīr is not known. According to popular and traditional accounts, he was born of a Brahmin widow. What is known as a fact is that the infant Kabīr, abandoned by his mother, was picked up from the Lahār Talāo in Benāras by a childless Muslim couple. He was brought up by them, and they were the only parents he had known.

23. Articulate expressions of mysticism can be traced back to the *Ṛig Veda* itself which is the most ancient scripture of the world.

24. The rapprochement between Sūfism and orthodox Islam was brought about by Abu Hamīd Al-Ghazālī (AD 1059–1111). His work *Ihyā-'ulum-al-dīn* (the revivification of religious sciences) proved very significant in this respect. Although Ghazālī recognized that the knowledge of the religious doctrine was a primary obligation, he attached great importance to intuitive knowledge also. He placed *ḥāl* (the state of soul or religious emotion) at par with *'ilm* (religious knowledge) and *'amal* (religious conduct). Mysticism of the Sūfis attained an honourable status in Islamic thought as a result of the writings of Al-Ghāzāli.

25. The trend was set in Hindi scholarship first. It started with the works of Rāmachandra Shukla, written during the period 1929–39. Shukla classified the Hindi bhakti literature under two heads, namely, Nirguṇa and Saguṇa bhakti. Since then, the bhakta poets have been grouped separately as the Nirguṇa and Saguṇa bhaktas in Hindi studies. Nevertheless, even in Hindi scholarship, the two groups are always linked together in all general accounts of the Bhakti movement and its antecedents.

26. Chaitanya can be cited as a rare exception. Perhaps he was the only Saguṇa bhakta who had actively led an anti-caste movement despite his adherence to the conventional religious modes connected with Vaishṇavism.

27. Tulsīdās is an arch example of this.

28. *Journal of the Economic and Social History of the Orient*, vol. IV, ii, pp. 198–224.

29. Kosambi, D. D. *The Culture and Civilization of Ancient India*, Delhi, 1970, p. 208.

30. R. S. Sharma, 'Problem of Transition from Ancient to Medieval in Indian History', *The Indian Historical Review*, vol. I, no. 1, March, 1974.

31. A somewhat similar attempt is made by Suvira Jaiswal to fix the 'material basis' of bhakti in the context of the ancient period of Indian history. Suvira Jaiswal, *The Origin and Development of Vaiṣṇavism*, New Delhi, 1967, pp. 38, 110 ff.

32. See Irfan Habib, *Agrarian System of Mughal India*, New Delhi, 1963, pp. 332 ff.

33. A similar mistake is committed regarding the social placement of Nānak by K. A. Nizami. Nizami commits a still greater error by including Chaitanya, a Brahmin, in the list of bhaktas who, according to him, belonged to the lower strata of Hindu society. K. A. Nizami, *Studies in Medieval Indian History and Culture*, Allahabad, 1966, pp. 92–3.

34. Irfan Habib, 'The Historical Background of the Popular Monotheistic Movements of the 15th–17th Centuries', paper presented at the Seminar on the History of Ideas held at Delhi University in November 1965.

35. Ibid.

36. Muhammad Habib, 'Introduction to Elliot and Dowson', *History of India*, vol. II, sec. edn, Aligarh, 1967.

37. Irfan Habib (1965).

38. Romila Thapar, *A History of India*, vol. I, Harmondsworth, 1966, pp. 68, 264, 308.

39. Whatever reasons scholars like Irfan Habib may have to offer for the conversion of the rural Jāts to Sikhism, the fact remains that the Jāts alone do not constitute the Sikh community. In fact, some of the liberal and independent minded men from higher castes had also responded to the new ideology. The Khatris formed an equally important constituent of the Sikh community founded by Nānak who was himself a Khatri.

40. To cite examples: (i) Irfan Habib sets apart Kabīr, Nānak, Dādū, etc., from the other bhaktas. He describes their movement as that of 'popular monotheism'. He connects the Saguṇa bhaktas with what he calls the 'conventional Bhakti Movement'. But he does not clarify as to what he means by bhakti, the Bhakti movement, and monotheism. Nor does he make any serious attempt to repudiate the existing opinion related to these themes while coining new epithets such as the 'conventional Bhakti Movement' and 'popular monotheism'. Besides, his rather careless use of the terms monotheism and pantheism confuses certain vital issues connected with the subject (Habib, 1965). (ii) Giving an account of the medieval bhaktas, Romila Thapar speaks of 'two broad groups': (a) those who confined themselves... to Hindu religious

activity, and (b) those who had been influenced by Islam. And yet, she treats the Bhakti movement as an integrated phenomenon while generalizing about it (which is invariably done by taking into account the second group only). Furthermore, she reiterates the conventional approach by linking the entire movement with the Tamil Ālvār (Vaishṇva) saints of the 6th and 7th centuries. Thapar, 1966, pp. 68, 186, 264, 304–5, 308.

41. In Hinduism, the sectarian efforts to retain the separate identities of the sects and the distinctiveness of their beliefs and conventions had always run parallel to the Brahminical drive towards an ideological synthesis to give it the semblance of oneness.

11

Imagined Religious Communities?

Ancient History and the Modern Search for a Hindu Identity*

Romila Thapar

My choice of subject for this lecture arose from what I think might have been a matter of some interest to Kingsley Martin, as also from my own concern that the interplay between the past and contemporary times requires a continuing dialogue between historians working on these periods. Such a dialogue is perhaps more pertinent to post-colonial societies where the colonial experience changed the framework of the comprehension of the past from what had existed earlier: a disjuncture which is of more than mere historiographical interest. And where political ideologies appropriate this comprehension and seek justification

* *Modern Asian Studies* 23, 2(1989): 209–31.

This is the text of the Kingsley Martin Lecture given in Cambridge on 1 June 1988.

I would like to thank K. N. Panikkar, N. Bhattacharya, and B. K. Matilal for their helpful criticism of an earlier draft of this lecture.

from the pre-colonial past, there, the historian's comment on this process is called for.

Among the more visible strands in the political ideology of contemporary India is the growth and acceptance of what are called communal ideologies. 'Communal', as many in this audience are aware, in the Indian context has a specific meaning and primarily perceives Indian society as constituted of a number of religious communities. Communalism in the Indian sense therefore is a consciousness which draws on a supposed religious identity and uses this as the basis for an ideology. It then demands political allegiance to a religious community and supports a programme of political action designed to further the interests of that religious community. Such an ideology is of recent origin but uses history to justify the notion that the community (as defined in recent history) and therefore the communal identity have existed since the early past. Because the identity is linked to religion, it can lead to the redefinition of the particular religion, more so in the case of one as amorphous as Hinduism.

Such identity tends to iron out diversity and insists on conformity, for it is only through a uniform acceptance of the religion that it can best be used for political ends. The attempt is always to draw in as many people as possible since numbers enhance the power of the communal group and are crucial in a mechanical view of democracy. This political effort requires a domination over other groups and where the numbers are substantially larger, there is a deliberate emphasis both on superiority and the notion of majority, a notion which presupposes the existence of various 'minority communities'. In the construction of what have been called 'imagined communities',[1] in this case identified by religion, there is an implied rejection of the applicability of other types of divisions in society, such as status or class.

In the multiplicity of communalisms prevalent in India today, the major one obviously is Hindu communalism since it involves the largest numbers and asserts itself as the dominant group. I shall therefore discuss only the notion of the Hindu community and not those of other religions. Nevertheless my comments on communal ideology and its use of history would apply to other groups claiming a similar ideology. I would like to look at those constituents of Hindu communal ideology which claim legitimacy from the past, namely, that there has always been a well-defined and historically evolved religion which we now call Hinduism and an equally clearly defined Hindu community. Implicit in this are the historical implications of Hindu communalism and I shall argue that it is in part a modern search for an imagined Hindu identity from the past, a search which has drawn on the historiography of the last two centuries. The historical justification is far from being the sole reason for the growth of communalism, but recourse to this justification fosters the communal ideology.

The modern description of Hinduism has been largely that of a *brāhmaṇa*-dominated religion which gathered to itself in a somewhat paternalistic pattern a variety of sects drawing on a range of Buddhists, Jainas, Vaiṣṇavas, Śāivas, and Śāktas. The texts and the tradition were viewed as inspirational, initially orally preserved, with multiple manifestations of deities, priests but no church, a plurality of doctrines with a seeming absence of controversies and all this somehow integrated into a single religious fabric. Differences with the Semitic religions were recognized and were seen as the absence of a prophet, of a revealed book regarded as sacred, of a monotheistic God, of ecclesiastical organization, of theological debates on orthodoxy and heresy and, even more important, the absence of conversion. But somehow the logic of these differences was not built into the construction of the history of the religion. Hinduism was projected largely in terms of its philosophical ideas, iconology, and rituals. It is ironic in some ways that these multiple religious sects were seldom viewed in their social and historical context even though this was crucial to their understanding. Histories of the 'Hindu' religion have been largely limited to placing texts and ideas in a chronological perspective with few attempts at relating these to the social history of the time. Scholarship also tended to ignore the significance of the popular manifestation of religion in contrast to the textual, a neglect which was remedied by some anthropological research, although frequently the textual imprint is more visible even in such studies.

The picture which emerges of the indigenous view of religion from historical sources of the early period is rather different. The prevalent religious groups referred to are two, Brahmanism and Śramanism with a clear distinction between them. They are organizationally separate, had different sets of beliefs and rituals, and often disagreed on social norms. That this distinction was recognized is evident from the edicts of the Mauryan king Aśoka[2] as well as by those who visited India and left accounts of what they had observed, as, for example, Megasthenes;[3] the Chinese Buddhist pilgrims Fa Hsien and Hsüan Tsang;[4] and Alberuni.[5] The Buddhist visitors write mainly of matters pertaining to Buddhism and refer to the *brāhmaṇas* as heretics. Patañjali, the grammarian refers to the hostility between Brahmanism and Śramanism as innate as is that between the snake and the mongoose.[6] Sometimes the *brāhmaṇas* and the *śramaṇas* are addressed jointly as in Buddhist texts and the Aśokan edicts. Here they are being projected as a category distinct from the common people. Such a bunching together relates to a similarity of concerns suggestive of a common framework of discourse but does not detract from the fundamental differences between the two systems. It might in fact be a worthwhile exercise to reconstruct Brahmanism from the references to it in Śramanic and other non-Brahmanical sources.

A historical view of early Indian religion would endorse this dichotomy and its continuity even in changed forms. Early Brahmanism demarcates the twice-born upper castes from the rest. The twice-born has to observe the precepts of *śruti*—the *Vedas*—and of *smṛti*—the auxiliary texts to the *Veda*s and particularly the *Dharmaśāstras*. *Dharma* lay in conforming to the separate social observances and ritual functions of each caste. The actual nature of belief in deity was left ambiguous and theism was not a requirement. The focus of worship was the sacrificial ritual. Brahmanism came closest to having a subcontinental identity largely through its ritual functions and the use of a common language, Sanskrit, even though it was prevalent among only a smaller section of people.

Śramanism, a term covering a variety of Buddhist, Jaina, Ājīvika, and other sects, denied the fundamentals of Brahmanism such as Vedic *śruti* and *smṛti*. It was also opposed to the sacrificial ritual both on account of the beliefs incorporated in the ritual as well as the violence involved in the killing of animals. It was characterized by a doctrine open to all castes and although social hierarchy was accepted, it did not emphasize separate social observances but, rather, cut across caste. The idea of conversion was therefore notionally present. The attitude to social hierarchy in most Śramanic sects was not one of radical opposition. In Buddhism, for example, recruitment to the *saṅgha* and support from lay followers were initially in large numbers from the upper castes and the appeal was frequently also made to such groups.[7] Nevertheless there were no restrictions on a lower caste recruitment and in later periods support from such groups was substantial. The founders of the Sramanic sects were not incarnations of deity. Buddhism and Jainism had an ecclesiastical organization, the *saṅgha*, and in most cases there was an overall concern with historicity.

In terms of numbers (there appears to have developed even greater support for the Śākta sects which were in many ways antithetical to early Brahmanism. The essentials of Śāktism are sometimes traced back to Harappan times and some of these elements probably went into the making of popular religion from the earliest historical period. Recognized sects gradually crystallized from the first millennium AD when they come to be referred to in the literature of the period. The centrality of worshipping the goddess was initially new to upper-caste religion. Some of these sects deliberately broke the essential taboos of Brahmanism relating to separate caste functions, commensality, rules of food and drink, and sexual taboos.[8] That some of the beliefs of the Śākta sects were later accepted by some *Brāhmaṇa* sects is an indication of a break with Vedic religion by these *Brāhmaṇa* sects although the legitimacy of the Vedic religion was sometimes sought to be bestowed on the new sects by them. Such religious compromises were not unconnected with the Brahmanical need to retain social ascendency. However, some Brahmanical sects remained orthodox.

As legitimizers of political authority, the *brāhmaṇa*s in the first millennium AD were given grants of land which enabled them to become major landowners. The institutions which emerged out of these grants such as the *agrahāras* became centres of control over rural resources as well as of Brahmanical learning and practice. It was probably this high social and economic status of the *brāhmaṇa* castes which encouraged the modern idea that Brahmanism and Hinduism were synonymous. But that Brahmanism had also to compromise with local cults is evident from the religious articulation of text and temple and from the frequency with which attempts were introduced into Brahmanism to purify the religion in terms of going back to *śruti* and *smṛti*. In the process of acculturation between Brahmanic 'high culture' and the 'low culture' of local cults, the perspective is generally limited to that of the Sanskritization of the latter. It might be historically more accurate on occasion to view it as the reverse, as, for example, in the cult of Viṭhṭhala at Pandharpur or that of Jagannātha at Puri.[9] In such cases, the deities of tribals and low-caste groups become, for reasons other than the purely religious, centrally significant and Brahmanism has to adapt itself to the concept of such deities. The domain of such deities evolves out of a span spreading horizontally, moving from a village to its networks of exchange and finally encompassing a region. The focal centre of such a cult takes on a political dimension as well in the nature of the control which it exercises, quite apart from ritual and belief. Pilgrimage then becomes a link across various circumferences.

The increasing success of Brahmanism by the end of the first millennium AD resulted in the gradual displacement of Śramanism—but not entirely. Local cults associated with new social groups led to the emergence of the more popular Puranic religion. Vedic deities were subordinated or ousted. Viṣṇu and Śiva came to be worshipped as the pre-eminent deities. The thrust of Puranic religion was in its assimilative and accommodating processes. A multitude of new cults, sects, and castes were worked into the social and religious hierarchy. Religious observance often coincided with caste identities.

By the early second millennium AD, a variety of devotional cults—referred to by the generic label *bhakti*—had come to form a major new religious expression. They drew on the Puranic tradition of Śaivism and Vaiśṇavism but were also in varying degrees the inheritors of the Śramanic religions. Their emphasis on complete loyalty to the deity has been seen as a parallel to feudal loyalties. But what was more significant was that *bhakti* cults and the sects which grew around them sought to underline dependence on and salvation through the deity. To this extent they indicate a departure from earlier indigenous religion. These cults were god-centred rather than man-centred. The ritual of sacrifice had been substituted by the worship of an icon. Some sects accepted, up to a point, Brahmanical *śruti* and *smṛti* whereas others vehemently denied it, a debate which continues to this day. Those sects in opposition to Brahmanism which sought to transcend caste and differentiated social observances, insisting that every worshipper was equal in the eyes of the deity, often ended up as castes, thus once again coinciding sect with caste. With the arrival of Islam in India, some drew from the ideas of Islam. Most of these sects were geographically limited and bound by the barriers of language. Possibly the beginnings of larger religious communities within what is now called the Hindu tradition date to the middle of the second millennium, such as perhaps some Vaiṣṇava sects, where, for example, the worship of Kṛṣṇa at Mathura drew audiences from a larger geographical region than before. This also heralds a change in the nature of Puranic religion, for Mathura attracts Vaiṣṇavas from eastern and southern India and becomes like Ayodhyā (for the worship of Rāma)[10] the focus of a search for sacred topography. It might perhaps be seen as an attempt to go beyond local caste and sect and build a broader community. The historical reasons for its happening at this juncture need to be explored.

Initial opposition from those of high-caste status also encouraged *bhakti* sects to inculcate a sense of community within themselves, particularly if they were economically successful, such as the Vīraśaivas. Even when such religious sects attempted to constitute a larger community, the limitations of location, caste, and language acted as a deterrent to a single, homogeneous Hindu community. In the continuing processes of either appropriation or rejection of belief and practice, the kaleidoscopic change in the constitution of religious sects was one which precluded the emergence of a uniform, monolithic religion.

The multiplicity of cults and sects also reflects a multiplicity of beliefs. Even in Brahmanism we are told that if two *śruti* traditions are in conflict then both are to be held as law.[11] This is a fundamentally different approach from that of religions which would like to insist on a single interpretation arising out of a given theological framework. This flexibility together with the emphasis on social observance rather than theology allowed of a greater privatization of religion than was possible in most other religions. Renunciatory tendencies were common, were respected, and often gave sanction to private forms of worship. The renouncer opted out of society, yet was highly respected.[12] The private domain of belief was always a permissible area of early Indian religion: a religion which is perhaps better seen as primarily the religious belief of social segments, sometimes having to agglomerate and sometimes remaining sharply differentiated. The coexistence of religious sects should not be mistaken for the absorption of all sects into an ultimately unified entity. But the demarcation was often more significant since it related both to differences in religious belief and practice as well as social status and political needs. The status of a sect could change as it was hinged to that of its patrons. Political legitimation through the use of religious groups was recognized, but the appeal was to a particular sect or cult or a range of these and not to a monolithic religion. Royal patronage within the same ruling family, extended to a multiplicity of sects, was probably conditioned as much by the exigencies of political and social requirements as by a religious catholicity. This social dimension as well as the degree to which a religious sect had its identity in caste or alternatively was inclusive of caste, has been largely ignored in the modern interpretation of early Hinduism. With the erosion of social observances and caste identity, there is now a search for a new identity and here the creation of a new Hinduism becomes relevant.

The evolution of Hinduism is not a linear progression from a founder through an organizational system, with sects branching off. It is rather the mosaic of distinct cults, deities, sects, and ideas and the adjusting, juxtaposing, or distancing of these to existing ones, the placement drawing not only on belief and ideas but also on the socio-economic reality. New deities could be created linked genealogically to the established ones, as in the recent case of Santoshi Ma, new rituals worked out, and the new sect could become the legitimizer of a new caste. Religious practice and belief are often self-sufficient within the boundaries of a caste and are frequently determined by the needs of a caste. The worship of icons was unthought of in the Vedic religion, but the idol becomes a significant feature of Puranic religion and therefore also in the eyes of contemporary Muslim observers. The consciousness of a similarity in ritual and belief in different geographical regions was not always evident. Thus *bhakti* cults were confined to particular regions and were frequently unaware of their precursors or contemporaries elsewhere. Recourse to historicity of founder and practice was confined within the sect and was not required of a conglomeration of sects which later came to be called Hinduism. This is in part reflected in the use of the term *sampradāya* for a sect where the emphasis is on transmission of traditional belief and usage through a line of teachers. The insistence on proving the historicity of human incarnations of deity, such as Rāma and Kṛṣṇa, is a more recent phenomenon and it may be suggested that there is a subconscious parallel with the prophet and the messiah. The identification of the *janma-bhūmi*s, the location of the exact place where Kṛṣṇa and Rāma were born, becomes important only by the mid-second millennium AD.

Religions such as Buddhism, Jainism, Islam, and Christianity see themselves as part of the historical process of the unfolding and interpreting of the single religion, and sects are based on variant interpretations of the original teaching. They build their strength on a structure of ecclesiastical organization. In contrast to this, Hindu sects often had a distinct and independent origin. Assimilation was possible and was sometimes expressed in the appropriation of existing civilizational symbols. What needs to be investigated is the degree to which such civilizational symbols were originally religious in connotation.

Civilizational symbols are manifested in many ways: from the symbol of the *svāstika* to the symbol of the renouncer as the noblest and most respected expression of human aspirations. The history of the *svāstika* goes back to the fourth millennium BC where it occurs on seals and impressions from north-west India and Central Asia. In the Indian subcontinent it is not a specifically Hindu symbol for it is used by a variety of religious groups in various ways, but in every case it embodies the auspicious. The Bon-po of the Himalayan borderlands reverse the symbol to distance themselves from the Buddhists. The two epics, the *Mahābhārata* and the *Rāmāyaṇa*, frequently treated as primarily the religious literature of the Vaiṣṇavas, are in origin as epics, civilizational symbols. They were, at one level, the carriers of ethical traditions and were used again by a variety of religious sects to propagate their own particular ethic, a situation which is evident from the diverse treatment of the theme of the *Rāmāyaṇa* in Vālmīki, in the Buddhist *Vessantara* and *Dasaratha Jātakas* and in the Jaina version—the *Paumacaryam* of Vimalasūri.[13] The epic versions were also used for purposes of political legitimation. The primarily Vaiṣṇava religious function of the epics develops gradually and comes to fruition in the second millennium AD, with clearly defined sects worshipping Rāma or Kṛṣṇa coinciding with the development of what has been called the Puranic religion. Subsequent to this were various tribal adaptations of the *Rāmayaṇa*, and these were less concerned with the Vaiṣṇava message and more with articulating their own social fears and aspirations.

Even on the question of beliefs about the after-life, although the concept of *karma* and rebirth was commonly referred to, there were distinct and important groups which believed in a different concept. The life after death of the hero in the heaven of Indra or Śiva, waited upon by *apsaras*, goes back to the Vedic belief in the *pitṛloka* or House of the Fathers. This belief is a major motivation in the widespread hero cults from the mid-first millennium AD onwards.[14] Here even the concept of after-life was conditioned by social birth and function. A different idea influences the way in which the ritual of *sati* changes its meaning over time. Initially a ritual which ensured that the faithful wife accompanied her hero-husband to heaven, and therefore associated largely with *kṣatriya* castes and those dying heroic deaths, its practice by other castes in the second millennium AD involved a change in eschatology. Ultimately the *sati* was deified, which meant that she neither went to heaven nor was subjected to the rules of *karma*.[15]

It has been suggested that there was a structural similarity in various rituals practised by people in different regions and therefore shared myths and shared ritual patterns can account for some unity in the varieties of the religious beliefs that we find in India over a long time.[16] This is certainly true. But nevertheless it is different from a shared creed, catechism, theology, and ecclesiastical organization.

The definition of Hinduism as it has emerged in recent times appears not to have emphasized the variant premises of Indian religion and therefore the difference in essence from the model of Semitic religions. This definition was the result of various factors: of Christian missionaries who saw this as the lacunae of religions in India and which they regarded as primitive; of some Orientalist scholarship anxious to fit the 'Hindu' process into a comprehensible whole based on a known model; the efforts also of Indian reform movements attempting to cleanse Indian religion of what they regarded as negative encrustations and trying to find parallels with the Semitic model. Even in the translation of texts from Sanskrit into English, where religious concepts were frequently used, the translation often reflected a Christian undertone. The selection of texts to be studied had its own purpose. The East India Company's interest in locating and codifying Hindu law gave a legal form to what was essentially social observance and customary law. The concept of law required that it be defined as a cohesive ideological code. The Manu *Dharmaśāstra*, for example, which was basically part of Brahmanical *smṛti* was taken as the laws of the Hindus and presumed to apply universally. In the process of upward social mobility during the late eighteenth and early nineteenth centuries, traders and artisanal groups emerged as patrons of temple building activities and the trend to conform to the Brahmanical model was reinforced by this comprehension of Hinduism.[17] The growth of the political concepts of majority and minority communities further galvanized the process.

The degree to which castes and sects functioned independently even in situations which would elsewhere have been regarded as fundamentally of theological importance, can perhaps be seen in attitudes to religious persecution and the manifestation of intolerance. Among the normative values which were highlighted in the discussion of Hinduism in recent times, has been the concept of *ahiṃsā* or non-violence. It has been argued that non-violence and tolerance were special features of Hinduism which particularly demarcated its ethics from those of Islam and to a lesser extent Christianity. Yet *ahimsā* as an absolute value is characteristic of certain Śramanic sects and less so of Brahmanism. The notion appears in the *Upaniṣads*, but it was the Buddhists and the Jainas who first made it foundational to their teaching, and their message was very different from that of the *Bhagvad-Gīta* on this matter. That Brahmanism and Śramanism were recognized as distinct after the period of the *Upaniṣads* further underlines the significance of *ahimsā* to Śramanic thinking. This is also borne out by the evidence of religious persecution.

In spite of what historians, ancient and modern, have written, there is a persistent, popular belief that the 'Hindus' never indulged in religious persecution. However, the Śaivite persecution of Śramanic sects is attested to and, on occasion, retaliation by the latter. Hsüan Tsang writing in the seventh century refers to this when he describes his visit to Kashmir.[18] That this was not the prejudiced view of the Buddhist pilgrim is made clear by the historian Kalhaṇa in the *Rājataraṅginī*, who even in the twelfth century refers to the earlier destruction of Buddhist monasteries and the killing of Buddhist monks by the Hūṇa king Mihīrakula and other ardent Śaivites.[19] That Mihīrakula was a Hūṇa is used by modern historians to excuse these actions, but it should be remembered that he gave large grants of land , *agrahāras*, to the *brāhmaṇas* of Gandhāra, which Kalhaṇa in disgust informs us they gratefully received. Clearly there was competition for royal patronage and the Śaiva *brāhmaṇas* triumphed over the Buddhists. The Buddhist association with the commerce between

India and Central Asia was one of the reasons for the material prosperity of the Buddhist *saṅgha*.[20] The Hūṇa disruption of the Indian trade with Central Asia may well have resulted in an antagonism between the northern Buddhists and the Hūṇas.

Elsewhere there is a variation on this story. In Tamil Nadu, for example, from the seventh century onwards, Śaiva sects attacked Jaina establishments and eventually succeeded in driving out the Śramanas.[21] In neighbouring Karnataka, at a somewhat later date, the Vīraśaivas or Liṅgāyatas, acquiring wealth and status in commerce, persecuted Jaina monks and destroyed Jaina images.[22] In some inscriptions, the Vīraśaivas claim that the Jainas began the trouble. In this case, the hostility can be traced not to competition for royal patronage but rather to control of the commercial economy over which the Jainas had a substantial hold. A further reason may also have been linked to the fact that the Jainas, maintaining high standards of literacy, may have been seen by the Vīraśaivas as rivals in the role of advisers and administrators at the royal court.

What is significant about this persecution is that it involved not all the Śaivas but particular segments of sects among them. The persecution was not a *jehād* or a holy war or a crusade in which all Hindu sects saw it as their duty to support the attack or to wage war against the Buddhists or the Jainas. Nor was there room for an inquisition in the Indian situation, for there dissidents could found a new sect and take on a splinter caste status. The notion of heresy evolved gradually. The term *pasamda* in the Aśokan edicts refers merely to any religious sect or philosophical school. By the time of the Puranic literature, *pāṣaṇḍa* quite clearly referred to sects in opposition to Brahmanism and carried with it the clear connotation of contempt.[23] Untouchability was also a form of religious persecution, for this exclusion was common to Brahmanism as well as to some Śramanic sects, the *Caṇḍāla* being a category apart. Vaiṣṇavism, although it had its episodes of enmity with Śaivism and others, seems to have been less prone to persecuting competitors. Instead it resorted to assimilating other cults and used the notion of the *avatāra* or incarnation of Viṣṇu to great effect in doing so. But even Vaiṣṇavism was less given to assimilating the Śramanic sects, preferring to absorb tribal and folk cults and epic heroes. Thus in spite of the reference to Buddha as among the ten incarnations, this, interestingly, does not become the focus of a large body of myths or Puranic texts as do the other incarnations. If acts of intolerance and violence against other religious sects reflecting the consciousness of belonging to a religious community did not form part of a Hindu stand against such sects, then it also raises the question of how viable is the notion of a Hindu community for this early period.

The notion of a Hindu community does not have as long an ancestry as is often presumed. Even in the normative texts of Brahmanism, the *Dharmaśāstras*, it is conceded that there were a variety of communities, determined by location, occupation, and caste, none of which were necessarily bound together by a common religious identity. The term for village, *grama*, referred to the collective inhabitants of a place and included cultivators and craftsmen. The control of this community lay in the hands of the *grāma-saṅgha*[24] and the *mahājana* and, in some cases, the *pañcakula*. Customary law of the village is referred to as *grāma-dharma*.[25] The sense of the village as the community was further impressed by the grants of land to *brāhmaṇa*s and officers in the late first millennium AD when they began to be given administrative and judicial rights over the villages granted to them. Community therefore had one of its roots in location and the law of the *janapada*/territory is listed among those which a king should observe.

In urban centres, craftsmen of the same profession or of related professions formed organizations and guilds, such as the *pūga, goṣṭhi*, and *śreṇī*. They were responsible for production and sale and gradually took on a community character. Thus donations were made at Buddhist *stūpa*s, as the one at Sanchi, by *goṣṭhi*s and *śreṇī*s which identified themselves as such.[26] These communities were part of the larger Buddhist community and the same *stūpa* was embellished from donations by a number of other such communities and by individuals. One can therefore speak of a Buddhist community which cuts across the boundaries of caste and locality. In contrast is the silk-weavers' guild at Mandasor which built a temple to Sūrya, the Sun-god, and renovated it in the late fifth century AD.[27] Even though the members of this guild had taken to a variety of alternative professions, they retained their identity as a guild for the purpose of building a temple. This religious edifice was built through the effort of a single group, identified as a guild and worshipping Sūrya, for no other Sun-worshippers were involved nor any other religious group which today would be called Hindu. It is unlikely that such a group saw itself as part of a larger Hindu community as its identity seems to have been deliberately limited. The Hūṇas established themselves in the region soon after and were known to be Sun-worshippers. A temple to the Sun was built at Gwalior in the early sixth century AD by a high-ranking individual.[28] Curiously there is neither contribution from nor reference to other Sun-worshipping communities in the area in the later inscription, barring the reference to the Hūṇa kings.

In urban life, the guild was a commanding institution acting as the nucleus of the urban community. The coins and seals of such guilds point to economic power and social status.[29] The *Nārada-smṛti*[30] clearly states that a guild could frame its own laws and these laws related both to administration and social usage. The customary law of the guild, the *śreṇī-dharma*, is particularly mentioned in the *Dharmaśāstras* and to which kings are required to conform. The importance of the guild also lies in the fact that some evolved into *jātis* or castes, becoming units of endogamous marriage uniting kinship and profession. Those not following a Śramanic religion maintained their own separate religious identity. We are also told that the king must respect *jāti-dharma*. The emphasis on the *dharma* of the *janapada* (locality or territory), *śreṇī* (guild), and *jāti* (caste) and the absence of reference to the *dharma* of various religious sects or of a conglomeration of religious sects are a pointer perhaps to what actually constituted the sense of community in the early past.

Identities were, in contrast to the modern nation-state, segmented identities. The notion of community was not absent but there were multiple communities identified by locality, language, caste, occupation, and sect. What appears to have been absent was the notion of a uniform, religious community readily identified as Hindu. The first occurrence of the term 'Hindu' is as a geographical nomenclature and this has its own significance.

This is not a quibble since it involves the question of the historical concept of 'Hindu'. Inscriptions of the Achaemenid empire refer to the frontier region of the Indus or Sindhu as Hi(n)dush.[31] Its more common occurrence many centuries later is in Arabic texts where the term is initially used neither for a religion nor for a culture. It refers to the inhabitants of the Indian subcontinent, the land across the Sindhu or Indus river. Al-Hind was therefore a geographical identity and the Hindus were all the people who lived on this land. Hindu thus essentially came to mean 'the other' in the eyes of the new arrivals. It was only gradually and over time that it was used not only for those who were inhabitants of India but also for those who professed a religion other than Islam or Christianity. In this sense Hindu included both the *brāhmaṇas* and the lower castes, an inclusion which was contrary to the precepts of Brahmanism. This all-inclusive term was doubtless a new and bewildering feature for the multiple sects and castes which generally saw themselves as separate entities.

The people of India curiously do not seem to have perceived the new arrivals as a unified body of Muslims. The name 'Muslim' does not occur in the records of early contacts. The term used was either ethnic, Turuṣka, referring to the Turks,[32] or geographical, Yavana,[33] or cultural, *mleccha*. Yavana, a back formation from *yona* had been used since the first millennium BC for Greeks and others coming from West Asia. *Mleccha* meaning impure, goes back to the Vedic texts and referred to non-Sanskrit speaking peoples often outside the caste hierarchy or regarded as foreign and was extended to include low castes and tribals. Foreigners, even of high ranks, were regarded as *mleccha*.[34] A late fifteenth-century inscription from Mewar refers to the Sultan of Malwa and his armies as *Śaka*s, a term used many centuries before for the Scythians, and therefore reflecting a curious undertow of historical memory.[35] These varying terms, each seeped in historical meaning, do not suggest a monolithic view, but rather a diversity of perceptions which need to be enquired into more fully.

For the early Muslim migrants, Indian society was also a puzzle, for it was the first where large numbers did not convert to Islam. There was, further, the unique situation that they were faced with a society which had no place for the concept of conversion, for one's birth into a caste defines one's religious identity and conversion is outside the explanation of belief.

Historians have posited two monolithic religions, Hinduism and Islam, coming face to face in the second millennium AD. This projection requires re-examination since it appears to be based on a somewhat simplistic reading of the court chronicles of the sultans. These spoke of Hindus sometimes in the sense of the indigenous population, sometimes as a geographical entity, and sometimes as followers of a non-Islamic religion. Such references should be read in their specific meaning and not as referring uniformly to the religion of India. Possibly the germ of the idea of a Hindu community begins when people start referring to themselves as Hindus, perhaps initially as a concession to being regarded as 'the other'. Such usage in non-Islamic sources is known from the fifteenth century. The literature of the *bhakti* sects registers a variation on this. Much that was composed in an indigenous tradition such as the *Rāmacaritamānas* of Tulsidās seems not to use the term Hindu. That which was clearly influenced by Islamic ideas such as the verses of Kabīr refers to Hindus and counterposes Hindus and Turuṣkas in a religious sense. Curiously both Tulsidās and Kabīr belonged to the Rāmānandin sect, yet expressed themselves in very different idioms.

Rānā Kumbha of Mewar ruling in the fifteenth century, on defeating the sultans of Dhilli and Gurjarātra, takes the title of *himdu suratrāna*,[36] *suratrāna* being the Sanskrit for sultan. In the context of the inscription in which it occurs, it is less a declaration of religious identity and more a claim to being a sultan of *al-hind*, superior to the other sultans. In another inscription, the sultan of Gujarata is referred to as the *gurjareśvara* and the *gurjarādhīṣvara*, but the virtually hereditary enemy, the sultan of Malwa, merely as *suratrāna*,[37] a subtle but significant distinction.

It would also be worthwhile to investigate when the term Muslim came to be used in what would now be called Hindu sources. One's suspicion is that Turuṣka and its variants and certainly *mleccha* were more commonly used as they are to this day. *Mleccha* does not have a primary religious connotation. It is a signal of social and cultural difference. Indian Muslims of course did not discontinue caste affiliations, particularly as the basis of marriage relations and often even occupations. Thus the gulf between the high-caste Muslims claiming foreign descent, such as the *ashrafs*, and the rest was not altogether dissimilar to the social difference between *brāhmaṇas* and non-*brāhmaṇas*. But the rank and file were often converted from lower castes, where an entire *jāti* would convert. These Muslims retained their local language in preference to Persian, were recognized by minor differences of dress and manner, and often incorporated their earlier rituals and mythology into Islamic tradition. Some of the *mangal-kābyas* in Bengali, for instance, are an example of such interlinks in the creation of what might be seen as a new mythology where Puranic deities intermingled with the personalities of the Qur'an.[38] This; becomes even more evident in the folk literature of regions with a large Muslim population. Elsewhere in Tamil Nadu, for instance, the guardian figures in the cult of Draupadī are Muslim.[39] This is not an anomaly if it is seen in terms of local caste relations.

This is not to suggest that the relationship was one of peaceful coexistence or total cultural integration but rather that the perception which groups subscribing to Hindu and Islamic symbols had of each other was not in terms of a monolithic religion, but more in terms of distinct and disparate castes and sects along a social continuum. Even the recognition of a religious identity does not automatically establish a religious community. Tensions, confrontations, and even persecutions at the level of political authority were not necessarily repeated all the way down the social scale nor were all caste and sectarian conflicts reflected at the upper levels. Clashes which on the face of it would now be interpreted as between Hindus and Muslims, would require a deeper investigation to ascertain how far they were clashes between specific castes and sects and to what degree did they involve support and sympathy from other castes and sects identifying with the same religion or seeking such identity.

The nineteenth-century definition of the Hindu community sought its justification in early history using Mill's periodization which assumes the existence of Hindu and Muslim communities and takes the history of the former back to the centuries BC. Its roots were provided by yet another nineteenth-century obsession, that of the theory of Aryan race.[40] It was argued that the Indo-Europeans who conquered India created the Hindu religion and civilization. In the theory of Aryan race, the nineteenth-century concern with European origins was transferred to India. The theory as applied to India emphasized the arrival of a superior, conquering race of Aryans used the mechanism of caste to segregate groups racially.[41] It underlined upper-caste superiority by arguing that they were the descendants of the Aryans and it therefore became an acceptable explanation of the origin of upper castes, could now also claim relationship to the European Aryans.[42] The lower castes were seen as the non-Aryan, indigenous people and were said to be of Dravidian and Austric origin. Aryanism was seen then to define the true and pure Hindu community. Other groups recruited into the caste structure at lower levels were regarded as polluting the pristine Hindu community.

Because of its centrality to both the notion of community and religion, the theory of Aryan race requires to be looked at critically by historians working on nineteenth-century ideas as well as historians of ancient India. The earlier evidence quoted in support of the theory as applied to India begins to fade with information from archaeology and linguistics. The notion of an Aryan race has now been generally discarded in scholarship and what we are left with is essentially a linguistic category: the Indo-Aryan speaking people. The archaeological picture takes the foundation of Indian civilization back to proto-history and the Harappa culture. The characteristic features of the latter do not mesh with those of the Vedic texts associated with the culture of the Indo-Aryan speakers.[43] The culture depicted in the Vedic texts seems increasingly to have drawn on local practices and beliefs, some going back to the Harappa culture or earlier, others drawing perhaps from the then contemporary society in India. There is virtually no evidence of the invasion and conquest of northwestern India by a dominant culture coming from across the border. Most sites register a gradual change of archaeological cultures. Where there is evidence of destruction and burning it could as easily have been a local activity and is not indicative of a large-scale invasion. The border lands of the north-west were in communication with Iran and Central Asia even before the Harappa culture with evidence of the passage of goods and ideas across the region.[44] This situation continued into later times and if seen in this light then the intermittent arrival of groups of Indo-European speakers in the north-west, perhaps as pastoralists or farmers or itinerant traders, would pose little problem. It is equally plausible that in some cases, local languages became Indo-Europeanized through contact. Such situations would require a different kind of investigation. If cultural elements from elsewhere are being assessed, then during the Harappan period, excavated evidence for contact with West Asia via the Gulf was more significant than that with eastern Iran and Central Asia and this raises another set of possibilities.

The more basic question for the historian is to explain the slow and gradual spread of the Indo-Aryan language across a large part of the Indian subcontinent. Here again the evidence from linguistics provides an interesting pointer. The claim that the earliest of the Vedic texts, the *Ṛg Veda* dating back to the second millennium BC, is linguistically purely Indo-Aryan is now under question for it is being argued that the text already registers the presence of non-Aryan speakers. The later Vedic texts show an even greater admixture of non-Aryan and specifically when dealing with certain areas of activity, such as agriculture.[45] The emergent picture might suggest that the speakers of Indo-Aryan may have been in a symbiotic relationship with speakers of non-Aryan languages, with a mutual adopting of not only vocabulary and linguistic structures in a bilingual situation but also technologies and religious practices and beliefs.[46] The exclusivity of *brāhmaṇa* ritual does not have to be explained on the basis of a racial segregation, but can be viewed as derived from the will to retain a certain kind of priestly power, which, claiming bestowal by the deities would ensure a separate and special status. Possibly the political hold of priestly power has its roots in the Harappa culture. In charting the spread of Indo-Aryan, it is worth remembering that Sanskrit not only underwent change in relation to other languages with which it had to co-exist and in relation to social change but that its use was initially restricted to *brāhmaṇa* ritual and elite groups.

The focus therefore is shifting to an investigation of the many ways in which a language gains acceptability. This would involve detailed studies of the juxtaposition of new technologies particularly in relation to ecological contexts, of demography, of kinship systems, and the ways in which social groups interact where stratification relates to lineage rather than to race. So deep has been the modern obsession with race that Pargiter as late as in the 1920s suggested the identification of even the traditional descent groups from the genealogies of the Puranic texts as Aryan, Dravidian, and Austric.[47] Thus the spread of the Indo-Aryan languages and the changes they manifest are a far more complicated study than that implied in the theory of spread by conquest. There is also a need to see the evolving of early Indian society as suggested by archaeological evidence independent of the attempt to impose Aryan identities on archaeological cultures. Only then can we hope to understand the social processes which went into the creation of early Indian society. In the texts, the term *ārya* generally refers to status indicating one who is to be respected. Whereas the connotation of *dāsa* may be said to contain racial elements, as, for example, in the emphasis on physical characteristics, such elements are not in the forefront of references to *ārya*. Thus in the Vedic texts there are *ārya*s of *dāsa* descent, the *dāsī-putrāḥ brāhmaṇas*,[48] or, politically powerful *dāsa* chiefs making gifts to the *brāhmaṇas*.[49] (It is interesting that one of the most respected lineages, that of the Pūrus is associated with sub-standard Sanskrit.[50] It is also said that Puru was an ancient king who was an Asura Rākṣasa and was overthrown by Bharata,[51] which can hardly be said to place the Pūrus in the category of the pure Aryans!) In the *Dharmaśāstra*s it is the observance of the complex *varnāśrama-dharma* which defines the *ārya*. To trace the emergence of caste would also involve a study of access to resources, kinship and clan networks, and notions of pollution.

Early history suggests the existence of multiple communities based on various identities. The need to create the idea of a single, Hindu community appears to have been a concern of more recent times which was sought to be justified by recourse to a particular construction of history. The new Hinduism which is now sought to be projected as the religion of this community is in many ways a departure from the earlier religious sects. It seeks historicity for the incarnations of its deities, encourages the idea of a centrally sacred book, claims monotheism as significant to the worship of deity, acknowledges the authority of the ecclesiastical organization of certain sects as prevailing over all, and has supported large-scale missionary work and conversion. These changes allow it to transcend caste identities and reach out to larger numbers. Religions indigenous to India which questioned Brahmanical belief and practice such as Buddhism and Jainism have been inducted into Hinduism and their separateness is either denied or ignored. Pre-Islamic India is therefore presented as a civilization characterized by an inclusive Hinduism, whereas it would seem that the reality perhaps lay in looking at it as a cluster of distinctive sects and cults, observing common civilizational symbols but with belief and ritual ranging from atheism to animism and a variety of religious organizations identifying themselves by location, language, and caste. Even the sense of religious identity seems to have related more closely to sect than to a dominant Hindu community.

The modern construction of Hinduism is often acclaimed as in the following defence of Orientalism: 'The work of integrating a vast collection of myths, beliefs, rituals, and laws into a coherent religion and of shaping an amorphous heritage into a rational faith known now as "Hinduism" were endeavours initiated by Orientalists.'[52] Given that religious traditions are constantly reformulated, the particular construction of Hinduism in the last two centuries has an obvious historical causation. Deriving largely from the Orientalist construction of Hinduism, emergent national consciousness appropriated this definition of Hinduism as well as what it regarded as the heritage of Hindu culture. Hindu identity was defined by those who were part of this national consciousness and drew on their own idealized image of themselves resulting in an upper-caste, *brāhmaṇa*-dominated identity. Even the counterposing of Hindu to other religious identities as an essential fact of social and historical reality grew out of this construction. But this construction not only deviates from the history of the religious groups involved but fails to encapsulate the essential differences within what is called the Hindu tradition whose presuppositions were distinct from other religions and closely entwined with social articulation. The search for coherence and rational faith was in terms of a perspective familiar to those who came from a Christian religious tradition and hardly reflected any attempt to understand the coherence of a different, indigenous religious tradition. The shape thus given to the latter has changed what originally existed and has made it difficult to recognize the actual earlier form.

The need for postulating a Hindu community became a requirement for political mobilization in the nineteenth century when representation by religious community became a key to power and where such representation gave access to economic resources. The competition for middle-class employment brought with it the argument that in all fairness, the size of the community should be taken into consideration. Communal representation of the religious kind firmed up the image. Once this argument was conceded it became necessary to recruit as many people as possible into the community. Here the vagueness of what constitutes a Hindu was to the advantage of those propagating a Hindu community. It encouraged an almost new perception of the social and political uses of religion. Conversion to Hinduism was invented largely to bring in the untouchables and the tribals. The notion of purification, *śuddhi*, permitted those who had been converted to Islam and Christianity to be reintroduced to the Hindu fold. A Hindu community with a common identity would be politically powerful. Since it was easy to recognize other communities on the basis of religion, such as Muslims and Christians, an effort was made to consolidate a parallel Hindu community. This involved a change from the earlier segmented identities to one which encompassed caste and region and identified itself by religion which had to be refashioned so as to provide the ideology which would bind the group. In Gramsci's terms, the class which wishes to become hegemonic has to nationalize itself and the new 'nationalist' Hinduism comes from the middle class.

The change implicit in the various levels of what is called modernization inevitably results in the refashioning of communities. Given that the notion of expansive communities may well be imagined, nevertheless the premises on which such communities are constructed are open to analysis and where they claim a historical basis, there the historian has perforce to be involved. This involvement becomes even more necessary when the concept of communities is brought into play in assigning positions to them in history either close to or distant from what are regarded as national aspirations. Thus the majority community tends to define national aspirations. The minority communities in varying degrees are viewed as disrupting society by their refusal to conform. The projection of such communities historically is that of their always having been alien to the dominant culture and therefore refusing to assimilate with the majority.

Minority communities pick up their cue in a similar reconstruction of history seeking to project a unified community stance in all historical situations. The fear of being overwhelmed by the majority community is expressed even in opposition to the making of homogeneous civil laws. These are treated as threats to a specific culture and practice, and there is a tendency to preserve even that which is archaic in an effort to assert a separate identity.

If the history of religions in India is seen as the articulation not only of ideas and rituals but also the perceptions and motivations of social groups, the perspectives which would follow might be different from those with which we are familiar. The discourse and the play between and among religious sects of various kinds has been a central fact of Indian religion and would reflect a more realistic portrayal of the role of religion in society. A historically analytical enquiry into the definition and role of religion and the concept of religious communities in pre-modern India could be juxtaposed with the way in which these have been perceived by interpreters of the past in the last couple of centuries. Incidentally such an assessment would be valuable not only to contemporary society in India but also to those societies which now host the vast Indian diaspora. Communal ideologies may be rooted in the homeland but also find sustenance in the diaspora.

It is possible now to look more analytically at the perspectives on early Indian society as available in the sources, keeping in mind the insights which we have, arising from research which, in a sense, is being gradually liberated from the polemics of the colonial age. Where institutions and ideologies of modern times seek legitimacy from the early past, at least there, the dialogue between historians working on these time periods becomes imperative.

Notes and References

1. B. Andersen, *Imagined Communities* (Vaso, 1983).

2. J. Bloch, *Les Inscriptions d'Asoka* (Paris, 1950), pp. 97, 99, 112.

3. J. W. McCrindle, *Ancient India as Described by Megasthenes and Arrian* (London, 1877). Arrian, *Indica*, XI.1 to XII.9; Strabo XV I.39–41, 46–9.

4. J. Legge, *Fa-hien's Record of Buddhistic Kingdoms* (Oxford, 1886); S. Beal, *Si-yu-ki; Buddhist Records of the Western World* (London, 1884).

5. E. C. Sachau (trans. and ed.), *Alberuni's India* (Delhi, 1964 reprint), p. 21.

6. S. D. Joshi (ed.), *Patañjali Vyākaraṇa Mahābhāṣya* (Poona, 1968), II.4.9; I.476.

7. N. Wagle, *Society at the Time of the Buddha* (Bombay, 1966), p. 74.

8. Curiously, the eating of meat and the drinking of intoxicants were part of the rejection of Brahmanism for these were now abhorent to Brahmanism, a rather different situation from that described in the Vedic texts where *brāhmaṇa*s consumed beef and took *soma*.

9. G. D. Sontheimer, 'Some Memorial Monuments of Western India', in *German Scholars in India*, II (New Delhi, 1976); S. G. Tulpule, 'The Origin of Viththala: A New Interpretation', *ABORI*, 1977–8, vols 58–9, pp. 1009–15: A. Dandekar, 'Pastoralism and the Cult of Viṭhṭhala', M. Phil. Dissertation, JNU; H. Kulke, *Jagannātha kult and Gajapati-Königtum* (Wiesbaden, 1979), p. 227; H. Kulke and D. Rothermund, *A History of India* (London, 1986), pp. 145ff.

10. A. Bakker, *Ayodhya* (Groningen, 1984).

11. Manu II, 14–15.

12. Romila Thapar, 'Renunciation: The Making of a Counter-Culture?', in *Ancient Indian Social History: Some Interpretations* (Delhi, 1978), pp. 63–104.

13. Romila Thapar, 'The Rāmāyaṇa: Theme and Variations', in S. N. Mukherjee (ed.), *India: History and Thought* (Calcutta, 1982), pp. 221–53.

14. Romila Thapar, 'Death and the Hero', in S. G. Humphreys and

H. King, *Mortality and Immortality: The Anthropology and Archaeology of Death* (London, 1981), pp. 293–316.

15. Romila Thapar, 'Sati in History', *Seminar*, no. 342 (February 1988).

16. Personal Communication from a friend.

17. H. Sanyal, *Social Mobility in Bengal* (Calcutta, 1981).

18. S. Beal, *Si-yu-ki*, I. xcix.

19. I. 307.

20. Xinru Liu, *Ancient India and Ancient China* (Delhi, 1988).

21. Romila Thapar, '*Cultural Transaction and Early India* (Delhi, 1987), pp. 17ff.

22. P. B. Desai, *Jainism in South India* (Sholapur, 1957), pp. 23, 63, 82–3, 124, 397–402; *Epigraphia Indica* V, pp. 142ff, 255; *Ep. Ind.* XXIX, pp. 139–44; *Annual Report of South Indian Epigraphy*, 1923, pp. 4ff.

23. Romila Thapar, 1978.

24. Manu, VIII.41.

25. *Aśvalāyana Gṛhasūtra* I.7.I; *Aśvalāyana Śrauta-sūtra* XII.8; Pāṇiṇi 6.2.62; *Amarakośa* 2.3.19; Buddhist texts speak more specifically of village boundaries (*Vinaya Piṭaka* I. 109.10; III.46.200). This was necessary in a system where the limits of areas for collecting alms had to be defined for each monastery.

26. See inscriptions from Sanchi as given in J. Marshall and A. Foucher, *Monuments of Sanchi* (Calcutta, 1940); also H. Lüders, *Ep. Ind.* X. nos 162–907; see also the Bhattiprolu inscription, Luders no. 1332.

27. J. F. Fleet (ed.), 'Inscriptions of the Early Gupta Kings and Their Successors,' *Corpus Inscriptionum Indicarum*, III (Varanasi, 1970 reprint), pp. 79ff.

28. *Ibid.*, pp. 162ff.

29. *Bṛhaspati* I. 28–30; *Kātyāyana* 2.82; 17.18; I. 126; *Archaeological Survey of India, Annual Report*, 1903–4; 1911–12.

30. *Nārada-smṛti*, X. 1–2; *Ep. Ind.* XXX, p. 169.

31. 'The Persepolis and Naqsh-i-Rustam inscriptions of Darius', in D. C. Sircar, *Select Inscriptions*, vol. I (Calcutta, 1965), p. 7.

32. Similarly Muslim women were often referred to as *Turuṣki*, as, for example, in Hemādri, *Caturvarga-cintāmaṇi*, Prāyaścitta-kāṇḍa.

33. e.g. Chateśvara temple inscriptions, where in the 13th century, a reference is made to a campaign against the *yavanas*. *Ep. Ind.* 1952, XXIX, pp. 121–2.

34. Romila Thapar, 'The Image of the Barbarian in Early India', in *Ancient Indian Social History*, pp. 152–92. A fourteenth-century inscription from Delhi refers to Shahab-ud-din, who was the first Turuṣka to rule Dhillika/Delhi, as a *mleccha*. D. D. R. Bhandarkar (ed.), Appendix to *Epi. Ind.* XIX–XXIII, no. 683.

35. Udaipur inscription of the time of Rajamalla in *Bhavnagar Inscriptions*, pp. 117ff. And see Bhandarkar (ed.), Appendix to *Ep. Ind.* XIX–XXIII, no. 862. It is ironic that it was earlier thought that these Rajput ruling families may in some cases have had their origin in the Śakas!

36. Sadadi Jaina inscription of the time of Kumbhakarṇa of Medapata in *Bhavnagar Inscriptions*, pp. 114ff and D. R. Bhandarkar, *op. cit.*, no. 784; D. Sharma, *Lectures on Rajput History and Culture* (Delhi, 1970), p. 55.

37. Kīrtistambha-praśasti, *ASIR*, XXIII, pp. 111ff.

38. Ashim Roy, *The Islamic Syncretistic Tradition in Bengal* (Princeton, 1983).

39. A. Heltebeitel, *The Cult of Draupadi* (Chicago, 1988).

40. Romila Thapar, 'Ideology and the Interpretation of Early Indian History', in K. S. Krishnaswamy *et al.* (eds), *Society and Change* (Bombay, 1977), pp. 1–19.

41. H. Risley, *The People of India* (London, 1908).

42. As, for example, in the writings of Keshab Chunder Sen, 'Philosophy and Madness in Religion', in *Keshab Chunder Sen's Lectures in India* (London, 1910).

43. Romila Thapar, 'The Study of Society in India', in *Ancient Indian Social History*, pp. 211–39; also, 'The Archaeological Background to the Agnicayana Ritual', in F. Staal, *Agni*, vol. II (Berkeley, 1983), pp. 3–40.

44. J. Jarrige, 'Excavations at Mehrgarh: their Significance for Understanding the Backgrond of the Harappan Civilisation', in G. Possehl (ed.), *Harappan Civilisation* (New Delhi, 1982), pp. 79ff.

45. T. Burrow, *The Sanskrit Language* (London, 1965), p. 379: M. M. Deshande and P. E. Hook (eds), *Aryan and non-Aryan in India* (Michigan, 1979).

46. Romila Thapar, *From Lineage to State* (New Delhi, 1984), pp. 21ff.

47. F. E. Pargiter, *Ancient Indian Historical Tradition* (London, 1922).

48. *Bṛhaddevatā* 4.11–15; 21–5; describes the birth of Dīrghatamas and his son Kakṡivant as the son of a *dāsī*. The *Aitereya Brāhmaṇa* 2.19 and the *Kausītaki Brāhmaṇa* 12.3 describe the Ṛg Vedic seer Kavasa Ailusa as a *dāsī-putraḥ*.

49. Romila Thapar, 1984, p. 43.

50. *Ṛg Veda*, VII. 18.13.

51. *Śatapatha Brāhmaṇa*, VI. 8.1.14.

52. D. Knopf, 'Hermeneutics versus History', *Journal of Asian Studies* 39.3 (1980): 495–505.

Index

Notes on Contributors

David N. Lorenzen is Professor of South Asian History at El Colegio de Mexico, Mexico City.

R. Champakalakshmi is Professor of History (retired) at Jawaharlal Nehru University, New Delhi.

The late *Burton Stein* was Professorial Research Associate, Department of History, School of Oriental and African Studies, University of London.

Richard M. Eaton is Professor of History at the University of Arizona (Tucson).

Mohammad Ishaq Khan is Professor of History at the University of Kashmir, Srinagar.

Sheldon Pollock is Professor of Sanskrit at the University of Chicago.

Brajadulal Chattopadhyaya is Professor of Historyat Jawaharlal Nehru University, New Delhi.

The late *Richard Burghart* was Professor of Anthropology at the University of Heidelberg.

The late *P. D. Barthwal* was Professor of Hindi at Banaras Hindu University.

The late *Hajariprasad Dvivedi* was Professor of Hindi at Banaras Hindu University.

Krishna Sharma was Principal of Gargi College, University of Delhi.

Romila Thapar is Emeritus Professor of History at Jawaharlal Nehru University, New Delhi.